POWER
AND
SOCIETY

An Introduction to the Social Sciences

6TH
EDITION

POWER AND SOCIETY

An Introduction to the Social Sciences

6TH EDITION

Thomas R. Dye
Florida State University
McKenzie Professor of Government
and Public Policy

Wadsworth Publishing Company
Belmont, California
A Division of Wadsworth, Inc.

Sponsoring Editor: Cynthia C. Stormer, Kris Clerkin
Editorial Associate Cathleen S. Collins
Production Editor: Marjorie Z. Sanders
Interior and Cover Designer: Roy R. Neuhaus
Print Buyer: Vena M. Dyer
Art Editor: Lisa Torri
Permissions Editor: Marie DuBois
Copy Editor: Laurie Vaughn
Photo Researcher: Stephen Forsling
Interior Illustration: Lotus Art
Cover Photo: Peter Gregoire/Index Stock Photography, Inc.
Compositor: GTS Graphics
Cover Printer: Phoenix Color Corp.
Printer: Arcata Graphics/Fairfield

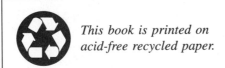

This book is printed on acid-free recycled paper.

1 2 3 4 5 6 7 8 9 10—97 96 95 94 93

Library of Congress Cataloging-in-Publication Data

Dye, Thomas R.
   Power and society : an introduction to the social sciences /
  Thomas R. Dye—6th ed.
     p.   cm.
   Includes bibliographical references and index.
   ISBN 0-534-19260-2
    1. Social sciences. 2. Power (Social sciences) I. Title.
  II. Title: Power and society.
H61.D95 1993   92-9973
300—dc20   CIP
ISBN 0-534-19260-2

Photo Credits: p. 20, Harry Wilks/Stock, Boston; p. 36, Thelma Shumsky/The Image Works; p. 222,
Bob Daemmrich/Stock, Boston.

In memory of James C. "Jeff" Dye

Preface

Power and Society: An Introduction to the Social Sciences is designed as a basic text for an introductory, interdisciplinary social science course. It is written specifically for first- and second-year students at community colleges and at four-year colleges and universities that offer a basic studies program.

Power and Society introduces students to central concepts in

anthropology	psychology
sociology	political science
economics	history

But more important, the text focuses these disciplinary perspectives on a central integrative theme—the nature and uses of power in society. In this way, students are made aware of the interdependence of the social sciences. Compartmentalization is avoided, and students are shown how each social science discipline contributes to an understanding of power.

Power and Society also introduces students to some of the central challenges facing American society:

ideological conflict	crime and violence
racism and sexism	urban affairs
poverty and powerlessness	defense and arms control

Each of these national challenges is approached from an interdisciplinary viewpoint, with *power* as the integrating concept.

Power has been defined as the capacity to modify the conduct of individuals through the real or threatened use of rewards and punishments. Doubtless there are other central concepts or ideas in the social sciences that might be employed to develop an integrated framework for an introduction to social science. But certainly *power* is a universal phenomenon that is reflected in virtually all forms of human interaction. Power is intimately related to many other key concepts and ideas in the social sciences—personality, behavior, aggression, role, class, mobility, wealth, income distribution, markets, culture, ideology, change, authority, oligarchy, the elite. Power is also a universal instrument in approaching the various crises that afflict human beings and their societies—racism, sexism, poverty, violence, crime, urban decay, and ideological and international conflict.

Several special features are designed to help the student understand the meaning of various concepts. The first such feature is the identification of specific masters of social thought and the clear, concise presentation of their central contributions to social science. Specific attention is given to the contributions of

Bertrand Russell	B. F. Skinner
Ruth Benedict	John Locke
Karl Marx	Charles Beard
Adam Smith	Frederick Jackson Turner
John M. Keynes	Martin Luther King, Jr.
Sigmund Freud	

The second special feature is the presentation of timely, relevant case studies in each chapter to illustrate important concepts. Topics include:

Explaining Presidential Approval Ratings
Women in the Work Force: Changing American Culture
Sociobiology: It's All in Your Genes
The Power Elite
Authority and Obedience: The "Shocking" Experiments
Watergate and the Limits of Presidential Power
Political Power and the Mass Media
Reconstruction and Black History
Vietnam: A Political History
The Rise and Fall of Communism in the Soviet Union
Affirmative Action or Reverse Discrimination?
Wilder of Virginia: Putting Race to Rest
Senior Power
The Death Penalty
Community Power Structures
American Military Power: "Desert Storm"

In addition, illustrative boxes throughout the text help maintain student interest, with brief discussion on such topics as

Are Social Mores in America Changing?
Religious Beliefs in America
The Incest Taboo

Telltale Behavior of Twins
The "Comparable Worth" Controversy
The CEOs: Who's at the Top
The "Best" and "Worst" Presidents
Americans: Liberal or Conservative?

A third special feature is the cross-national perspectives provided on important aspects of life in the United States. As this book introduces students to the social sciences with principal reference to the American experience, discussions in each chapter endeavor to place this experience in a global context.

Thus, "Cross-National Perspective" sections include:

World Population
Global Inequalities
Suicide
GNP and Standards of Living
Capitalism and Socialism in the World
The Rise and Fall of Communism
Women in the Labor Force
Murder and Homicide
Worldwide Urbanization
Tax Burdens

as well as anthropological observations on power among Polar Eskimos, power among Crow Indians, and power in the Aztec Empire.

Another important special feature is the running study guide provided in the wide page margins throughout the text. The study guide defines key vocabulary items and outlines central arguments, keeping pace with the student's progress through the text.

The sixth edition of *Power and Society* continues to resist the lamentable tendency in introductory college textbooks to "dummy" material for undergraduate students. It "smartens" material in every chapter, introducing more social science research studies to describe and explain human behavior, as well as providing cross-national perspectives on the American experience. Chapter 2, "Social Sciences and the Scientific Method," describes scientific research designs and experimental, survey, case-study, and aggregate-data analysis. It discusses the difficulties in applying scientific research designs to human behavior and provides illustrative case studies: "An Experiment in Crime Fighting" and "Explaining Presidential Approval Ratings." It also encourages students to evaluate survey results for themselves and to use the *Statistical Abstract of the United States* and other common sources of social science data for their own investigations. The new feature of the sixth edition, its effort to bring cross-national perspectives to the American experience, places an additional challenge on students. The sixth edition continues the book's tradition of focusing on the conditions of minorities and women in American society. In addition to its material on such topics as "Reconstruction and Black History," "Martin Luther King, Jr.: The Power of Protest," "Hispanic Power," "Women in the Labor Force," and "The 'Comparable Worth' Controversy," it adds new material on "Wilder of Virginia: Putting Race to Rest."

I am particularly grateful for the many constructive comments and criticisms made at various stages of this work. Assistance in preparing the sixth edition was provided by Thom Amnotte, Eastern Maine Technical College; John DeBrizzi, Jersey City State College; James L. Gibson, University of Houston; Harry Holloway, University of Oklahoma; John D. Molloy, Michigan State University.

Thomas R. Dye

About the
Author

Thomas R. Dye (Ph.D., University of Pennsylvania) is McKenzie Professor of Government and Public Policy at Florida State University. He is the author of numerous books and articles on American government and public policy, including *The Irony of Democracy,* now in its ninth edition; *Politics in States and Communities* and *Understanding Public Policy,* both now in their seventh editions; and *Who's Running America?* His books have been translated into many languages, including Russian and Chinese.

Dye has served as President of the Southern Political Science Association, President of the Policy Studies Organization, and Secretary of the American Political Science Association. He is a member of Omicron Delta Kappa and Phi Kappa Phi and is listed in most major biographical directories, including *Who's Who in America.*

Contents

4

CHAPTER   **Power and Social Class**   **69**

5

CHAPTER   **Power and Personality**   **97**

6
CHAPTER   **Power and the Economic Order**   **125**

III
PART THE USES OF POWER 223

9
CHAPTER Power and Ideology 225

10
CHAPTER Power, Race, and Gender 247

11
CHAPTER

Poverty and Powerlessness

275

12
CHAPTER

Power, Crime, and Violence

293

13
CHAPTER **Power and Community** 319

14
CHAPTER **Power and the International System** 345

THE NATURE AND STUDY OF POWER

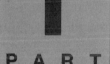

PART

The purpose of this book is to introduce you to the social sciences. Because power in society is a theme that pervades each of the social sciences, as well as the problems they study, we have chosen this theme as the focal point for our presentation. Part I is designed to familiarize you with the notion of power, with the nature of each of the social sciences, and with the scientific methods they employ. You will find that Chapter 1 reflects the structure of the entire text. Like the book as a whole, its first part focuses on the nature of power, its second part on the individual social sciences and the particular ways in which they contribute to our understanding of power, and its third and final part on the problems with which the social sciences are concerned. Chapter 2 is devoted to a discussion of the methods used in social science research.

Power,
Society,
and Social
Science

The Nature of Power

Ordinary men and women are driven by forces in society that they neither understand nor control. These forces are embodied in governmental authorities, economic organizations and markets, social values and ideologies, accepted ways of life, and learned patterns of behavior. However diverse the nature of these forces, they have in common the ability to modify the conduct of individuals, to control their behavior, to shape their lives.

Power is the capacity to affect the conduct of individuals through the real or threatened use of rewards and punishments. Power is exercised over individuals or groups by offering them some things they value or by threatening to deprive them of those things. These values are the *power base,* and they can include physical safety, health, and well-being; wealth and material possessions; jobs and means to a livelihood; knowledge and skills; social recognition, status, and prestige; love, affection, and acceptance by others; a satisfactory self-image and self-respect. To exercise power, then, control must be exercised over the things that are valued in society.

Power is a special form of influence. Broadly speaking, influence is the production of intended effects. People who can produce intended effects by any means are said to be influential. People who can produce intended effects by the real or threatened use of rewards and punishments are said to be powerful.

Power can rest on various resources. The exercise of power assumes many different forms—the giving or withholding of many different values. Yet power bases are usually *interdependent*—individuals who control certain resources are likely to control other resources as well. Wealth, economic power, prestige, recognition, political influence, education, respect, and so on, all tend to "go together" in society.

Power is never equally distributed. "There is no power where power is equal." For power to be exercised, the "powerholder" must control some base values. By *control* we mean that the powerholder is in a position to offer these values as rewards to others or to threaten to deprive others of these values.

Power is a relationship among individuals, groups, and institutions in society. Power is not really a "thing" that an individual possesses. Instead, power is a relationship in which some individuals or groups have control over certain resources.

The *elite* are the few who have power; the *masses* are the many who do not. The elite are the few who control what is valued in society and use that control to shape the lives of all of us. The masses are the many whose lives are shaped by institutions, events, and leaders over which they have little control. Political scientist Harold Lasswell wrote, "The division of society into elites and masses is universal," and even in a democracy, "a few exercise a relatively great weight of power, and the many exercise comparatively little."[1]

Power is exercised in interpersonal relations. Psychologist Rollo May wrote that "power means the ability to affect, to influence, and to change other persons."[2] He argued that power is essential to one's "sense of significance"—one's conviction that one counts for something in the world, that one has an effect on others, and that one can get recognition of one's existence from others. Power is essential to

---

power

the capacity to affect the conduct of others through the real or threatened use of rewards and punishments

power

based on control of valued resources

unequally distributed

exercised in interpersonal relations

exercised through large institutions

elite and masses

the few who have power and the many who do not

the development of personality. An infant who is denied the experience of influencing others or of drawing their attention to its existence withdraws to a corner of its bed, does not talk or develop in any way, and withers away physiologically and psychologically.

Power is exercised in large institutions—governments, corporations, schools, the military, churches, newspapers, television networks, law firms, and so on. Power that stems from high positions in the social structures of society is stable and far-reaching. Sociologist C. Wright Mills observed: "No one can be truly powerful unless he has access to the command of major institutions, for it is over these institutional means of power that the truly powerful are, in the first instance, powerful."[3] Not all power, it is true, is anchored in or exercised through institutions. But institutional positions in society provide a continuous and important base of power. As Mills explained:

> If we took the one hundred most powerful men in America, the one hundred wealthiest, and the one hundred most celebrated away from the institutional positions they now occupy, away from their resources of men and women and money, away from the media of mass communication that are now focused upon them—then they would be powerless and poor and uncelebrated. For power is not of a man. Wealth does not center in the person of the wealthy. . . . To have power requires access to major institutions, for the institutional positions men occupy determine in large part their chances to have and to hold these valued experiences.[4]

Power and the Social Sciences

Social science is the study of human behavior. Actually, there are several social sciences, each specializing in a particular aspect of human behavior and each using different concepts, methods, and data in its studies. Anthropology, sociology, economics, psychology, political science, and history have developed into separate "disciplines," but all share an interest in human behavior.

social science
the study of human behavior

Power is *not* the central concern of the social sciences, yet all the social sciences deal with power in one form or another. Each of the social sciences contributes to an understanding of the forces that modify the conduct of individuals, control their behavior, and shape their lives. Thus, to fully understand power in society, we must approach this topic in an *interdisciplinary* fashion—using ideas, methods, data, and findings from all the social sciences.

Anthropology

Anthropology is the study of people and their ways of life. It is the most comprehensive of the social sciences. Some anthropologists are concerned primarily with people's biological and physical characteristics; this field is called *physical anthropology*. Other anthropologists are interested primarily in the ways of life of both ancient and modern peoples; this field is called *cultural anthropology.*

Culture is all the common patterns and ways of living that characterize society. The anthropologist tries to describe and explain a great many things: child rearing

anthropology
the study of people and their ways of life

culture
all the common patterns and ways of living that characterize society

and education; family arrangements; language and communication; technology; ways of making a living; the distribution of work; religious beliefs and values; social life; leadership patterns; and power structures.

Power is part of the culture or the way of life of a people. Power is exercised in all societies, because all societies have systems of rewards and sanctions designed to control the behavior of their members. Perhaps the most enduring structure of power in society is the family: power is exercised within the family when patterns of dominance and submission are established between male and female and between parents and children. Societies also develop structures of power outside the family to maintain peace and order among their members, to organize individuals to accomplish large-scale tasks, to defend themselves against attack, and even to wage war and exploit other peoples.

In our study of power and culture, we shall examine how cultural patterns determine power relationships. We shall also examine patterns of authority in traditional and modern families and the changing power role of women in society. We shall examine the origins and development of power relationships, illustrating them with examples of societies in which power is organized by family and kinship group (polar Eskimos), by tribe (Crow Indians), and by the state (the Aztec empire). Finally, as a case study, we shall look at the controversy over "sociobiology"— that is, the extent to which genetics or culture determines behaviors.

Sociology

sociology
the study of relationships among individuals and groups

Sociology is the study of relationships among individuals and groups. Sociologists describe the structure of formal and informal groups, their functions and purposes, and how they change over time. They study social institutions (such as families, schools, churches), social processes (for example, conflict, competition, assimilation, change), and social problems (crime, race relations, poverty, and so forth). Sociologists also study social classes.

All societies have some system of classifying and ranking their members—a system of *stratification*. In modern industrial societies, social status is associated with the various roles that individuals play in the economic system. Individuals are ranked according to how they make their living and the power they exercise over others. Stratification into social classes is determined largely on the basis of occupation and control of economic resources.

social stratification
the classification and ranking of members of a society

Power derives from social status, prestige, and respect, as well as from control of economic resources. Thus, the stratification system involves the unequal distribution of power.

In our study of power and social class, we shall describe the stratification system in America and explore popular beliefs about "getting ahead." We shall discuss the differing lifestyles of upper, middle, and lower classes in America and the extent of class conflict. We shall examine the ideas of Karl Marx about the struggle for power among social classes. We shall describe the differential in political power among social classes in America. Finally, we shall explore the ideas of sociologist C. Wright Mills about a "power elite" in America that occupies powerful positions in the governmental, corporate, and military bureaucracies of the nation.

Psychology

Psychology may be defined as the study of the behavior of people and animals. Behavior, we know, is the product of both "nature and nurture"—that is, a product of both our biological makeup and our environmental conditioning. We shall examine the continuing controversy over *how much* of our behavior is a product of our genes versus our environment. There is great richness and diversity in psychological inquiry. For example, *behavioral psychologists* study the learning process—the way in which people and animals learn to respond to stimuli. Behavioral psychologists frequently study in experimental laboratory situations, with the hope that the knowledge gained can be useful in understanding more complex human behavior outside the laboratory. *Social psychologists,* on the other hand, study interpersonal behavior—the ways in which social interactions shape an individual's beliefs, perceptions, motivations, attitudes, and behavior. Social psychologists generally study the whole person in relation to the total environment. *Freudian psychologists* study the impact of subconscious feelings and emotions and of early childhood experiences on the behavior of adults. *Humanistic psychologists* are concerned with the human being's innate potential for growth and development. Many other psychologists combine theories and methods in different ways in their attempts to achieve a better understanding of behavior.

Personality is all the enduring, organized ways of behavior that characterize an individual. Psychologists differ over how personality characteristics are determined—whether they are learned habits acquired through the process of reinforcement and conditioning (behavioral psychology), products of the individual's interaction with the significant people and groups in his or her life (social psychology), manifestations of the continuous process of positive growth toward "self-actualization" (humanistic psychology), the results of subconscious drives and long-repressed emotions stemming from early childhood experiences (Freudian psychology), or some combination of all these.

In our study of power and personality, we will examine various theories of personality determination in an effort to understand the forces shaping the individual's reaction to power. Using a Freudian perspective, we shall study the "authoritarian personality"—the individual who is habitually dominant and aggressive toward others over whom he or she exercises power but is submissive and weak toward others who have more power; the individual who is extremely prejudiced, rigid, intolerant, cynical, and power-oriented. We shall explore the power implications of B. F. Skinner's ideas of behavioral conditioning for the control of human behavior. To gain an understanding of humanistic psychology's approach to power relationships, we shall examine Rollo May's formulation of the functions of power for the individual and Abraham Maslow's theory of a "hierarchy of needs." Finally, in our case study, we shall describe the startling results of an experiment designed to test the relationship between authority and obedience.

Economics

Economics is the study of the production and distribution of scarce goods and services. There are never enough goods and services to satisfy everyone's demands,

psychology
the study of the behavior of people and animals

personality
all the enduring, organized ways of behavior that characterize an individual

economics
the study of the production and distribution of scarce goods and services

and because of this, choices must be made. Economists study how individuals, firms, and nations make these choices about goods and services.

Economic power is the power to decide what will be produced, how much it will cost, how many people will be employed, what their wages will be, what the price of goods and services will be, what profits will be made, how these profits will be distributed, and how fast the economy will grow.

Capitalist societies rely heavily on the market mechanism to make these decisions. In our study of economic power, we shall explore both the strengths and weaknesses of this market system, as well as the ideas of economic philosophers Adam Smith and John Maynard Keynes. In addition, we shall consider the role of government in the economy, which has increased over the years. We shall then turn to an examination of America's vast wealth—how it is measured, where it comes from, and where it goes. We shall examine the relationship between wealth and the quality of life, which are not always equivalent things. We shall also examine the concentration of corporate power in America. Finally, in our case study, we shall discuss the power of the corporate managers, the "CEOs," and whether they use that power to benefit the stockholders or themselves.

Political Science

political science
the study of government and politics

authority
the legitimate use of physical force

Political science is the study of government and politics. Governments possess *authority,* a particular form of power; that is, the legitimate use of physical force. By *legitimate,* we mean that people generally consent to the government's use of this power. Of course, other individuals and organizations in society—muggers, street gangs, the Mafia, violent revolutionaries—use force. But only government can legitimately threaten people with the loss of freedom and well-being to modify their behavior. Moreover, governments exercise power over all individuals and institutions in society—corporations, families, schools, and so forth. Obviously the power of government in modern society is very great, extending to nearly every aspect of modern life—"from womb to tomb."

Political scientists from Aristotle to the present have been concerned with the dangers of unlimited and unchecked governmental power. We shall examine the American experience with limited, constitutional government and the meaning of democracy in modern society. We shall observe how the U.S. Constitution divides power, first between states and the national government, and second among the legislative, executive, and judicial branches of government. We shall examine the growth of power in Washington, D.C., and the struggle for power among the different branches. We shall also explore competition between political parties and interest groups and popular participation in decision making through elections. Finally, in our case study "Political Power and the Mass Media," we shall examine the growing power of television in American politics.

History

history
the recording, narrating, and interpreting of human experience

History is the recording, narrating, and interpreting of human experience. The historian recreates the past by collecting recorded facts, organizing them into a narrative, and interpreting their meaning. History is also concerned with change over time. It provides a perspective on the present by informing us of the way people lived in the past. History helps us understand how society developed into what it is today.

The foundations of power vary from age to age. As power bases shift, new groups and individuals acquire control over them. Thus, power relationships are continuously developing and changing. An understanding of power in society requires an understanding of the historical development of power relationships.

In our consideration of the historical development of power relationships, we shall look at the changing sources of power in American history and the characteristics of the individuals and groups who have acquired power. We shall describe the people of power in the early days of the republic and their shaping of the Constitution and the government it established. We shall discuss Charles Beard's interpretation of the Constitution as a document designed to protect the economic interests of those early powerholders. We shall also discuss historian Frederick Jackson Turner's ideas about how westward expansion and settlement created new bases of power and new powerholders. We shall explore the power struggle between northern commercial and industrial interests and southern planters and slave owners for control of western land, and the Civil War, which resulted from that struggle. In addition, we shall explore the development of an industrial elite in America after the Civil War, the impact of the depression on that elite, and the resulting growth of New Deal liberal reform. In a brief case study, "Reconstruction and Black History," we shall examine how history occasionally overlooks the experiences of powerless minorities and later reinterprets their contributions to society. Finally, we shall undertake a brief historical study, "Vietnam: A Political History," which argues that despite military victory, this war was "lost" through failures of America's political leadership.

Social Sciences and Social Problems

Social problems—the major challenges confronting society—include ideological conflict, racism, sexism, poverty, crime, violence, urban decay, and international conflict. These problems do not confine themselves to one or another of the disciplines of social science. They spill over the boundaries of anthropology, economics, sociology, political science, psychology, and history—they are *interdisciplinary* in character. Each of these problems has its *historical* antecedents, its *social* and *psychological* roots, its *cultural* manifestations, its *economic* consequences, and its impact on *government* and public policy. The origins of these social problems, as well as the various solutions proposed, involve complex power relationships.

interdisciplinary study
the use of theory, methods, or findings from more than one social science

Ideological Conflict

Ideas have power. Indeed, whole societies are shaped by systems of ideas that we call *ideologies*. The study of ideologies—liberalism, conservatism, socialism, communism, fascism, radicalism—is not a separate social science. Rather, the study of ideologies spans all the social sciences, and it is closely related to philosophy. Ideologies are integrated systems of ideas that rationalize a way of life, establish stan-

ideology
an integrated system of ideas that rationalize and justify the exercise of power in society

dards of "rightness" and "wrongness," and provide emotional impulses to action. Ideologies usually include economic, political, social, psychological, and cultural ideas, as well as interpretations of history.

Ideologies rationalize and justify power in society. By providing a justification for the exercise of power, the ideology itself becomes a base of power in society. Ideology "legitimizes" power, making the exercise of power acceptable to the masses and thereby adding to the power of the elite. However, ideologies also affect the behavior of the elite, because once an ideology is deeply rooted in society, powerholders themselves are bound by it.

In our study of power and ideology, we shall first explore the ideology of *classical liberalism*—an ideology that attacked the established power of a hereditary aristocracy and asserted the dignity, worth, and freedom of the individual. Classical liberalism and capitalism justify the power of private enterprise and the market system. Whereas classical liberalism limits the powers of government, *modern liberalism* accepts governmental power as a positive force in freeing people from poverty, ignorance, discrimination, and ill health. It justifies the exercise of governmental power over private enterprise and the establishment of the welfare state. In contrast, *modern conservatism* doubts the ability of the governmental planners to solve society's problems; conservatism urges greater reliance on family, church, and individual initiative and effort.

We shall then look at ideologies that have influenced other societies. *Fascism* is a power-oriented ideology that asserts the supremacy of a nation or race over the interests of individuals, groups, and other social institutions. *Marxism* attacks the market system, free enterprise, and individualism; it justifies revolutionary power in overthrowing liberal capitalist systems and the establishment of a "dictatorship of the proletariat." *Socialism* calls for the evolutionary democratic replacement of the private enterprise system with government ownership of industry.

We shall describe the current crisis of communism and the reasons for its collapse in eastern Europe and the former Soviet Union, and communism's unpopularity among the Chinese people. We shall also record the recent historic events of democratic movements in communist nations and shall provide a case study, "The Rise and Fall of Communism in the Former Soviet Union."

Racial and Sexual Inequality

Historically, no social problem has challenged the United States more than racial inequality. It is the only issue over which Americans ever fought a civil war. We shall describe the American experience with racism and the civil rights movement, which brought about significant changes in American life. We want to understand the philosophy of that movement, particularly the "nonviolent direct action" philosophy of Nobel Peace Prize winner Dr. Martin Luther King, Jr. We shall describe the recent successes of blacks in acquiring political power. However, we shall also examine continuing inequalities between blacks and whites in income, employment, and other conditions of life in the United States. Our case study describes the political rise of Douglas Wilder, the nation's first black governor. In addition, we confront sexism in American life, particularly in the economy. And we shall examine the arguments both for and against government efforts to assure "comparable worth" in the labor market. We shall describe the successes and failures of the women's movement in recent years and examine the constitutional status of abortion laws. Finally, we shall examine the controversy over "affirmative action" and "reverse discrimination" and its implication for how America is to achieve real equality.

Bertrand Russell: Power Is to the Social Sciences What Energy Is to Physics

Bertrand Russell (1872–1970), English philosopher and mathematician, is regarded as one of the twentieth century's greatest thinkers, mainly because of his contributions to mathematics and symbolic logic. However, Russell possessed a great breadth of interest that included history, economics, and political science, as well as education, morals, and social problems. He received the Nobel Prize in literature "in recognition of his many-sided and significant authorship, in which he has constantly figured as a defender of humanity and freedom of thought." He summarized his views about the importance of power in society in a book significantly entitled *Power: A New Social Analysis.**

First of all, power is fundamental to the social sciences:

The fundamental concept in the social sciences is power, in the same sense in which energy is the fundamental concept in physics.

Second, the desire for power as well as wealth motivates people:

When a moderate degree of comfort is assured, both individuals and communities will pursue power rather than wealth: they may seek wealth as a means to power, or they may forgo an increase of wealth in order to secure an increase of power, but in the former case as in the latter their fundamental motive is not economic. . . .

Third, power takes many forms:

Like energy, power has many forms, such as wealth, armaments, civil authority, influence on opinion. No one of these can be regarded as subordinate to any other, and there is no one form from which the others are derivative. The attempt to treat one form of power, say wealth, in isolation can only be partially successful. . . . To revert to the analogy of physics: power, like energy, must be regarded as continually passing from any one of its forms into any other, and it should be the business of social science to seek the laws of such transformations.

Finally, power produces social change:

Those whose love of power is not strong are unlikely to have much influence on the course of events. The men who cause social changes are, as a rule, men who strongly desire to do so. Love of power, therefore, is a characteristic of the men who are causally important. We should, of course, be mistaken if we regarded it as the sole human motive, but this mistake would not lead us so much astray as might be expected in the search for causal laws in social science, since love of power is the chief motive producing the changes which social science has to study.

Poverty and powerlessness: searching through trash bags for food on West Houston Street in New York City.
Source: Spencer Grant/Photo Researchers

Poverty and Powerlessness

powerlessness
a social–psychological condition of hopelessness, indifference, distrust, and cynicism

The American economy has produced the highest standard of living in the world, yet a significant number of Americans live in poverty. We shall observe that poverty can be defined as *economic hardship* or as *economic inequality* and that each definition implies a different governmental approach to the problem. Poverty can also be defined as *powerlessness*—a social–psychological condition of hopelessness, indifference, distrust, and cynicism. We shall then discuss whether or not there is a culture of poverty—a way of life of the poor that is passed on to future generations—and what its implications for government policy are. We shall describe government efforts to cope with poverty and discuss whether or not some government policies encourage poverty. We shall focus special attention on homelessness in America. Finally, we shall examine the future of the Social Security program in a look at "Senior Power."

Crime and Violence

a problem of democratic government
to protect its citizens without violating individual liberty

Governmental power must be balanced against *individual freedom.* A democratic society must exercise police powers to protect its citizens, yet it must not unduly restrict individual liberty. We shall explore the problem of crime in society, the constitutional rights of defendants, the role of the courts, and the relationship between drug use and crime. We shall also describe briefly the history of violence in American society and the continuous role that violence has played in American struggles for power. We shall summarize social-psychological explanations of vio-

Power in international affairs: U.S.-led coalition forces liberate Kuwait from Iraqi occupation in the Gulf War.
Source: Jacques Langevin/Sygma

lence, violence as a form of political activity, and violence as an aspect of lower-class culture. Finally, we shall examine the arguments for and against the death penalty as society's ultimate sanction.

Urban Life

A variety of social problems affect the quality of life in the United States. The solution to these problems, if there is any solution, depends in great part on how government chooses to exercise its powers. We shall explore the growth of urban and suburban populations in the United States. We shall also explore the social patterns of urban life—the characteristic forms of social interaction and organization that typically emerge in a large metropolis—and the socioeconomic conflicts between cities and suburbs. We shall observe how our nation's communities are governed. We shall focus special attention on the social and economic problems of the inner city and how the concentration of social problems can make them worse. Finally, we shall present a case study, "Community Power Structures," to compare power structures in different cities.

International Conflict

The struggle for power is global. It involves all the nations and peoples of the world, whatever their goals or ideals. Nearly 200 nations in the world claim *sovereignty:* authority over their internal affairs, freedom from outside intervention,

sovereignty
authority over internal affairs, freedom from outside intervention, and recognition by other nations

and political and legal recognition by other nations. But sovereignty is a legal fiction; it requires power to make sovereignty a reality. Over the years nations have struggled for power through wars and diplomacy. The struggle has led to attempts to maintain a fragile balance of power among large and small nations, as well as to attempts to achieve collective security through the United Nations and other alliances. Despite its internal problems, Russia remains a nuclear "superpower," together with the United States. In our discussion of the international system, we shall describe the nuclear "balance of terror" and the "triad" of weapons that maintains this balance. We shall describe the history of the Strategic Arms Limitations Talks (SALT) between the United States and the Soviet Union, the Intermediate-Range Nuclear Forces (INF) Treaty, and the major reductions in nuclear forces agreed to in the Strategic Arms Reduction Talks (START) Treaty. The collapse of communism in eastern Europe brought an end to the Soviet-dominated Warsaw Pact and changed the balance of power in Europe. We shall describe the NATO alliance and speculate on the future of the new Europe. The United States continues to face challenges around the world; we shall describe various regional mini-balances of power, notably in the Middle East. Finally, we shall observe the continuing need for U.S. military power in our case study, "American Military Power: Desert Storm."

Notes

1. Harold Lasswell and Abraham Kaplan, *Power and Society* (New Haven, Conn.: Yale University Press, 1950), p. 219.
2. Rollo May, *Power and Innocence* (New York: Norton, 1977), p. 20.
3. C. Wright Mills, *The Power Elite* (New York: Oxford University Press, 1956), p. 9.
4. Ibid., p. 10.

About This Chapter

Power in society is not just an abstract concept or a convenient focus for academic exercise. Nor is power something that is located exclusively in the nation's capitals. Power is very much a real factor that affects the lives of each of us. We experience it in some form in our families, in school, and at work; we feel its effects in the grocery store and on the highway. And we each react to it in characteristic ways. Our aim in this chapter was to understand just what power *is*. We also saw why it provides us with a useful perspective from which to gain a unified view of the social sciences and the social problems that concern us all.

Now that you have read this chapter, you should be able to

- define power in society and describe its characteristics;
- define the area of study of each of the social sciences; as well as their common focus, and discuss how each relates to power in society;
- identify the major social problems that the social sciences study and explain why they are interdisciplinary in nature and how they relate to power.

Discussion Questions

1. How would you define power? What characteristics of power deserve to be discussed in any definition of power?

2. Consider the power relationships that directly and indirectly affect your life. On the basis of your experiences and observations, assess the validity of these statements by Bertrand Russell: "The fundamental concept in the social sciences is power, in the same sense in which energy is the fundamental concept in physics. . . . When a moderate degree of comfort is assured, both individuals and communities will pursue power rather than wealth. . . . Love of power is the chief motive producing the changes which social science has to study."

3. Identify and briefly define the area of study of each of the social sciences. Discuss how you would study power from the perspective of each of these disciplines.

4. What is meant by the *interdisciplinary* study of social problems?

5. Choose two of the following social problems and briefly explain how they involve power: (a) racial and sexual inequality, (b) poverty, (c) crime and violence, (d) international conflict.

Social Sciences and the Scientific Method

2

CHAPTER

Science and the Scientific Method

A *science* may be broadly defined as any organized *body of knowledge,* or it may be more narrowly defined as a discipline that employs the *scientific method.* If we use the broad definition, we can safely say that all the social sciences are indeed sciences. However, if we narrow our definition to only those disciplines that employ the scientific method, then some questions arise about whether the social sciences are really scientific. In other words, if science is defined as a *method of study,* rather than a *body of knowledge,* then not all studies in the social sciences are truly scientific.

The *scientific method* is a method of explanation that develops and tests theories about how observable facts or events are related. What does this definition really mean? How is this method of study actually applied in the social sciences? To answer these questions, let us examine each aspect of the scientific method separately.

scientific method
a method of explanation that develops and tests theories about how observable facts or events are related

Explaining Relationships

The goal of the scientific method is explanation. When using this method, we seek to answer *why.* Any scientific inquiry must begin by observing and classifying things. Just as biology begins with the careful observation, description, and classification of thousands upon thousands of different forms of life, the social sciences also must begin with the careful observation, description, and classification of various forms of human behavior. But the goal is explanation, not just description. Just as biology seeks to develop theories of evolution and genetics to explain the various forms of life upon the earth, the social sciences seek to develop theories to explain why human beings behave as they do.

To answer the question of *why,* the scientific method searches for *relationships.* All scientific *hypotheses* assert some relationship between observable facts or events. The social sciences seek to find relationships that explain human behavior. The first question is whether two or more events or behaviors are related in any way—that is, do they occur together consistently? The second question is whether either event or behavior *causes* the other. Social scientists first try to learn whether human events have occurred together merely by chance or accident, or whether they occur together so consistently that their relationship cannot be a mere coincidence. A relationship that is not likely to have occurred by chance is said to be *significant.* After observing a significant relationship, social scientists next ask whether there is a *causal relationship* between the phenomena (that is, whether the facts or events occurred together because one is the cause of the other), or whether both phenomena are being caused by some third factor. Box 2-1 explains some of the terms used in scientific study of data.

hypothesis
a tentative statement about a relationship between observable facts or events

significant
not likely to have occurred by chance

Developing and Testing Hypotheses

The scientific method seeks to develop statements (hypotheses) about how events or behaviors might be related and then determine the validity of these statements by careful, systematic, and logical tests. Scientific tests are really exercises in logic.

For example, if we wanted to find out something about the relationship between race and party voting, we might collect and record data from a national sample of black and white voters chosen at random (see the discussion of survey research later in this chapter). If our data showed that *all* blacks voted Democratic and *all* whites Republican, it would be obvious that there was a perfect relationship between race and voting. In contrast, if both blacks and whites voted Republican and Democratic in the *same* proportions, then it would be obvious that there was *no* relationship. But in the social sciences we rarely have such obvious, clear-cut results. Generally our data will show a mixed pattern. For example, in the 1992 presidential election between Democrat Bill Clinton and Republican George Bush, 82 percent of blacks voted Democratic and only 11 percent voted Republican. In that same election, 41 percent of whites voted Republican and only 39 percent voted Democratic. If there had been *no* relationship between race and voting, then blacks and whites would have voted Democratic and Republican in roughly the *same* proportions. But as we have just noted, blacks voted Democratic in far heavier proportions (82 percent) than whites (39 percent). This difference is not likely to have occurred by chance—thus we consider it "significant." The same pattern of heavy Democratic voting among blacks can be observed in other elections (see Table 2-1). So we can make the *inference* that race is related to voting.

However, the existence of a statistically significant relationship does not prove cause and effect. We must employ additional logic to find out which fact or event caused the other, or whether both were caused by a third fact or event. We can eliminate as illogical the possibility that voting Democratic causes one to become black. That leaves us with two possibilities: being black may cause Democratic voting, or being black and voting Democratic may both be caused by some third condition. For example, the real causal relationship may be between low incomes and Democratic voting: low-income groups, which would include many blacks,

inference
a causal statement based on data showing a significant relationship

---

BOX 2-1

The Vocabulary of Social Science

Social science researchers use many special terms in their work, some of which have already been defined. It helps in reading social science research reports to understand the specific meanings given to the following terms:

Theory: A causal explanation of relationship between observable facts or events. A good theory fits the facts, explains why they occur, and allows us to predict future events.

Hypothesis: A tentative statement about a relationship between facts or events. The hypothesis should be derived from the theory and should be testable.

Variable: A characteristic that varies among different individuals or groups.

Independent variable: Whatever is hypothesized to be the cause of something else.

Dependent variable: Whatever is hypothesized to be the effect of something else.

Significant: Not likely to have occurred by chance.

Correlation: Significant relationships found in the data.

Spurious: Describing a relationship among facts or events that is *not* causal, but is a product of the fact that both the independent and dependent variables are being caused by a third factor.

Case study: An in-depth investigation of a particular event. A good case study should suggest theories and hypotheses that can then be used to study other cases.

An Experiment in Crime Fighting

Let us consider an example of applying the classic scientific research design to a specific social problem—neighborhood crime. A local government is considering the installation of street lighting in residential neighborhoods to combat crime. The hypothesis is that increased lighting will reduce crime rates. Before spending large sums of money to light up the entire city without knowing whether the plan will work, the city council decides to put the program to a scientific test. The council selects several neighborhoods that have identical characteristics (crime rate, land use, population density, unemployment, population age, income, racial balance, and so forth). Some of the areas are randomly selected for the installation of new street lighting. Crime rates are carefully measured before the installation of streetlights in those neighborhoods that received new lighting and in those neighborhoods that did not receive streetlights (see Figure 2-1). After several months of new lighting, crime rates are again carefully measured in the experimental neighborhoods (which received lights) and the control neighborhoods (which did not). The results are compared. If a significant reduction in crime occurred in the neighborhoods with new lights but did not occur in the neighborhoods without lights, and no other changes can be identified in the neighborhoods that might account for the differences, then the city can have some confidence that lighting reduces crime. An expansion of lighting to the rest of the city would then seem appropriate.

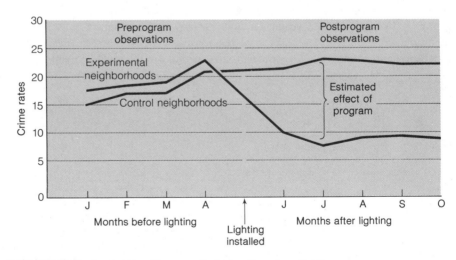

FIGURE 2-1 A scientific research design for crime fighting

tend to identify with the Democratic party. We can test this new hypothesis by looking at the voting behavior of other low-income groups to see if they voted Democratic in the same proportions as did blacks. It turns out that blacks vote more heavily Democratic than white low-income groups, so we can reject the low-income explanation. We may therefore infer that race is independently related to voting

TABLE 2-1   Voting by Race in Presidential Elections, 1968–1992

| Testing the hypothesis: Blacks tend to vote Democratic | | | | |
Election year	Candidates	All	Whites	Blacks
1992	Republican Bush	38	41	11
	Democrat Clinton	43	39	82
	Independent Perot	19	20	7
1988	Republican Bush	54	60	11
	Democrat Dukakis	46	40	89
1984	Republican Reagan	59[a]	66	9
	Democrat Mondale	41	34	90
1980	Republican Reagan	51	56	10
	Democrat Carter	41	36	86
	Independent Anderson	7	7	2
1976	Republican Ford	48	52	15
	Democrat Carter	50	46	85
1972	Republican Nixon	62	68	13
	Democrat McGovern	38	32	87
1968	Republican Nixon	44	47	12
	Democrat Humphrey	43	38	85
	Independent Wallace	13	15	3

[a]Figures are percentages of the vote won by each candidate. Percentages in each election may not add up to 100 because of voting for minor-party candidates.

Source: Data from the *Gallup Opinion Index* (December 1984), the *New York Times* (November 10, 1988), and the *New York Times* (November 5, 1992).

Computerized telephone opinion surveys collect and record social science data.
Source: Lara Hartley

behavior. But there are many other possible alternatives to our explanation of the relationship between race and voting behavior. Social scientists must test as many alternative explanations as possible before asserting a causal relationship.

Every time we can reject an alternative explanation for the relationship we have observed, we increase our confidence that the relationship (as between race and voting behavior) is a causal one. Of course, in the areas of interest to social scientists someone can always think of new alternative explanations, so it is generally impossible to establish for certain that a causal relationship exists. Some social scientists react to the difficulties of proving "cause" by refusing to say that the relationships they find are anything more than *correlations,* or simply statistical relationships. The decision whether or not to call a relationship "causal" is difficult. Statistical techniques cannot guarantee that a relationship is causal; social scientists must be prepared to deal with probabilities rather than absolutes.

correlations
significant relationships that may or may not be causal

Dealing with Observable Phenomena

empirical
referring to observable facts and events; what is

The scientific method deals only with observable—empirical—facts and events. In other words, the scientific method deals with what *is,* rather than what *should be.* It cannot test the validity of values, norms, or feelings, except insofar as it can test for their existence in a society, group, or individual. For example, the scientific method can be employed to determine whether voting behavior is related to race, but it cannot determine whether voting behavior *should be* related to race. The latter question is a *normative* one (dealing with "ought" and "should"), rather than an empirical one (dealing with "is"). The scientific method is *descriptive* and *explanatory,* but not *normative.* The social sciences can explain many aspects of human behavior but cannot tell human beings how they ought to behave. For guidance in values and norms—for prescriptions about how people should live—we must turn to ethics, religion, or philosophy.

normative
referring to values or norms; what should be

Developing Theory

The scientific method strives to develop a systematic body of theory. Science is more than crude empiricism—the listing of facts without any statement of relationships among them. Of course, especially in the early stages of a science, research may consist largely of collecting data; but the ultimate goal of the scientific method is to develop verifiable statements about relationships among facts and events. It is the task of social scientists to find patterns and regularities in human behavior, just as it is the task of physicists and chemists to find patterns and regularities in the behavior of matter and energy. The social scientist's use of the scientific method, then, assumes that human behavior is not random, but rather that it is regular and predictable.

theories
explanations of facts or events

Theories are developed at different *levels of generality.* Theories with low levels of generality explain only a small or narrow range of behaviors. For example, the statement that blacks tend to vote Democratic is a fairly low-level generality about political behavior. Theories with higher levels of generality explain a greater or wider range of behavior. For example, the statement that racial differences cause political conflict has a higher level of generality. Strictly speaking, *a theory is a set of interrelated concepts at a fairly high level of generality.* Some social scientists concentrate on theory building rather than on empirical research; they try to develop sweeping social theories to explain all, or a large part, of human behavior. Still other social theorists provide insights, hunches, or vague notions that suggest possible explanations of human behavior, thus developing new hypotheses for empirical research.

Maintaining a Scientific Attitude

Perhaps more than anything else, *the scientific method is an attitude of doubt or skepticism.* It is an insistence on careful collection of data and systematic testing of ideas; a commitment to keep bias out of one's work, to collect and record all relevant facts, and to interpret them rationally regardless of one's feelings. For the social scientist, it is the determination to test explanations of human behavior by careful observations of real-world experiences. It is a recognition that any explanation is tentative and may be modified or disproved by careful investigation. Even the scientific theories that constitute the core knowledge in any discipline are not regarded as absolutes by the true social scientist; rather, they are regarded as probabilities or generalizations developed from what is known so far.

scientific attitude doubt or skepticism about theories until they have been scientifically tested

Why the Social Sciences Aren't Always "Scientific"

Not all the knowledge in social science is derived scientifically. A great deal of knowledge about human behavior comes to us through insight, intuition, random observation, folklore, and common sense rather than through careful scientific investigation. The scientific method we have just described was devised in the physical and biological sciences. There are many difficulties in applying this method to the study of individuals, groups, economies, classes, governments, nations, or whole societies. Let us examine some of the obstacles to the development of truly *scientific* social sciences.

Personal Bias

Social science deals with subjective topics and must rely on interpretation of results. Social scientists are part of what they investigate—they belong to a family, class, political party, interest group, profession, nation; they earn money and consume goods like everybody else. If the topic is an emotional one, the social scientist may find it much harder to suppress personal bias than does the investigator in the physical sciences: it is easier to conduct an unbiased study of migratory birds than of migrant workers.

It is difficult to conduct *value-free research.* Even the selection of a topic reveals the values of the researcher. Researchers study what they think is important in society, and what they think is important is affected by their personal values. If it were only in the selection of the topic that researchers' values were reflected, there would be no great problem in social science research. But researchers' values are also frequently reflected in their perceptions of the data, in their statement of the hypoth-

value-free research scientific work unaffected by the values of society or the scientist

value intrusion
values may affect selection of topic for research

perceptions of the data

formulation of hypotheses

construction of tests

interpretation of findings

eses, in their design of the test for the hypotheses, and in their interpretation of the findings. *Value intrusion* can occur in many stages of the research process, which is why social scientists studying the same problems and using the same methods frequently end up with contradictory results.

Perhaps it is impossible to separate facts and values in social science research. As sociologist Louis Wirth explains:

> Since every assertion of a "fact" about the social world touches the interests of some individual or group, one cannot even call attention to the existence of certain "facts" without raising objections of those whose very raison d'etre in society rests upon a divergent interpretation of the "factual" situation.[1]

Public Attitudes

Another problem in the scientific study of human behavior centers on public attitudes toward social science. Few people would consider arguing with atomic physicists or biochemists about their respective fields, but most people believe they know something about social problems. Many people think they know exactly what should be done about juvenile delinquency, expanding welfare rolls, and race relations. Very often their information is limited, and their view of the problem is simplistic. When a social scientist suggests that a problem is very complex, that it has many causes, and that information on the problem is incomplete, people may believe that the social scientist is simply obscuring matters that seem obvious.

Social science sometimes develops explanations of human behavior that contradict established ideas. Of course, the physical and biological sciences have long faced this same problem: Galileo faced the opposition of the established church when he argued that the earth revolved around the sun, and Darwin's theory of evolution continues to be a public issue. But social science generates even more intense feelings when it deals with poverty, crime, sexual behavior, race relations, and other heated topics.

Limitations and Design of Social Science Research

Another set of problems in social science centers on the limitations and design of social science research. It is not really possible to conduct some forms of controlled experiments on human beings. For example, we cannot deliberately subject people to poverty and deprivation just to see if it makes them violent. Instead, social researchers must find situations of poverty and deprivation in order to make the necessary observations about causes of violence. In a laboratory, we can control all or most of the factors that go into the experimental situation. But in real-world observations, we cannot control factors; this makes it difficult to pinpoint what it is that causes the behavior we are studying. Moreover, even where some experimentation is permitted, human beings frequently modify their behavior simply because they know they are being observed in a social science experiment. This phenomenon, which is known as the *Hawthorne effect,* makes it difficult to determine whether the observed behavior is a product of the stimulus being introduced or merely a product of the experimental situation itself.

Hawthorne effect
people modify their behavior simply because they know they are being observed by social scientists

Complexity of Human Behavior

Perhaps the most serious reservation about social science research is that human behavior is shaped by so many different forces that it resists scientific explanation. A complete understanding of such a complex system as human society is beyond our current capabilities. At present, human behavior can be as well understood through art, literature, and music as through scientific research.

What Is a "Fact"?

In the social sciences very few statements can be made that apply to *every* circumstance. We cannot say, for example, that "all blacks vote Democratic." This is a *universal statement* covering every black person, and universal statements are seldom true in the social sciences. Moreover, it would be difficult to examine the voting behavior of every black person in the past and in the future to prove that the statement is true.

universal statement
a statement that applies to every circumstance

A more accurate statement might be: "Most blacks vote Democratic." This is a *probabilistic statement* covering "most" blacks, but it does not exclude the possibility that some blacks vote Republican. An even more accurate statement would be that "82 percent of blacks cast their ballots for Democratic candidate Bill Clinton in the 1992 presidential election." This means there was an 82 percent *probability* of a black voter's casting his or her ballot for Democrat Bill Clinton.

probabilistic statement
a statement that applies to some proportion of circumstances

A probabilistic statement is a fact, just like a universal statement. Students in the physical sciences deal with many universal statements—for example, "Water boils at 100°C." Water always does this. But students of the social sciences must be prepared to deal with probabilistic statements—for example, "Blacks are three times more likely to experience poverty than whites." Social science students must learn to think in probabilities rather than in absolute terms.

Social scientists must also beware of substituting individual cases for statements of probability. They must be careful about reasoning from one or two observed cases. A statement such as "I know a black family that always votes Republican" may be true, but it would be very dangerous to generalize about the voting habits of all black voters on the basis of this one case. We always build tentative generalizations from our own world of experiences. However, as social scientists, we must ensure that our own experiences are typical. We should keep in mind that the "facts" of the social sciences are seldom absolute—they rarely cover the complexity of any aspect of human behavior. So we must be prepared to study probabilities.

The Classic Scientific Research Design

An *experiment* is a scientific test that is controlled by the researcher and designed to observe the effect of a specific program or treatment. The *classic scientific research design* involves the comparison of specific changes in two or more care-

experiment
a scientific test controlled by the researcher to observe effects of a specific program or treatment

fully selected groups, both of which are identical in every way, except that one has been given the program or treatment under study while the other has not.

This design involves the following:

1. Identification of the goals of the study and the selection of specific hypotheses to be tested.

2. Selection of the groups to be compared—the *experimental group*, which will participate in the program or undergo the treatment being studied, and the *control group*, which is similar to the experimental group in every way except that it will *not* participate in the program or undergo the treatment being studied.

3. Measurement of the characteristics of both the experimental and control groups *before* participation in the experiment.

4. Application of the program or treatment to the experimental group, but not to the control group. (Members of the control group may be given a *placebo*— some activity or program known to have no effect—to make them believe they are participating in the experiment. Indeed, the scientific staff administering the experiment may not know which group is the real experimental group and which group is the control group. When neither the staff nor the group members themselves know who is really receiving the treatment, the experiment is called a *double-blind experiment.*)

5. Measurement of the condition of both the experimental and control groups *after* the program or treatment. If there are measurable differences between the experimental and control groups, the scientist can begin to infer that the program or treatment has a specific effect. If there are *no* measurable differences, then the scientist must accept the *null hypothesis*—the statement that the program or treatment has no effect.

6. Comparison of the preprogram/pretreatment status versus the postprogram/posttreatment status in both groups. This is a check to see if the difference between the experimental and control groups occurred during the experiment. This method, used alone, is sometimes called a "before–after" study.

7. A search for plausible explanations for differences after treatment between the control and experimental groups that might be due to factors other than the treatment itself.

The classic research design is not without its problems. Social scientists must be aware of the more difficult problems in applying this research design to social science research and must be prepared on occasion to change their procedures accordingly. These problems include the following:

1. As noted earlier, members of the experimental group may respond differently to a program if they know it is an experiment. Because of this Hawthorne effect, members of a control group are often told they are participating in an experiment, even though nothing is really being done to the control group.

2. If the experimental group is only one part of a larger city, state, or nation, the response to the experiment may be different from what it would have been had all parts of the city, state, or nation been receiving the program. For example, if only one part of a city receives streetlights, criminals may simply operate as usual (even with the lights), and total crime rates will be unaffected.

---

control group
a group, identical to the experimental group, that does not undergo treatment; used for comparison

null hypothesis
a statement that the program or treatment has no effect

3. If persons are allowed to *volunteer* for the experiment, then experimental and control groups may not be representative of the population as a whole.

4. In some situations, political pressures may make it impossible to provide one neighborhood or group with certain services while denying these same services to the rest of the city, state, or nation. If everyone *thinks* the program is beneficial before the experiment begins, no one will want to be in the control group.

5. It may be considered morally wrong to provide some groups or persons with services, benefits, or treatment while denying the same to other groups or persons (control groups) who are identical in their needs or problems.

6. Careful research is costly and time-consuming. Public officials often need to make immediate decisions. They cannot spend time or money on research even if they understand the long-term benefits of careful investigation. Too often, politicians must operate on "short-run" rather than "long-run" considerations.

Gathering Social Science Data

How do social scientists go about observing the behaviors of individuals, groups, and societies? There are a variety of methods for gathering data; some fields rely more heavily on one method than on another. The *controlled experiment,* described earlier, is often used in psychology; the *survey* is frequently employed in political science and sociology; *field research,* or participant observation, is a major source of data in anthropology; and *secondary data analysis* is employed in all social sciences.

Survey Research

Most surveys ask questions of a representative sample of the population rather than question the entire population. A selected number of people, the *sample,* are chosen in a way that ensures that they are representative of the whole group of people, the *universe,* about which information is desired. In order to ensure that the sample is representative of the universe, most surveys rely on random selection. *Random sampling* means that each person in the universe has an equal chance of being selected for interviewing. Random sampling improves the likelihood that the responses obtained from the sample would be the same as those obtained from the universe if everyone were questioned. Hypothetically, we must obtain a random sample of American voters by throwing every voter's name in a giant box and blindly picking out 1,000 names to be interviewed. A more common method is to randomly select telephone area codes and then numbers from across the nation.

There is always the chance that the sample selected will *not* be representative of the universe. But survey researchers can estimate this *sampling error* through the mathematics of probability. The sampling error is usually expressed as a range above and below the sample response, within which there is a 95-percent likelihood that the universe response would be found if the entire universe were questioned. For example, if 63 percent of the people questioned (the sample) say they "approve" of the way the president is handling his job, and the sampling error is

universe
the whole group about which information is desired

random sample
each person in the universe has an equal chance of being selected for interviewing

sampling error
the range of responses in which a 95-percent chance exists that the sample reflects the universe

calculated at plus or minus 3 percent, then we can say that there is a 95-percent likelihood that the president's approval rating among the whole population (the universe) stands somewhere between 60 and 66 percent.

Large samples are not really necessary to narrow the sampling error. Large samples are not much more accurate than small samples. A sample of a few thousand— maybe even 1,000—is capable of reflecting the opinions of 1 million or 100 million voters fairly accurately. For example, a random sample of 1,000 voters across the United States can produce a sampling error (plus or minus) of only 3 percent.

survey research problems
unformed opinions
weakly held opinions
changing opinions

When polls go wrong, it is usually because public opinion is unformed, weakly held, or changing rapidly. If public opinion is really unformed on a topic, as may be the case in early presidential preference polls, people may choose a familiar name or a celebrity who is frequently mentioned in the news. Their thoughts about the presidential race are still largely unformed; as the campaign progresses, candidates who were once unknown and rated only a few percentage points in early polls can emerge as front-runners. Weakly held opinions are more likely to change than strongly held opinions. Political commentators sometimes say a particular candidate's support is "soft," meaning that his or her supporters are not very intense in their commitment, and, therefore, the polls could swing quickly away from the candidate. Finally, widely reported news events may change public opinion very rapidly. A survey can only measure opinions at the time it is taken. A few days later public opinion may change, especially if major events are receiving heavy television coverage. Some political pollsters conduct continuous surveys until election night in order to catch last-minute opinion changes.

A common test of the accuracy of survey research is the comparison of the actual vote in presidential elections to the predictions made by the major polls. Discrepancies between the actual and predicted vote percentages are sometimes used as rough measures of the validity of surveys. Most forecasts have been fairly accurate, but the 1980 Carter–Reagan presidential contest was an exception (see Table 2-2). Opinion was extraordinarily volatile during the campaign; the lead changed several times. Last-day media coverage of the one-year anniversary of the Iranian seizure of the U.S. embassy and detention of American personnel reminded people of Carter's weaknesses. Polling conducted on Sunday failed to catch persons who switched to Reagan by Tuesday (election day). It was not a problem of sample size or accuracy, but rather one of rapidly changing voter opinion.

The wording or phrasing of public opinion questions can often determine the outcome of a poll. Indeed, "loaded" or "leading" questions are often asked by unprofessional pollsters simply to produce results favorable to their side of an argument. They are hoping to inspire a "bandwagon effect," convincing people that most of the nation favors or opposes a particular candidate or viewpoint and therefore they should as well. Ideally, questions should be clear and precise, easily understood by the respondents, and as neutral and unbiased as possible. But because all questions have a potential bias, it is usually better to examine changes over time in responses to identically worded questions. (The case study on "Explaining Presidential Approval Ratings" examines responses to the same presidential popularity question asked over a period of over twenty-five years.)

TABLE 2-2   Forecasting Errors by Major Polls in Presidential Elections

	Predicted vote for winner (%)	Actual vote for winner (%)	Error
1992	Clinton	Clinton	1.0
USA Today/CNN	44.0	43.0	1.0
Gallup	44.0	43.0	1.0
1988	Bush	Bush	
USA Today/CNN	55.0	54.0	1.0
CBS/*N.Y. Times*	53.0	54.0	1.0
1984	Reagan	Reagan	
Gallup	59.3	59.0	0.3
CBS/*N.Y. Times*	60.9	59.0	1.9
ABC/*Washington Post*	59.3	59.0	0.3
1980	Reagan	Reagan	
Gallup	47.0	51.7	4.7
CBS/*N.Y. Times*	38.9	51.7	12.8
NBC/AP	48.0	51.7	3.7
1976	Carter	Carter	
Gallup	48.0	50.0	2.0
Roper	51.0	50.0	1.0
NBC	49.0	50.0	1.0

Even the most scientific surveys are not error-free, however. We have already noted that weakly held opinions can change rapidly. Some surveys ask questions about topics that most people had never considered before being interviewed. Then the pollsters report responses as "public opinion," when, in fact, very few people really had any opinion on the topic at all. Many respondents do not like to admit they do not know anything about the topic, so they give a meaningless response. Many respondents give "good citizen" responses, whether the responses are truthful or not. For example, people do not like to admit that they do not vote or that they do not care about politics. Surveys regularly report higher percentages of people *saying* they voted in an election than the *actual* number of ballots cast would indicate. Many people give socially respectable answers, even to an anonymous interviewer, rather than answers that suggest prejudice, hatred, or ignorance.

Field Research

Fieldwork is the cornerstone of modern anthropology. Many sociologists and political scientists also obtain their information through fieldwork. These social scientists study by direct, personal observation of people, events, and societies. *Field research* is essentially going where the action is, watching closely, and taking notes.

field research
directly observing social behavior

Fieldwork is usually less structured than either experimental or survey research. The scientist is not able to control many variables, as in experimental research. Nor

CASE STUDY

Explaining
Presidential
Approval
Ratings

President watching is a favorite pastime among political scientists. Regular surveys of the American people ask the question: "Do you approve or disapprove of the way _____ is handling his job as president?" By asking this same question over time about presidents, political scientists can monitor the ups and downs of presidential popularity. Then they can attempt to explain presidential popularity by examining events that correspond to changes in presidential approval ratings.

One hypothesis that helps explain presidential approval ratings centers on the election cycle. The hypothesis is that presidential popularity is highest immediately after election or reelection, but it steadily erodes over time. Note that this hypothesis tends to be supported by the survey data in Figure 2-2. This simple graph shows, over time, the percentage of survey respondents who say they approve of the way the president is handling his job. Election dates are shown on the graph to correspond to high approval ratings for the winner. Presidents and their advisers generally know about this "honeymoon" period hypothesis and try to use it to their advantage by pushing hard for their policies in Congress early in the term.

Another hypothesis centers on the president's responsibility for national and international events. The hypothesis is that presidential popularity falls when national or international events threaten the nation's well-being. The Vietnam War eroded President Johnson's initial high approval ratings. American ground combat troops were sent to Vietnam in early 1965, but by 1968 the war appeared "unwinnable." President Nixon began the withdrawal of U.S. troops from Vietnam, but casualties continued and his popularity also eroded. Nixon's highest ratings came in early 1973 when the Paris Peace Accords were signed, ending U.S. involvement in Vietnam. However, Nixon's popularity was short-lived, as the Watergate scandal unfolded. Nixon's low approval ratings in early 1974 contributed to his decision to resign. President Carter's ratings were adversely affected by Iran's seizure of U.S. embassy personnel in 1979; he experienced a brief upturn when the Soviet Union invaded Afghanistan, but his generally low ratings contributed to his election defeat in 1980. President Reagan suffered through the recession in 1982, but he was a very popular president until 1987, when details of the arms-for-hostages negotiations with Iran and the diversion of profits to the Contras were revealed. Yet Reagan recovered from the Iran-Contra affair and left office with the highest approval rating of any president at the end of his term.

George Bush's highest ratings have occurred during international crises. He won high approval ratings following the U.S. invasion of Panama in December 1989, and his ratings also rose following the Iraqi invasion of Kuwait and his decision to sponsor a UN embargo against Saddam Hussein's aggression. But his popularity quickly declined thereafter with the onset of an economic recession at home. Bush's highest ratings—the highest approval ratings ever accorded a modern president—came with the decisive U.S. military victory against Iraq in the Persian Gulf War.

(continued)

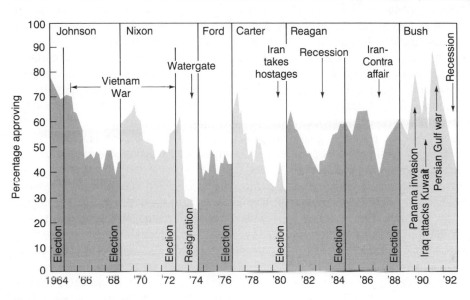

FIGURE 2-2 Presidential approval survey

is the scientist able to know whether the peoples or societies being studied are truly representative of all other peoples or societies, as in survey research. However, careful field reports can provide qualitative information that is often missing from experimental and survey research. Researchers can report on emotions, feelings, and beliefs that underlie people's behavioral responses. Researchers can also report on attitudes, myths, symbols, and interpersonal relationships that could not be detected by other research methods. Most important, they can observe individuals, groups, and societies as they live in their subjects' environment.

Fieldwork research often involves *participant-observation,* where the researcher both observes and participates in the society being studied. Direct participation (moving to Appalachia and getting a job as a coal miner) can provide insights that would otherwise escape a researcher. However, personal participation can also interfere with the detachment required for scientific inquiry. There is also the question of whether the scientist should identify himself or herself as a researcher, which could change the behavior of the people being studied, or conceal his or her identity, which could encourage people to act naturally but raises ethical questions. Some behavior simply cannot be observed if social scientists are identified as researchers. Consider the dilemma of the sociologist who wanted to study homosexual behavior in public toilets. It was not really feasible for him to go on field trips to public toilets identifying himself as a sociologist, asking people if they were homosexuals seeking contacts, and, if so, could he watch. So instead he began vis-

participant-observation
researchers both observe and participate in the behavior being studied

iting public toilets where he suspected homosexual activity was taking place and volunteering to act as a "lookout" for those engaging in the action. He discovered that a lookout was an acceptable, even important, position, and he took advantage of it to study homosexual behavior. Later, after the publication of his study, he came under attack by homosexuals and others for deceiving his subjects.[2]

Anthropology relies heavily on field research. To describe cultures accurately, many anthropologists chose to live among the people they were studying, directly observing and participating in their lives. Many early anthropological studies were intuitive: they produced in-depth, firsthand, long-term observations of societies, but these observations were not very systematic. Some would focus on child rearing, or religion, or art, or language, or particularly strange or bizarre practices. Later, anthropological fieldwork became more disciplined, and anthropologists began systematic comparisons of cultures.

ethnography
systematic description of a society's customary behaviors, beliefs, and attitudes

Ethnography is the systematic description of a society's customary behaviors, beliefs, and attitudes. Ethnographic studies are usually produced by anthropologists who have spent some time living with, interviewing, and observing the people. Anthropologists in the field can test hypotheses by directly asking and observing the people and learning about the context of their behavior and beliefs. For example, an anthropologist in the field may think the society he or she is studying practices polygamy (one man marries more than one woman simultaneously) because it has more women than men. But as ethnographic studies are gradually acquired for a larger number of different cultures, anthropologists can begin to test hypotheses by cross-cultural comparisons. They may find reports of some societies that practice polygamy even though the number of men and women is equal. This finding would cast doubt on the hypothesis that polygamy is caused by gender-ratio imbalances.

case study
in-depth investigation of a particular event in order to understand it as fully as possible

A *case study* is an in-depth investigation of a particular event in order to understand it as fully as possible. A case study may involve an examination of a single governmental decision, or a single business firm, or a single town, or a single society. A hypothesis may be tested in a case study, but researchers know that a single case is not sufficient to make generalizations about other cases. A single case study is more useful for generating hypotheses to be explored later in comparative studies involving larger numbers of cases. However, some case studies involve limited comparisons, as when two, three, or four cases are studied simultaneously.

Secondary Source Data

Social scientists do not always collect their own data, that is, primary source data. Often, social scientists rely on data collected by government agencies, other organizations, or other researchers (see Box 2-2 for international sources); these data are known as secondary source data. One of the most important sources of data for social scientists is the U.S. Census Bureau, which not only provides the decennial census data on the population of the United States, but also regularly collects and publishes data on governments, housing, manufacturing, and so on. Each year, the Census Bureau also publishes the *Statistical Abstract of the United States,* which summarizes facts about birthrates and death rates, education, income, health, welfare, housing, election outcomes, government taxing and spending, crime, national

BOX 2-2

Cross-National Perspectives

Social scientists are also obliged to rely on governments and international organizations, notably the United Nations, for information on nations. This is particularly true when comparative data on a number of nations are desired. The U.S. Bureau of the Census prepares a *World Population Profile* annually, and the United Nations Educational, Scientific, and Cultural Organization (UNESCO) prepares a *Statistical Yearbook*. Table 2-3 is drawn from these sources. The population of the world was estimated to be over 5 billion in 1990—5,332,824,000. Only 250 million people, or about 5 percent of the world's population, live in the United States. Well over 1 billion people, or about 21 percent of the world's population, live in China.

However, there are many problems in cross-national comparisons. Many of the less developed nations do not possess the technical capabilities to collect and report data on their people. Even their population figures are only estimates, because not all nations can afford a regular, careful, and accurate census of their populations. Moreover, definitions of data and methods of collection differ around the world, rendering direct comparisons among nations difficult. The United Nations sometimes adjusts figures reported by some nations to make them more comparable with figures from other countries. Finally, some governments occasionally hide or misrepresent data they believe may reflect badly on their system of government.

While remaining aware of these problems, social scientists nonetheless can learn a great deal from comparing data from nations around the world. Even if we are interested primarily in life in the United States, we can obtain a better perspective on ourselves by comparing how others live. And as improved transportation, communication, technology, and trade increasingly bring the peoples of the world together, looking beyond our own borders becomes increasingly important.

TABLE 2-3   The World's Most Populous Nations Ranked by Population Size, 1950–2050

Shifting population size in developed and developing nations is causing dramatic changes in the ranking of countries by population. In 1950 Iran was 28th in size, moved to 21st in 1987, and is projected to be the 10th largest country by 2025. Nigeria and Pakistan, ranked 13th and 14th in 1950, are expected to become the 3rd and 4th largest countries by 2050. As populations in developing countries continue to increase, populations in developed regions have already begun to decline and are projected to continue decreasing. The United Kingdom was 8th in size in 1950, dropped to 16th in 1987, and is projected to be 27th by 2025, and not on the list of top 30 countries by 2050. Similarly, West Germany dropped from 9th position in 1950 to 14th in 1987 and is projected to be 29th by 2025 and not on the list by 2050.

1950	1987	2025	2050
1. China	1. China	1. China	1. India
2. India	2. India	2. India	2. China
3. Soviet Union	3. Soviet Union	3. Commonwealth*	3. Nigeria
4. United States	4. United States	4. Indonesia	4. Pakistan
5. Japan	5. Indonesia	5. Nigeria	5. Commonwealth*
6. Indonesia	6. Brazil	6. United States	6. Brazil
7. Brazil	7. Japan	7. Brazil	7. Indonesia
8. United Kingdom	8. Nigeria	8. Pakistan	8. United States
9. West Germany	9. Bangladesh	9. Bangladesh	9. Bangladesh
10. Italy	10. Pakistan	10. Iran	10. Iran
11. Bangladesh	11. Mexico	11. Ethiopia	11. Ethiopia
12. France	12. Vietnam	12. Mexico	12. Philippines
13. Nigeria	13. Philippines	13. Philippines	13. Mexico

(continued)

BOX 2-2

(continued)

TABLE 2-3 *(continued)*

1950	1987	2025	2050
14. Pakistan	14. West Germany	**14. Vietnam**	**14. Vietnam**
15. Mexico	15. Italy	15. Japan	**15. Kenya**
16. Spain	16. United Kingdom	**16. Egypt**	**16. Zaire**
17. Vietnam	17. France	**17. Turkey**	**17. Egypt**
18. Poland	**18. Thailand**	**18. Zaire**	**18. Tanzania**
19. Egypt	**19. Turkey**	**19. Kenya**	**19. Turkey**
20. Philippines	**20. Egypt**	**20. Thailand**	20. Japan
21. Turkey	**21. Iran**	**21. Tanzania**	**21. Saudi Arabia**
22. South Korea	**22. Ethiopia**	**22. Burma**	**22. Thailand**
23. Ethiopia	**23. South Korea**	**23. South Africa**	**23. Uganda**
24. Thailand	24. Spain	**24. Sudan**	**24. Sudan**
25. Burma	**25. Burma**	**25. South Korea**	**25. Burma**
26. East Germany	26. Poland	26. France	**26. South Africa**
27. Argentina	**27. South Africa**	27. United Kingdom	**27. Syria**
28. Iran	**28. Zaire**	28. Italy	**28. Morocco**
29. Yugoslavia	**29. Argentina**	29. West Germany	**29. Algeria**
30. Romania	**30. Colombia**	**30. Uganda**	**30. Iraq**

Note: Developing countries are shown in **bold.**

*Commonwealth of Independent States: states of the former Soviet Union including Russia, Ukraine, and Bylorusse, minus Latvia, Lithuania, and Estonia.

Source: U.S. Bureau of the Census, *World Population Profile: 1987* (1987).

defense, employment, prices, business, transportation, agriculture, trade, and manufacturing. Footnotes to the data summarized in the *Statistical Abstract* tell where additional data can be found on each topic. (See Box 2-3, "Using the *Statistical Abstract.*")

BOX 2-3

Using the *Statistical Abstract*

The *Statistical Abstract of the United States* is published annually by the U.S. Census Bureau. Statistics in each edition are for the most recent year or period available by October of the preceding year. Each new edition contains nearly 900 tables. Most of the tables are updated versions of tables that appeared in previous editions. The original source of the data is provided in footnotes to each table, and headnote references indicate where historical data on the same topic can be found.

For example, Table 2-4 is a reproduction of Table 283 in the *Statistical Abstract of the United States 1990,* which summarizes U.S. crime rates from 1979 to 1988. The headings along the top of the table are column headings, and the headings at the left are row headings. In this table the column headings indicate the total and type of crime, while the row headings indicate the number of crimes, the percentage of change, and the rate (number

(continued)

BOX 2-3

(continued)

of crimes per 100,000 inhabitants) for the years 1979 through 1988. So, for example, we can see there were 20,700 murders in the United States in 1988 (note that the number of offenses is given in thousands), and we can see that is somewhat *fewer* than the 23,000 murders in 1980. We can also observe that the murder rate per 100,000 inhabitants declined from 10.2 in 1980 to 8.4 in 1986.

It is possible to construct charts of the changes in crime rates from 1978 through 1988 using the data provided in this table. For example, the Census Bureau used these data to construct the two charts in Figure 2-3; one

chart depicts the violent crime rate (violent crimes are defined as murder, forcible rape, robbery, and aggravated assault) and one chart shows the rate for nonviolent crime (larceny, burglary, and motor vehicle theft).

The original source of these data is indicated in the footnote—annual publication by the Federal Bureau of Investigation, *Crime in the United States*. For more detailed data, social scientists would go to a library to find this publication or write to the U.S. Government Printing Office in Washington, D.C., and request a copy.

TABLE 2-4   Crimes and Crime Rates, by Type, 1979–1988

		Violent Crime				Property Crime			
Item and Year	Total	Total	Murder[a]	Forcible rape	Robbery	Aggra-vated assault	Total	Burglary	Larceny/ theft	Motor vehicle theft
Number of offenses (1,000):										
1979	12,250	1,208	21.5	76.4	481	629	11,042	3,328	6,601	1,113
1980	13,408	1,345	23.0	83.0	566	673	12,064	3,795	7,137	1,132
1981	13,424	1,362	22.5	82.5	593	664	12,062	3,780	7,194	1,088
1982	12,974	1,322	21.0	78.8	553	669	11,652	3,447	7,143	1,062
1983	12,109	1,258	19.3	78.9	507	653	10,851	3,130	6,713	1,008
1984	11,882	1,273	18.7	84.2	485	685	10,609	2,984	6,592	1,032
1985	12,431	1,329	19.0	88.7	498	723	11,103	3,073	6,926	1,103
1986	13,212	1,489	20.6	91.5	543	834	11,723	3,241	7,257	1,224
1987	13,509	1,484	20.1	91.1	518	855	12,025	3,236	7,500	1,289
1988	13,923	1,566	20.7	92.5	543	910	12,357	3,218	7,706	1,433
Percent change, number of offenses:										
1979–1988	13.7	29.7	−3.6	21.1	13.0	44.6	11.9	−3.3	16.7	28.8
1984–1988	17.2	23.0	10.6	9.8	12.0	32.8	16.5	7.8	16.9	38.8
1987–1988	3.1	5.5	2.9	1.5	4.9	6.4	2.8	−.6	2.7	11.2
Rate per 100,000 inhabitants:										
1979	5,566	549	9.7	34.7	218	286	5,017	1,512	2,999	506
1980	5,950	597	10.2	36.8	251	299	5,353	1,684	3,167	502
1981	5,858	594	9.8	36.0	259	290	5,264	1,650	3,140	475
1982	5,604	571	9.1	34.0	239	289	5,033	1,489	3,085	459
1983	5,175	538	8.3	33.7	217	279	4,637	1,338	2,869	431
1984	5,031	539	7.9	35.7	205	290	4,492	1,264	2,791	437
1985	5,207	557	7.9	37.1	209	303	4,651	1,287	2,901	462

(continued)

BOX 2-3

(continued)

TABLE 2-4   *(continued)*

Item and Year	Total	Violent Crime					Property Crime			
		Total	Murder[a]	Forcible rape	Robbery	Aggra-vated assault	Total	Burglary	Larceny/ theft	Motor vehicle theft
1986	5,480	618	8.6	37.9	225	346	4,863	1,345	3,010	508
1987	5,550	610	8.3	37.4	213	351	4,940	1,330	3,081	529
1988	5,664	637	8.4	37.6	221	370	5,027	1,309	3,135	583
Percent change, rate per 100,000 inhabitants:										
1979–1988	1.8	16.1	−13.4	8.4	1.1	29.4	.2	−13.4	4.5	15.3
1984–1988	12.6	18.2	6.3	5.3	7.5	27.6	11.9	3.6	12.3	33.3
1987–1988	2.1	4.5	1.2	.5	3.9	5.4	1.8	−1.5	1.7	10.1

Note: Data refer to offenses known to the police. Rates are based on the Bureau of the Census estimated resident population as of July 1, except 1980, enumerated as of April 1. Annual totals for years prior to 1984 were adjusted in 1984 and may not be consistent with those in prior editions. See source for details. Minus sign (−) indicates decrease. For definitions of crimes, see text, section 5. See *Historical Statistics, Colonial Times to 1970,* series H 952-961 for related data.

[a]Includes nonnegligent manslaughter.

Source: U.S. Federal Bureau of Investigation, *Crime in the United States,* annual.

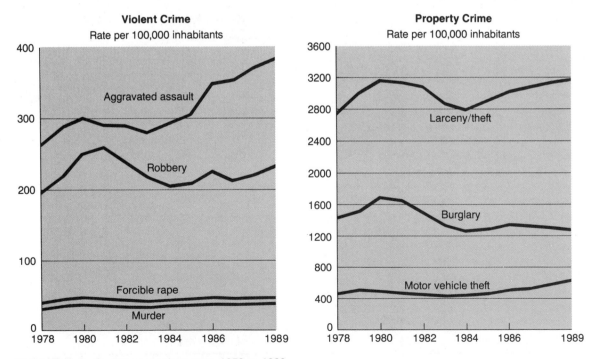

FIGURE 2-3   Selected crime rates, 1978 to 1988
        Source: Chart prepared by U.S. Bureau of the Census. For data, see Table 2-4.

Notes

1. Louis Wirth, preface to *Ideology and Utopia: An Introduction to the Sociology of Knowledge,* by Karl Mannheim (New York: Harcourt Brace Jovanovich, 1936), p. vii.
2. Laud Humphreys, *Tearoom Trade: Impersonal Sex in Public Places* (Chicago: Aldine, 1970), cited in *Sociology: An Introduction,* 2nd ed., ed. Earl R. Babbie (Belmont, Calif.: Wadsworth, 1980).

About This Chapter

What is a science, and what is the scientific method? How can the subject matter of the social sciences be studied scientifically? What are the obstacles to the scientific study of human behavior and social relations? How can theories and hypotheses be tested in social science research? How can data be collected? For example, how can a psychologist accurately and objectively measure a person's reaction to authority or a sociologist identify someone's social status? How can a political scientist be sure that a reduction in crime is the result of a government program and not the incidental effect of some other factor? Social scientists are often accused of not being truly scientific. Are they guilty as charged, and if so, why? What are the problems, the promise, and the sometimes paradoxical effects of social science research?

These are the questions that Chapter 2 addressed. Now that you have read it, you should be able to

- define science and describe the scientific method,
- illustrate how social scientists develop and test hypotheses,
- describe the classic research design and discuss some of the problems that social scientists have in applying this design and the scientific method to their research.

Discussion Questions

1. You are about to begin a social science research project, and you want it to be scientific rather than normative. Describe the method you would choose, explaining how it works and what its goals are. Using this method, will you be able to prove cause and effect? Why or why not?

2. Discuss some of the difficulties the social scientist has in applying the scientific method to the study of social problems.

3. Suppose you are a school psychologist who wishes to determine if students learn more when television is used in the classroom than when only conventional teaching methods are used. Construct a classic research design for this purpose. Describe some of the problems you might encounter in applying the design.

POWER AND
THE SOCIAL
SCIENCES

PART II

In Part II we shall take a close look at the ways in which each of the social sciences contributes to our understanding of power in society. In so doing, we hope to gain some feel not only for the different topics, theories, methods, and data of each of the social sciences but also for the goal they share in common—that is, an improved understanding of human behavior.

In Chapter 3 we shall focus on what *anthropology*, with its concern for culture, has to tell us about the growth of power relationships in societies. In Chapter 4 we shall examine the *sociology* of relationships between power and social class, particularly as evidenced by stratification in American society. In Chapter 5 we shall attempt to determine how and why individuals react in characteristic and different ways to power and authority. Here we shall turn to the theories of personality determination offered by various schools of *psychology*. Control of economic resources is an important base of power in any society, and in Chapter 6 we shall turn our attention to *economics*. In Chapter 7 we shall examine government and power from the point of view of *political science*. Finally, in Chapter 8 we shall look at how the perspective of *history* can increase our understanding of power in society.

Power and
Culture

The Origins of Power

Power is exercised in all societies. Every society has a system of sanctions, whether formal or informal, designed to control the behavior of its members. Informal sanctions may include expressions of disapproval, ridicule, or fear of supernatural punishments. Formal sanctions involve recognized ways of censuring behavior—for example, ostracism or exile from the group, loss of freedom, physical punishment, mutilation or death, or retribution visited upon the offender by a member of the family or group that has been wronged.

Power in society is exercised for four broad purposes:

functions of power in society

maintain internal peace

organize and direct community enterprises

conduct warfare

rule and exploit

1. to maintain peace within the society
2. to organize and direct community enterprises
3. to conduct warfare, both defensive and aggressive, against other societies
4. to rule and exploit subject peoples

Even in the most primitive societies, power relationships emerge for the purposes of maintaining order, organizing economic enterprise, conducting offensive and defensive warfare, and ruling subject peoples.

At the base of power relationships in society is the family or kinship group. Power is exercised, first of all, within the family, when work is divided between male and female and parents and children, and when patterns of dominance and submission are established between male and female parents and children. In the simplest societies, power relationships are found partially or wholly *within* family and kinship groups. True political (power) organizations begin with the *development* of power relationships *among* family and kinship groups. As long as kinship units are relatively self-sufficient economically and require no aid in defending themselves against hostile outsiders, political organization has little opportunity to develop. But the habitual association of human beings in communities or local groups generally leads to the introduction of some form of political (power) organization. The basic power structures are voluntary alliances of families and clans who acknowledge the same leaders, habitually work together in economic enterprises, agree to certain ways of conduct for the maintenance of peace among themselves, and cooperate in the conduct of offensive and defensive warfare. Thus, power structures begin with the development of cooperation among families and kinship groups.

Warfare frequently leads to another purpose for power structures: ruling and exploiting peoples who have been conquered in war. Frequently, primitive societies that have been successful in war learn that they can do more than simply kill or drive off enemy groups. Well-organized and militarily successful tribes learn to subjugate other peoples for purposes of political and economic exploitation, retaining them as subjects. The power structure of the conquering tribe takes on another function—that of maintaining control over and exploiting conquered peoples.

Culture: Ways of Life

culture

ways of life common to a society

The ways of life that are common to a society make up its *culture*. The culture of any society represents *generalizations* about the behavior of many members of that society; culture does not describe the personal habits of any one individual. Common ways of behaving in different societies vary enormously. For example, some societies view dog meat as a delicacy, whereas others find the idea of dog meat nauseating. Some people paint their entire bodies with intricate designs, while others paint only the faces of the females. In some cultures a man is required to support, educate, and discipline his children, and in others these functions belong to the children's uncle.

The concept of culture is basic to what *anthropology* is all about. One could say that anthropology is the study of culture. Anthropologist Clyde Kluckhohn has defined culture as all the "historically created designs for living, explicit and implicit, rational, irrational, and nonrational which may exist at any given time as potential guides for the behavior of man."[1] In contrast with psychologists, who are interested primarily in describing and explaining individual behavior, anthropologists tend to make *generalizations about behavior in a whole society.* Of course, generalizations about behavior in a whole society do not describe the personal habits of any one individual. Some of them apply only to a portion of that society's membership. In other words, there may be *variations* in ways of life among different groups within one society, variations frequently referred to as *subcultures.*

Anthropologists believe culture is learned. They believe culture is transferred from one generation to another, but it is *not* genetically transmitted. Culture is passed down through the generations because people in different societies are brought up differently. Individuals learn from other people how to speak, how to think, and how to act in certain ways.

The Components of Culture

Anthropologists often subdivide a culture into various components in order to simplify thinking about it. These components of culture—symbols, beliefs, values, norms, sanctions, and artifacts—are closely related in any society.

Symbols play a key role in culture. The creation and use of symbols—including words, pictures, and writing—distinguish human beings from other animals. A symbol is anything that has meaning bestowed on it by those who use it. Words are symbols, and language is symbolic communication. Objects or artifacts can also be used as symbols: a cross may be a symbol of Christianity. The color red may stand for danger, or it may be a symbol of revolution. The creation and use of such symbols enable human beings to transmit their learned ways of behaving to each new generation. Children are not limited to knowledge acquired through their own experiences and observations; they can learn about the ways of behaving in society through symbolic communication, receiving, in a relatively short time, the result of centuries of experience and observation. Human beings therefore can learn more rapidly than other animals, and they can employ symbols to solve increasingly complex problems. Because of symbolic communication, human beings can transmit a body of learned ways of life accumulated by many people over many generations.

Beliefs are generally shared ideas about what is true. Every culture includes a system of beliefs that are widely shared, even though there may be some disagreement with these beliefs. Culture includes beliefs about marriage and family, religion and the purpose of life, and economic and political organization. (In Chapter 9, "Power and Ideology," we shall discuss the importance of belief systems in organizing the economic and political systems of societies.)

anthropology
the study of cultures

subcultures
variations in ways of life within a society

symbols
anything that communicates meaning, including language, art, music

beliefs
shared ideas about what is true

Religious beliefs are evident in all known cultures (see Box 3-1, "Religious Beliefs in America"). Although there are differences between societies in the nature of their religious beliefs, all cultures include some beliefs about supernatural powers (powers not human and not subject to the laws of nature) and about the origins of life and the universe.[2] Various theories have arisen about why religious beliefs are universal. Some theories contend that religious beliefs arise out of human anxieties about death and the unknown or out of human curiosity about the meaning, origins, and purpose of life. Other theories stress the social functions of religion, providing goals, purposes, rituals, and norms of behavior for people.

values
shared ideas about what is good and desirable

Values are shared ideas about what is good and desirable. Values tell us that some things are better than others; values provide us with standards for judging ways of life. Values may be related to beliefs. For example, if we believe that human beings were endowed by God with rights of life, liberty, and property, then we will value the protection of these rights. Thus, belief can justify our values. But values can conflict with each other (that is, the value of individual freedom conflicts

BOX 3-1

Religious Beliefs in America

Social science cannot assist us in determining the truth or falsity of any religious belief. Social science cannot investigate the supernatural, determine the meaning or purpose of life, or evaluate competing religious beliefs. We must rely on faith, scripture, or revelation for our religious beliefs. However, social science *can* try to assess the prevalence of religious belief in a society and even theorize about the relationships between characteristics of societies and the nature of religious beliefs.

The United States is one of the most religious societies in the world in terms of the proportion of people who say they believe in God (94%), belong to an organized religion (70%), and regularly attend church (40%). These beliefs and practices are wholly voluntary in the United States; the First Amendment to the Constitution prohibits the official "establishment of a religion" and guarantees the "free exercise" of religion.

The professed importance of religion and church attendance has declined only slightly over recent decades in the United States. The figures that follow summarize national poll results to questions that attempt to track religious beliefs and practices over time:

Question: Do you believe in God or a Universal Spirit?

	1947	1967	1986
Yes	94%	97%	94%

Question: How important would you say religion is in your life?

	1952	1965	1989
Very important	75%	70%	55%

Question: Did you yourself happen to attend church or synagogue in the last seven days?

	1958	1967	1977	1987
Yes	49%	43%	41%	40%

There are modest differences in regular church attendance between age groups and religions. Church attendance has declined slightly over the past thirty years.

Question: How often do you attend religious services?

Percent who attend nearly every week or more

	1972–1974	1980–1982	1986–1988
National	38	35	34
Age			
18–24	24	24	24
40–69	41	37	35
Over 70	46	52	50
Religion			
Protestant	37	35	36
Catholic	53	46	42

Sources: Reported in *Public Opinion* (September/October 1988), pp. 24–25; and *The American Enterprise* (May/June 1990), p. 100.

with the need to prevent crime), and not everyone in society shares the same values. Yet most anthropologists believe that every society has some widely shared values.

Norms are shared rules and expectations about behavior. Norms are related to values in that values justify norms. If, for example, we value freedom of speech, we allow people to speak their minds even if we do not agree with them. The norm of tolerance derives from the value we place on individual freedom. Fairly trivial norms, like lining up at ticket windows instead of pushing to the front, are called *folkways.* Folkways may determine our style of clothing, our diet, or our manners. *Mores* (pronounced "morays") are more important norms. These are rules of conduct that carry moral authority; violating these rules directly challenges society's values. Yet, like values and beliefs, some norms within a given culture conflict with each other, and not everyone shares a belief in all of society's norms.

Sanctions are the rewards and punishments for conforming to or violating cultural norms. Rewards—praise, affection, status, wealth, reputation—reinforce cultural norms. Punishments—criticism, ridicule, ostracism, penalties, fines, jail, executions—discourage violations of cultural norms. But conformity to cultural norms does not depend exclusively on sanctions. Most of us conform to our society's norms of behavior even when no sanctions are pending, even when we are alone. We do so because we have been taught to do so, because we do not envision any alternatives, because we share the values on which the norms are based, and because we view ourselves as part of society (see Box 3-2).

An *artifact* is a physical product of a culture. An artifact can be anything from a piece of pottery or a religious object from an ancient culture to a musical composition, a high-rise condominium, or a beer can from a modern culture. But usually we think of an artifact as a physical trace of an earlier culture about which we have little written record. Anthropologists and archaeologists try to understand what these early cultures were like from the study of the artifacts they left behind.

norms
shared rules and expectations about behavior

sanctions
rewards and punishments for conforming to or violating norms

artifact
physical product of a culture

Power, Authority, and Legitimacy

Legitimacy is the belief that the exercise of power is "right" or "proper," that people are morally obligated to submit to it. Legitimacy depends on people believing that the exercise of power is necessary and valuable to society. As long as people believe in the legitimacy of the institutions in which power is lodged and believe that power is being used rightfully and properly, then force will seldom be required. People feel obliged to obey laws, follow rules, and abide by decisions that they believe to be legitimate. But if people begin to question the legitimacy of institutions (that is, governments, corporations, churches, the military, and so on), and if people come to believe that laws, rules, and decisions are no longer rightful or proper, then they will no longer feel morally obligated to abide by them. Institutional power will then rest on sheer force alone, as, for example, when unpopular, "illegitimate" governments rely on repression by police or military forces to exercise power over their populations.

Authority refers to power that is exercised legitimately. Not all power is legitimate: a thief who forces us to turn over money at gunpoint is exercising power, not authority. A tax collector from the Internal Revenue Service who forces us to

legitimacy
the belief that the exercise of power is right and proper

authority
power that is exercised legitimately

turn over money under threat of a fine or jail sentence is exercising authority—power that is perceived as legitimate. Authority, then, is a special type of power that is believed to be rightful and proper.

Authority and legitimacy depend on beliefs, attitudes, and values of the masses. Authority, like beauty, is in the eye of the beholder. The elite know this, so they try to influence mass beliefs and values in order to maintain the legitimacy of institutions they control and to reinforce their own authority. The elite do not like to rely on force alone.

What are the sources of legitimacy? Years ago a German sociologist, Max Weber (pronounced "Vayber"), suggested three general sources of legitimacy:

sources of legitimacy
tradition
charisma
legality

1. *Tradition:* Legitimacy rests on established beliefs in the sanctity of authority and the moral need to obey leaders.

BOX 3-2

Are Social Mores in America Changing?

It is easy to believe that social mores in America are "breaking down." Television news and entertainment shows regularly tell us that America's values are changing—that extramarital sex, homosexuality, or pornography are simply "alternative lifestyles" or legitimate "sexual preferences." But survey research indicates that Americans find these behaviors morally unacceptable and that opinion is *not* changing over time. Large majorities of Americans believe that extramarital sex and homosexual relations are "always wrong" or "almost always wrong." Most Americans would outlaw pornography for persons under eighteen, and over 40 percent would outlaw it altogether.

Can laws change public mores? A change in the laws can affect popular values, but only over time. Changes in the law were an important stimulus to reductions in racism in American society (see Chapter 10). The U.S. Supreme Court decided in 1962[3] that prayer and Bible reading in the public schools violated the "no establishment of religion" clause in the Constitution. But ten years later, over two-thirds of the American people disagreed with that decision. Disagreement has declined over time, but even today more than half of the public continues to disagree. Views on abortion are not changing much (see Table 3-1): when the Supreme Court decided in 1973 that all women had a constitutional right to obtain an abortion for any reason, only about 40 percent of the general public agreed. Today, this figure has changed very little, and abortion remains a sensitive moral issue.

TABLE 3-1   Changing Social Mores? Survey Research Results

	Percentage of respondents in agreement	
	1973	1987
Extramarital sex always wrong/ almost always wrong	85	90
Homosexual relations always wrong/almost always wrong	81	81
There should be laws against the distribution of pornography—to		
persons under 18	92	96
whatever the age	43	40
Disapprove of Supreme Court's ruling against Lord's Prayer and Bible reading in public schools	68	56
It should be possible for a woman to obtain a legal abortion—		
if she is married and does not want any children	40	42
if the woman's own health is endangered	87	88

Source: Reported in *Public Opinion* (September/October 1987), pp. 26–27, by permission of the American Institute for Public Policy Research.

2. *Charisma:* Legitimacy rests on the personal heroic qualities of a particular leader.
3. *Legality:* Legitimacy is based on a commitment to rules that bind both leaders and the people.

Historically, most elites have depended on tradition for their authority. The rule of tribal chieftains, pharaohs and kings, and feudal lords and ladies has been accepted as right because "it has always been that way." Some have relied on charismatic leadership—from Napoleon to Hitler to Gandhi to Mao Zedong. The authority of these leaders was based on the faith of their followers. Still other elites depend on legitimacy conferred by rules agreed on by both leaders and followers. Weber referred to this as rational–legal authority. The elite exercise their authority not because of tradition or personal charisma but because of the office or position they occupy.

The Functions of Culture

Culture assists people in adapting to the conditions in which they live. Even ways of life that at first glance appear quaint or curious may play an important role in helping individuals or societies cope with problems (see Box 3-3). Many anthropologists approach the study of culture by asking what function a particular institution or practice performs for a society. How does the institution or practice serve individual or societal needs? Does it work? How does it work? Why does it work? This approach is known as *functionalism.*[4]

Functionalism assumes that there are certain minimum *biological needs,* as well as *social and psychological needs,* that must be satisfied if individuals and society

functionalism
the assumption that cultural institutions and practices serve individual or societal needs

---

BOX 3-3

Understanding the !Kung

Someone not very knowledgeable about the !Kung* of the Kalahari Desert of South Africa might decide that those people are inferior savages. The !Kung wear little clothing, have few possessions, live in meager shelters, and enjoy none of our technological niceties. But let us reflect on how a typical American community might react if it awoke to find itself in an environment similar to that in which the !Kung live. The Americans would find that the absence of arable and pasture land makes both agriculture and animal husbandry impossible, and they might have to think about adopting a nomadic existence. They might then discard many of their material possessions so they could travel easily in order to take advantage of changing water and wild food supplies. Because of the extreme heat and the lack of extra water for doing laundry, they might find it more practical to be almost naked than to wear clothes. They would undoubtedly find it impossible to build elaborate homes. For social security, they might start to share the food brought into the group. Thus, if they survived at all, they might end up looking and acting far more like the !Kung than like typical Americans.

*The exclamation point in the name !Kung signifies a clicking sound made with the tongue.

Source: Carol R. Ember and Melvin Ember, *Cultural Anthropology,* 5th ed., © 1988, p. 10. Reprinted by permission of Prentice-Hall, Inc., Englewood Cliffs, N.J.

are to survive. The biological needs are fairly well defined: food, shelter, bodily comfort, reproduction, health maintenance, physical movement, and defense. Despite great variety in the way these needs are met in different cultures, we can still ask how a culture goes about fulfilling them and how well it does so. Social and psychological needs are less well defined, but they probably include affection, communication, education in the ways of the culture, material satisfaction, leadership, social control, security, and a sense of unity and belonging. Functionalists tend to examine every custom, material object, idea, belief, and institution in terms of the task or function it performs.

To understand a culture functionally, we have to find out how a particular institution or practice relates to biological, social, or psychological needs and how it relates to other cultural institutions and practices. For example, a society that fulfills its biological needs by hunting may fulfill its psychological needs by worshiping animals. Similarly, we find an agricultural society worshiping a sun-god or a rain-god. The function of magic is to give human beings courage to face the unknown; myth preserves social traditions; religion fosters individual security and social solidarity; and so forth.

Technology, with its tools, weapons, and artifacts, underlies nearly all these human activities. Variations in ways of life reflect different attempts by human beings to adjust or adapt to their environment. Technology can be viewed as a cultural screen that people set up between themselves and their environment. While most animals simply use the environment for food and shelter, changing it very little in the process, human beings alter or transform their environment. As a result human beings, who probably originated as tropical animals, can live almost anywhere on the earth's surface. Of course, peoples differ widely in the degree to which they exploit environmental resources. A society without means of transportation is restricted to a single area and depends on that area's resources. The technologies of "primitive" societies are not necessarily simple; the products of Eskimo technology, for example, are often ingenious and complex and require great skill to manufacture.

Anthropology helps us appreciate other cultures. It requires impartial observation and testing of explanations of customs, practices, and institutions. Anthropologists cannot judge other cultures by the same standards that we use to judge our own. *Ethnocentrism,* or judging other cultures solely in terms of one's own culture, is an obstacle to good anthropological work.

ethnocentrism
judging other cultures solely in terms of one's own culture

cultural relativity
uncritical acceptance of customs, practices, and institutions of other cultures

But *cultural relativity*—uncritical acceptance of customs, practices, and institutions of other cultures—leads to moral dilemmas for scholars and students. While it is important to assess the elements of a culture in terms of how well they work for their own people in their own environment, an uncritical or romantic view of other cultures is demoralizing. Consider, for example, the practice of female infanticide, a common practice in many cultures, including India (before infanticide was declared illegal by British rulers in 1870). Anthropologists might explain the preference for sons in terms of economic production based on hard manual labor in the fields. But understanding the functional relationship between female infanticide and economic conditions must not be viewed as a moral justification of the practice.

Some elements of a culture not only differ from those of another culture, but are *better.* The fact that all peoples—Asians, Europeans, Africans, Native Americans, and others—have often abandoned features of their own culture in order to replace them with elements from other cultures implies that the replacements served peoples' purposes more effectively.[5] Arabic numerals are not simply different from Roman numerals, they are *better*. This is why the European nations, whose own culture derived from Rome, replaced Roman numerals with numerals derived from Arab culture (which had learned them from the Hindus of India). It is inconceivable today that we would express large numbers in Roman numerals; for example, the year of American independence—MDCCLXXVI—requires more than twice as many Roman numerals as Arabic numerals and requires subtracting as well as adding numbers, depending on their place in the sequence. So it is important for scholars and students to avoid the assumption of cultural relativity—that all cultures serve their people equally well.

Authority in the Family

The family is the principal agent of socialization into society. It is the most intimate and important of all social groups. Of course, the family can assume different shapes in different cultures, and it can perform a variety of functions and meet a variety of needs. But in *all* societies, the family relationship centers on sexual and child-rearing functions. A cross-cultural comparison reveals that in all societies the family possesses these common characteristics:[6]

1. sexual mating
2. childbearing and child rearing
3. a system of names and a method of determining kinship
4. a common habitation
5. socialization and education of the young
6. a system of roles and expectations based on family membership

characteristics of the family

These common characteristics indicate why the family is so important in human societies. It replenishes the population and rears each new generation. Within the family, the individual personality is formed. The family transmits and carries forward the culture of the society. It establishes the primary system of roles with differential rights, duties, and behaviors. And it is within the family that the child first encounters *authority*.

Family arrangements vary. First of all, the marriage relationship may take on such institutional forms as monogamy, polygyny, and polyandry. *Monogamy* is the union of one husband and one wife; *polygyny*, the union of one husband and two or more wives; *polyandry*, the union of one wife and two or more husbands. Throughout the world, monogamy is the most widespread marriage form, probably because the *gender ratio* (number of males per 100 females) is near 100 in all societies, meaning there is about an equal number of men and women.

monogamy
marriage union of one husband and one wife

To an anthropologist, marriage does not necessarily connote a wedding ceremony and legal certificate. Rather, *marriage* means a socially approved sexual and economic union between a man and a woman, intended to be more or less permanent and implying social roles between the spouses and their children. Marriage is found in all cultures, and anthropologists have offered a variety of explanations for its

marriage
a socially approved sexual and economic union between a man and a woman, intended to be lasting, and implying social roles between the spouses and their children

CASE STUDY

Ruth Benedict: Patterns of Culture

The concept of culture helps us to understand ourselves by allowing us to see ourselves in relation to individuals in other societies and other cultures. Not only does culture explain many of the regularized behaviors of people—for example, eating, sleeping, dress, or sexual habits—but, perhaps more important, it helps us gain a wider perspective on our own behavior. Through the study of diverse cultures we realize that there are many different ways of living—many different ways in which people can satisfy their social and psychological needs as well as their biological requirements; that our culture is not the only possible way of life.

Perhaps this perception of the diversity of human existence was the most important contribution of cultural anthropologist Ruth Benedict in her widely read *Patterns of Culture*. As professor of anthropology at Columbia University, Ruth Benedict (1887–1947) popularized the notion that different cultures can be organized around characteristic purposes or themes. "A culture, like an individual, is a more or less consistent pattern of thought and action. Within each culture there come into being characteristic purposes not necessarily shared by other types of societies."[7] According to Benedict, each culture has its own patterns of thought, action, and expression dominated by a certain theme that is expressed in social relations, art, and religion.

For example, Benedict identified the characteristic themes of life among Zuñi Pueblo Indians as moderation, sobriety, and cooperation. There was little competition, contention, or violence among tribal members. In contrast, the Kwakiutls of the northwestern United States engaged in fierce and violent competition for prestige and self-glorification. Kwakiutls were distrustful of one another, emotionally volatile, and paranoid. Members of the Dobu tribe of New Guinea, too, were suspicious, aggressive, and paranoid:

> Life in Dobu fosters extreme forms of animosity and malignancy which most societies have minimized by their institutions. Dobuan institutions, on the other hand, exalt them to the highest degree. The Dobuan lives out without repression man's worst nightmares of the ill-will of the universe, and according to his view of life virtue consists in selecting a victim upon whom he can vent the malignancy he attributes alike to human society and to the powers of nature. All existence appears to him as a cut-throat struggle in which deadly antagonists are pitted against one another in a contest for each one of the goods of life. Suspicion and cruelty are his trusted weapons in the strife and he gives no mercy, as he asks for none.[8]

Yet Benedict was convinced that *abnormality* and *normality* were relative terms. What is "normal" in Dobuan society would be regarded as "abnormal" in Zuñi society, and vice versa. She believed that there is hardly a form of abnormal behavior in any society that would not be regarded as normal in some other society. Hence, Benedict helped social scientists realize the great variability in the patterns of human existence. People can live in competitive as well as cooperative societies,

(continued)

CASE STUDY

(continued)

in peaceful as well as aggressive societies, in trusting as well as suspicious societies.

Today many anthropologists have reservations about Benedict's idea that the culture of a society reflects a single dominant theme. There is probably a multiplicity of themes in any society, and some societies may be poorly integrated. Moreover, Benedict may have underestimated the fact that regardless of the importance of culture in shaping individual behavior, even within a single culture wide variations of individual behavior exist.

universality. One theory explaining marriage focuses on the prolonged infant dependency of humans. In most cultures infants are breast-fed for up to two years. This results in a division of roles between the female nurturer and the male protector that requires some lasting agreement between the partners. Another theory focuses on sexual competition among males. Marriage minimizes males' rivalry for female sexuality and thus reduces destructive conflict. The incest taboo further reduces sexual conflict (see Box 3-4). Still another theory focuses on the economic division of labor between the sexes. Males and females in every culture perform somewhat different economic activities; marriage is a means of sharing the products of their divided labor.

The Family in Agricultural Societies

In most agricultural societies the family is *patriarchal* and *patrilineal:* the male is the dominant authority and kinship is determined through the male line. The family is an economic institution, as well as a sexual and child-rearing one; it owns land,

the patriarchal family
the male is the dominant authority and kinship is determined through the male line

BOX 3-4

The Incest Taboo

All cultures enforce the incest taboo—a prohibition against sexual relations or marriage among close family members. The universality of this taboo has inspired anthropologists to develop a variety of explanatory theories. One of the oldest theories focuses on the potential genetic damage of inbreeding within the family. Inbreeding multiplies recessive genes and increases the likelihood of malformed offspring in animals and humans. Perhaps, over millions of years, natural selection favored cultures with the incest taboo. Another theory focuses on the importance of maintaining stable family life and avoiding sexual competition within the family. Sexual rivalry and

tension within the family might disrupt and destroy its nurturing functions. Still another theory focuses on the value of the incest taboo in promoting cooperation among family groups and in helping communities survive. Marrying outside of the family broadens kinship ties and encourages competition between families.

Finally, it has been noted that children raised together in the same family, even when not biologically related, show less sexual interest in each other than in persons outside of the family. Children raised together on collective farms (kibbutzim) in Israel rarely selected mates from their own group.[9]

Combining paid work with child rearing creates multiple burdens for women.
Source: Michael Weisbrot

produces many artifacts, and cares for its old as well as its young. Male family heads exercise power in the wider community; patriarchs may govern the village or tribe. Male authority frequently means the subjugation of both women and children. This family arrangement is buttressed by traditional moral values and religious teachings that emphasize discipline, self-sacrifice, and the sanctity of the family unit.

Women face a lifetime of childbearing, child rearing, and household work. Families of ten or fifteen children are not uncommon. The property rights of a woman are vested in her husband. Women are taught to serve and obey their husbands and are not considered as mentally competent as men. The husband owns and manages the family's economic enterprise. Tasks are divided: men raise crops, tend animals, and perform heavy work; women make clothes, prepare food, tend the sick, and perform endless household services.

The Family in Industrialized Societies

effects of industriali-
zation on the family

Industrialization alters the economic functions of the family and brings about changes in the traditional patterns of authority. In industrialized societies the household is no longer an important unit of production, even though it retains an economic role as a consumer unit. Work is to be found outside the home, and industrial technology provides gainful employment for women as well as for men. This means an increase in opportunities for women outside the family unit and the possibility of economic independence. The number of women in the labor force increases; today in the United States more than 60 percent of adult women are employed outside the home.

role of women

The patriarchal authority structure that typifies the family in an agricultural economy is altered by the new opportunities for women in an advanced industrial nation. Not only do women acquire employment alternatives, but their opportunities for education also expand. Independence allows them to modify many of the more oppressive features of patriarchy. Women in an advanced industrialized society have fewer children. Divorce becomes a realistic alternative to an unhappy marriage. The trend in divorce rates in industrialized societies is upward.

At the same time, governments in industrialized societies assume many of the traditional functions of the family, further increasing opportunities for women. The government steps into the field of formal education—not just in the instruction of reading, writing, and arithmetic, but in support of home economics, driver training, health care, and perhaps even sex education, all areas that were once the province of the family. Governmental welfare programs provide assistance to dependent children when a family breadwinner is absent or unable to provide for the children. The government undertakes to care for the aged, the sick, and others incapable of supporting themselves, thus relieving families of still another traditional function.

role of government

Despite these characteristics of industrial society, however, *the family remains the fundamental social unit.* The family is not disappearing; marriage and family life are as popular as ever. But the father-dominated authority structure, with its traditional duties and rigid gender roles, is changing. The family is becoming an institution in which both husband and wife seek individual happiness rather than the perpetuation of the species and economic efficiency. Many women still choose to seek fulfillment in marriage and child rearing rather than in outside employment. The important point is that now this is a *choice* and not a cultural requirement.

family as fundamental social unit

The American Family

The American family endures. Its nature may change, but the family unit nonetheless continues to be the fundamental unit of society.

Today there are more than 66 million families in America, and 215 million of the nation's 250 million people live in these family units.[10] Only about 13 percent of the population lives outside family units.

However, the nature of the family unit has indeed been changing. Husband–wife families compose 79 percent of all families, whereas 21 percent of all families consist of a single adult and children. Female-headed families with no spouse present have risen from 9.9 percent of all families in 1970 to 16.5 percent of all families in 1990. (See Figure 3-1.) The birthrate has declined from 3.7 births per woman of childbearing age in the 1950s to 2.4 in the 1970s and to only 1.8 in 1990. This last figure is *below* the projected zero population growth rate (2.1 children per female of childbearing age). In addition, there are about four abortions for every ten live births in the United States.

It is not really clear what factors are contributing to these changes in the American family. Certainly new opportunities for women in the occupational world have increased the number of women in the work force and altered the "traditional" patterns of family life. Less than half of today's mothers stay at home and devote full time to child rearing. Economic concerns may be an even more important factor: families must increasingly depend on the incomes of both husband and wife to maintain a middle-class lifestyle.

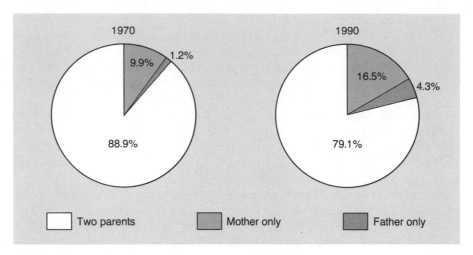

FIGURE 3-1   The changing American family

Divorce

Almost all societies allow for the separation of husband and wife. Many primitive societies have much higher divorce rates than the United States and other advanced industrialized societies. In 1990 in the United States, there were 4.8 divorces per 1,000 population, compared with 9.7 marriages. At this rate, we would expect nearly half of all marriages to end in divorce. The U.S. divorce rate has moderated somewhat in recent years; it was slightly higher at 5.2 divorces per 1,000 population in 1970. The median duration of marriages that end in divorce is seven years.

Women are more burdened by divorce than men. Most mothers retain custody of children. Although both spouses confront reduced family income from the separation, the burden falls more heavily on the mother who must both support herself and rear the children. Divorced fathers are generally required by courts to provide child support payments; however, these payments rarely amount to full household support, and significant numbers of absent fathers fail to make full payments.

Most divorced persons eventually find new spouses, but these remarriages are even more likely to end in divorce than first marriages.

Power and Gender

gender role differences in most cultures

Although some societies have reduced sexual inequalities, no society has entirely eliminated male dominance.[11] *Gender role differentiation* in work differs among cultures (see Table 3-2), but the most common pattern is for women to work close to home. Moreover, comparisons of numbers of different cultures studied by anthropologists reveal that men rather than women are usually dominant in *political leadership and warfare.* A cross-cultural survey reports that in 85 percent of the societies studied, *only* men were political leaders.[12] In the other 15 percent of societies studied, female leaders were either outnumbered by male leaders or were less pow-

Women's demanding roles
continue to receive media
attention. This cover of *Ms.
Magazine* is from March
1978.
Source: Carl Fischer/Courtesy,
Matilda Publications

erful than the males. In 88 percent of the world's societies women never participate
in war.

Why have men dominated in politics and war in most cultures? There are many
theories on this topic.

A theory of *physical strength* suggests that men prevail in warfare, particularly
in primitive warfare, which relies mainly on physical strength of the combatants.

**theories to explain
male dominance**
physical strength
hunting
child care
aggression

TABLE 3-2   Division of Labor by Gender: A Cross-Cultural Comparison

	Numbers of cultures dominated by				
	Men always	*Men usually*	*Either gender equally*	*Women usually*	*Women always*
Hunting	166	13	0	0	0
Herding	38	4	4	0	5
Fishing	98	34	19	3	4
Planting	31	23	33	20	37
Harvesting	10	15	35	39	44
Cooking	5	1	9	28	158
Carrying water	7	0	5	7	119

Source: Adapted from George P. Murdock, "Comparative Data on the Division of Labor by Sex," *Social Forces* 15 (May 1985):
551–553.

Because men did the fighting, they also had to make the decisions about whether or not to engage in war. Decisions about whether to fight or not were vital to the survival of the culture; therefore, decisions about war were the most important political decisions in a society. Dominance in those decisions assisted men in other aspects of societal decision making and led to their general political dominance.

A related *hunting* theory suggests that in most societies men do the hunting, wandering far from home and using great strength and endurance. The skills of hunting are closely related to the skills of war; people can be hunted and killed in the same fashion as animals. Because men dominated in hunting, they also dominated in war.

A *child care* theory argues that women's biological function of bearing and nursing children prevents women from going far from home. Infants cannot be taken into potential danger. (As we stated earlier in this chapter, in most cultures women breast-feed their children for up to two years.) This circumstance explains why women in most cultures perform functions that allow them to remain at home—for example, cooking, harvesting, and planting—and why men in most cultures undertake tasks that require them to leave home—hunting, herding, fishing. Warfare, of course, requires long stays away from home.

Still another theory, an *aggression* theory, proposes that males on the average possess more aggressive personalities than females. Some anthropologists contend that male aggression is biologically determined and occurs in all societies. Even at very young ages, boys try to hurt others and establish dominance more frequently than girls; these behaviors seem to occur without being taught and even when efforts are made to teach boys just the opposite.[13]

All these theories are arguable, of course. Some theories may be thinly disguised attempts to justify an inferior status for women—for keeping women at home and allowing them less power than men. Moreover, these theories do not go very far in explaining why the status of women varies so much from one society to another.

Although these theories help explain male dominance, we still need to explain: *Why do women participate in politics in some societies more than in others?* Generally, women exercise more political power in societies where they make substantial contributions to economic subsistence. Thus, women have less power in societies that depend on hunting or herding and appear to have less power in societies that frequently engage in warfare. Finally, some evidence exists that women have more power in societies that rear children with greater affection and nurturance.[14]

Stages of Development of Power Relationships

As a general guide to the study of the development of power relationships in society, we can identify the following stages:

family and kinship   1. Societies in which no separate power organization exists outside the *family or kinship* group. In these societies there is no continuous or well-defined system of leaders over or above those who head the individual families. These societies do not have any clear-cut division of labor or economic organization outside the family, and there is no structured method for resolving differences and maintaining peace among members of the group. Further, these societies do not engage in organized offensive or defensive warfare. They tend to be small and widely dispersed,

Women in the
Work Force:
Changing
American
Culture

Women are increasingly
entering traditionally male-
dominated occupations such
as oil refinery worker.
Source: Lorraine Rorke/The
Image Works

The number of American women who work has been rising steadily since 1947.
Responding both to changing views of their role in society and to economic pressures on family budgets, women have entered the U.S. labor force at an unprece-
dented rate (see Table 3-3). Not even in World War II, in the days of Rosie the
Riveter, did so many women work outside the home. Nearly 60 percent of American women aged sixteen to sixty-four held jobs or were actively looking for work
in 1988. It is estimated that by 1995 more than 75 percent of adult women will
work outside the home.

   Like all complex social changes, the back-to-work movement has been shaped
by many economic and cultural forces. A number of factors other than economic
need coupled with the rising divorce rate have contributed to the increased number
of working women. These factors include (1) more effective means of birth control
and the trend toward fewer children, (2) the increased life expectancy of women,
(3) the greater number of college-educated women, and (4) the widespread use of
                                                                    (continued)

(continued)

TABLE 3-3 Women in the Work Force

Year	Number (add 000)	Percentage of adult female population[a]	Percentage of married female population[b]
1940	13,840	27.4	16.7
1950	17,795	31.4	24.8
1960	22,516	34.8	31.7
1970	31,233	42.6	41.4
1980	44,934	51.1	50.7
1984	49,210	53.3	52.2
1986	51,732	54.7	55.0
1988	53,987	55.9	56.8

[a] Age 16 and over

[b] Includes married with spouse absent

Source: U.S. Bureau of the Census, *Statistical Abstract of the United States 1990* (Washington, D.C.: U.S. Government Printing Office, 1990), p. 384.

labor-saving devices in the home. Other factors are (5) the expansion of the white-collar job market in which most women are employed, (6) the increase in opportunities for part-time employment, and (7) legal action prohibiting job discrimination based on gender.

Women's pay has increased significantly in recent years, but it is still well below the pay of men (see Figure 3-2). Currently for all year-round full-time workers, the median earnings of women is 66 percent of that of men.

This wage gap reflects the continued concentration of women in relatively low-skilled, low-paying jobs. More than two-fifths of all female workers were employed in just ten job categories: secretary, retail sales worker, bookkeeper, private household worker, elementary school teacher, waitress, typist, cashier, sewer and stitcher, and registered nurse.

Occupational segregation stems from many sources—discrimination, cultural conditioning, and the personal choices of women themselves. The jobs women have traditionally held are frequently related to the work they perform in the home—teaching children and young adults, nursing the sick, preparing food, and assisting their husbands and other men.

Despite statistics indicating that the majority of women work because of economic need, many employers still hold to the traditional view that men ought to be paid more than women. Because they see women as temporary entries in the labor force, many employers tend to shuttle women into jobs in which the skills can be quickly learned and that hold little opportunity for advancement.

(continued)

(continued)

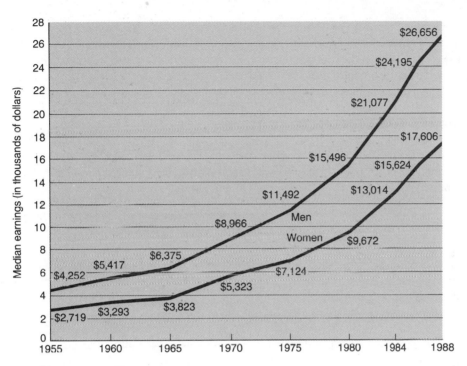

FIGURE 3-2   The earnings gap

Source: U.S. Bureau of the Census, *Statistical Abstract of the United States 1990* (Washington, D.C.: U.S. Government Printing Office, 1990), p. 411.

TABLE 3-4   Women in Traditionally Male Occupations

	Percentage of women	
	1960	*1988*
Physicians	10	20
Lawyers	4	19
Engineers	1	7
College professors	28	38
Chemists	10	24
Architects	3	15
Computer analysts	11	30

Source: Statistical Abstract of the United States 1990 (Washington, D.C.: U.S. Government Printing Office, 1990), pp. 389–390.

(continued)

CASE STUDY

(continued)

Growing numbers of women are gaining access to such traditionally male-dominated professions as law, medicine, architecture, business, and engineering. Consider, for example, the changes over nearly thirty years in various traditionally male occupations (see Table 3-4).

However, the trend toward work and careers outside the home has placed a double burden on many married women. Sociological studies consistently show that women in the United States perform many more hours of housework than men even when both hold full-time paid jobs. Moreover, families with small children require much more housework than families without children, yet men typically do not assume much of the additional work themselves. The same findings have been reported for the former Soviet Union, China, and many other nations.[15]

to have economies that yield only a bare subsistence, and to lack any form of organized defense. Power relationships are present, but they are closely tied to family and kinship.

bands and tribes

2. Societies in which families are organized in larger *bands, tribes,* or confederacies that have organized sets of power arrangements extending beyond family ties. In these societies population tends to be somewhat more concentrated; the economy yields a richer subsistence but no real surplus; and warfare, although frequent and often of great importance, is usually a matter of raiding between neighboring societies. When wars are decisive, they result in the killing or driving off of enemy tribes rather than in their conquest for exploitation.

state
a defined territory and a recognized organization to make and enforce rules of conduct

3. Societies that are organized as permanent *states* and that have a more or less well-defined territory and a recognized organization to make and enforce rules of conduct. In these societies populations are large and highly concentrated; the economy produces a surplus; and there are recognized rules of conduct for the members of the society, with positive and negative sanctions. These societies have an organized military establishment for offensive and defensive wars. In war, conquered people are not usually destroyed, but instead are held as tributaries or incorporated as inferior classes into the state. In the vast majority of these societies, power is centered in a small, hereditary elite.

These stages of development of power relationships in societies certainly do not exhaust the variety of current and past power arrangements. They represent only broad divisions, each of which can be subdivided. (For example, a state can be classified in Aristotelian fashion as a *monarchy, aristocracy,* or *democracy*—rule by the one, the few, or the many.) Sharp lines cannot be drawn among these three stages; each stage shades into the next, and there are many transitional forms.

Let us consider three examples of societies in which power is organized by these broad divisions: (1) family and kinship group (polar Eskimos), (2) tribe (Crow Indians), and (3) state (the Aztec Empire).

Power among the Polar Eskimos

Societies lacking formal power organizations are found today only in the very mar-   **environment**
ginal areas of the world. These societies, with no formal power structures beyond
family and kinship groups, exist only in the most difficult environments, where
physical hardship and a lack of adequate food resources keep the human population
small and thinly scattered. Among the polar Eskimos of northern Greenland, for
example, a harsh environment and a limited food supply, together with a limited
technology, force families to wander great distances to maintain themselves. Inadequate food resources make it physically impossible for these Eskimos to maintain,
except temporarily, any groupings larger than one or two families. As a result, there
is little in the way of power organization outside the family.

Anthropologists who have observed Eskimo culture note that it has just two   **economy**
social units: the primary family, a small but autonomous kinship group; and the
winter village, an unstable association of primary families who are not necessarily
linked by kinship ties. The winter village is only partially a power grouping. Its
member families do not stay together long enough or undertake the common enterprises necessary for the development of a stable leadership system. Ordinarily the
families in a winter village, though temporarily united by common residence, act
independently of one another. Their technology, whether in food gathering or house
building, requires no high degree of cooperative labor. In times of stress, when a
storm or lack of game reduces food stores to the danger point, a *shaman,* respected
for his supernatural powers, may call the families together to participate in a ceremony intended to restore the food supply. But the shaman's authority is limited
to such occasions; at other times he has no right to direct or command.

A strong and aggressive hunter may gain the esteem and respect of his fellows,   **leadership**
but there are few occasions when he may capitalize on this prestige to assume a
position of leadership. In short, the winter village has little need for leadership outside the family. There is not even the occasion of warfare to call for the organization
of families for offensive or defensive action. Leadership resides only within the
primary family, where it is shared by husband and wife, each in his or her sphere
of activity. The family maintains itself largely through its own efforts. It is linked
to other families through intermarriage, remote kinship, or ties of mutual affection
and regard. Conflicts are often resolved by song sessions in which the disputants
lampoon each other in songs, which they sing before an audience of their neighbors.
More aggressive behavior is inhibited by fear of retaliation by kinsmen of the victims. Protracted disputes may be resolved among some Eskimos by one party's
moving to another winter village, although an overbearing and abusive individual
may be speared while on a hunt.

Among these Eskimos, then, there is no structure of power outside the family   **organization**
group. Cooperation among families in joint enterprises is rare. Leadership outside
the family is seldom evidenced, usually only during a crisis, when some particularly
able member of the community takes charge. Ecological circumstances prohibit
large permanent groupings of people, and the technology of the society is so simple
that it utilizes individual rather than group effort. Variations on this fundamental
type of power system that exists solely within the family group are also found
among other primitive peoples living in harsh environments.

A Crow peace delegation, 1872.
Source: Smithsonian Institution National Anthropological Archives

Power among the Crow Indians

Perhaps the simplest form of power arrangement outside the family is a *band, clan,* or *tribe.* Although its members may be linked by kinship, such a group is generally made up of many family units, not all of which need to be related by marriage. These groups form the next stage of development in power relationships above that of the family or kinship groups. The band, clan, or tribe consists of numbers of individuals and families who (1) live and travel together; (2) regularly engage in one or more large community enterprises—for example, an organized hunt; (3) regulate conflict and maintain order among themselves; and (4) organize to protect themselves from their enemies and wage war against them.

leadership   Within the band there is usually an acknowledged leader—a chief—together with other respected individuals who assist in implementing authority. This authority may be backed by force, but more often it rests on the ability of the leadership to *persuade* and *influence* its followers. The leaders generally owe their status to their personal achievements as hunters or warriors.

warfare   Anthropological research on the American Crow Indians in the early nineteenth century provides an example of the development of power relationships at the tribal level. The Crow were more or less continually hostile to their neighbors. Any non-Crow was automatically an enemy. Warfare, however, was largely a matter of small-scale raiding, either to steal horses or to avenge the death of a tribesman. Horse-stealing parties tried to take as many horses as they could without disturbing the enemy camp; they fought only when necessary to defend themselves. When revenge was the object of a war party, however, they tried to surprise the enemy and kill as many as possible without losing any of their own men. A war leader, whether he set out to capture horses or to get revenge, was not considered successful unless he brought his own party home intact.

Success in warfare was very important. Crow men achieved reputation and prestige through the slow accumulation of war honors. War honors were clearly defined. They were awarded for (1) leading a successful war party, (2) capturing an enemy's weapon in actual combat, (3) being first to strike an enemy in the course of a fight, and (4) driving off a horse tethered in an enemy encampment. A man who performed all these deeds became, in Crow terms, a "good and valiant man," and his status increased as the number of his earned war honors increased. A Crow who had not yet attained the minimum four honors was regarded as not yet a man, but only an untried youth.

The warriors formed a kind of military aristocracy that made up the band council. One of their number, usually an older man with many war honors, was recognized as chief. He decided when the band was to move or settle down in its yearly wanderings in search of food and when war parties were to be sent out. He directed the annual buffalo hunt, a cooperative endeavor in which the whole band united to secure a store of winter food. **economy**

However, the chief's authority was by no means absolute; he was "neither a ruler nor a judge." In effect, the chief was a leader rather than a ruler; it was his function to persuade and influence rather than to command. On some occasions, mainly the annual buffalo hunts, the chief and other council warriors had the authority to resort to force rather than persuasion to maintain order. In such instances the senior warriors "severely whipped anyone who prematurely attacked the herd, broke his weapons, and confiscated the game he had illegally killed."[16] The need for a winter's supply of food, and the fact that this need could not be adequately served without the closest coordination of effort, clearly justified, in Crow eyes, the chief's authority over his tribesmen. However, apart from such special occasions as the community buffalo hunt, members of the band were allowed to act pretty much as they pleased, subject only to the discipline of public opinion. The threat of ridicule and the obligations imposed by kinship were normally sufficient deterrents to antisocial behavior. **authority**

Band or tribal organizations similar to that of the Crow are widespread among nonliterate peoples. As environment and technology permit higher concentrations of population, bands form into larger tribes. From this stage there emerge even larger political units with recognized power structures.

Power and the Aztec Empire

The most fully developed system of power relationships is the state—the last of our major categories. Power in the state is employed to maintain order among peoples and to carry on large-scale community enterprises, just as in the band or tribe. But power in the state is also closely linked to defense, aggression, and the exploi-

The Great Temple of México–Tenochtitlán as reconstructed by the twentieth-century pre-Conquest architectural historian Ignacio Marquina, according to the plans of Bernardino de Sahagún and Diego Durán.
Source: Department of Library Services/American Museum of Natural History, Neg. No. 326597

tation of conquered peoples. Frequently states emerge in response to attacks by others. Where there is a fairly high density of population, frequent and continuing contact among bands, and some commonality of language and culture, there is the potential for "national" unity in the form of a state. But a state may not emerge if there is no compelling motivation for large-scale cooperation. Motivation is very often provided initially by the need for defense against outside invasion.

authority
the legitimate use of force

States differ from bands or tribes to the extent that there is a *centralized authority* with recognized power, backed by force, to carry out its decrees. This *legitimate use of force* distinguishes the state as a form of power structure from the band or tribe, in which power depends largely on persuasion or the personal achievements of individuals. Power in the state is a more impersonal kind of authority.

economy
specialization of labor and trade

The Aztec Empire, which was conquered by the Spaniards under Cortés in 1521, is an excellent example of an early state. Anthropologists have been able to trace its beginnings to an earlier tribal order confined to the valley of Mexico. The rich agricultural economy developed by the Aztecs produced far in excess of their immediate needs. With the exchangeable surplus, there soon evolved a complex specialization of labor and an extensive trade that brought the Aztecs into frequent and profitable contact with neighboring groups.

warfare and exploitation

Early in the fifteenth century, the Aztecs embarked on a series of military conquests that led ultimately to their economic and political control over most of central and southern Mexico. The Aztecs did not destroy the cities and states they had conquered. On the contrary, the commercially minded Aztecs permitted those cities and states to retain local autonomy, demanding only political allegiance and a yearly tribute in goods and services to the Aztec emperor. It was this economic empire, politically a loose aggregate of city-states controlled from the Aztec capital city of Tenochtitlán, that Cortés took over in 1521.

The early Aztec power structure, although more complicated than that of primitive tribes, still retained a measure of democratic procedure. The core of the Aztec Empire was ruled by its citizens, the members of the *calpulli,* small groups composed of nuclear families that farmed their own land. Although the positions of chief and king were in part hereditary (they were customarily chosen from particular families), the choice of a leader also depended on reputation and ability. The king had great power as a military leader in a state more or less continuously at war, but his power was modified by councils of family heads.

As the Aztecs grew wealthier from their numerous conquests and ever-widening control of trade, however, the power structure underwent a gradual change. Most important, a class division developed in Aztec society along socioeconomic lines. An upper class appeared, composed of honorary lords known as *tecutin.* These were **upper class** men, calpulli members, who were given titles for outstanding services to the state as warriors, merchants, public officials, or priests. They were universally esteemed; had many privileges, including certain exemptions from taxation; were preferred for high governmental and military positions; and were given large estates and shares of tribute by the king, to be held as private property during their lifetime. These rewards clearly made the tecutin economically independent of their calpulli and, moreover, allied them with the king, who, while he gave the tecutin their honors, also had the power to withdraw them.

A middle class also emerged, made up of calpulli members who were not tecu- **middle class** tin. These formed the bulk of the population of the capital city. They were self-supporting through their membership in the calpulli and had a voice in the government through their representatives in the state and great councils. Often they rented their calpulli lands, and some acquired great wealth.

Finally, a lower class was divided into propertyless freemen and serfs. The latter were attached to the lands of the nobility as slaves. The former were men exiled **slaves** from the calpulli for various crimes and who thus had no way of making a living except by hiring themselves out as agricultural laborers or as porters in the caravans of the merchants. Slaves were similarly dependent for a living on their own labor. Neither slaves nor propertyless freemen had a voice in the government. Though initially small, the lower class grew as conquests increased.

As class lines become more sharply drawn, Aztec government moved inevitably in the direction of an absolute *hereditary monarchy.* Tecutin clearly supported this **hereditary monarchy** tendency to their advantage and increasingly, by various devices, managed to pass **and nobility** on their titles and private property to their heirs. Slowly a *hereditary nobility* arose. At the time of the conquest, the Aztec Empire was essentially an emerging feudal order, with political power centered more and more in the king and his tecutin rather than in the elected representatives of the calpulli.

Power and Society: Some Anthropological Observations

Let us summarize the contributions that anthropological studies can make to our understanding of the growth of power relationships in societies. First, it is clear that the *physical environment* plays an important role in the development of power sys- **power and the physi-** tems. Where the physical environment is harsh and the human population must of **cal environment**

CASE STUDY

Sociobiology:
It's All in Your
Genes

A highly controversial topic in the social sciences is *sociobiology*. Sociobiology may be defined as the branch of biology that deals with the biological basis of social behavior in all kinds of organisms, including human beings. In general, sociobiologists argue that at least some aspects of human behavior are based on *genetics;* that is, these behaviors are the result of millions of years of heredity and evolution. Some sociobiologists, whose ranks include biologists and zoologists as well as social scientists, believe that genetics largely determines culture—from educational and child-rearing practices to sexual behavior.

In 1975 Harvard zoologist Edward Wilson's book *Sociobiology: The New Synthesis* brought many of the insights of the rapidly advancing field of genetics to the study of human social behavior. The book and the field of sociobiology are highly controversial. Some people claim that the field is reactionary and denies the possibility of improving social conditions because of the pull of the genes. Others fear that genetic explanations of human behavior may be used to justify racism or sexual discrimination.

Sociobiologists, however, claim that their research builds on our scientific knowledge of genetic evolution and applies this knowledge to animal and human behavior. They maintain that many of the behavioral patterns of humans, as well as of other animals, are not "learned" but are instead the results of genetic coding. Songbirds that have been raised in complete isolation from any other members of their own species can sing the exact melody that their species sings, even though the isolated birds never had any opportunity to "learn" the melody. The melody is built into the DNA sequences in their genes. Many similar animal experiments reveal that behaviors occur in a species even though the animal has never had the opportunity to "learn" the behaviors.

Sociobiology, Natural Selection, and the Selfish Gene

Sociobiology is related to Darwin's theory of evolution, which holds that all animals (including humans) evolve by *natural selection*—those that are better adapted to their environment survive and reproduce; the rest tend to become extinct. Darwin, however, in attempting to explain natural selection, focused on the animal itself rather than its particular genetic code. Sociobiologists, on the other hand, focus on the genetic coding, for they believe that it is within this coding that natural selection takes place. The genes struggle *within* the animal to protect themselves. Darwin was never really able to explain why some animals (including humans) acted altruistically—giving up their own lives to save others. Such behavior— birds risking their own lives to cry out to warn the flock of danger, dolphins swimming beside an injured companion to keep it from drowning, ants giving up their lives fighting for the colony—seems to contradict the theory of natural selection.

(continued)

(continued)

Sociobiologists explain this altruism by claiming that the genetic coding of each animal in these particular species includes directions to save the others in order to protect the same genes. In other words, altruism is really *genetic selfishness*. More-over, most sociobiologists argue that animals will act more altruistically to save relatives (who share more of their own genes) than nonrelatives. Altruism extended to general charitable acts (even by human beings) may simply be a genetic code that urges individuals to risk their lives to save their genes. Many true heroes who feel they acted on impulse in risking their lives to save others may really have been obeying genetically coded directions.

Sociobiological Explanations of Various Behavior

Sociobiologists do *not* necessarily agree that humans are always instinctively aggressive (as suggested by Konrad Lorenz in his popular book *On Aggression*). The optimal genetic coding for survival will include just enough aggression not to be beaten out by others, but not too much to waste energy and risk death by point-less fighting. In other words, genetic coding includes a rough cost-benefit analysis for aggression.

Is it possible that upper social classes acquire power because they have acquired superior genes? Responsible sociobiologists reject this notion. It requires millions of years for any significant change to occur in the genetic coding of a group. Cul-ture moves too fast for genes to be able to create any permanent class system. Even the two-thousand-year-old castes of India are not genetically different, despite their prohibitions on intermarriage and rigid separation between castes (restrictions that have been lifted since India's independence). On the other hand, sociobiologists may attribute an individual's success in such areas as sports, business, war, or sci-ence to the individual's genetic makeup.

Sociobiologists also offer genetic explanations for sexual behavior. They contend that the object of sexual behavior in animals and humans is to pass on as many of their own genes to succeeding generations as possible, at the lowest possible cost in energy and time. Because a male can start thousands of pregnancies, thus ensur-ing that some of his offspring will survive, he can ignore the nurturing of his off-spring. But a female can give birth only a limited number of times during her life-time and therefore must invest more time in nurturing her young in order to ensure their survival. Thus, promiscuity among males of many species is common, as is the nesting urge of females. Females of many species stay near the nest, while males roam far in search of opportunities to breed. Moreover, males often engage in openly aggressive behavior against other males, not only to beat out the com-petition for available females, but also to impress females with the strength of their genes. Over millions of years of evolution, the result, say the sociobiologists, is a different and stronger male physique. Of course, these views have irritated many

(continued)

(continued)   women, who fear that sociobiologists are telling them to stay home and mind the babies.

It is difficult to estimate how much human behavior is genetically directed (as the sociobiologists contend) and how much is learned from parents and others (as cultural anthropologists contend). It is impossible to say, for example, that 20 or 30 percent of human behavior is genetically based and the rest is culturally based. All we know now is that both genetics and culture affect human behavior.

necessity be spread thinly, power relationships are restricted to the family and kinship groupings. Larger political groupings are essentially impossible. The elite emerge only after there is some concentration of population, where food resources permit groupings of people larger than one or two families.

power and the economy

Second, power relationships are linked to the *economic patterns* of a culture. In subsistence economies, power relationships are limited to the band or tribal level. Only in surplus-producing economies do we find states or statelike power systems. Developed power systems are associated with *patterns of settled life,* a certain degree of *technological advance,* and *economic surplus.*

power and warfare

Third, *patterns of warfare* are linked to the development of power relationships. Warfare is rare or lacking among people such as the Eskimos who have no real power system outside the family. Where power relationships emerge at the band or tribal level, as in the culture of the Crow, warfare appears to be continuous, in the form of periodic raiding for small economic gains or the achievement of personal glory and status; victory assumes the form of killing or driving off enemy groups. Only at the state level is warfare well organized and pursued for the purpose of conquest and economic exploitation. This does not mean necessarily that statelike power systems *cause* war, but rather, that some common factor underlies both the rise of state power systems and organized warfare. Warfare and conquest are not essential to the maintenance of the state; in fact, in the modern world, warfare between major states may slowly give way to other forms of competition, if only because of the increasing threat of total destruction.

power in advanced societies

Fourth, anthropological research makes it clear that power relationships exist in simple forms in primitive societies and that *no society is void of a power structure.* Power structures become more complex and hierarchical, and more impersonal and based on physical force, as societies move from the subsistence level with simple technology to a surplus-producing level with advanced technology and large cooperative enterprises. The simpler power systems are frequently headed by chiefs and councils selected for their age, wisdom, or demonstrated capacity as hunters or warriors. These leaders tend to rule more by example and persuasion than by formal decree or force. As more complex state systems emerge, leaders are endowed with the exclusive right to coerce. Characteristically, political and economic power in the state is concentrated in a small hereditary elite. Modern representative government, in the form of European and American democracies, is relatively rare in the history of human societies.

Notes

1. Clyde Kluckhohn and William Kelly, "The Concept of Culture," in *The Science of Man in the World Crisis,* ed. Ralph Linton (New York: Columbia University Press, 1945), p. 97.
2. Carol R. Ember and Melvin Ember, *Cultural Anthropology,* 6th ed. (Englewood Cliffs, N.J.: Prentice-Hall, 1990), pp. 196–221.
3. *Engle* v. *Vitale, 370* U.S. 421 (1962).
4. This approach was developed by Bronislaw Malinowski in *A Scientific Theory of Culture and Other Essays* (Chapel Hill: University of North Carolina Press, 1944).
5. See the argument presented by Thomas Sowell in "Cultural Diversity: A World View," *The American Enterprise* 2 (May/June 1991): 44–55.
6. William W. Stephens, *The Family in Cross-Cultural Perspective* (New York: Holt, Rinehart & Winston, 1963).
7. Ruth Benedict, *Patterns of Culture* (Boston: Houghton Mifflin, 1934), p. 46.
8. Ibid., p. 172.
9. Yonima Talmon, "Mate Selection in Collective Settlements," *American Sociological Review* 29 (1964): 491–508; cited in Ember and Ember, p. 183.
10. U.S. Bureau of the Census, *Statistical Abstract of the United States, 1990* (Washington, D.C.: U.S. Government Printing Office, 1990), p. 45.
11. Ember and Ember, *Cultural Anthropology,* ch. 9; George P. Murdock and Caterina Post, "Factors in the Division of Labor by Sex: A Cross-Cultural Analysis," *Ethnology* 12 (1973): 203–225.
12. Martin K. Whyte, "Cross-Cultural Codes Dealing with the Relative Status of Women," *Ethnology* 17 (1978): 217.
13. Beatrice B. Whiting and Carolyn P. Edwards, "A Cross-Cultural Analysis of Sex Differences in the Behavior of Children Aged Three Through Eleven," *Journal of Social Psychology* 91 (1973): 171–188; Eleanor E. MacCoby and Carol N. Jacklin, *The Psychology of Sex Differences* (Stanford, Calif.: Stanford University Press, 1974).
14. Marc H. Ross, "Female Political Participation: A Cross-Cultural Explanation," *American Anthropologist* 88 (1986): 841–858.
15. Jean Stockard and Miriam M. Johnson, *Sex Roles, Sex Inequality, and Sex Role Development* (Englewood Cliffs, N.J.: Prentice-Hall, 1980).
16. Robert H. Lowie, *The Crow Indians* (New York: Rinehart, 1935), p. 5.

About This Chapter

Anthropologists, in their study of human culture, have been able to document that the exercise of power and the division of labor within the family constitute the most basic power relationship, the one from which true political power structures develop. What causes these structures to develop? Why should we need to control each other's behavior, and how do we manage to do it? How do anthropologists document the growth of power relationships? How, in fact, do they approach the study of something as diverse as human culture?

These questions were the focus of Chapter 3. Now that you have read it, you should be able to

- describe how power in society is exercised and for what purposes,
- discuss how and why the family is the fundamental social unit in which power relationships originate,
- discuss the changing roles of women in American society,
- discuss the stages of development of power relationships and the factors that influence this development, and
- discuss anthropological approaches to the study of culture.

Discussion Questions

1. Describe how societies attempt to control the behavior of their members. Discuss the four broad purposes for which societies exercise power.

2. Describe how power and relationships begin within the family and how they develop into political organizations. What effect can warfare have on the power structure?

3. Choose a "subculture" that is familiar to you. If you were asked to explain in anthropological terms what sets this subculture apart from the society at large, what cultural categories would you examine? Identify the variations in lifestyle that make this a subculture.

4. Describe how an anthropologist of the functionalist school would approach the study of culture.

5. Discuss Ruth Benedict's contributions to anthropology.

6. Identify the characteristics of marriage that are found in all societies. Explain why the family is the most important social group.

7. "In all societies the child's first experience with authority is within the family. . . . Differences in the type of authority exercised, and whether or not the authority is exercised primarily by the mother or father, can shape the character and personality of the growing individual." Describe the type of adult woman you might expect to have grown up within a family in an agricultural society, and contrast her with an adult woman who has grown up within a family in an industrialized society. Describe the influences contributing to the development of both women.

8. Discuss changes in the American family. Comment on the continuing strength of family life, the number of families with a single adult, and the declining birthrate.

9. Discuss the changing roles of women in American society, particularly their changing role in the work force.

10. Describe the broad stages of development of power relationships and the power groups associated with them. Compare these groups in terms of leadership, economic systems, patterns of warfare, population density, and patterns of settlement. How have anthropological studies contributed to our understanding of these power relationships?

11. "Culture is learned. . . . Culture is transferred from one generation to another, but . . . it is *not* genetically transmitted." What arguments do sociobiologists advance against this contention? Why does sociobiology arouse so much controversy? Identify the areas of human social behavior that sociobiologists believe may be genetically directed. Discuss your opinions about the relative effects on human behavior of genetics and culture.

Power and Social Class

Power Pyramids and Pecking Orders

stratification
classifying people and
ranking the classifica-
tions on a superiority–
inferiority scale

All known societies have some system of ranking their members along a superiority–inferiority scale. Although some societies claim to grant "equality" to their
members, in no society have people in fact been considered equal. The *stratification*
of society involves the *classification* of individuals and the *ranking* of classifications on a superiority–inferiority scale. This system of classification and ranking
is itself a source of prestige, wealth, income, authority, and power.

Individuals can be classified on a wide variety of characteristics—physical
strength, fighting prowess, family lineage, ethnic or racial category, age, gender,
religion, birth order, and so on. But *the most important bases of stratification in a
modern industrial society are the various roles that individuals play in the economic
system.* Individuals are ranked according to how they make their living and how
much control they exercise over the livelihood of others. Ranking by occupation
and control of economic resources occurs not only in the United States but in most
other modern nations as well.[1]

**stratification results
in unequal**
deference
styles of life
wealth and income
power

The evaluation of individuals along a superiority–inferiority scale means, of
course, a differential distribution of prestige. Thus, the elite strata will receive the
deference of individuals who are ranked below them. Deference may take many
forms: acquiescence in the material advantages or privileges of the elite (the use of
titles and symbols of rank, distinctive clothing, housing, and automobiles); accordance of influence and respect; acceptance of leadership in decision making; and
so on. The stratification system also involves *different styles of life:* foods eaten,
magazines and books read, places of residence, favorite sports, schools attended,
pronunciation and accent, recreational activities, and so forth. In addition, of course,
the stratification system is associated with the *uneven distribution of wealth and
income:* in every society higher-ranking persons enjoy better housing, clothing,
food, automobiles, and other material goods and services than persons ranked lower
on the scale.

Finally, the stratification system involves the *unequal distribution of power—*
the ability to control the acts of others. Sociologists agree that power and stratification are closely related, but they disagree on the specific value of this relationship. Some theorize that power is a *product* of economic well-being, prestige, or
status. Others believe that power *determines* the distribution of wealth, prestige,
and status.[2]

social class
a category and ranking
in the stratification system

The stratification system creates social classes. The term *social class* simply
refers to all individuals who occupy a broadly similar category and ranking in the
stratification system. Members of the same social class may or may not interact or
even realize that they have much in common. Because all societies have stratification systems, all societies have social classes.

functional theory
inequality is necessary
to get people to work
harder in more
demanding jobs that
require longer training
and greater skills

Why Do We Have Social Classes?

Sociologists disagree on why societies distribute wealth, power, and prestige unequally. On one side are the *functional theorists,* who argue that stratification is
necessary and perhaps inevitable for maintaining society. On the other side are the

conflict theorists, who argue that stratification results from the selfish interests of groups trying to preserve their advantages over others.

The functional argument might be summarized as follows:

1. Certain positions are more important to a society's survival than other positions and require special skills. For example, in most societies, occupations such as governor, physician, teacher, and priest are considered vital.
2. Only a few persons in society have the ability (intelligence, energy, personality) to perform well in these positions.
3. These positions require persons who do have ability to undergo extensive training and education before they occupy these positions.
4. In order to motivate able people to endure the training and to sacrifice their time and energy for education, society must provide them with additional rewards.
5. The result is social inequality, with some classes receiving more rewards than others. Inequality is inevitable and essential in order to "insure that the most important positions are conscientiously filled by the most qualified persons."[3]

In other words, an expectation of inequality is essential in getting people to work harder in more difficult jobs that require longer training and greater skill.

In contrast, *conflict theory* focuses on the struggle among competing groups in society over scarce resources. Conflict theorists have argued as follows:

conflict theory
inequality is imposed on society by those who want to retain their wealth and power

1. People who possess property, income, power, or prestige—the upper classes— simply wish to protect their position in society. Thus, the stratification system is perpetuated.
2. There are many "functionally important" positions in society that are *not* highly rewarded. It might be argued that an electrician, an auto mechanic, or a plumber is just as important to the survival of society as is a doctor or a lawyer.
3. Many persons in the lower classes have the ability to perform in high-status occupations, but because of unequal educational opportunities they never get the chance to do so.
4. Wealth is not the only way of motivating people. Conceivably, societies might reward people merely by recognizing their services. Cooperation could then replace competition as a motivating force.
5. Stratification negatively affects the thinking of members of the lower class. Stratification may even be "dysfunctional" to society if it fosters feelings of suspicion, hostility, and disloyalty to society among those in the lower classes.

In short, the stratification system is imposed on society by those at the top. It allows them to use their power and prestige to keep what they have. Later in this chapter we will examine the ideas of Karl Marx, who argued that the struggle between classes was the driving force in history and politics.

Stratification in American Society

Social classes are of interest to sociologists, with their concern for the relationships among individuals and groups. Sociologists have devised several methods of identifying and measuring social stratification. These include: (1) the *subjective method,*

methods of identifying and measuring stratification

in which individuals are asked how they see themselves in the class system; (2) the *reputational method,* in which individuals are asked to rank positions in the class system; and (3) the *objective method,* in which social scientists observe characteristics that discriminate among patterns of life they associate with social class.

The American ideology encompasses the notion that status should be based on personal qualities and achievements. Individuals in a free society should have the opportunity to achieve the social rankings they can earn by ability, effort, and moral worth. These individuals are supposed to rise or fall according to their merits. The American ideology does not deny the existence of a superiority–inferiority scale for evaluating people in society, nor does it call for *absolute equality,* or *"leveling,"* with all people given equal income, wealth, position, and prestige regardless of their individual merit. But it does call for *equality of opportunity;* that is, all should have an equal opportunity to achieve high position in accordance with their individual merits and endeavors. In the American ideal, "anyone who has the drive and the ability can get ahead." The logical sequel to this is that those at the top are worthy of being there because of their talents and efforts.

In view of this ideology, it is not surprising that most Americans think of themselves as middle class. Nearly nine out of ten will describe themselves as middle class when they are forced to choose between this term and either upper or lower class. It is apparent that to characterize oneself as upper class is regarded as "snobbish," and to view oneself as lower class is to admit that one is a loser in the great game of life. Even people who admit to being poor consider it an insult to be called "lower class."[4]

However, the fact that most Americans label themselves as middle class does not mean that American society is one big middle-class society. In fact, when *working class* is added to the list of choices, and individuals are asked for subjective evaluations of their own class membership, a different picture emerges. When given the option, about 43 to 48 percent of Americans identify themselves as "working class," and roughly the same proportions identify themselves as "middle class." About 4 to 6 percent say they are "lower class," and even fewer, 3 to 4 percent, say they are "upper class."[5]

Social scientists have spent a great deal of time studying the prestige ranking of occupations as a measure of the stratification system of modern society. Individuals are asked in national surveys to make a superiority–inferiority ranking of specific occupations. The resulting prestige scores for one hundred separate occupations are shown in Table 4-1. Note that prestige is not the equivalent of income. Apparently prestige is awarded on the basis of ability, education, and training required for an occupation. Generally "white-collar" occupations that involve mental activity are awarded greater prestige than "blue-collar" occupations that require physical labor. These rankings have remained stable for several decades.

The principal *objective criteria* of social class are income, occupation, and education. If sociologists are correct in the assumption that occupation and control of economic resources are the source of stratification in society, then these indexes are the best available measures of class. Certainly income, jobs, and education are unequally distributed in American society, as they are in all other societies.

Table 4-2 shows that slightly more than 20 percent of the adults in the United States are college graduates. Approximately 76 percent are high school graduates,

equality of opportunity versus absolute equality, or "leveling"

subjective identification
individuals identify their own social class

reputational method
individuals ranking the prestige of occupations

objective identification
ranking by occupation, income, or education

TABLE 4-1 Occupational Prestige in the United States

White-collar occupations	Prestige score	Blue-collar occupations
Physician	82	
College/university professor	78	
Lawyer	76	
Dentist	74	
Physicist/astronomer	74	
Bank officer	72	
Architect	71	
Aeronautical/astronautical engineer	71	
Psychologist	71	
Airplane pilot	70	
Clergy	69	
Chemist	69	
Electrical engineer	69	
Geologist	67	
Sociologist	66	
Secondary school teacher	63	
Mechanical engineer	62	
Registered nurse	62	
Dental hygienist	61	
Pharmacist	61	
Radiologic technician	61	
Chiropractor	60	
Elementary school teacher	60	
Veterinarian	60	
Postmaster	58	
Union official	58	
Accountant	57	
Economist	57	
Drafter	56	
Painter/sculptor	56	
Actor	55	
Librarian	55	
Statistician	55	
Industrial engineer	54	
Forester and conservationist	54	
Surveyor	53	
Dietician	52	
Funeral director	52	
Social worker	52	
Athlete	51	
Computer specialist	51	
Editor/reporter	51	
	51	Locomotive engineer
Radio/TV announcer	51	
Bank teller	50	
Sales manager	50	

(continued)

TABLE 4-1 *(continued)*

White-collar occupations	Prestige score	Blue-collar occupations
	49	Electrician
	48	Aircraft mechanic
	48	Machinist
	48	Police officer
Bookkeeper	48	
Insurance agent	47	
Musician/composer	46	
	46	Secretary
	44	Fire fighter
Adult education teacher	43	
Air traffic controller	43	
	42	Mail carrier
	41	Apprentice electrician
	41	Farmer
Buyer/shipper, farm products	41	
	41	Tailor
Photographer	41	
	40	Carpenter
	40	Telephone operator
	40	Welder
Restaurant manager	39	
Building superintendent	38	
	37	Auto body repairperson
	36	Brick/stone mason
	35	TV repairperson
	34	Baker
	33	Hairdresser
	33	Bulldozer operator
Auctioneer	32	
	32	Bus driver
	32	Truck driver
Cashier	31	
File clerk	30	
	30	Upholsterer
	29	Drill-press operator
	29	Furniture finisher
Retail salesperson	29	
	23	Midwife
	22	Gas station attendant
	22	Security guard
	22	Taxi driver
	21	Elevator operator
	20	Bartender
	20	Waiter/waitress
	18	Clothing presser
	18	Farm laborer

(continued)

TABLE 4-1   *(continued)*

White-collar occupations	Prestige score	Blue-collar occupations
	18	Household servant
	17	Car washer
	17	Freight handler
	17	Garbage collector
	16	Janitor
	14	Bellhop
	09	Shoe shiner

Source: Adapted from *General Social Surveys, 1972–1989: Cumulative Codebook* (Chicago: National Opinion Research Center, 1989), pp. 685–698.

about 24 percent having dropped out of formal education without a high school degree.

Table 4-3 reveals the distribution of income in the United States, as well as the distribution of income by education. Generally individuals with prestigious occupations and good educations enjoy high incomes. Table 4-3 shows that individuals who have acquired higher educations tend to enjoy higher annual incomes. However, Table 4-3 also shows that there are two separate scales by which income is distributed—one white and one black. Blacks with equivalent educations tend to earn less than whites. These disparities between blacks and whites are changing slowly over time, but there is still considerable racial inequality in the distribution of income in America.

Inequality in America

Income is a key component of stratification, and income is unequally distributed in all societies. As long as societies reward skills, talents, knowledge, hard work, innovation, initiative, and risk taking, there will be inequalities of income. But the

TABLE 4-2   Distribution of Formal Education among the Adult Population (Persons Aged 25 and over) in the United States

	Percentage of adult population
Not a high school graduate	23.8
0–7 years	6.8
8 years	5.2
9–11 years	11.7
High school graduate	76.2
High school only	35.9
Some college	17.0
College graduate or more	20.3

Source: U.S. Bureau of the Census, *Statistical Abstract of the United States 1990* (Washington, D.C.: U.S. Government Printing Office, 1990), p. 134.

TABLE 4-3 Distribution of Family Income in the United States

Family income	Percentage of families
Less than $5,000	6.9
$5,000–$14,999	22.1
$15,000–$24,999	19.2
$25,000–$49,999	33.3
Over $50,000	18.5
Median family income in 1987 = $25,986	

	Median family income	
Education	White	Black
Less than eight years	$11,431	$12,494
Eight years school	17,816	13,143
One to three years high school	22,759	14,112
Four years high school	30,065	21,139
One to three years college	35,646	26,078
Four years college or more	51,689	37,700

Source: U.S. Bureau of the Census, *Statistical Abstract of the United States 1990* (Washington, D.C.: U.S. Government Printing Office, 1990), pp. 445–446.

question remains how much inequality is required to provide adequate rewards and incentives for education, training, work, enterprise, and risk.

measuring inequality
percentage of total national income received by each fifth of income earners

Let us try to systematically examine income inequality in America. Table 4-4 divides all American families into five groups—from the lowest one-fifth in personal income to the highest one-fifth—and shows the percentage of total family personal income received by each group over the years. (If perfect income equality existed, each fifth would receive 20 percent of all family personal income, and it would not even be possible to rank fifths from highest to lowest.) The poorest one-fifth received 3.5 percent of all family personal income in 1929; in 1987, this group received 4.6 percent of all family personal income. (Most of the increase occurred during World War II.) The highest one-fifth received 54.4 percent of all family personal income in 1929; in 1987, however, the percentage had declined to 43.7. This was the only income group to lose in relation to other income groups. The middle classes improved their relative income position even more than the poor.

Note, however, an *increase* in inequality in the United States since 1970. Social scientists and policy makers have voiced concern over this reversal of the historical trend toward greater income equality. This recent increase in inequality appears to be a product of several social and economic trends: (1) the relative decline of the manufacturing sector of the economy, with its middle-income blue-collar jobs, and the ascendancy of the information and service sectors, with a combination of high-paying and low-paying jobs; (2) an increase in the number of two-wage families, making single-wage households relatively less affluent; and (3) demographic trends that include larger proportions of aged and larger proportions of female-headed families.

equality of opportunity
equal chances for success based on ability, work, initiative, and luck

But most Americans are concerned more with equality of opportunity than with equality of results (see Table 4-5). *Equality of opportunity* refers to the ability to make of oneself what one can, to develop talents and abilities, and to be rewarded

TABLE 4-4   Percentage Distribution of Family Personal Income, by Quintiles, and Top 5 Percent of Consumer Units in Selected Years, 1929–1987

Quintiles	1929	1950	1960	1970	1980	1987
Lowest	3.5	4.5	4.8	5.4	5.2	4.6
Second	9.0	12.0	12.2	12.2	11.6	10.8
Third	13.8	17.4	17.8	17.6	17.5	16.9
Fourth	19.3	23.4	24.0	23.9	24.1	24.1
Highest	54.4	42.7	41.2	40.9	41.5	43.7
Top 5 percent ratio	30.0	17.3	15.9	15.6	15.6	16.9

Source: U.S. Bureau of the Census, *Statistical Abstract of the United States 1990* (Washington, D.C.: U.S. Government Printing Office, 1990), p. 451.

for work, initiative, and achievement. Equality of opportunity means that everyone comes to the same starting line in life with the same chance of success, that whatever differences develop over time do so as a result of abilities, talents, initiative, hard work, and perhaps good luck. Americans do not generally resent the fact that physicians, engineers, airline pilots, or others who have spent time and energy acquiring particular skills make more money than those whose jobs require fewer skills and less training. Nor do most Americans resent the fact that people who risk their own time and money to build a business, bring new or better products to market, and create jobs for others make more money than their employees. Nor do many Americans begrudge multimillion-dollar incomes to sports figures, rock singers, or movie stars, whose talents entertain the public. Indeed, few Americans object when someone wins a million-dollar lottery, as long as everyone had an equal chance at winning.

Equality of results refers to the equal sharing of income and material rewards regardless of one's condition in life. Equality of results means that everyone starts *and finishes* the race together, regardless of ability, talent, initiative, or work. Most Americans support a "floor" on income and material well-being—a level below which no one, regardless of their condition, should be permitted to fall. But very few Americans want to place a "ceiling" on income or wealth. This unwillingness to limit top income extends to nearly all groups in America, the poor as well as the rich.[6] Generally Americans want people who cannot provide for themselves to be well cared for, especially children, the elderly, the ill, and the disabled. However, most Americans believe that a "fair" economic system rewards people for ability and hard work (see Box 4-1).

equality of results
equal incomes regardless of ability, work, or initiative

Social Mobility: The Ups and Downs

Although all societies are stratified, societies differ greatly in social mobility—that is, in the opportunity people have to move from one class to another. The *social mobility* of individuals may be *upward,* when they achieve a status higher than that of their parents, or *downward,* when their status is lower. In the United States, there is a great deal of social mobility, both upward and downward.

upward mobility
downward mobility

The results of one study of social mobility in America are presented in Table 4-6. This study compared the occupational status of sons and fathers in two different years, 1962 and 1973. A majority of the sons of upper white-collar fathers (53.8 percent in 1962 and 52 percent in 1973) were themselves in upper white-collar occupations. But the rest of those sons descended to less prestigious occupations than their fathers' (downward mobility). At the other end of the scale, only

BOX 4-1

The American Ideology: Equality of Opportunity

In the American ideal, anyone who works hard ought to get ahead, does get ahead, and in getting ahead proves that hard work is justified. The American ideology is one of equality of opportunity. Its major points are:

1. the belief in an open opportunity structure in the United States, with equality of chances for upward and downward mobility;

2. personal responsibility for movement upward or downward in the class system, with movement based largely on personal effort, ambition, hard work, skill, and education;

3. relative accessibility of education to everyone who has the ability; and

4. the impartial functioning of the political and legal systems.

Do Americans believe in this ideology? A majority of them endorse it when it is presented to them in very general statements. However, Americans are also realistic in their appraisal of differences in opportunities between rich and poor and white and black (see Table 4-5).

TABLE 4-5   Beliefs about Equality and Opportunity

Perceived general equality of opportunity		*Beliefs about equality*	
How good a chance do you think a person has to get ahead today, if the person works hard?		Everyone in America should have an equal opportunity to get ahead.	
A very good chance	25%	Agree	99%
A good chance	38	Disagree	2
Some chance	26		
Little chance	9		
No chance at all	2		
Do you think most Americans have a fair opportunity to make the most of themselves in life, or does something usually hold them back?		Under a fair economic system:	
		All people would earn about the same	7%
		People with more ability would earn higher	
Fair opportunity	70%	salaries	78
Held back	30	Decline to choose	15
America is the land of opportunity where everyone who works hard can get ahead.		Which would be fairer, to pay people according to:	
		Their economic needs	6%
Strongly agree	14%	How hard they work	71
Agree	56	Decline to choose	23
Disagree	27		
Strongly disagree	4		

(continued)

BOX 4-1

(continued)

TABLE 4-5   *(continued)*

Perceived equality of opportunity for rich, poor, working class, blacks, and women

Compared to the average person in America, what do you think the chance of getting ahead is for

	Much better (%)	*Better (%)*	*Average (%)*	*Worse (%)*	*Much worse (%)*
People who grew up in rich families	35	48	14	0	3
People who grew up in poor families	2	17	47	5	29
People who grew up in working-class families	3	20	69	0	8
Blacks	6	22	45	3	25
A woman working full-time compared to a man at the same job	2	12	46	2	37

Source: Left column adapted with permission from James R. Kluegel and Eliot R. Smith, *Beliefs About Inequality: Americans' Views of What Is and What Ought to Be* (New York: Aldine de Gruyter). Copyright © 1986 by James R. Kluegel and Eliot R. Smith. Right column from Herbert McClosky and John Zaller, *The American Ethos* (Cambridge, Mass.: Harvard University Press, 1984), pp. 83–84.

TABLE 4-6   Social Mobility in America

Year and Father's Occupation	Upper white-collar (%)	Lower white-collar (%)	Upper manual (%)	Lower manual (%)	Farm (%)	Father's percentage totals
1962						
Upper white-collar	53.8	17.6	12.5	14.8	1.3	16.5
Lower white-collar	45.6	20.0	14.4	18.3	1.7	7.6
Upper manual	28.1	13.4	27.8	29.5	1.2	19.0
Lower manual	20.3	12.3	21.6	43.8	2.0	27.5
Farm	15.6	7.0	19.2	36.1	22.2	29.4
Son's percentage totals	27.8	12.4	20.0	32.1	7.7	100.0
1973						
Upper white-collar	52.0	16.0	13.8	17.1	1.1	18.2
Lower white-collar	42.3	19.7	15.3	21.9	0.8	9.0
Upper manual	29.4	13.0	27.4	29.0	1.1	20.5
Lower manual	22.5	12.0	23.7	40.8	1.0	29.7
Farm	17.5	7.8	22.7	37.2	14.8	22.6
Son's percentage totals	29.9	12.7	21.7	31.5	4.1	100.0

Note: Mobility from father's (or other family head's) occupation to current occupation: U.S. men in the experienced civilian labor force aged 20 to 64 in 1962 and 1973.

Source: The basic source of information is David Featherman and Robert Hauser, *Opportunity and Change* (New York: Academic Press, 1978). Data are from March 1962 and March 1973, "Current Population Surveys and Occupational Changes in a Generation Survey." Occupation groups are upper white-collar: professional and kindred workers and managers, officials, and proprietors, except farm; lower white-collar: sales, clerical, and kindred workers; upper manual: craftspeople, forepersons, and kindred workers; lower manual: operatives and kindred workers, service workers, and laborers, except farm; farm: farmers and farm managers, farm laborers and forepersons.

about 40 percent of the sons of lower manual workers (43.8 percent in 1962 and 40.8 percent in 1973) ended up in the same occupational category as their fathers. This means that nearly 60 percent of those sons rose to more prestigious occupations than their fathers' (upward mobility). Box 4-1 illustrates how Americans feel about the opportunity for social advancement.

Overall, there has been more upward mobility than downward mobility over the years. This upward movement is made possible by economic growth. However, the rate of upward mobility appears to be slowing down. This trend may reflect slower rates of economic growth in the 1980s and jobs in industry and technology lost to foreign competition.

Class as a Determinant of Style of Life

Life in each social class is different. Differences in ways of life mean differences in culture, or rather (because the style of life in each class is really a variant of one common culture in American society) a division of the culture into *subcultures*. Class subcultures have been described by many sociologists. Class differences exist in almost every aspect of life: health, hygiene, vocabulary, table manners, standards of right and wrong, recreation and entertainment, religion, sexual activity, family and child-rearing practices, political beliefs and attitudes, club memberships, dress, birthrates, attitudes toward education, toilet training, reading habits, and so on. It is impossible to provide a complete description of all the class differences that have been reported by sociologists. Moreover, class lifestyles overlap, and in America there are no rigid boundaries between classes. Class subcultures should be thought of as being on a *continuous scale* with styles of life that blend; thus there are many "in-between" positions. And finally, it should be remembered that any generalizations about broad classes in the United States do not necessarily describe the style of life of any particular individuals; the following paragraphs are merely a general summary of the subcultures.

The Upper Class

The typical upper-class individual is future-oriented and cosmopolitan. Persons of this class expect a long life, look forward to their future and the future of their children and grandchildren, and are concerned about what lies ahead for the community, the nation, and mankind. They are self-confident, believing that within limits they can shape their own destiny and that of the community. They are willing to invest in the future—that is, to sacrifice some present satisfaction in the expectation of enjoying greater satisfaction in time to come. They are self-respecting; they place great value on independence and creativity and on developing their potential to the fullest. In rearing their children, they teach them to be guided by abstract standards of social justice rather than by conformity to a given code. ("Do things not because you're told to but because you take the other person into consideration.") Child rearing is permissive, and the only coercive measures taken against the child are verbal and emotional. Instructions to the child are always rationalized. Upper-class parents are not alarmed if their children remain in school

Upper-class entertainment—patrons of a Palm Beach, Florida, polo club.
Source: Polly Brown/Actuality

or travel until the age of thirty. Women enjoy nearly equal status with men in family relationships. The goals of life include individuality, self-expression, and personal happiness. Wealth permits a wide variety of entertainment and recreation: theater, concerts, art, yachting, tennis, skiing, travel abroad, and so on.

Upper-class individuals take a tolerant attitude toward unconventional behavior in sex, the arts, fashions, lifestyles, and so forth. They deplore bigotry and abhor violence. They feel they have a responsibility to "serve" the community and to "do good." They are active in "public service" and contribute time, money, and effort to worthy causes. They have an attachment to the community, the nation, and the world, and they believe they can help shape the future. This "public-regardingness" inclines them toward "liberal" politics; the upper classes provide the leadership for the liberal wings of both the Republican and Democratic parties.

The Middle Class

Middle-class individuals are also future-oriented; they plan ahead for themselves and their children. But they are not likely to be as cosmopolitan as the upper-class person, because they are more concerned with their immediate families than with "humanity" in the abstract. They are confident about their ability to influence their own futures and those of their children, but they do not really expect to have an effect on community, state, or national events. They show some independence and creativity, but their taste for self-expression is modified by their concern for "getting ahead."

The middle-class individual is perhaps even more self-disciplined and willing to sacrifice present gratification for future advantage than the upper-class individual. In the lower middle class, investing time, energy, and effort in self-improvement and getting ahead is a principal theme of life. Middle-class people strongly want their children to go to college and acquire the kind of formal training that will help them get ahead. Child rearing in the middle class is slightly less permissive than in the upper class; it is still based largely on verbal and emotional punishment. This can be quite severe, however, and the middle-class child may be more closely supervised and disciplined than either upper- or lower-class children. Authority is rationalized for the child, but values and standards of behavior are drawn from surrounding middle-class society rather than from abstract concepts of social justice. In matters of sex the middle-class individual is outwardly conventional. The middle-class adolescent experiences first intercourse at a later age than the lower-class youth. However, in adult life, vis-à-vis lower-class individuals, the middle-class person enjoys greater variety in sexual activity, women have greater equality in the family, and the family has fewer children (though home activities are frequently child-centered). Recreation and entertainment include golf, swimming, movies, sports events, and travel in the United States. In general, the middle-class person is less able than the upper-class one to afford an interest in theater, art, symphonies, or travel abroad.

As a rule, middle-class individuals deal with others according to established codes of conduct and behavior. They are likely to be middle-of-the-road or conservative in politics; they tend to vote Republican. They have regard for the rights of others and generally oppose bigotry and violence. However, they do not hold those attitudes as strongly as do members of the upper class, nor do they feel as much responsibility to the community as the upper-class individual does. Though they join voluntary organizations, many of which are formally committed to community service, they are less willing to give their time, money, and effort to public causes.

The Working Class

Working-class individuals do not invest heavily in the future; they are much more oriented toward the present. They expect their children to make their own way in life. They have less confidence than the middle class in their ability to shape the future and a stronger sense of being at the mercy of fate and other uncontrollable forces. They are self-respecting and self-confident, but these feelings extend over a narrower range of matters than they do in middle-class individuals. The horizon of the working class is limited by job, family, immediate friends, and neighborhood. Self-improvement or getting ahead is not a major concern of life; there is more interest in having a "good time" with family and companions. The working-class family has more children than do middle-class or upper-class families.

Working-class individuals work to maintain themselves and their families; they do not look at their jobs as a means of getting ahead and certainly not as a means of self-expression. In rearing their children, they emphasize the virtues of neatness, cleanliness, honesty, obedience, and respect for authority. They seldom rationalize authority over their children ("Because I said so, that's why") and sometimes use physical punishment. They are not interested in stimulating their children to self-expression, but rather in controlling them—teaching them traditional family values. They would like their children to go to college, but if they do not, it is no great matter. The working-class youth experiences first sexual intercourse at an earlier age than do middle- and upper-class young people; young working-class men are more likely to categorize women as "good" or "bad" depending on their sexual

The working class generally finds entertainment of a different type, such as this carnival.
Source: Alan Carey/The Image Works

activity. The working-class woman is relegated to a subordinate role in sexual and family affairs. Frequently a double standard allows promiscuity in the man, whereas a woman's engaging in extramarital sex can be the cause of family disruption.

In relationships with others the working-class individual is often intolerant and sometimes aggressive. Open bigotry is more likely to be encountered in the working class than in the middle or upper classes. Violence is less shocking to the working class than to middle-class persons; indeed, sometimes it is regarded as a normal expression of a masculine style. To the working class, the upper class appears somewhat lacking in masculinity. The working-class individual's deepest attachment is to family. Most visiting is done with relatives rather than friends. Working-class persons do not belong to many organizations other than union and church. Whether Protestant or Catholic, their religious beliefs are fundamentalist in character; they believe in the literal meaning of the scriptures and respect the authority of the church. In their views toward others in the community, they are very "private-regarding"; they believe they work hard for a living and feel others should do the same. They are not interested in public service or "do-goodism"; they look down on people who accept welfare or charity unless those people are forced to do so by circumstances over which they have no control. When they vote, they generally vote Democratic, but they are often apathetic about politics. They are liberal on economic issues (job security, fair labor standards, government guarantees of full employment, and so on) but conservative on social issues (civil rights, welfare, drug use, and so forth). The working-class position in politics is motivated not by political ideology but by ethnic and party loyalties, by the appeal of personalities, or by occasional favors. For recreation the working-class individual turns to bowling, stock-car racing, circuses, fairs, and carnivals.

CASE STUDY

Karl Marx: The Class Struggle

Conflict between social classes is a central feature of communist ideology. In the opening of his famous *Communist Manifesto,* Karl Marx wrote:

> The history of all hitherto existing society is the history of class struggles. Freeman and slave, patrician and plebeian, lord and serf, guild-master and journeyman, in a word, oppressor and oppressed, stood in constant opposition to one another, carried on an uninterrupted, now hidden, now open fight, a fight that each time ended, either in a revolutionary reconstitution of society at large, or in the common ruin of the contending classes. . . . Our epoch, the epoch of the bourgeoisie, possesses, however, this distinctive feature: it has simplified the class antagonisms. Society as a whole is more and more splitting up into two great hostile camps, into two great classes directly facing each other: Bourgeoisie and Proletariat.[7]

Karl Marx was born in Prussia in 1818. His parents were Jews who converted to Christianity when Marx was a child. He studied history, law, and philosophy at Bonn, Berlin, and Jena and received his doctor of philosophy degree in 1841. Soon after, he entered revolutionary socialist politics as a journalist and pamphleteer; he was expelled from Prussia and engaged in conspiratorial activities in France and Belgium from 1843 to 1849. *The Communist Manifesto,* written with Friedrich Engels, appeared in 1848 as a revolutionary pamphlet. In 1849 Marx fled to London, where he spent the remainder of his life writing occasional pamphlets on socialism, advising socialist leaders, and setting forth his views in a lengthy work, *Das Kapital.* He lived largely on the money given him by Friedrich Engels, who was the son of a wealthy textile manufacturer.

According to Marx, social classes develop on the basis of the different positions that individuals fulfill in the prevailing "mode of production"—that is, the economy. In an agricultural economy, the principal classes are landowner and tenant, serf, or slave; in a handicraft economy, guild-master and apprentice; and in an industrial economy, the capitalist (owner of the factory) and the non–property-owning worker. Marx believed that one's position in the economy determines one's interests, beliefs, and actions. The bourgeoisie who own the factories have an interest in maximizing profit and seek to keep for themselves the surplus of profit that has been created by the worker. Workers are exploited in that they produce more than they receive in wages; this "surplus value" is stolen from the workers by the capitalists. In the long run bourgeois society is doomed to destruction because gradually the workers will realize they are being exploited, will become aware of their historic role and will act collectively to improve their situation, and ultimately will take over the ownership of the instruments of production in violent revolution. In Marx's opinion it was inevitable that the development of capitalism would lead eventually to the proletarian revolution. He believed that as the capitalist became richer, the workers would become poorer.

Marx viewed class consciousness as an important prerequisite to successful proletarian revolution. Class consciousness would increase as the proletariat grew in

(continued)

(continued)

numbers, as factories concentrated the proletariat in greater masses, as workers communicated among themselves and achieved solidarity in unions and political organizations, and as conflict between workers and owners intensified. The bourgeoisie would not relinquish their control over the means of production without a fight, and therefore violent revolution was necessary and inevitable. Marx said little about the details of revolution; this aspect of communist ideology was developed later by Lenin (see Chapter 9). But after the successful proletarian revolution, Marx envisioned a society without social classes. This *classless society* would be a "dictatorship of the proletariat" with all other social classes eliminated. The state would control the means of production, and everyone would be in the same relationship to the state as everyone else. Only when all were employees of the state would true equality exist. Class distinctions and class antagonisms would then be abolished. Social relations would be based on the rule: "From each according to his ability; to each according to his needs." The state, which functions in bourgeois society to help the bourgeoisie oppress the masses, would gradually wither away in a communist society. As soon as there was no longer any social class to be held in subjection, the special repressive force, the state, would no longer be necessary.

The truth is, of course, that neither capitalist societies nor communist societies conformed to Marx's analysis. There are several reasons the capitalist society of the United States failed to meet Marx's expectations. First, Americans do not define their interests strictly on the basis of their class membership. Allegiances to church, ethnic group, racial category, voluntary organizations, union, occupational group, and so forth prevent the emergence of a militant class consciousness. Second, and perhaps more important, the workers in the United States did not become poorer over time but improved their standard of living. It turned out that capitalism provided workers with considerable material comfort. Third, American society provided a great deal of social mobility that enabled many individuals in the working class to move into the middle class. Marx did not foresee this growth of the middle class. Moreover, the social mobility of American society encouraged people in the working class to work within the system to improve their lives and the lives of their children rather than to organize to destroy the system.

With regard to the failure of communist societies to conform to Marx's analysis, even though the bourgeois class was eliminated at great cost in human lives, communist party rulers emerged who were more oppressive than the former bourgeoisie. Communist party officials, government bureaucrats, and military officers monopolized power, prestige, and wealth. The state did not wither away at all, but instead became all-encompassing and all-powerful.

The Lower Class

Lower-class individuals live from day to day, with little interest in the future. They have no confidence in their ability to influence what happens to them. Things happen *to* them; they do not *make* them happen. They do not discipline themselves to sacrifice for the future because they have no sense of future. They look for immediate gratification, and their behavior is governed largely by impulse. When they work, it is often from payday to payday, and they frequently drift from one unskilled job to another, taking scant interest in the work. Their self-confidence is low, and occasionally they even suffer from feelings of self-contempt. In relations with others, they are suspicious, hostile, and aggressive. They feel little attachment to community, neighbors, and friends and resent all authority (for example, that of policemen, social workers, teachers, landlords, and employers). Lower-class individuals are nonparticipants—they belong to no voluntary organizations, attend church infrequently, have no political interests, and seldom vote.

The lower-class family is frequently headed by a woman. Lower-class women not only have more children than middle- or upper-class women but also have them earlier in life. A woman may have a succession of mates who contribute intermittently to the support of the family but who take almost no part in rearing children. In child rearing, the mother (or the grandmother) is impulsive; children may be alternately loved, disciplined, and neglected, and often do not know what to expect next. The mother may receive welfare or work at a low-paying job, but in either case children are generally unsupervised once they have passed babyhood. Physical punishment is frequent. When these children enter school, they are already behind other children in verbal abilities and abstract reasoning. For the male offspring of a lower-class matriarchal family, the future is often depressing, with defeat and frustration repeating themselves throughout his life. He may drop out of school in the eighth or ninth grade because of lack of success. Without parental supervision, and having little to do, he may get into trouble with the police. The police record will further hurt his chances of getting a job. With limited job skills, little self-discipline, and low aspiration levels, the lower-class male is not likely to find a steady job that will pay enough to support a family. Yet he yearns for the material standard of living of higher classes—a car, a television set, and other conveniences. He may tie up much of his income in installment debts; because of his low credit rating he will be forced to pay excessive interest rates, and sooner or later his creditors will garnishee his salary. If he marries, he and his family will live in overcrowded, substandard housing. As pressures mount, he may decide to leave his family, either because his inability to support a wife and children is humiliating, or because he is psychologically unprepared for a stable family relationship, or because only in this way will his wife and children be eligible for welfare payments.

Frequently, to compensate for defeat and frustration, the lower-class male will resort to risk taking, conquest, and fighting to assert his masculinity. Lower-class life is violent. The incidence of mental illness is greater in the lower class than in any other class. The lower-class youth may have engaged in sexual activities from a very early age, but these activities are stereotyped in a male-dominant—female-subordinate fashion. Entertainment may be limited to drinking and gambling. Many aspects of lower-class culture are unattractive to women. Sociologist Herbert Gans wrote:

> The woman tries to develop a stable routine in the midst of poverty and deprivation;
> the action-seeking man upsets it. In order to have any male relationships, however,
> the woman must participate to some extent in his episodic lifestyle. On rare occasions,

she may even pursue it herself. Even then, however, she will try to encourage her children to seek a routine way of life. Thus the woman is much closer to working class culture, at least in her aspirations, although she is not often successful in achieving them.[8]

BOX 4-2

Cross-National Perspective: Global Inequalities

Three of every four persons in the world today live in a Third World culture. The term *Third World* refers to poor, agrarian societies. *First World* refers to industrial societies with free-market economics, democratic governments, and high standards of living. These societies include the United States, Western Europe, and Japan. *Second World* refers to industrial societies with government-directed socialist economies, one-party authoritarian governments, and generally lower standards of living. Until recently these societies included the states of the former Soviet Union and all of eastern Europe; but the nations of eastern Europe ousted their communist democrated governments in 1989 and introduced free-market economic reforms. Russia, Ukraine, Belarus, and other former Soviet states have also introduced market reforms and greater democracy. (See Chapter 9 for an understanding of socialism as well as of changes taking place in Russia.) The Third World encompasses most of the globe: all of South and Central America; all of Africa, with the exception of the white minority of South Africa; the Middle East, with the exception of Israel; and Asia, with the exception of Japan and the rapidly developing "Four Dragons"—Hong Kong, South Korea, Taiwan, and Singapore.

While these broad categories of "worlds" are commonly used by social scientists and others, it is important to remember that each category encompasses societies with different languages, diverse people, and distinct cultures. Nonetheless, there are common characteristics of Third World societies that can be observed by visitors as well as by social scientists. Americans can better appreciate their own society by knowing how the majority of the world's population lives.

Poverty

Poverty in the Third World is widespread and severe. The vast majority of the world's population lives well below the standard of living of America's poorest families. Hunger, starvation, and ill-health are common. It is estimated that one out of every five persons in the world today does not eat enough to enable him or her to work; one child in four dies before reaching the age of five. Life expectancy is short (see Table 4-7).

Inequality

The limited resources of Third World societies are unequally distributed, with small elites controlling large proportions of land and wealth. In some societies a caste system determines one's social position at birth with no opportunity for upward social mobility. The subordination of women in Third World societies is very pronounced; women are commonly denied education, land ownership, and a voice in public affairs.

Traditionalism

Third World cultures generally place great value on traditional ways of life passed down, virtually unchanged, from generation to generation. Traditionalism also means the acceptance of one's life and one's fate, however poor. It also means resisting innovation and change.

High Fertility

Birthrates are generally very high in the Third World. Family reliance on human labor, high infant mortality rates, the low status of women, and the absence of birth control information or technology all contribute to high birthrates. China has attempted to force families to have only one child; sterilization and abortion are common, but so also are abortion of female fetuses only and female infanticide.

Primitive Technology

Most energy in Third World societies is directly supplied by human and animal muscle power. A lifetime of hard manual labor, just to meet minimum needs, confronts most of the people of the world. Animal labor is more common than farm machinery.

(continued)

BOX 4-2

(continued)

TABLE 4-7 Cross-National Perspective: Life in the Third World

	GNP per person (U.S. $)	Birthrate[a]	Life expectancy (years)	Infant mortality rate[b]
United States	18,570	15.1	76.1	11
Mexico	1,701	30.3	70.1	42
Argentina	2,467	20.3	70.6	26
Colombia	1,105	27.3	65.8	42
Bolivia	563	35.6	54.3	105
Egypt	1,370	35.5	59.6	93
Nigeria	214	46.2	48.1	121
Zaire	165	44.7	52.6	107
Kenya	340	51.1	61.1	70
Ghana	354	46.2	53.9	91
Mali	238	49.0	45.8	151
China	438	22.5	69.3	34
India	307	30.6	57.3	91
Pakistan	327	43.0	54.2	120
Bangladesh	163	42.7	53.2	138

[a]Live births per 1,000 population per year.

[b]Number of deaths of children under one year of age per 1,000 live births per year.

Source: U.S. Bureau of the Census, *Statistical Abstract of the United States 1990* (Washington, D.C.: U.S. Government Printing Office, 1990), pp. 835–836, 840.

Social Classes: Conflict and Conciliation

class consciousness
believing that all members of one's class have similar political and economic interests, adverse to those of other classes

An awareness of class membership is not the same as class consciousness. *Class consciousness* is the belief that all members of one's social class have similar economic and political interests that are adverse to the interests of other classes and ought to be promoted through common action. As we have already seen, Americans are *aware* of class membership, but members of the same class do not always share political interests, feel that collective class action is necessary, or see themselves as locked in a struggle against opposing classes. Few Americans believe in the militant ideology of class struggle. Americans do not have a strong sense of class consciousness.

Nonetheless, there is some evidence of awareness of class interest in voting behavior. Although Democratic and Republican candidates draw their support from all social classes in America, social-class bases of the Democratic and Republican parties are slightly different (see Chapter 7). Professional and managerial groups and other white-collar employees give greater support to the Republican party than do skilled, semiskilled, and unskilled workers. Likewise, people with some college education tend to vote Republican more often than persons with a high school or grade school education do. Of course, not all the upper-class vote goes to the Republican party, and not all the lower-class vote goes to the Democratic party. In fact, the differences in voter support are not very great. But there is some indication that class has an impact on voting behavior.

Why is there no militant class consciousness in America? This is a difficult question to answer precisely, but we can summarize some of the factors that appear to help stabilize the existing class system in America and reduce class conflict:

1. the high level of real income of Americans of all social classes and the relatively wide distribution of a very comfortable standard of living;
2. a great deal of upward mobility in the American system, which diverts lower-class attention away from collective class action and focuses it toward individual efforts at "getting ahead";
3. the existence of a large middle-income, middle-prestige class;
4. widespread belief in the legitimacy of the class structure and the resulting acceptance of it;
5. many cross-cutting allegiances of individuals to churches, communities, races, unions, professional associations, voluntary organizations, and so forth, which interfere with class solidarity.

factors in American life reducing class conflict
high standard of living

upward mobility

large middle class

widespread belief in the system

many cross-cutting allegiances

In stabilizing the class system, these factors also stabilize the existing distribution of power in America.

The American system has produced a high level of material comfort for the great majority of the population. The real possibilities of acquiring greater income and prestige have reinforced efforts to strive within the system rather than to challenge it. Even individuals who realize that their own social mobility is limited can transfer their hope and ambition to their children. A large middle class, diverse in occupation and ambiguous in political orientation, helps to blur potential lines of class identification and conflict. This class stands as a symbol and an embodiment of the reality of opportunity. A widely accepted set of ideologies, beliefs, and attitudes supports the existing system. Finally, cleavages caused by religious affiliations, ethnic backgrounds, and racial categories, as well as by other types of diversity (region, skill level, occupational group), have all worked against the development of a unified class movement.

Social Class and Political Power

Government leadership is recruited mainly from the upper social classes. Most government officials, particularly at the national level (cabinet officers, presidential advisers, congressional representatives, Supreme Court judges, and so on), are members of the well-educated, prestigiously employed, successful, and affluent upper and upper middle classes (see Box 4-3). With few exceptions, they are the children of professionals, business owners and managers, or successful farmers and landowners. Only a small minority are the children of wage earners or salaried workers. The occupational characteristics of representatives also show that they are generally of higher social standing than their constituents; professional and business occupations dominate the halls of Congress. One reason is, of course, that con-

social class and legislative power

gressional candidates are more likely to win the election if their occupations are socially "respectable" and provide opportunities for extensive public contacts. The lawyer, insurance agent, farm implement dealer, and real estate agent establish in their businesses the wide circle of friends necessary for political success. Another, subtler, reason is that candidates and elected legislators must come from occupational groups with flexible work responsibilities. Lawyers, landowners, and business owners can adjust their work to the campaign and legislative schedules, whereas office managers cannot.

lawyers in politics

The overrepresentation of lawyers as an occupational group in Congress and other public offices is particularly marked, since lawyers constitute no more than two-tenths of 1 percent of the labor force. Lawyers have always played a prominent role in the American political system. Twenty-five of the fifty-two signers of the Declaration of Independence and thirty-one of the fifty-five members of the Continental Congress were lawyers. The legal profession has also provided 70 percent of the presidents, vice-presidents, and cabinet officers of the United States and approximately half of all U.S. senators and members of the House of Representatives. Lawyers are in a reasonably high-prestige occupation, but so are physicians,

---

BOX 4-3

Social Backgrounds of Cabinet-Level Appointees in Presidential Administrations

	Truman through Carter	Reagan	Bush
Education			
Advanced degree	69%	68%	80%
Law degree	40	26	40
Ivy League degree	48	58	50
Ph.D.	19	16	25
No college degree	0	0	0
Average age	53 yrs	55 yrs	56 yrs
Women	4%	5%	10%
Blacks	4	5	5
Occupations			
Law	28%	11%	40%
Business	28	32	55
Government	16	16	5
Education	19	16	25
Military	3	5	10

Sources: For Reagan and Bush administrations, see Thomas R. Dye, *Who's Running America?* 5th Edition (Englewood Cliffs, N.J.: Prentice Hall) 1990; for Truman through Carter see Phillip H. Burch, Jr., *Elites in American History* vol. 3 (New York: Holmes and Meier) 1980.

The most popular and controversial analysis of power in the United States is *The Power Elite,* by sociologist C. Wright Mills. Since its appearance in 1956, most writers have been unable to discuss national power without reference to this important study.

The Power Elite

According to Mills, power in the United States is concentrated at the top of the nation's corporate, governmental, and military organizations, which closely interlock to form a single structure of power: *a power elite.* Power rests in these three domains: "the corporation chieftains, the political directorate, and the warlords." Occasionally there is tension among them, but they share a broad consensus about the general direction of public policy and the main course of society. Other institutions (the family, churches, schools, and so forth) are subordinate to the three major institutions of power:

> Families and churches and schools adapt to modern life; governments and armies and corporations shape it; and, as they do, they turn these lesser institutions into means for their own ends.[9]

The *emergence* of the power elite is a product of *technology, bureaucratization, and centralization.* The economy—once a scatter of many small competing units—is now dominated by a few hundred giant corporate and financial institutions. The political system—once a decentralized structure of states and communities with a small central government—has become a giant centralized bureaucracy in Washington that has assumed power over nearly every aspect of American life. The military—once a slim establishment depending largely on citizen-soldiers to meet specific crises—has become the largest and most expensive function of government and a sprawling bureaucratic domain.

> The history of modern society may readily be understood as the story of the enlargement and the centralization of the means of power—in economic, in political, and in military institutions.[10]

As these sectors of society enlarged and centralized, they increasingly came together to coordinate decision making.

> At the pinnacle of each of the three enlarged and centralized domains, there have arisen those higher circles which make up the economic, the political, and the military elites. At the top of the economy, among the corporate rich, there are the chief executives; at the top of the political order, the members of the political directorate; at the top of the military establishment, the elite of soldier-statesmen clustered in and around the Joint Chiefs of Staff and the upper echelon. As each of these domains has coincided with the others, as decisions tend to become total in their consequences, the leading men in each of the three domains of power—the warlords, the corporation chieftains, the political directorate—tend to come together, to form the power elite of America.[11]

(continued)

CASE STUDY

(continued)

The power elite holds power because of its position at the top of the institutional structures of society. These people are powerful *not* because of any individual qualities—wealth, prestige, skill, or cunning—but because of the *institutional positions* they occupy. As society has concentrated more and more power in a few giant institutions, the people in command of these institutions have acquired enormous power over all of us.

> If we took the one hundred most powerful men in America, the one hundred wealthiest, and the one hundred most celebrated away from the institutional positions they now occupy, away from their resources of men and women and money, away from the media of mass communication that are now focused upon them—then they would be powerless and poor and uncelebrated. For power is not of a man. Wealth does not center in the person of the wealthy. Celebrity is not inherent in any personality. To be celebrated, to be wealthy, to have power requires access to major institutions, for the institutional positions men occupy determine in large part their chances to have and to hold these valued experiences.[12]

Mills is aware that his description of power in the United States conflicts with the "pluralist" interpretation. But he believes that notions of powerholders who balance and compromise interests or who engage in competition between parties and groups apply to middle-level powerholders in America and not to the top power elite. Political journalists and scholars write about middle levels because this is all they know about or understand; these levels provide the noisy content of most "political" news and gossip. The major directions of national and international policy are determined by persons beyond the "clang and clash of American politics." Political campaigns actually distract attention from the really important national and international decisions.

The *unity* of the top elite rests on several factors. First of all, these people are recruited from the same upper social classes; they have similar education, wealth, and upbringing. Moreover, they continue to associate with each other, reinforcing their common feelings. They belong to the same clubs, attend the same parties, meet at the same resorts, and serve on the same civic, cultural, and philanthropic committees. Members of the elite incorporate into their own viewpoints the viewpoints, expectations, and values of those who "count." Factions exist and individual ambitions clash, but their community of interest is far greater than any divisions among them. Perhaps what accounts for their consensus more than anything else is their experience in command positions in giant institutions. "As the requirements of the top places in each of the major hierarchies become similar, the types of men occupying these roles at the top—by selection and by training in the jobs—become similar."

Mills finds American democracy severely deficient, and his work is frequently cited by radical critics of American society. According to Mills, the power elite is

(continued)

CASE STUDY

(continued)

guilty of "a higher immorality" that is not necessarily personal corruption or even mistaken policies and deeds, but rather is the moral insensitivity of institutional bureaucracy. More important, it is the failure of the power elite to be responsive and responsible to "knowledgeable publics." Mills implies that true democracy is possible only where persons in power are truly responsible to "men of Knowledge." He is not very specific about who the "men of Knowledge" are, but the reader is left with the impression that he means intellectuals like himself.

businesspeople, and scientists. Why, then, do lawyers, rather than members of those other high-prestige groups, dominate the halls of Congress?

It is sometimes argued that lawyers bring a special kind of skill to Congress. Since their occupation is the representation of clients, they make no great change in occupation when they move from representing clients in private practice to representing constituents in Congress. Also, they are trained to deal with public policy as it is reflected in the statute books, so they may be reasonably familiar with public policy before entering Congress. But professional skills alone cannot explain the dominance of lawyers in public office. Another answer is that of all those in high-prestige occupations, only lawyers can really afford to neglect their careers for political activities. For the physician, the corporate businessperson, and the scientist, such slighting of their vocations is very costly. However, for the lawyer, political activity can be a positive advantage in terms of occupational advancement; free public advertising and opportunities to make contacts with potential clients are two important benefits. Yet another answer is that lawyers naturally have a monopoly on public offices in the legal and judicial system, and the office of judge or prosecuting attorney often provides a stepping stone to higher public office, including Congress.

Members of Congress are among the most educated occupational groups in the United States. They are much better educated than most members of the populations they represent. Of course, their education reflects their occupational background and their middle- and upper-class origins.

To sum up, information on the occupational background of legislators indicates that more than high social status is necessary for election to Congress. It is also helpful to have experience in interpersonal relations and public contacts, easy access to politics, and a great deal of free time to devote to political activity.[13]

Power in the *executive branch,* which most analysts now see as more important than Congress in policy formulation, is also exercised by individuals from the upper and upper middle classes. Cabinet secretaries, under-secretaries, and top civil servants tend to come from eastern Ivy League schools; most are lawyers or businesspeople at the time of their appointment; many accept lower salaries out of a sense of obligation to perform "public service."[14] The same class origins are found among judges in federal courts, particularly the Supreme Court.[15]

social class and executive and judicial power

elitist view of society

We know that political power is largely in the hands of individuals from upper social classes, but what does this really mean for the great majority of Americans? We might *infer* that people drawn from upper social classes share values and interests different from those of the majority of people. We might also infer that this elite will use their power to implement the values of the upper social classes and that, consequently, public policy will reflect upper-class values more than mass values.

On the other hand, several factors may modify the impact of upper social classes in politics. First, there may be considerable conflict among members of upper social classes about the basic directions of public policy—that is, despite similarity in social backgrounds, individuals may *not* share a consensus about public affairs. Competition rather than consensus may characterize their relationships.

Second, the elite may be very "public-regarding" in their exercise of power; they may take the welfare of the masses into account as an aspect of their own sense of well-being. Indeed, there is a great deal of evidence that America's upper classes are liberal and reformist and that "do-goodism" is a widespread impulse. Many public leaders from very wealthy families of the highest social status (for instance, Franklin D. Roosevelt, Adlai Stevenson, and John F. Kennedy) have championed the interests of the poor and the downtrodden. Thus, upper-class values may foster public service rather than political exploitation.

Third, upper-class leaders, whatever their values, can be held accountable for their exercise of power by the majority in elections. Our system of parties and elections forces public officials to compete for mass support to acquire public office and the political power that goes with it. This competition requires them to modify their public statements and actions to fit popular preferences. Hence, in a democracy the fact that the upper social classes tend to hold public office does not necessarily mean that the masses are oppressed, exploited, or powerless.

Notes

1. Melvin M. Tumin, *Social Stratification: The Forms and Functions of Social Inequality* (Englewood Cliffs, N.J.: Prentice-Hall, 1985).
2. Gerhard Lenski, *Power and Privilege* (New York: McGraw-Hill, 1966); Jack Roach, Llewellyn Gross, and Orville R. Gursslin, *Social Stratification in the United States* (Englewood Cliffs, N.J.: Prentice-Hall, 1969).
3. Kingsley Davis and Wilbert Moore, "Some Principles of Stratification," *American Sociological Review* 10 (April 1945): 243.
4. Richard Centers, *The Psychology of Social Classes* (Princeton, N.J.: Princeton University Press, 1949).
5. *Public Opinion* (November/December 1986), p. 14.
6. See Sidney Verba and Gary R. Orren, *Equality in America* (Cambridge, Mass.: Harvard University Press, 1985).
7. Karl Marx, *The Communist Manifesto,* ed. A. J. P. Taylor (New York: Penguin, 1967), p. 79.
8. Herbert Gans, *The Urban Villagers* (New York: Free Press,

1962), p. 246. See also Edward C. Banfield, *The Unheavenly City* (Boston: Little, Brown, 1968), ch. 3.
9. C. Wright Mills, *The Power Elite* (New York: Oxford University Press, 1956), p. 6.
10. C. Wright Mills, "The Structure of Power in American Society," in *Power, Politics and People: The Collected Writings of C. Wright Mills,* ed. Irving L. Horowitz (New York: Oxford University Press, 1963), p. 24.
11. Mills, *The Power Elite,* pp. 8–9.
12. Ibid., p. 10.
13. See Joseph A. Schlesinger, *Ambition and Politics* (Chicago: Rand McNally, 1968).
14. David T. Stanley, Dean E. Mann, and Jameson W. Doig, *Men Who Govern* (Washington, D.C.: Brookings, 1966).
15. John Schmidhauser, "The Justices of the Supreme Court: A Collective Portrait," *Midwest Journal of Political Science* 3 (1959).

About This Chapter

After traveling to the new American nation in 1835, the French social commentator Alexis de Tocqueville wrote:

> When it is birth alone, independent of wealth, which classes men in society, every one knows exactly what his own position is upon the social scale; he does not seek to rise, he does not fear to sink. . . . [But in America] as the social importance of men is no longer ostensibly and permanently fixed by blood, and is infinitely varied by wealth, ranks still exist, but it is not easy clearly to distinguish at a glance those who respectively belong to them.[a]

Thus, Tocqueville acknowledged that there were social classes in America, but unlike Europe at the time, class membership was based on respect and wealth, not birth, and individuals could rise or fall in social position.

In this chapter we looked at how Americans "stratify" themselves into social classes, how sociologists measure this stratification, the functions ideology serves, and the relationship between social class and power. Now that you have read Chapter 4, you should be able to

- describe the stratification system and the methods sociologists use to identify and measure stratification,
- describe functional and conflict explanations of social classes,
- discuss the functions of ideology and describe how the American ideology influences social stratification,
- define class consciousness and identify the factors that help to stabilize the existing class system in America,
- discuss the basic notions set forth by Karl Marx about social classes and describe what some of the problems are in Marxist analysis,
- discuss the relationships between social class and lifestyle and between social class and political power.

Discussion Questions

1. Discuss the social stratification system. Include in your discussion a description of the bases used for stratification, as well as the characteristics associated with the stratification system.

[a] Alexis de Tocqueville, *Democracy in America* (New York: New American Library, 1956), p. 40.

2. Describe the functional and conflict theories of social class.

3. If you were studying social class, what methods might you use to identify and measure social stratification? If in the course of your study you were to ask average Americans how they see themselves in the class system, what class would they choose, and why? How might the respondents' subjective evaluations differ from the results you as a social scientist obtained? What are the objective criteria you would use to identify social class?

4. Discuss the functions of the ideology of a stratification system. Describe the American ideology and the attitudes of Americans toward that ideology.

5. Choose two of the American social classes and contrast them according to orientation toward life, individual self-confidence, child-rearing practices, sexual attitudes, women's roles, activities and interests, and political participation and party identification.

6. Contrast class consciousness with class awareness. Discuss the factors that appear to stabilize the existing class system in the United States and reduce class conflict.

7. Distinguish between inequality and social mobility. How is inequality usually measured? How can we measure mobility?

8. Discuss Karl Marx's views of economic roles and class consciousness in the struggle for power among social classes. What sort of society did Marx envision, and what are the reasons for the failure of capitalist and communist societies to conform to his vision?

9. Political power in the United States is largely in the hands of individuals from upper social classes. Discuss the factors that account for this, what impact it might have on the "masses," and what factors may modify the impact. In your discussion distinguish between the "elitist" view of society and the "pluralist" view of society.

10. Define the *power elite* that was identified by C. Wright Mills and describe the factors that contribute to the emergence of such an elite. What is its actual base of power, and on what factors does its unity rest? How does Mills's interpretation of power in the United States conflict with the "pluralist" interpretation?

Power and Personality

CHAPTER

Personality and Individual Responses to Power

Individuals react toward power and authority in characteristic ways. In many different situations their responses to power and authority are fairly predictable. Some individuals regularly seek power and authority, whereas others avoid seeking them. Some individuals are submissive to authority, whereas others are habitually rebellious. Some individuals try to conform to the expectations of other people, and others are guided by internalized standards. Some individuals feel powerless, helpless, and isolated; they believe they have little control over their own lives. Other individuals are self-assured and aggressive; they speak out at meetings, organize groups, and take over leadership positions. Some individuals are habitually suspicious of others, unwilling to compromise; they prefer simple, final, and forceful solutions to complex problems. Some individuals are assertive, strong-willed, and self-confident; others are timid, submissive, and self-conscious. There are as many different ways of responding to power as there are types of personalities.

personality
characteristic ways of behaving; the enduring and organized responses that individuals habitually make to particular stimuli

Personality is all the characteristic ways of behaving that an individual exhibits; it is the enduring and organized sets of responses an individual habitually makes when subjected to particular stimuli. By *characteristic* and *habitual* we mean that individuals tend to respond in a similar fashion to many separate situations. For example, their attitudes toward authority in general may affect their response to any number of different leaders, supervisors, directors, or other authority figures in different situations. By *enduring* we mean that these characteristic ways of behaving may operate over a long time, perhaps through youth, young adulthood, and maturity. Attitudes toward authority in the home may carry over to school, university, job, church, government, and so forth. By *organized* we mean that there are relationships between various elements of an individual's personality. A change in one element (let us say, a growing need for social approval) would bring about a change in another element (let us say, an increased willingness to conform to group norms). Thus, personality is not just a bundle of traits but an *integrated pattern of responses.*

Nature versus Nurture

Children often have the same personality characteristics as their parents. Is the similarity a result of what they learned in the home? Or do children inherit personality characteristics from their parents? Actually, this is not an "either–or" question: psychologists generally acknowledge that personality is shaped by *both* heredity and environment. The only question is what is the relative influence of these factors on personality.

The question of the relative influence of heredity versus environment on personality is part of a larger controversy about the influence of genetics on behavior. (We encountered this same controversy in our discussion of sociobiology in Chapter 3.) Some psychologists attribute greater influence to heredity in determining many personality characteristics by chemical and hormonal balances, the functioning of the senses (sight, hearing, smell, taste, touch), and physique. Other psychologists attribute greater influence to environment. The influence of the environment may

Research on the behavior of identical twins suggests the importance of genetic influences.
Source: Jim Whitmer/Stock, Boston

begin even before birth, depending, for example, on whether the mother has a good diet, avoids smoking, alcohol, and drugs, is active or inactive, and is in good emotional health. Infants respond to their earliest environment and acquire characteristic ways of responding—that is, personality—very early in life.

It is very difficult to determine whether a specific personality characteristic shared by a parent and child has been genetically inherited or transferred through social interaction in the home. However, some studies of twins have suggested that heredity plays an important role in personality. Identical twins (who have the same genetic composition) score more alike on standard personality tests than fraternal twins (whose genetic composition is different).[1] Identical twins reared in separate families tend to share more personality and behavior characteristics than fraternal twins raised in the same household (see Box 5-1). According to one study, separated identical twins shared the same smoking and eating habits and scored similarly on tests of intelligence, extroversion, and neuroticism.[2]

The mother is probably the single most important influence in anyone's early environment. We cannot deprive human babies of contact with their mothers for the sake of experimentation, but psychologists have placed newborn monkeys in isolation and observed their development. The results showed abnormal and irreversible behavior: extreme fear, anxiety, avoidance of all social contact with other monkeys, and emotional and intellectual retardation.[3]

Some psychologists argue that early mother–child relationships are instinctual. Newborn babies possess five instinctual responses: sucking, crying, smiling, clinging, and following. Together these responses bind the child to the mother and the mother to the child. Some psychologists contend that these inherited responses were acquired over millions of years by natural selection.[4] There is also evidence that clinging and following are inherited responses. Infant monkeys reared in isolation from their mothers were supplied with two surrogate mother figures. One was made of wire mesh, while the other was made of soft "cuddly" cloth. The baby monkeys chose to be near the soft surrogate, even when the wire mesh surrogate had a bottle attached to it for feeding.[5]

As we examine personality in this chapter, we should remember that both heredity and environment play important roles in shaping human beings. We will examine some theories of personality that emphasize instincts and heredity, others that emphasize early childhood experiences, and still others that emphasize continuing growth and development over a lifetime. There is no single "right" theory of personality.

BOX 5-1

Telltale Behavior of Twins

There is a mystique about twins, especially about identical twins reared apart. Stories of twins meeting for the first time capture the imagination. . . .

Over the years, scientists have reported provocative similarities in identical twins brought up separately. In 1962, for instance, the British investigator James Shields described the case of Herta and Berta, who were reared on different continents without even a first language in common. Nevertheless, both reported a tendency toward the dramatic, enjoyed artistic pursuits, and were prone to excitability and depression. They had been given the same nickname, "Pussy"—in different languages—because each purred like a cat when she was contented. . . .

Alfred and Harry . . . both nodded their heads in the same way as they spoke, and each closed his eyes as he turned his head. Jacqueline and Beryl had the same firm handshakes and made the same half-thoughtful, half-humorous face before answering a question. James and Robert both tapped on the table to make points; both flicked their fingers when unable to think of an answer immediately. Kathleen and Jenny laughed, giggled, and wept over the same things and reported that they often found themselves sitting in the same positions. Olwen and Gwaldys had the same wild look about them, their eyes darting from place to place. Their expressions and gestures mirrored each other, and their hands frequently went to their mouths in a tense finger-biting gesture. Both held

their fingers stiffly for fingerprinting. One of the more interesting mannerisms was reported for Madeline and Lilian, whose husbands were impressed with the similarities in their movements; particularly, each twin had a habit of rubbing her nose and rocking when tired. They had developed the habit with no knowledge of each other. . . .

My speculation is that when families have identical twins, they treat them in subtly different ways, probably without consciously intending to do so, in an attempt to differentiate them. For instance, if one twin is quicker to walk in infancy and is generally more active physically, parents may assign that twin the role of "athlete," while the quiet child becomes the "intellectual." The twins themselves, as we know from observation and from their own reports, seesaw between close identification with each other and exaggerated independence. If one does well in math, the other maps out territory elsewhere, simply out of a need for individuality. . . .

Overall, the findings underscore the significance of individuality. If twins reared in even moderately different homes remain markedly alike, what more do we need in order to acknowledge the genetic uniqueness of each individual? Similarly, if twins make themselves "artificially" different as a result of contact with each other, what more do we need to indicate the need of each individual to be an individual, separate unto himself and clearly bounded?

Source: Excerpted from Susan Farber, "Telltale Behavior of Twins," *Psychology Today,* January 1981, pp. 59–80. Reprinted with permission from *Psychology Today* magazine. Copyright © 1981 (Sussex Publishers, Inc.)

Approaches to Psychology and Personality

Psychologists differ over the precise meaning of personality. Definitions tend to be linked to major theories or approaches to individual behavior and to the major approaches within psychology itself.[6]

Clinical psychology focuses on the treatment of psychological disorder. It is closely related to *psychiatry* in that both clinical psychologists and psychiatrists deal with the diagnosis and treatment of psychological disorders. (The psychiatrist, however, is also a medical doctor.) Clinicians deal with real people with real psychological problems. They enter the patient's world and concern themselves with the subjective human experience, including wishes, fears, anxieties, ambitions. Clinical psychology stresses therapy, ranging from chemical therapy and shock treatment to various behavior therapies and insight therapies.

Psychoanalysis is a type of insight-oriented therapy that encourages patients to think about themselves—their problems, dreams, memories—so they can gain insight into the causes of their own difficulties. Psychoanalysis enables patients to talk about early childhood experiences and thus to reveal unconscious motivations, emotions, and conflicts. The psychoanalytic approach to personality emphasizes *childhood experiences* and *unconscious feelings* as determining factors in personality development. Although the practice of psychoanalysis has always been the domain of the Freudian-trained psychiatrist, many clinical psychologists do use *psychoanalytic theory* in their approach to therapy.

Experimental psychology, another major division of psychology, is concerned with the scientific study of the behavioral responses of human beings to various stimuli. Experimental psychology focuses on observed behavior; it is frequently termed *behavioral psychology.* Its setting is the academic laboratory, and rats and pigeons are frequent subjects of experimentation. There is an emphasis on careful observation, quantitative data, and statistical methods. Behavioral psychology relies heavily on *learning theory* (stimulus–response theory), which views all behavior as a product of learning or conditioning. Behavioral patterns are learned through a process whereby a stimulus evokes a response that is either rewarded or punished, and habits are formed. The behavioral approach to personality views personality as a *pattern of learned, reinforced responses.*

Social psychology is concerned with the individual's relationship with other individuals and groups. The social psychologist studies the whole person and the impact of the social world on the person—the world of social interaction and group life, which constantly shapes and modifies the individual's goals, perceptions, attitudes, and behavior. The social–psychological approach to personality emphasizes the individual's *socialization*—the development of individual identity through *interpersonal experiences* and the *internalizing of the expectations of significant others.*

Humanistic psychology focuses on human experience and human fulfillment; it emphasizes the individual's innate potential to grow and develop. According to the humanists, human beings are unique among animals because they alone have psychological as well as biological needs. The individual is internally motivated to fulfill those needs, to grow and develop and to expand the capacity for creativity. Humanistic psychology views personality development as a *continuous process of*

clinical psychology
treatment of psychological disorder

psychoanalysis
insight-oriented therapy

experimental psychology
scientific study of behavioral responses to stimuli

social psychology
the study of the individual's relationships with other individuals and groups

humanistic psychology
the study of human experience and human fulfillment

CASE STUDY

Sigmund Freud:
Psychoanalytic
Theory

Perhaps no other scholar has had a greater impact on the social sciences than the Viennese psychiatrist Sigmund Freud (1856–1939). Freud specialized in the treatment of nervous disorders; he studied hypnosis because he learned that neurotic symptoms could be removed during hypnotic trance. But he soon found that patients did not really need to be in a full hypnotic trance so long as they felt relaxed and uninhibited. He encouraged them to engage in *free association*—that is, to say anything that came into their minds without regard to organization, logic, or embarrassment over socially unacceptable ideas. He wanted to make the patient's *unconscious* motives, drives, feelings, and anxieties *conscious* ones. The goal of psychoanalysis, as it was called, was to help patients attain *insight,* or self-knowledge. Once that was achieved, the neurotic symptoms tended to disappear.

According to Freud, the personality is composed of three major systems: the *id,* the *ego,* and the *superego.* The *id* is the basic system of life instincts, or drives—hunger, thirst, sex, rest, pain avoidance, and so on. The id is in close touch with the body's needs; these needs produce psychic energy, which is experienced as uncomfortable states of tension. The id operates on the *pleasure* principle, but the id has no knowledge of objective reality. A newborn baby's personality is almost pure id. It seeks immediate gratification of bodily urges and has no knowledge of reality or morals.

The *ego* is the part of the personality that is in contact with objective reality. It directs the energies of the id toward real-world objects that are appropriate for the satisfaction of the urge and the reduction of tension. The ego operates on the *reality* principle, formulating plans for the satisfaction of needs, testing the plans, and deciding what needs will be satisfied first and in what manner.

The *superego,* the last part of the personality to develop, is the internal representative of the values, standards, and morals the child is taught. The superego is the *moral* arm of the personality and develops through rewards and punishments that the parents impose upon the child and through the child's identification with the parents' standards. The superego decides what is right and wrong, rewarding the individual with feelings of pride or punishing with feelings of guilt. It inhibits the impulses of the id, persuades the ego to direct energies toward moralistic goals rather than realistic ones, and strives for moral perfection.

Anxiety is a state of tension that results from an apprehension of impending pain or danger, whether physical or psychological. Anxiety reduction is a drive like hunger or thirst, the difference being that it results from psychological, rather than bodily, discomfort. When its intensity and nature are appropriate to the real situation, the anxiety is *normal.* When there does not seem to be adequate cause for it in the real world, when it is caused by unconscious or irrational fears, and when it interferes with the person's functioning, the anxiety is *neurotic.*

Identification is important as a process in early personality development and as a way of reducing anxiety. The infant imitates the characteristics of the persons in

(continued)

(continued)

its environment who satisfy its needs. These characteristics—for example, a parent's way of walking or talking—are incorporated into the child's developing personality. As we have noted, identification is also important in the development of the superego, as the child identifies with and incorporates the parents' moral values.

Children (or adults) may also identify with persons whom they perceive as aggressive, threatening, or all-powerful, and it is in this sense that identification is used to reduce anxiety. By becoming like the feared person who causes the anxiety, one is able to perceive the aggression as if it were one's own and under one's own control. This type of identification is known as *identification with the aggressor,* and it constitutes one type of defense against anxiety. Hostages sometimes identify with their terrorist kidnappers in order to reduce anxiety.

The most important of the *defense mechanisms* that the body uses, often unconsciously, to reduce anxiety and tension is *repression:* the ego protects the individual from unbearable impulses by forcing them out of consciousness. This defensive maneuver may occur when an impulse would endanger life, risk punishment, or risk feelings of guilt. But there are costs to repression. A severely repressed individual who has denied many strong impulses may suffer fatigue, nervousness, or depression. Repression can even interfere with the functioning of the body; in a male, sexual impotence can result from severely repressed sexual impulses.

Freud never drew up a comprehensive list of instincts or needs. However, he was convinced that of all of our many instincts, sex and aggression were the most seriously repressed by society. This repression begins with the newborn infant and extends through adulthood. If we feel hunger, we can immediately go out and buy a hamburger; but if we feel a sexual urge, it usually must be denied until an appropriate outlet is found. Aggressive impulses are also severely restricted. Thus, Freud's seeming emphasis on sex was a product not of his belief that this drive was any more powerful than others, but of his view that it was the most repressed and therefore the source of many personality disorders.

Perhaps no other social science theory has been subjected to such searching and bitter criticism as Freudian theory. The criticism ranges from charges that Freud was a "sex maniac" (Freud was a dedicated father and husband whose marriage lasted a lifetime; Freud's daughter, Anna, became a distinguished psychoanalyst herself) to more serious scientific reservations. One criticism centers on psychoanalytic therapy: it can be long and costly, and it is not always successful. Drugs and behavioral therapy frequently produce more complete results in less time and at less expense. Another criticism is that Freud's observations were based on abnormal, clinical cases rather than on normal adults; most of his patients were middle-class Europeans; and he worked in a cultural period when sexual repression in society was much greater than it is today. All these factors may have produced distortions in his theory.

Another problem with Freudian theory is that it is difficult to test scientifically.

(continued)

CASE STUDY

(continued)   Freudian explanations proceed from observed behavior *back* to unconscious feelings and childhood experiences; but they do not permit exact predictions of future behavior from these factors. For example, Freudian theory might hypothesize that a boy who has a severe Oedipus complex (a male child's attraction to his mother) and cannot "cut the apron strings" and identify with his father may cope with this problem by becoming a homosexual. But Freudian theory might also hypothesize that the same Oedipus complex could lead the boy to become a Don Juan, with a string of sexual conquests to prove his masculinity to himself. A scientist may object that Freudian theory provides two completely different behaviors with the same explanation. It does not predict which of the two behaviors may result from an Oedipus complex; hence it is "bad" scientific theory. Nevertheless, psychologist William McDougall concluded, "In my opinion Freud has, quite unquestionably, done more for the advancement of our understanding of human nature than any other man since Aristotle."[7]

Box 5-2 offers a glossary of selected Freudian terminology.

BOX 5-2

Developing Your Psychoanalytic Vocabulary

Id

The component of the personality that is completely unconscious and contains all the instincts. It is the animalistic portion of the personality and is governed by the pleasure principle.

Ego

The executive of the personality, whose job is to satisfy the needs of both the id and the superego by engaging in appropriate environmental activities. The ego is governed by the reality principle.

Superego

The moral component of the personality.

Anxiety

The general feeling of uneasiness one experiences when one engages in, or thinks of engaging in, activities that violate the internalized values of the superego.

Ego defense mechanisms

Unconscious processes that falsify or distort reality in order to reduce or prevent anxiety.

Identification

The incorporation of another person's values and/or characteristics either to enhance one's self-esteem or to minimize that person as a threat.

Repression

The ego defense mechanism by which anxiety-provoking thoughts are held in the unconscious mind, thereby preventing a conscious awareness of them.

Free association

Called by Freud "the Fundamental Rule of Psychoanalysis," it entails instructing the patient to say whatever comes to his or her mind, no matter how irrelevant, unimportant, or nonsensical it seems to be.

Freudian slip

A verbal "accident" that is thought to reveal the speaker's true feelings, such as occurred when Dr. Freud was introduced as "Dr. Fraud."

positive growth in which the individual, having fulfilled a lower need, pursues the fulfillment of a higher one.

In the following pages we will see how each of these approaches can contribute to our understanding of personality and individual reactions to power and authority. We will begin with an exploration of psychoanalytic (Freudian) theory and a consideration of the Freudian approach to power relationships, as exemplified by the study *The Authoritarian Personality*. We will then examine behavioral psychology's reliance on learning (stimulus–response) theory and the ideas of behavioral psychologist B. F. Skinner about the need to control human behavior. Next we will consider how social psychology uses interpersonal-interaction theory to explain personality. We will then briefly describe humanistic psychology's theory of personality and Abraham Maslow's construction of a "hierarchy of needs." We will examine differences of suicide rates among nations and consider Emile Durkheim's classic explanation of these differences. We will then look at a case study of authority and obedience; this case study describes the startling results of one of the most interesting social science experiments of recent times. To conclude this chapter, we will describe Rollo May's views of power and powerlessness.

The Authoritarian Personality

The Freudian approach to power relationships focuses on the channeling and blocking of drives; the conflicts among the id, ego, and superego; unconscious processes; and early childhood determinations of habitual responses to power and authority. Power motives—for example, a need to dominate others or, the opposite, comfort in accepting direction—are organized into the personality early in life. The real motives for people's public behavior are largely unconscious, so they *rationalize* their behavior in terms of the public interest.

the Freudian approach to power relationships

An early influential study of power, authority, and personality, one that was conducted mainly within the framework of Freudian theory, was the landmark study *The Authoritarian Personality*.[8] This study was undertaken after World War II by a group of psychologists who sought to identify potentially antidemocratic individuals—those whose personality structures render them particularly susceptible to authoritarian appeals. One of the tools developed in the course of the study was the F (fascism) Scale, now widely used by social scientists to identify authoritarianism. Part of the original F Scale is reproduced in Table 5-1. Persons who agree with all or most of the items in the F Scale are said to be authoritarian.

characteristics of the authoritarian personality
dominance and submission
orientation toward power
rigidity
exaggerated concern with strength
anti-introception
cynicism
ethnocentrism

The central attitudes of authoritarianism are *dominance* and *submission*—dominance over subordinates in any power hierarchy and submissiveness toward superiors. Authoritarians are highly ambivalent in their attitudes toward authority. They are outwardly servile toward those they perceive as their superiors, but in fact they also harbor strong negative feelings toward them. Their repressed rage toward their superiors is redirected into hostility toward the weak and inferior.

Authoritarians are *oriented toward power.* They tend to think in power terms, to be acutely sensitive in any situation to questions of who dominates whom. They are very uncomfortable when they do not know what the chain of command is. They need to know whom they should obey and who should obey them.

Authoritarians are *rigid.* They are "intolerant of ambiguity." They like order and

TABLE 5-1   Items from the F (Fascism) Scale

Conventionalism
Rigid adherence to conventional middle-class values.
Obedience and respect for authority are the most important virtues children should learn.
A person who has bad manners, habits, and breeding can hardly expect to get along with
      decent people.

Authoritarian submission
Submissive, uncritical attitude toward idealized moral authorities of the in-group.
What this country needs most, more than laws and political programs, is a few coura-
      geous, tireless, devoted leaders in whom the people can put their faith.

Authoritarian aggression
Tendency to be on the lookout for and to condemn, reject, and punish people who violate
      conventional values.
What the youth needs most is strict discipline, rugged determination, and the will to work
      and fight for family and country.
An insult to our honor should always be punished.

Anti-introception
Opposition to the subjective, the imaginative, the tender-minded.
When people have problems or worries, it is best for them not to think about it, but to
      keep busy with more cheerful things.
Nowadays more and more people are prying into matters that should remain personal and
      private.
If people would talk less and work more, everybody would be better off.

Power and "toughness"
Preoccupation with the dominance–submission, strong–weak, leader–follower dimension;
      identification with power figures; overemphasis upon the conventionalized attributes of
      the ego; exaggerated assertion of strength and toughness.
No weakness or difficulty can hold us back if we have enough willpower.
What the youth needs most is strict discipline, rugged determination, and the will to work
      and fight for family and country.
People can be divided into two distinct classes: the weak and the strong.

Destructiveness and cynicism
Generalized hostility, vilification of the human.
Human nature being what it is, there will always be war and conflict.
Familiarity breeds contempt.

Source: Abridgement of Table 7 (pp. 255–257), "The F (Fascism) Scale," from T. W. Adorno et al.,
The Authoritarian Personality. Copyright 1950 by The American Jewish Committee. Reprinted by
permission of HarperCollins, Inc.

are uncomfortable in the presence of disorder. When matters are complex, they
impose their own rigid categories on them. Their thinking, therefore, is largely in
stereotypes.

Authoritarians show *exaggerated concern with strength.* Feelings of personal
weakness are covered with a facade of toughness. They are unusually preoccupied
with masculine virtues, and they stereotype women as feminine and soft.

Authoritarians are *anti-introceptive.* They are impatient with and opposed to the
subjective and tender-minded. They are unimaginative and reluctant to acknowledge their own feelings and fantasies.

Authoritarians are *cynical*. They distrust the motives of others and are generally pessimistic about human nature. They are disposed to believe that the world is a jungle and that various conspiracies exist to threaten them and their ways of life.

Authoritarians are *ethnocentric*. They view members of social groups other than their own as outsiders who are different, strange, unwholesome, and threatening. They hold an exalted opinion of their own groups. They reject outsiders and project many of their own aggressive impulses on them. They place stereotyped labels on outsiders.

A great deal of research followed *The Authoritarian Personality* study, much of it using the F Scale to identify authoritarians and then observing related attitudes, environments, and behaviors. Some of the subsequent research on authoritarianism raised serious criticisms and reservations about the original work. First, it was observed that poorly educated persons tend to agree with F Scale statements more frequently than do well-educated persons. This finding does not necessarily mean that a lack of education causes authoritarianism, but it does suggest that differences in F Scale scores may be a product of education and *not* of personality development. Well-educated persons, whether they are authoritarian or not, simply know enough not to agree with the obviously biased statements on the F Scale.

Another problem is that the F Scale tests only for *right-wing* (fascist) authoritarianism and fails to identify *left-wing* authoritarianism. Yet there is ample evidence of exaggerated submission to authority in revolutionary and communist movements; aggression and sadism practiced by left-wing authoritarians against the hated out-group: the "bourgeoisie"; rigidity, toughness, and an orientation toward power among revolutionaries; extreme cynicism toward society among leftists, as well as conspiratorial views about politics; and rigid conformity to stereotyped Marxist ideas. Unfortunately, the F Scale equates authoritarianism with only fascist ideas.

Another criticism is that authoritarianism is not really a complete and separate syndrome; some of the attitudes of authoritarianism are found in individuals who do not exhibit other attitudes of the supposed syndrome. For example, ethnocentricity is frequently encountered in individuals who are not dominant–submissive. Ethnocentric attitudes may be acquired in a family or subculture that is otherwise warm and affectionate. Thus, stable and loving individuals may have ethnocentric, stereotyped views of out-groups and even harbor suspicion toward them, simply because their culture or subculture has taught them to do so. In other words, ethnocentricity may be part of a culture or subculture rather than a component of a personality syndrome. The same may be true of superstition, rigidity, and conventionalism.

Despite these reservations, *The Authoritarian Personality* provides us with valuable insights into the psychological mechanisms by which some individuals adjust themselves to power and authority.

criticisms of *The Authoritarian Personality*
educated persons recognize bias in the F Scale

fails to identify left-wing authoritarians

not really a complete and separate syndrome

Behaviorism and Learning Theory

Behavioral psychology is heavily indebted to learning theory or, more precisely, stimulus–response (SR) theory. It is not an overstatement to say that rats have had

behaviorism
an approach to psychology that asserts that only observable behavior can be studied

Pavlov's dogs

conditioned response
a behavior that is elicited by a previously neutral stimulus

conditioned SR linkage requires
drive
cue
response
reinforcement

more to do with shaping this theory than human beings; SR theory grew out of experimental laboratory studies with animals. Academic psychology is based largely on SR theory; most college courses in psychology are oriented toward this approach. Behavioral psychology asserts that the goal of psychologists should be to study *behavior* by employing the same *scientific* tests as the natural sciences. Behavioral psychologists discount Freudian notions about the mind or the personality, which cannot be directly observed. For the behaviorists, one is what one does; personality *is* behavior, a pattern of learned, reinforced responses.

The founder of modern stimulus–response theory was the Russian physiologist Ivan Petrovich Pavlov (1849–1936), who had already won a Nobel Prize for his studies of digestive glands before he undertook his landmark experiments with salivating dogs. Pavlov's early experiments established the notion of *conditioning*. Saliva flows when meat is placed in a dog's mouth. If a bell is consistently sounded just a moment before the meat is placed in its mouth, the dog will soon begin to salivate merely upon hearing a bell even if the meat is not given. Dogs do not normally salivate at the sound of a bell, so such a response is a *conditioned response*. The bell and the meat have become associated in the dog's mind by their occurring together.

The learning process is a bit more complex than it first appears. *To establish a linkage between a conditioned stimulus and response,* there must be a *drive*, a *cue*, a *response*, and *reinforcement*. Learning depends on the establishment of this SR linkage. In simple terms, in order to learn, one must want something as a result of one's action (*drive*). For example, for a rat that is placed in a box and given electric shocks through a wire grid floor, reinforcement is the relief of pain. Pain provides the *drive*, which is the first factor that must be present if learning is to occur. Hunger, thirst, or curiosity may also provide the drive to learn. In our example, the electric shocks that the rat receives are accompanied by a buzzer. The buzzer provides the *cue*, the stimulus associated with the response. The stimulus may be visual (objects, colors, lights, designs, printed words), auditory (bells, whistles, spoken words), or related to any of the other senses. Of course, for a response to be linked to a cue, a response must first occur. A critical stage in the learning process is the production of the *appropriate response*. The rat experiencing an electric shock and hearing the buzzer will make a variety of responses; eventually it may pull on the lever that turns off the current. The particular response that satisfies the drive is likely to recur the next time the same situation is encountered. Learning takes place gradually, not so much through "trial and error" as through "trial and success." The rat's first success in pulling the lever will be an accident. After several shocking experiences, however, the rat will learn to pull the lever immediately to stop the current.

reinforcement
repeating conditioned stimulus and response

The key to the learning process is the *reinforcement* of the appropriate behavior. Reinforcement occurs each time the behavior is accompanied by reduction in the drive. The cue itself will eventually elicit the same response as the original drive. Thus, the rat will pull the lever when it hears the sound of the buzzer whether it is shocked or not. In this way a previously neutral stimulus (the buzzer) becomes a *conditioned stimulus,* the rat having learned to respond to it in a particular way.

The *strength* of the SR linkage depends on (1) the strength of the original drive, (2) the closeness of the drive reduction to the response, and (3) the number of

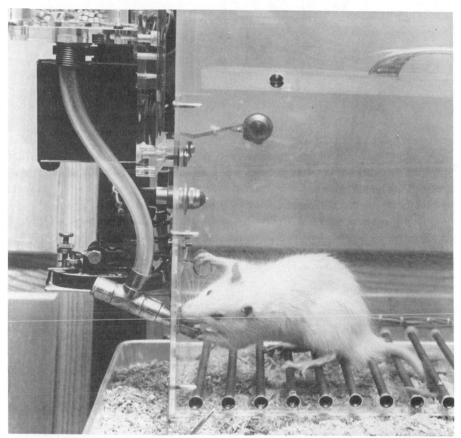

This rat's stimulus−response behavior is reinforced with food pellets.
Source: Photo Researchers

consistently reinforced trials. Thus the combination of a strong shock, the quick elimination of the shock after the rat pulls the lever, and a large number of trials makes a well-trained rat.

Higher-order learning takes place when an organism establishes complex and abstract linkages between stimulus and response. Higher-order conditioning occurs, for example, when a child learns to associate the written word *bell* spelled on a card with the sound of a bell. Cues become stimuli that provoke a response, which in turn becomes a cue to still another response. Certainly *language* can be viewed as an abstract set of cues. By labeling and naming events, things, and experiences, people can increase their powers of stimulus generalization and discrimination.

In recent years behavioral psychologists have come out of the laboratory to engage in some types of treatment for mental disorders. Behaviorists define disorders in terms of the undesirable behaviors that are exhibited. Behavioral psychologists seldom talk about anxiety or repression; they talk in terms of *functional* (desirable) and *dysfunctional* (undesirable) behaviors. They believe neurotic behavior has been learned—generally by inconsistent use of rewards and punishment. (Hungry rats that are shocked when they pull a lever that previously produced food

strength of SR linkage depends on
strength of drive

immediate drive reduction

number of trials

higher-order learning
complex and abstract linkages between stimulus and response

develop symptoms similar to "nervous breakdowns"!) Undesirable behaviors can be extinguished by withholding rewards or by administering punishment. Neurotic behavior can be unlearned by the same combination of principles by which it was taught. Behavioral psychotherapy establishes a set of conditions by which neurotic habits are unlearned and nonneurotic habits learned. The behavioral therapist is regarded as a kind of teacher and the patient as a learner. Thus, the behavioral therapist may reward patients in mental hospitals for good behavior with tokens to be used to buy small luxuries. A therapist of this school believes that smokers can learn avoidance reaction by having thick, obnoxious cigarette smoke blown in their faces; or that bed wetters can unlearn their habit by sleeping on a wire blanket that produces a mild shock when it becomes wet. Even repression (viewed by the behaviorists as "learned nonthinking") can be overcome by forcing individuals to confront situations, events, or experiences they have repressed.

behavioral therapy
treatment based on learning or unlearning behavior

Social Psychology—the Self in Relation to Others

Social psychology is concerned primarily with interpersonal interactions—how the individual interacts with others. The social psychologist studies the individual as a whole person interacting with the environment, rather than studying particular responses, behaviors, or reflexes. Many social psychologists are critical of the "reductionism" of behavioral psychology—the tendency to reduce individual behavior to a series of stimulus–response linkages. Social psychology is strongly influenced by early *Gestalt psychologists,* who argued that the whole person is an entity that cannot be understood by breaking it into sensory elements. (The German word *Gestalt* means "whole," "pattern," or "configuration.")

Gestalt psychology
the study of the whole individual

Social psychologists view *interpersonal interaction* as the critical determinant of personality development. Indeed, an individual develops an awareness of *self* only by interaction with the environment. The newborn infant cannot distinguish its own body from the outer world. It acquires an identity—a sense of self—only by moving out into the world and relating to other people. As the infant observes and responds to its mother, the mother becomes a meaningful object, bringing pleasure, frustration, pain, and so on. The infant becomes aware of itself only in relation to others. An infant who is totally ignored withdraws to a corner of its crib, does not talk or develop in any way, and withers away physiologically and psychologically. The emergence of self-identity requires interpersonal interaction; without others there is no self.

self
the individual's awareness of himself or herself derived from interpersonal interaction

The process by which an individual internalizes the values, attitudes, and judgments of others is called *socialization.* By *interacting* with others, people come to understand what is expected of them and *internalize* these expectations as part of their personalities. George Herbert Mead conceived the notion of *roles* to explain how the individual internalizes the expectations of others and acquires the values of society. The essential process in the development of self is the individual's taking on the roles of others.

socialization
assuming the roles expected of us by others

Years ago Charles H. Cooley described the self as a *system of ideas drawn from the social world.* The "looking-glass" self is a product of the following:

Self-awareness develops through early interpersonal interactions.
Source: Elizabeth Crews/The Image Works

1. Our image of how we appear to others. We all try to see how we are regarded
   by others—how our actions are viewed and interpreted.
2. Our image of the judgment of others. We each imagine how others are evaluating us.
3. Our self-feeling. We all react to our perceptions of others' judgments with feelings of pride, shame, guilt, self-esteem, self-hate, and so forth.[9]

In short, our self-concept derives from *interaction* with others from infancy through
adulthood.

Through interaction with its parents, the child learns that certain sounds, such
as "Mama" and "Daddy," gain favorable attention. The child begins to repeat these
sounds because of the response they evoke in others and in this way begins to learn
language. Children also learn that the things they do are meaningful to those around
them, and thus they develop a sense of *self*. Infants who are ignored fail to develop
either language or self-identity. Later the small child at play tries on a variety of
roles—"mother," "father," "fire fighter," "soldier"—and increases self-realization in the process. Even such basic social roles as male and female may be viewed
as products of socialization rather than biology. Masculine and feminine traits
develop through the child's internalization of the expectations of others and through
role playing. Schools, games, and group activities provide more and more role-
playing opportunities. Of course, not all the "others" in one's life are equally influential in shaping self-identity; each person has some *significant others* whose judgments carry more weight than the judgments of others. As socialization continues,

role playing
developing a sense of
self by trying on a vari-
ety of roles

CASE STUDY

B. F. Skinner:
The Control of
Human
Behavior

Power is the capacity to control human behavior. What if behavioral science learns to control human behavior and develops a "behavioral technology" to do so? Who will apply this technology and for what purposes? Will the behavioral scientist acquire the ultimate power in society?

Behavioral psychologist B. F. Skinner (1904–1990) believed that society could no longer afford individual freedom and self-determination. He argued that human behavior must be controlled to ensure the survival of humanity and that *behavioral conditioning* must be employed on a massive scale to remold human beings and human culture. In the Skinnerian world, people would be conditioned to be humanitarian rather than selfish and to refrain from polluting, overpopulating, rioting, and making war. Behavioral conditioning would create a utopian society of communal ownership, egalitarian relationships, and devotion to art, music, and literature. Outmoded ideas of individual freedom and self-determination would be discarded in favor of a scientifically designed culture that would condition people to be "good."

Skinner believed that the freedom and dignity of an autonomous human being are "illusions" anyhow. All behavior is determined by prior conditioning. The apparent freedom of human beings is merely inconspicuous control: a permissive government is simply relying on other sources of control—family, church, schools, values, ideologies. If people behave well without government control, it is because they are being controlled by these other agencies. There is, however, ample evidence—war, crime, poverty, racism—that existing control mechanisms are inadequate for survival. Behavioral conditioning replaces imperfect and haphazard control methods with a more effective technology of behavioral control. *Brainwashing* is attacked by scholars who otherwise support changing people's minds by less obvious control mechanisms. Yet, according to Skinner, brainwashing is an effective means of accomplishing *behavioral modification*.

> A common technique is to build up a strong aversive condition, such as hunger or lack of sleep, and, by alleviating it, to reinforce any behavior which "shows a positive attitude" toward a political or religious system. A favorable "opinion" is built up simply by reinforcing favorable statements.[10]

Skinner believed that all attitudes are developed in this way; the only difference is that formal behavioral conditioning appears obvious and conspicuous.

Skinner developed his ideas through a lifetime of laboratory research on behavioral conditioning. He was the inventor of the famous "Skinner box," a soundproof enclosure with a food dispenser that can be operated by a rat pressing a lever or a pigeon pecking at a bar. Skinner had long been preoccupied with the ideas of conditioning and control:

> I've had only one idea in my life—a true idée fixe. To put it as bluntly as possible— the idea of having my own way. "Control" expresses it. The control of human behavior. In my early experimental days it was a frenzied, selfish desire to dominate. I

(continued)

(continued)

remember the rage I used to feel when a prediction went awry. I could have shouted at the subjects of my experiments, "Behave, damn you! Behave as you ought!"[11]

Skinner pioneered in the development of teaching machines and programmed instruction, which employ conditioning principles by reinforcing correct answers with a printed statement that the student's response is correct.

Can behavioral conditioning be used on a massive scale? Serious dilemmas of power are raised by Skinner's proposals. Who is to determine what is "good" and "bad" behavior? What standards will be used? In Skinner's utopia immense power would be placed in the hands of the behavioral scientist who designs the culture. Skinner's utopia, although benevolent, is totalitarian. Can the behavioral scientist always be trusted to be "good"? How can the power entrusted in the scientist be checked if the scientist has full capacity to manipulate human behavior? Moreover, what kind of human beings would be produced under a system that manipulates behavior, choices, tastes, and desires? If we believe individual freedom and dignity are essential components of humanity, then behavioral conditioning on a massive scale is dehumanizing. Giving up freedom and dignity to achieve a secure, comfortable, unpolluted, egalitarian world may be too high a price to pay.

knowledge of roles and attitudes of others becomes more generalized, and we gradually unify and consolidate the many roles we have played into a generalized self-conception. At this point the mature personality emerges.

Over time an individual acquires a distinctive pattern of *interpersonal response traits,* relatively consistent and stable dispositions to respond in a distinctive way toward others. These interpersonal response traits constitute the *personality.* (See Box 5-3 for a discussion of how the personalities of U.S. presidents may affect their job performance.) They represent the sum of one's socialization, one's role experiences, and one's history of successes and failures with various interpersonal responses. Table 5-2 presents twelve interpersonal response traits.

Many social psychologists believe that interpersonal-interaction theory provides a basis for the treatment of *personality disorders.* They define an *integrated personality* as one in which the individual plays fairly well-defined and stable roles that are not incompatible or conflicting and that are consistent with the values of the groups and culture in which the individual lives. *Personality disorganization* occurs when people find themselves in conflicting roles. Most people can handle mildly conflicting roles, such as being mother and office worker simultaneously; but serious role conflicts, such as an inability to assume fully either a male or a female identification, create deeper problems. Another source of personality disorganization may be an abrupt change in roles—caused, for example, by the loss of a job by a breadwinner, the loss of a wife or husband by a devoted spouse, a change from rural to urban living, even war and natural disaster. Failure to be adequately "socialized" in the first place is another recognized source of personality

interpersonal response traits
the sum of all of an individual's socializing experience, or personality

causes of personality disorder
conflicting role expectations

abrupt changes in roles

inadequate socialization

desocialization: consistent defeat, frustration, and withdrawal

TABLE 5-2   Some Interpersonal Response Traits

Role dispositions

Ascendance (*social timidity*): defends one's rights; does not mind being conspicuous; is not self-reticent; is self-assured; forcefully puts self forward.

Dominance (*submissiveness*): assertive; self-confident; power-oriented; tough; strong-willed; order-giving or directive leader.

Social initiative (*social passivity*): organizes groups; does not stay in background; makes suggestions at meetings; takes over leadership.

Independence (*dependence*): prefers to do own planning, to work things out in own way; does not seek support or advice; emotionally self-sufficient.

Sociometric dispositions

Acceptance of others (*rejection of others*): nonjudgmental in attitude toward others; permissive; believing and trustful; overlooks weaknesses and sees best in others.

Sociability (*unsociability*): participates in social affairs; likes to be with people; outgoing.

Friendliness (*unfriendliness*): genial, warm; open and approachable; approaches other people easily; forms many social relationships.

Sympathy (*lack of sympathy*): concerned with the feelings and wants of others; displays kindly, generous behavior; defends underdog.

Expressive dispositions

Competitiveness (*noncompetitiveness*): sees every relationship as a contest in which other people are rivals to be defeated; self-aggrandizing; noncooperative.

Aggressiveness (*nonaggressiveness*): attacks others directly or indirectly; shows defiant resentment of authority; quarrelsome; negativistic.

Self-consciousness (*social poise*): embarrassed when entering a room after others are seated; suffers excessively from stage fright; hesitates to volunteer in group discussions; bothered at work when people watch; feels uncomfortable if different from others.

Exhibitionism (*self-effacement*): is given to excess and ostentation in behavior and dress; seeks recognition and applause; shows off and behaves in odd ways to attract attention.

Note: Opposite trait appears in parentheses.

BOX 5-3

Power, Personality, and the Presidency

How does the personality of a president—especially the characteristic ways of responding toward power and politics—affect that president's job performance? Political scientist James David Barber wrote that because the issues are always changing, we should be concerned somewhat less with the policy stands a candidate takes than with the candidate's character.[12]

Barber claimed we can classify presidents and would-be presidents according to their activism (how active and assertive they are) on the one hand and their enjoyment of politics and public service on the other. With these two dimensions we can predict presidential performance fairly well. Table 5-3 shows Barber's classification scheme and how he assessed most twentieth-century presidents.

Barber held that the people best suited for the presidency are politicians who creatively shape their environment and enjoy the give-and-take exchanges of political life. He called them "active–positives." Beware, he told us, of the active–negative types. They are the driven personalities, compelled to feverish activity, yet doomed by rigidity and personal frustration in the way they approach their jobs. Wilson, Hoover, Johnson, and Nixon are illustrative cases. Barber considers Ford an active–positive type, but others think of Ford as somewhat more of a passive–positive type. Some observers think Carter belongs as much in the negative category as in the positive. Still others think that the contradictory conclusions about

(continued)

BOX 5-3

(continued)

where to place individual presidents merely demonstrate that this scheme is more confusing than helpful—and is more likely to tell us about the classifiers than about the classified.

Our understanding of personality and character, however, may not yet be sufficiently developed that we can make accurate predictions about suitable presidential candidates. Moreover, critics doubt that Barber's generalizations are based on sufficient evidence. Many people judge Reagan to be an "active" and not a "passive," at least in Barber's terms. Still others, at least partially persuaded by Barber's analysis, doubt we can be guided by it during most elections. For whom should we vote, for example, if all the candidates are "active–positive"? Further, using strict character criteria to screen candidates probably would have prevented the moody and often-depressed Abraham Lincoln from winning office. In addition to a

presidential candidate's character, voters want and deserve to know the candidate's policy positions. It also helps to know the kind of people a candidate seeks out as advisers.

Perhaps too much emphasis is placed on presidential personality and character. Psychologists, of course, tend to emphasize the personal more than the institutional. But the personality of the president is but one factor, and Barber's classifications are so lacking in precision that they predict little and explain less. Presidential success or failure is probably due more to social, economic, and political forces at work in the nation during presidents' terms than to presidents' personalities. This is not to say that the president's character, integrity, and leadership or management styles are unimportant. But these considerations are only one set of concerns, and they may be less important than our institutional structures and processes.

TABLE 5-3   Barber's Classification of Presidential Character

		Energy level in politics	
		Active	*Passive*
Emotional attitude toward politics	*Positive*	Franklin Roosevelt Harry Truman John F. Kennedy Gerald Ford Jimmy Carter	William H. Taft Warren G. Harding Ronald Reagan
	Negative	Richard Nixon Lyndon Johnson Herbert Hoover Woodrow Wilson	Dwight Eisenhower Calvin Coolidge

disorder—for example, the adult who exhibits childlike behavior, or adolescents who cannot "find themselves," that is, find mature responsible roles for themselves in society. *Desocialization* occurs when an individual, encountering consistent defeat and frustration in interpersonal situations, withdraws from contacts with others. Thus, social psychologists tend to view mental disorders in terms of people's relationships to their social environment—whether they are well adjusted and capable of functioning in a socially acceptable fashion.

Humanistic Psychology—the Innate Human Potential

humanistic psychology
a focus on individual development and self-fulfillment

Humanistic psychology, like social psychology, focuses on the *whole* person, rather than on particular defensive structures or behavioral responses. However, while social psychology focuses on the process of socialization as the key factor in determining personality, humanistic psychology emphasizes the individual's innate potential for development, the human need for self-fulfillment.

humanistic psychology as an alternative to psychoanalysis and behaviorism

Humanistic psychology represents a reaction against behaviorism and psychoanalytic theory, the two forces that dominated psychology for many years. Humanistic psychology rejects behaviorism's insistence on using the strictly scientific, objective, value-free methods of the natural sciences. It views behaviorism as lacking in concern for the meaningfulness of human experience; behaviorism, with its narrow focus on behavior itself and its disregard of the subjective human experience, is unable to explain the totality of the person. Humanistic psychology also rejects the Freudian emphasis on the biological needs, or drives, of the body and on the defensive structure of the personality. For the humanists, the basic "self" is not a negative force that must be repressed or controlled; the self is good and has the innate and unique capacity to grow and to develop and expand its creativity.

According to the humanists, we are unique among animals because we alone have psychological as well as biological needs. Psychological needs include the need for safety and security, for friendships and intimacies, for self-esteem and self-expression. The highest psychological need is the need for *"self-actualization."*

the need to "self-actualize"

Human beings are internally motivated to fulfill these needs, to realize their potential; they have an innate propensity toward self-actualization. Personality development is the continuous process of positive growth in search of fulfilling ever-higher needs, the ultimate goal being self-actualization.

factors in personality development

Self-actualization requires first of all that individuals be aware of their own feelings; without such self-awareness, they can never know themselves, let alone realize their innate potential. In addition, self-actualization is affected by social, or environmental, factors. Like the social psychologists, humanistic psychologists believe that an individual's concept of "self" is in large measure socially determined, that others in one's world have an important impact on the way one feels about oneself. Although all people have the innate need to realize their potential, certain types of "socialization" experiences may prevent the individual from achieving self-actualization. If one is fully and unconditionally accepted as a person, then one develops positive feelings about oneself; if, on the other hand, acceptance is contingent on certain types of behavior, then one may experience anxiety and the need to function defensively, to close oneself off from feelings and a subjective experience of the world. This type of functioning interferes with the process of self-actualization.

humanistic therapies

Because of its orientation toward a "good" human nature and its emphasis on the need for openness and self-awareness, humanistic psychology does not talk in terms of "personality disorder" or "mental illness." Nor does it concern itself with past experiences; the primary focus is on "the here and now." People are not "sick" but simply in need of ridding themselves of anxiety and the defensive functioning that closes them off from subjective experience. The various forms of therapy that fall under the umbrella of humanistic psychology range from individual psychotherapy to consciousness-raising and encounter groups, sensitivity training, biofeedback, and meditation. What these therapies have in common is a focus on

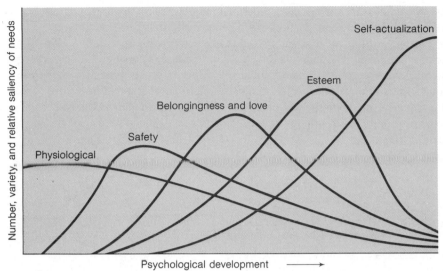

FIGURE 5-1   Maslow's hierarchy of needs, showing progressive changes in number, variety, and relative importance of needs

promoting self-acceptance and an openness in experiencing the world. Positive personality change is accomplished by bringing people into touch with their feelings, by helping them accept themselves and others, and by showing them how to assume full responsibility for the direction of their lives. This, in turn, opens the way to self-actualization.

Power and the Hierarchy of Human Needs

From the point of view of humanistic psychology, the ultimate power of the individual might be regarded as the ability to achieve self-actualization. Abraham Maslow, one of the foremost spokespersons of the humanistic movement, devised a *hierarchy of needs* that distinguishes between the "higher" and "lower" needs inherent in each individual. The highest need is, of course, self-actualization. However, before one can fulfill the higher needs, one must first satisfy the lower needs. Individual behavior at any time is determined by the individual's strongest need at that time. The higher needs reflect later stages of personality development. Figure 5-1 shows Maslow's formulation of the hierarchy of needs. (Note that the peak of an earlier main class of needs must be passed before the next "higher" need can begin to assume a dominant role. Note also that as psychological development takes place, the number and variety of needs increase.)

At the base of Maslow's hierarchy are *physiological needs* (food, clothing, shelter). These basic needs must be satisfied first. Once they have been satisfied, other levels of needs become important and begin to motivate individual behavior. Above physiological needs are the needs for *safety* and *security*. These needs may not always be apparent to the individual; they may be subconscious and not easily identified. A need for safety or security may become highly motivating, depending on early childhood experiences. The insecure child may later prefer occupations that offer insurance, retirement, protection from layoffs, and a predictable life. In con-

hierarchy of needs
the arrangement of needs from lowest to highest in potency

physiological needs
the most basic cluster of needs; include water, food, oxygen, sleep, elimination, and sex

safety needs
include order, security, and predictability

belongingness and love needs
include affiliation with others and the feeling of being loved

trast, the adult who had a secure childhood may prefer occupations that offer continuing challenges to imagination and ingenuity and that penalize failure.

Once physiological and safety needs are fairly well satisfied, *social needs* become dominant. The individual, according to Maslow, now seeks group acceptance, friendships, and intimacies. Indeed, studies of group dynamics suggest that group approval may occasionally become so important that it tends to override realistic appraisal of other sources of action. The individual may actually become a victim of group pressures in his or her search to satisfy social needs and find acceptance in life.

BOX 5-4

Cross-National Perspective: Suicide

Suicide is an individual act. At first glance, it would appear to be solely a product of internal conflicts within the individual. But the pioneering sociologist Emile Durkheim, writing a century ago, argued convincingly that social relations played a major role in the incidence of suicide. Durkheim studied records of suicide in various regions of Europe and observed that some categories of people were much more likely than others to commit suicide. Durkheim found that males, Protestants, wealthy people, and unmarried people all had higher suicide rates than females, Catholics and Jews, poor people, and married people. Durkheim theorized that differences in social integration—the strength of social attachments—explained differences in suicide rates. Lower rates were found among people who forged stronger bonds with others, and higher rates were found among people whose lifestyles were typically individualistic and autonomous. Durkheim reasoned that because men have more autonomy in most societies than women, they are more likely to kill themselves. Because Catholic life fosters family, church, and community ties, Catholics are less likely to commit suicide than Protestants, whose doctrine emphasizes individual and autonomous life. The wealthy have more independence than the poor, who are frequently dependent on others, but the result of this independence is a higher suicide rate. Finally, Durkheim reasoned that single people's suicide rates were higher because they usually had fewer and weaker social attachments than married people.

A century later, Durkheim's general observations still hold true. In the United States, the suicide rate for white

males (22.3 per 100,000 persons) is much higher than black males (11.1), and the rates for both white and black males are higher than those for white females (5.9) and black females (2.3).

Cross-national comparisons also tend to confirm Durkheim's original theory. Suicide rates are higher for men than for women in all the nations for which we have reliable data (see Table 5-4). Suicide rates are generally higher in richer and predominantly Protestant nations.

TABLE 5-4   Suicide Rates (Rate per 100,000 Population)

	Male	*Female*
United States	20.6	5.4
Australia	19.1	5.6
Austria	40.1	15.7
Canada	22.8	6.4
Denmark	35.6	19.9
France	32.9	12.9
Italy	12.2	4.7
Japan	25.6	13.8
Netherlands	13.9	8.2
Poland	22.3	4.7
Sweden	27.1	10.1
United Kingdom	11.6	4.5
Germany	26.7	11.8

Source: U.S. Bureau of the Census, *Statistical Abstract of the United States 1990* (Washington, D.C.: U.S. Government Printing Office, 1990), p. 838.

A significant theme in the study of human behavior has been the reaction of individuals who were commanded to inflict pain, injury, or death upon others. An estimated six million Jews—men, women, and children—were murdered in Nazi death camps in World War II by individuals who frequently claimed they were "only carrying out orders."

Authority, as we have noted, is a form of power that is perceived as legitimate by society. Doubtless, throughout the ages more pain, injury, and death have been inflicted on humanity by "authorities" than by recognized "criminals." The criminal's claim to power is sanctioned only by guns, knives, fists, or fraud, not by "legitimacy." But what are the psychological mechanisms that provide legitimacy to the exercise of power, and how far will ordinary Americans go in inflicting pain, injury, or even death if they believe they are acting legitimately?

These are some of the questions explored by psychologist Stanley Milgram in a series of experiments at Yale University in which experimenters told subjects to administer electric shocks to other people.[13] The subjects in these experiments were all adult males of various ages and represented a cross section of occupations. Each subject was told that he was participating in a "learning experiment"; the "learner" (actually an associate of the experimenter) was strapped into an "electric chair" and given a list of questions and answers to memorize. The subject was told by the experimenter to administer an ever-increasing electric shock every time the "learner" made a mistake. Thirty separate voltage levers were used, with signs reading from 15 to 450 volts. Signs also announced that the shocks ranged from "Slight Shock" to "Danger: Severe Shock." Actually the "learner" did not receive any shocks at all, but the subject did not know this. Moreover, the subject could watch the "learner" through a window and hear any sounds the "learner" made. Starting with 75 volts the "learner" began to twitch, grunt, and groan with each shock. At 150 volts the "learner" demanded that he be let out of the experiment. At 180 volts the "learner" screamed that he could no longer stand the pain. At 300 volts the "learner" slumped over, refused to provide any more answers to questions, and appeared in dire distress. In response to each of the acts by the "learner," the experimenter told the subject, who was administering the shocks: "You have no choice, you must go on!"

Before the experiments began, Professor Milgram asked forty psychiatrists at a leading medical school to predict the behavior of most subjects; these psychiatrists were asked to predict specifically when the subject would break off the experiment and refuse to administer any more pain to the "learner." These psychiatrists predicted that *most* subjects would refuse to continue beyond the 150-volt level and that only one-tenth would continue to the full 450-volt level. However, the shocking results of the "shocking" experiments were that 62 percent of the subjects obeyed the experimenter's commands completely and proceeded to administer the highest shock level on the board (450 volts). Only 38 percent of the subjects broke off the

(continued)

(continued)

experiment when the "learner" groaned, screamed, demanded to be released, and finally pretended to be near death.

Many subjects expressed concern about their "learner" victims and about their part in the experiments but continued the experiment anyway:

150 volts	"You want me to keep going?"
165 volts	"That guy is hollering in there. He's liable to have a heart attack. You want me to go on?"
180 volts	"He can't stand it. I'm not going to kill that man in there! You hear him hollering. He's hollering. He can't stand it. What if something happens to him? . . . I mean who is going to take the responsibility if something happens to that gentleman?"
	(The experimenter says he will accept responsibility.)
195 volts	"You see he's hollering. Hear that? Gee, I don't know."
	(The experimenter says, "The experiment requires that you go on.")
210 volts	
225 volts	
240 volts	"Aw, no. You mean I've got to keep going up the scale? No, sir. I'm not going to kill that man! I'm not going to give him 450 volts!"
	(The experimenter repeats, "The experiment requires that you go on.")
	The subject proceeds to the highest shock level, 450 volts.*

One point made in these experiments is that the subjects were not simply sadistic. They were average men selected from all walks of life. Most objected verbally to what they were doing at some point in the experiment. But in the context of *authority* (an experimenter who told them to continue no matter what happened) and *legitimacy* (the idea that they were participating in a scientific experiment at a prestigious university), these individuals performed acts of brutality that they would not otherwise consider doing.

Psychologist Milgram concluded:

With numbing regularity good people were seen to knuckle under to the demands of authority and perform actions that were callous and severe. Men who are in everyday life responsible and decent were seduced by trappings of authority, by the control of their perceptions, and by uncritical acceptance of the experimenter's definition of the situation, into performing harsh acts.

What is the limit of obedience?[14]

It is not clear how far we can generalize from these experiments. But it is certainly not far-fetched to suspect that under the right conditions otherwise normal people can become unusually cruel. If those who are invested with authority and legitimacy encourage sadistic behavior toward others, we can reasonably expect that a substantial proportion of the population will engage in such behavior. Another holocaust is not impossible.

*Excerpt from *Obedience to Authority,* by Stanley Milgram. Copyright © 1974 by Stanley Milgram. Reprinted by permission of HarperCollins, Inc.

Assuming that an individual's social needs are reasonably well satisfied, a fourth need comes into prominence: *esteem.* Failure to understand this need may lead parents to complain, "We've given our child everything—a good home, stable family, all the things he ever asked for, even our own time and assistance—yet he is still dissatisfied." However, it may be that it is precisely because such children have had the three basic needs sufficiently satisfied that a fourth need emerges—recognition of worth as an individual. Like the need for security or social needs, the need for personal esteem appears in a variety of forms; a search for *recognition* is one manifestation of the need for personal esteem.

esteem needs
include status, prestige, competence, and confidence

Evidence from studies of large corporate and governmental organizations suggests that recognition or symbols of prestige may be more important in motivating management employees than money. Most employees of these organizations make enough money to satisfy their physiological and security needs, and their social needs may be satisfied in relationships with family, work group, neighborhood, church, and so on. But their job performance suffers when they feel they do not receive personal recognition from their supervisors for their work. Their salary carries some prestige value, but often an impressive-sounding title (for example, "vice-president for operations," "director of planning," or "deputy secretary") is even more important. In business organizations it is frequently remarked that "a name on the door and a rug on the floor" are the key to recognition. Many individuals will sacrifice salary to achieve these symbols of esteem.

When the first four needs are more or less satisfied, we can expect to witness the emergence of Maslow's fifth and final need: the need for *self-actualization.* It is not always clear what self-actualization really is. According to Maslow, "Self-actualizing people are, without one single exception, involved in a cause outside of their own skin, in something outside of themselves."[15]

self-actualization
the highest level in the hierarchy, reached only if the preceding need levels have been adequately satisfied; the self-actualizing individual operates at full capacity

Despite problems in defining self-actualization, it does seem true that at some point in life, frequently in the late thirties or early forties, many individuals feel a vague sense of dissatisfaction. This "mid-life crisis" may be related to the need for self-actualization. Individuals who have provided well for themselves and their families; who face no serious threats to their security; who are well accepted by their family, friends, and neighbors; and who have won recognition in their field of work may nonetheless feel that something is "missing." These individuals may have been content while striving to achieve their position in life, but once they have achieved this position, they ask, "Is that all there is?" According to Maslow, these individuals have reached a point at which they must turn to their fifth and final need, self-actualization.

Powerlessness and Mental Health

There is a common adage that "power tends to corrupt, and absolute power corrupts absolutely." It reflects our negative view of power and our association of power with abuse. But the distinguished psychologist Rollo May, whose contributions to the humanistic movement are highly significant, contends that power is a fundamental aspect of the life process. Indeed, he believes that *powerlessness* corrupts the human personality by robbing the individual of a sense of meaning and significance.

Rollo May's argument is that power occurs in an individual's life in five functional forms.[16] The first is the *power to be*. The word *power* comes from the Latin root meaning "to be able." The newborn infant must have the power to make others respond to its needs—it cries and waves its arms violently as signs of its discomfort. An infant who cannot elicit a response from others fails to develop as a separate personality. *Power as self-affirmation* is the recognition of one's own worth and significance in life. Some power is essential for self-esteem and self-belief. *Power as self-assertion* makes it clear who we are and what we believe. It gives us the potential to react to attack and protect ourselves from becoming victims. Power also occurs in everyone's life as *aggression*—thrusting out against a person or thing seen as an adversary. The constructive aspects of aggression include cutting through barriers to initiate relationships; confronting another person, not with the intent to hurt, but in order to penetrate that individual's consciousness; and actualizing one's own self in a hostile environment. The destructive side of aggression, of course, includes thrusting out to inflict injury and taking power simply to increase one's own range of control. Finally, power occurs as *violence*. May believes that violence is an attempt to exercise power. Violence may result from a failure at self-affirmation or self-assertion, or it may accompany aggression. Nonetheless, it can be regarded as functional to the individual if there is no other way for that person to gain significance in life.

It is May's belief that modern mass society impairs the individual's self-esteem and self-worth. The feeling of personal powerlessness is widespread.

> To admit our own individual feelings of powerlessness—that we cannot influence many people; that we count for little; that the values to which our parents devoted their lives are to us insubstantial and worthless; that we feel ourselves to be "faceless others," insignificant to other people and therefore not worth much to ourselves—that is, indeed, difficult to admit.[17]

He believes that much irrational violence—riots, assassinations, senseless murders—is a product of feelings of powerlessness.

Notes

1. I. J. Gottesman, "Heritability of Personality," *Psychological Monographs* 77 (1963): 1–21.
2. J. Shields, *Monozygotic Twins Brought Up Apart and Brought Up Together* (London: Oxford University Press, 1962).
3. Harry F. Harlow, "Learning to Love," *American Scientist* 54 (1966): 244–272.
4. John Bowlby, "The Nature of the Child's Tie to His Mother," *International Journal of Psychoanalysis* 39 (1958): 350–373.
5. Harry F. Harlow and R. R. Zimmerman, "Affectionate Responses in the Infant Monkey," *Science* 130 (1959): 421–432.
6. Gordon Allport, *Personality* (New York: Holt, 1937), pp. 24–54.
7. William McDougall, quoted in *Handbook of Social Psychology,* vol. I, ed. Gardner Lindzey (Reading, Mass.: Addison-Wesley, 1954), p. 144.
8. T. W. Adorno et al., *The Authoritarian Personality* (New York: Harper, 1950).
9. Charles H. Cooley, *Human Nature and the Social Order* (New York, Scribner's), 1902.
10. B. F. Skinner, *Beyond Freedom and Dignity* (New York: Knopf, 1971), p. 5.
11. Ibid., p. 96.
12. James David Barber, *The Presidential Character,* 3rd ed. (Englewood Cliffs, N.J.: Prentice-Hall, 1985). See evaluations of this study by Alexander L. George, "Assessing Presidential Character," *World Politics,* January 1974, pp. 234–282; and by Alan C. Elms, *Personality in Politics* (Harcourt Brace Jovanovich, 1976), ch. 4. See also Michael Nelson, "James David Barber and the Psychological Presidency," *Virginia Quarterly Review* 56 (Autumn 1980): 650–667.
13. Stanley Milgram, "Some Conditions of Obedience and Disobedience to Authority," *Human Relations* 18 (February 1965), 57–76.

14. Ibid., p. 74.
15. A. H. Maslow, *The Farther Reaches of Human Nature* (New York: Viking Press, 1971), p. 43.
16. Rollo May, *Power and Innocence* (New York: Norton, 1972).
17. Ibid., p. 21.

About This Chapter

An understanding of personality, of individual behavioral responses and their determinants, is essential to a full understanding of power in society. In this chapter we have explored the meaning of personality and various psychological theories regarding the determinants of personality. We also saw what various schools of psychology have to say about the relationship between personality and power. Now that you have read Chapter 5, you should be able to

- describe the "nature versus nurture" controversy in the shaping of personality;
- discuss how psychoanalytic (Freudian) theory views personality and its development and how this theory interprets individual responses to power and authority;
- discuss behavioral psychology's use of learning theory in its approach to the study of personality, and B. F. Skinner's ideas for the control of human behavior;
- describe humanistic psychology's view of the "self," Abraham Maslow's construction of a "hierarchy of needs," and Rollo May's concept of powerlessness;
- discuss how power in the form of authority and legitimacy can command obedience, and the implications of such obedience.

Discussion Questions

1. Describe the "nature versus nurture" controversy over the determination of personality. How does research on the personality characteristics of identical twins help us learn more about the relative effects of heredity versus environment on human behavior?

2. Discuss the psychoanalytic (Freudian) view of the determinants of behavior. Identify the three major systems that Freudians believe compose the personality and describe the roles played by each of these systems. Differentiate between normal and neurotic anxiety and describe the functions of identification.

3. Describe the authoritarian personality. What are some psychoanalytic explanations of the authoritarian personality? Discuss the criticisms of the *Authoritarian Personality* study.

4. How would a behavioral psychologist define personality and the goal of psychology? Describe how a linkage between a conditioned stimulus and response is established.

5. Describe how a social psychologist would approach the study of personality. Identify the processes that social psychologists believe are critical determinants of personality development. Discuss the meaning of the *looking-glass self* and *interpersonal response traits*.

6. Discuss humanistic psychology's view of the individual, Rollo May's formulation of the functions of power, and Abraham Maslow's "hierarchy of needs."

7. Discuss the results of the experiments that psychologist Stanley Milgram carried out at Yale University. What do these results tell us about the power of authority and legitimacy to command obedience? What are the implications of such obedience?

8. If you were interested in becoming a clinical psychologist, which type of therapy do you think you would want to practice—psychoanalytic therapy, behavioral therapy, a therapy based on the principles of interpersonal-interaction theory, or one that uses the approach of humanistic psychology? Describe how the theory you would choose views "personality disorder."

9. Which of the theories studied do you think provides the most cogent view of personality and the relationship between personality and power? Discuss your reasoning, including any criticisms you may have about any of these theories.

Power
and the
Economic
Order

CHAPTER

Power and Economic Organization

A great deal of power in the United States is centered in large economic organizations—corporations, banks, utilities, investment firms, and government agencies charged with the responsibility of overseeing the economy. Not all power, it is true, is anchored in or exercised through these institutions; power is also embodied in class, cultural, political, and ideological institutions and processes, as discussed elsewhere in this volume. *But control of economic resources provides a continuous and important base of power in any society.*

Economics is the study of the production and distribution of scarce goods and services. Economics decides the following questions:

1. *What should be produced?* What goods and services should be produced and in what quantities? Should we produce more automobiles or more trains and subways, more food and fertilizer or more clean air and water, more B-1 bombers or higher Social Security benefits? Should we produce more for immediate consumption, or should we save and invest more now in order to be able to enjoy even more later? Every economic system must answer questions like these.

2. *How will goods and services be produced?* The decision to produce particular goods and services does not accomplish the task. Resources must be organized and allocated, and people must be motivated to work. Various combinations of resources—land, labor, capital (factories, machinery, supplies), and technology—might be used to produce a particular item. Wheat might be grown with less land and labor if more fertilizer and machinery and better technology are employed. And all these resources must be organized for production, either by providing economic incentives (wages and profits) or by threats of force.

3. *For whom will goods and services be produced?* Who will consume these products and services? Economists refer to this question as the question of *distribution.* Should people be paid according to their skills, or knowledge, or contribution to the production of goods and services? Or should everyone be paid equally regardless of their skills, knowledge, or contribution to production? Should people be allowed to bid for goods and services, with the most going to the highest bidders? Or should goods and services be distributed by government, with the most going to those who are best able to influence government decisions?

In general, there are two ways of making these economic decisions: (1) individually, through the market system; or (2) collectively, through governments.

The *market* system allows individuals and firms to make their own decisions about who gets what and how. Markets implement decisions through voluntary exchange. Markets work through unregulated prices and decentralized decisions of many separate individuals and businesses.

Governments also decide who gets what and how by *collective decision making.* Governments implement decisions through coercion (fines, penalties, imprisonment) and threats of coercion. In democracies, collective decisions are influenced by individual voters, interest groups, and parties; in nondemocratic governments, the decisions are influenced primarily by ideology and the interests of government leaders themselves.

In most economies, including that of the United States, economic decisions are made by *both* the market system and the government.

---

economics
the study of the production and distribution of scarce resources

economic decisions
what to produce

how to produce it

for whom it will be produced

economic decision making
markets: individually through voluntary exchange

governments: collectively through coercion

The Market System, Hard-Boiled and Impersonal

The economic system consists of the *institutions and processes by which a society produces and distributes scarce resources.* There is not enough of everything for all of us to have all we want. If nature provided everything that everyone wanted without work, there would be no need for an economic system. But resources are "scarce," and some scheme must be created to decide who gets what. Scarcity, together with the problem of choice it raises, is the fundamental question of economics.

The American economic system is a capitalist, free enterprise system. It is largely "unplanned"; no government bureau tells all 115 million workers in the United States where to work, what to do, or how to do it. On the whole, the private enterprise economy organizes itself, with a minimum of centralized planning or direction. The American system relies chiefly on private individuals, in search of wages and profits, to get the job done. No government agency directs that shirts be produced: If people want shirts, then there is profit to be made in producing them, and businesspeople who recognize the potential profit will begin turning them out. No government agency directs how many shirts will be produced: As shirt output increases, a point is reached at which there are so many shirts that the price that people are willing to pay falls below the cost of producing them, and businesspeople then begin curtailing their production of shirts. This same production-in-search-of-profits goes on for thousands of other products simultaneously.

A private enterprise economy decides what is to be produced, how it is to be produced, and how it is to be distributed, all in a fashion that is for the most part automatic and impersonal. Everyone, by following self-interest, decides who gets what. The absence of planning and control does not mean chaos. Rather, it means a complex system of production and distribution that no single mind, and probably no government planning agency, could organize or control in all its infinite detail.

A *market* is any place or arrangement that enables people to exchange money for goods, services, or labor. The exchange rate is called the *price*. Under the private enterprise system, the *market determines what is to be produced, how much it will cost, and who will be able to buy it.* Consumers decide what should be produced by expressing their preferences in terms of the amount of money they spend on various goods and services (*consumer demand*). When consumers *are willing and able to pay* for something, they will bid up the *price* of that item. The price is an indication of how much of the item consumers want produced. Businesses are out to make *profits.* Profits motivate producers to satisfy consumer demands. Profits drive the free enterprise system. Profits occur when selling prices are higher than the costs of production. Businesspeople move into industries in which consumers bid up prices. Where consumer demand bids up prices, businesspeople can afford to pay higher wages; and workers tend to move toward those industries with higher pay and better working conditions. Thus, consumer demand shifts both business and labor into industries in which prices are high. Businesspeople play a key role in a private enterprise system because they channel production toward industries having the strongest consumer demand and organize productive activity in the most efficient (lowest-cost) way possible. Profits are the mainspring of the market system. In seeking profits, businesspeople perform a vital economic function.

Who gets the goods that are produced? The price system allocates goods to those

economic system
institutions and processes by which society produces and distributes scarce resources

private enterprise economy
private individuals in search of wages and profit, acting on their own, without government direction

market
arrangement that enables people to exchange money for goods, services, and labor

consumer demand
preferences for goods and services, expressed by willingness to pay

profits
motivate producers to satisfy consumer demand and to produce goods and services in the most efficient way possible

Markets can be small sidewalk enterprises.
Source: Michael Weisbrot

who have both the *willingness to pay* and the *ability to pay.* The willingness to pay determines the desirability of producing a certain item. No government agency determines whether we "need" goods and services; the market reveals whether individuals are willing to pay for them. Consumers, however, must also have the ability to pay: They must earn incomes by working to produce goods and services that consumers want. The *labor market* largely determines where people will work and how much they will be paid. The income received for their labor depends primarily on their worth to the businesses that employ them. They are worth more when they contribute more to production and profit. Where production and profits are low, wages will be low and individuals will be frequently unemployed.

The market is hard-boiled and impersonal. If a business produces too much of a particular item—more than consumers are willing to buy at a particular price—the price will have to be lowered or production (supply) will have to be cut back. Competition among businesses also checks prices, for a business that sets a price higher than that set by competitors will lose sales. Thus *consumer demand, product supply, and competition determine prices.* In the absence of interfering factors, the *price* depends on a relationship of supply and demand at any given time. If demand increases, prices tend to rise; if demand decreases, prices tend to fall. If supply increases, prices tend to fall; if supply decreases, prices tend to rise.

The market reconciles the interests of buyers and sellers, labor and business, in the process of getting people to agree on prices. The market in a free enterprise system undertakes this reconciliation automatically, without assistance from outside individuals or forces. The ideal conditions for a market operation are these:

1. The existence of a perfect competition, in which the market has so many buyers and sellers that no single trader has any control over the price of the good or service being exchanged, and the price is made by the market through the imper-

prices
allocate goods and services by willingness and ability to pay

determined by consumer demand, product supply, and competition

The New York Stock Exchange is a market on a larger scale.
Source: Peter Menzel/Stock, Boston

sonal forces of supply and demand. (If one or a few sellers have control over supply, the market is said to be *monopolistic;* if one or a few buyers have control over demand, the market is said to be *monopsonistic.*)

2. The ability of a buyer of the good to exclude others from the satisfactions that good provides so no one can enjoy the benefits of someone else's purchase. (When people benefit from the purchases of others, there are said to be *spillover effects,* as, for example, in the case of national defense products, which cannot be sold on the open market.)

3. The complete mobility of resources and labor so they can move in response to changes in prices. (In a completely mobile economy, each individual [or business] is prepared to alter the pattern of spending and working in response to changes in prices of goods and labor.)

In other words, in an ideal market there is a great deal of competition, and prices are determined solely by supply and demand. All must pay for the goods and benefits they receive, and resources and labor shift easily in response to changes in prices and wages.

ideal conditions for a market operation
competition among many buyers and sellers

ability of buyer to exclude others from benefits of purchase

mobility of resources and labor

Supply, Demand, and the Market Price

Let us illustrate what happens in a true market economy, where price is governed by supply and demand.

Along with many other commodities, millions of bushels of wheat are bought and sold every day at the Chicago Board of Trade. Let us suppose that the first buyer of the day offers $2 per bushel for wheat (see Table 6-1). Let us also suppose

an example of market pricing

CASE STUDY

Adam Smith:
Laissez Faire
Economics

In the same year the Declaration of Independence was signed, Adam Smith, a Scottish professor of philosophy, published his *Wealth of Nations* and thereby secured recognition as the founder of free enterprise economics. Today the economic model set forth by Adam Smith is frequently referred to as *classical economics* or *laissez faire economics* (from the French phrase meaning "allow to do as one pleases"). Smith wrote *The Wealth of Nations* as an attack on the *mercantilism* of nations in his day, that is, the attempt of governments to intervene in the economy with special tariffs, regulations, subsidies, and exclusive charters to businesses, all designed to maximize the acquisition of gold and silver in government treasuries. Smith argued against mercantilism and for *free competition* in the marketplace. He believed that a worldwide market, *unfettered by government restrictions or subsidies,* would result in lower prices and high standards of living for all. A free market would allow the businesses and nations most capable of producing particular goods cheaply and efficiently to do so. There would be greater specialization as each business and nation concentrated on what it did best. The outcome of the specialization and efficiency created by free competition would be a high standard of living for everyone. Thus, pursuit of private profit was actually in the public interest.

> Every individual endeavors to employ his capital so that its produce may be of greater value. He generally neither intends to promote the public interest, nor knows how much he is promoting it. He intends only his . . . own gain. He is in this led by an invisible hand to promote an end which was no part of his intention. By pursuing his own interest he frequently promotes that of society more effectively than if he really intended to promote it.[1]

Laissez faire economics is based on the idea that people are rational, that they will pursue their own economic self-interest, and that they are mobile and able to shift their resources and labor as the market demands. According to this economic system, there should be no artificial blocks to the most efficient use of people and materials. The market has a large number of competitors buying and selling products, services, and labor; and no one alone has control over supply, demand, or price. Buyers buy from producers who make the best goods at the lowest price. Thus, efficiency is rewarded and inefficiency driven out of the economy. As competition increases supply and lowers prices, some producers shift to more lucrative lines. The market continuously corrects unproductive use of resources. The system is *self-adjusting* and *self-regulating.*

Smith objected to government interference in the natural operations of the marketplace. Government should do only two things: (1) create an environment for an orderly marketplace, that is, maintain law and order, protect private property, enforce contracts, and provide a monetary system; and (2) supply those services the marketplace cannot provide, such as defense, public works, and care of widows, orphans, and other helpless people.

(continued)

(continued)

Laissez faire economics has much in common with *traditional democracy*. It is important to realize that at the same time that Adam Smith was setting forth a model economic system that stressed individual rationality, freedom of choice, and limited government intervention, democrats in America were developing a model political system emphasizing individual responsibility, freedom of expression, rational voter choice, and limitations on governmental power over individual liberty. The free enterprise economic system *paralleled* the democratic political system. In politics, every person was to be free to speak out, to form a political party, and to vote as he or she pleased—to pursue political interests as he or she thought best. In economic life, every person was to be free to find work, start a business, and spend money as he or she pleased—to pursue economic self-interest as he or she thought best. The ballot box in politics and the market in economics were the impartial arbiters of conflict in society. Government was to be restricted in both its power over individual liberty and its power over economic life.

Today many "classical" economists echo Adam Smith's ideas. Although it is now widely recognized that government must play an important role in stabilizing the economy (avoiding both inflation and depression), protecting consumers, regulating business and labor practices, and assisting individuals who cannot care for themselves, classical economists nonetheless argue that economic planning by government is incompatible with *personal freedom*. They contend that bureaucratic intervention in the economy not only is inefficient and wasteful but also gradually erodes individual freedom and initiative.

This fear is not unfounded; political scientist J. Roland Pennock warns of the political consequences of a government-controlled economy:

> The existing freedom to choose one's vocation, one's employer, and the way one would manage his savings or spend his income would give way in greater and lesser degree to regimentation in all these areas by governmental fiat. It might provide greater security or more equality, but it could hardly fail to reduce liberty.[2]

Thus the appeal of laissez faire economics is based not only on the efficiency of the marketplace in channeling labor and resources into their most productive uses, but also on the personal freedom this system guarantees.

that there are buyers for 20 million bushels of wheat at this low price (demand). However, few owners are willing to sell at this price, and therefore there are only 10 million bushels of wheat offered at $2 per bushel (supply). The result is an imbalance in supply and demand, a 10-million-bushel shortfall in supply at the low $2 price. Those still wishing to buy must therefore raise their price to attract more wheat to the market. Let us suppose that the price then shoots up to $4 per bushel. At this price there are fewer buyers (let us say only an 8-million-bushel demand) and many more sellers (let us say an 18-million-bushel supply). The result is an

TABLE 6-1 An Example of Supply and Demand

Supply: Bushels of wheat offered for sale (millions)	Price (dollars)	Demand: Bushels of wheat demanded (millions)
18	4.00	8
16	3.50	11
14	3.00	14
12	2.50	17
10	2.00	20

excess supply of 10 million bushels at the high price; this excess will eventually push prices back down.

Thus, the price tends to stabilize at a point low enough to attract sufficient demand for wheat but high enough to attract an equivalent supply of wheat. In our example (Table 6-1), this price is $3 per bushel, where 14 million bushels are demanded and 14 million bushels are offered.

Figure 6-1 shows our example of supply and demand in graphic form. The supply curve is low at a low price, but it increases as the price increases. Demand is high at a low price, but it declines as the price increases. The two lines for supply and demand intersect at a price where the amount demanded just matches the amount supplied. This will tend to be the market price. In our example, it is set at $3 per bushel. Any other price will produce either an excess supply (at a higher price) or an excess demand (at a lower price).

Government and the Economy

The free enterprise system we have just described is subject to major modifications by the activities of government. In fact, government is now so involved in the economy that we might call the American economic system a *mixed* economy rather than a *private enterprise* economy. Government intervenes in the free market for many reasons:

reasons for government intervention

assure fair competition

set minimum wages

regulate public industries

protect consumers

provide public services

care for persons not in the marketplace

stabilize the market

1. To assure competition among businesses by breaking up monopolies and prohibiting unfair competitive practices;
2. To set minimum standards for wages and working conditions;
3. To regulate industries (like communications, broadcasting, and transportation) in which there is a strong public interest and in which unbridled competition may hurt more than it helps;
4. To protect the consumer from phony goods and services and false or misleading advertising;
5. To provide a wide range of public services (defense, education, highways, police protection) that cannot be reasonably provided on a private-profit basis;
6. To provide support and care (welfare, Social Security, unemployment compensation, Medicare, health care, and so forth) to individuals who cannot supply these things for themselves through the market system;
7. To ensure that the economic system functions properly and avoids depression, inflation, or unemployment.

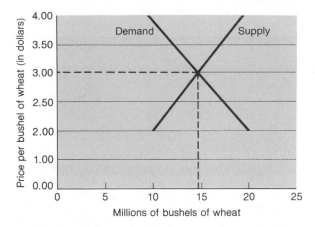

FIGURE 6-1   An example of supply and demand

The Government and Economic Stabilization: Cushioning the Ups and Downs

Today the government of the United States is fully committed to preserving economic prosperity and using fiscal and monetary policies to try to offset the effects of inflation and recession (see Box 6-1, "Achieving Economic Stability"). This much of Keynesian economics is contained in the *Employment Act of 1946,* which specifically pledges the federal government "to promote maximum employment, production, and purchasing power."

The act created the *Council of Economic Advisers* (CEA) to "develop and recommend to the president national economic policies." The CEA is composed of three economists, appointed by the president, and a staff of analysts who collect data on the economy and advise the president on what to do to offset cycles of inflation or recession. The act also requires the president to submit to Congress an annual economic report assessing the state of the economy and recommending economic legislation.

Employment Act of 1946
pledged the federal government to use all practicable means to promote maximum employment, production, and purchasing power

Council of Economic Advisers
advises the president on national economic policies

Fiscal Policy

In Keynesian theory, during recessions when consumer demand must be increased, Congress should increase government spending, thereby adding to the total demand, or it should cut taxes, thereby putting more money into the pockets of consumers. Conversely, during inflation, when strong consumer demands are pushing prices up, Congress should cut its own spending, thereby reducing total demand, or it should raise taxes, thereby restricting the spending power of consumers. During recessions the government must run a deficit (debt) in order to pour money into the economy. During inflations the government must cut its spending or raise taxes and create a surplus in its budget: that is, it must take money out of the economy and reduce its debt in order to lower consumer demand and stabilize prices.

fiscal policy
government taxing and spending

CASE STUDY

John M. Keynes: The Mixed Economy

The Great Depression of the 1930s significantly altered American thinking about laissez faire economics. It is difficult to realize today what a tremendous economic disaster befell the nation in those days. Following the stock market crash of October 1929 and in spite of President Herbert Hoover's assurances that prosperity lay "just around the corner," the American economy virtually collapsed. Businesses failed, factories shut down, new construction practically ceased, banks closed, and millions of dollars in savings were wiped out. One out of four American workers was unemployed, and one out of six was receiving welfare relief. Persons who had never before known unemployment lost their jobs, used up their savings or lost them when the banks folded, cashed in their life insurance, and gave up their homes or farms because they could not continue the mortgage payments. Fear was widespread that violent revolution would soon sweep the country. Many lost faith in the free enterprise system and urged the abandonment of the market economy. The "solutions" of fascism in Italy and Germany and communism in the Soviet Union were looked to as alternatives to a "doomed" capitalist system.

In 1936 John M. Keynes, a British economist, wrote a landmark book called *The General Theory of Employment, Interest and Money.* Keynes attacked the basic notion of classical economics—that the free enterprise system was a self-adapting mechanism that tended to produce full employment and maximum use of resources. He believed that not all savings went into investment. When there was little prospect of profit, savings were likely to be hoarded and not used. This removal of money from the economy brought depression. Moreover, he argued, low interest rates would not necessarily stir businesses to reinvest; the expectation of *profit,* not the availability of money, motivated investment. Keynes believed that as confidence in the future diminishes, investment will decline, regardless of interest rates.

In Keynes's view only *government* can reverse a downward economic cycle. Private businesses cannot be expected to invest when consumer demand is low and there is no prospect of profit. And consumers cannot be expected to increase their purchases when their incomes are falling. So the responsibility rests on the government to take *countercyclical* action to increase income and consumption.

Government can act, first of all, by means of *fiscal policy,* that is, by making decisions regarding government expenditures, taxes, and debt. In recessions government can *increase its own expenditures or lower taxes or do both* in order to raise total demand and private income. Government purchases add directly to total demand and stimulate production and employment. Government payments to individuals in the form of Social Security, unemployment compensation, or welfare make more money available to individuals for consumption. Reducing taxes also makes more money available to individuals for purchasing. Of course, increasing expenditures or lowering taxes or both means an *increase in government debt,* but only in this fashion can government pump money into the economy.

At the same time, government can act in a countercyclical way by means of

(continued)

(continued)

monetary policy, that is, by making decisions regarding the availability of money and credit and rates of interest. To encourage investment, government can expand the money supply by *lowering interest rates and increasing the amount of money available for circulation.* However, monetary policy may not have a really direct or immediate impact on the economy if businesses do not take advantage of the availability of cheaper money. Thus *Keynes relied more heavily on fiscal policy than monetary policy to bring about economic recovery during recessions.*

Keynes also argued that governments should pursue countercyclical fiscal and monetary policies to offset inflation as well as depression. *Inflation* means a general rise in the price level of goods and services. Inflation occurs when total demand exceeds or nears the productive capacity of the economy. An excess of demand over supply forces prices up.

Keynes believed that when inflation threatens, government should gear its fiscal policy toward *reducing its own expenditures or increasing taxes or both.* Reducing government purchases would reduce total demand and bring it back into equilibrium with supply. Raising taxes would reduce the money available for consumption and therefore also help bring demand back into equilibrium with supply. These fiscal policies (to be pursued during inflationary times) would enable the government to reduce its debt (which is incurred during depressions).

Keynes was no revolutionary. On the contrary, he wished to preserve the private enterprise system by developing effective governmental measures to overcome disastrous economic cycles. In December 1933 he wrote an open letter to President Roosevelt emphasizing the importance of saving the capitalist system:

> You have made yourself the trustee for those in every country who seek to mend the evils of our condition by reasoned experiment within the framework of the existing social system. If you fail, rational change will be gravely prejudiced throughout the world, leaving orthodoxy and revolution to fight it out.[3]

Automatic Stabilizers

Automatic stabilizers are government programs that act automatically to counter the effects of economic cycles. For example, since income taxes increase in proportion to one's earnings, the income tax automatically restricts spending habits in times of prosperity by taking larger bites of income. In times of adversity and low earnings, taxes drop automatically. Welfare programs also act automatically to counter economic cycles: In recessions, more people apply for welfare and unemployment payments, and those payments help offset declines in income.

automatic stabilizers government programs that act to counter economic cycles

Monetary Policy

Because banks are the major source of money and credit, the government can control investment spending by making it easy or difficult to borrow money from

monetary policy controlling the supply of money

BOX 6-1

Achieving Economic Stability

Socialist critics of free market economies have long argued that the "internal contradictions of capitalism" would eventually bring about the downfall of free markets. They contended that economic cycles of inflation and depression would undermine public support for free markets and pave the way for socialism. And indeed, before 1950, economic cycles in the United States pro-duced extreme ups and downs, with double-digit swings in real gross national product (GNP). In recent decades, however, economic fluctuations have been more moderate. We still experience economic cycles, but many economists believe that countercyclical government fiscal and monetary policy has succeeded in achieving greater stability. (See Figure 6–2.)

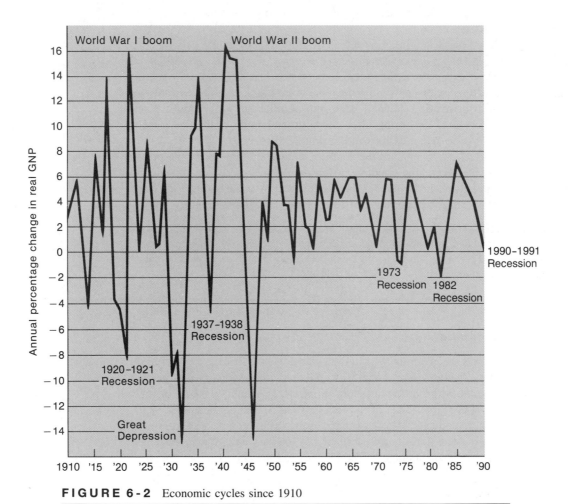

FIGURE 6-2   Economic cycles since 1910

Lee Iacocca celebrates Chrysler's "independence" when federally guaranteed notes are paid off.
Source. UPI/Bettmann Newsphotos

banks. The *Federal Reserve Board* (the Fed) was created in 1913 to regulate the nation's supply of money through its *power to control the amount of money that commercial banks can lend.* The Fed is headed by a seven-person board of governors, appointed by the president, for overlapping terms of fourteen years. In periods of *recession,* the Fed can *loosen controls* on lending and encourage banks to lend more money to businesspeople at lower interest rates. During *inflation,* the Fed can pursue *tight money policies,* policies that make it more difficult for banks to lend money, and thus reduce inflationary pressures.

Government Use of Countercyclical Tools

In practice there have been many difficulties in government use of fiscal and monetary policy.

   1. *Economic prediction is not an exact science;* honest economists will admit to a lot of uncertainty about just what policy should be adopted and when. Actions taken by the government may not have an impact on the economy until many months later, when conditions have changed from those that existed at the time the policy was adopted. There is a "lag" between government action and its effect.

   2. Presidents and members of Congress are afraid of being blamed for a depression. Inflation frequently goes unchecked because *public officials fear that "tight money," reduced spending, or higher taxes might set off a recession.* Besides, these counterinflationary actions are politically unpopular. Hence, deficit spending continues even when the nation is not confronting a recession.

problems with countercyclical policy

economic predictions not exact

politicians reluctant to counter inflation

overreactions to monetary policy changes

conflicts between fighting inflation and fighting recession

occasional lack of coordination between Congress (fiscal policy) and Federal Reserve Board (monetary policy)

political problems in halting inflation

3. Monetary policy often results in *overreaction to short-run economic distur-bances* and contributes to long-run instability. Very tight money can check an infla-tion, but it may later cause a recession. Likewise, easy credit may check a tem-porary downswing but contribute to long-run inflation. Economist Milton Friedman has suggested that the money supply be stabilized through thick and thin. This would allow minor economic fluctuations but would avoid big swings.

4. *Inflation and recession can occur at the same time* if prices are pushed up by union demands for higher wages and if business anticipates that inflation is a permanent way of life. Thus, even with high unemployment, prices can continue to climb. In such a situation, the government is forced into the difficult choice of fighting inflation at the cost of continued high unemployment or reducing unem-ployment at the cost of runaway inflation.

5. Fiscal and monetary policy must be *effectively coordinated* for optimal results. Unless they are, one may offset the other. But the president and Congress largely determine fiscal policy, while the independent Federal Reserve Board deter-mines monetary policy. Occasionally, the Fed has disagreed with politicians about what policy should be applied at what time. The Fed is frequently more concerned with inflation than are the president and Congress (who are usually more concerned with unemployment).

It is difficult for any democratically elected government to curb inflation by deliberate "belt tightening," that is, by cutting down government spending, increas-ing taxes, and holding down the supply of money and credit. Although these pol-icies are *economically* sound in an inflationary period, they are *politically* unpop-ular. Members of Congress (and elected officials in other democratic nations) are reluctant to cut favorite spending programs, to confront their constituents with a tax increase, or to allow unemployment to rise as a result of cutbacks in the supply of money and credit for business expansion and home buying. In short, good eco-nomics is not always good politics.

Supply-Side Economics

supply-side econom-ics
government policies designed to increase the supply of goods and services through incentives to work, save, and produce

Keynesian economics emphasizes the *demand side* of the economy—increasing government spending and expanding the money supply in periods of recession and doing the opposite in periods of inflation. In other words, Keynesian economics calls for government manipulation of aggregate (total) demand for goods and ser-vices. However, today many economists are calling for increased attention to the *supply side* of the economy—to government activities that affect the aggregate sup-ply of goods and services. High government tax rates and costly regulations reduce incentives for Americans to work, save, invest, and produce. Supply-side econo-mists believe that government should act to increase incentives to produce. Increased production will keep prices down (reduce inflation) and open up new employment opportunities (avoid recession).

marginal tax rates
tax rates applied to additional income

Central to supply-side economics is the idea of reducing *marginal rates of tax-ation.* (The marginal rate of taxation is the rate at which *additional* income is taxed.) Before 1981, the marginal rates of the federal personal income tax ranged

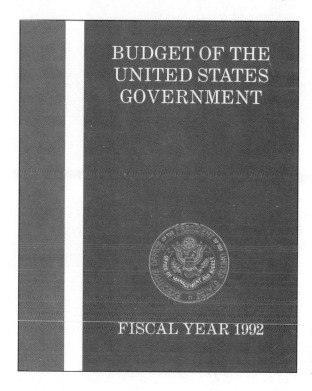

BUDGET OF THE
UNITED STATES
GOVERNMENT

FISCAL YEAR 1992

The president submits 2,000
pages of budget
recommendations to Congress.

from 14 to 70 percent. Supply-side economists argued that these high marginal rates of taxation (especially the 50- to 70-percent brackets) reduced economic output and productivity. People will prefer leisure time over extra work if, for example, 50 percent of the additional money they make from the extra work is "snatched away" by income taxes. Individuals will not risk their money in new business investments if, for example, 70 percent of the income from the investment will be taken away by income tax. High marginal tax rates also encourage people to seek out "tax shelters," special provisions in the tax laws that reduce personal income taxes. Tax shelters direct money to special investments (municipal bonds, commercial property, movies, horse farms, and so on) that are not really important for the nation's economic health. In addition, a large "underground economy" flourishes when tax rates are high; in the underground economy people hide their real incomes and/or trade goods and services rather than conduct transactions out in the open where they will be subject to taxation.

Taxes discourage work, productivity, investment, and economic growth. If tax rates are reduced, the paradoxical result may be to *increase* government revenue because more people will work harder and start new businesses knowing they can keep a larger share of their earnings. Economist Arthur Laffer developed the diagram, known as the *Laffer curve,* shown in Figure 6-3. If the government imposed a zero tax rate, of course, the government would receive no revenue (point A). Initially, government revenues rise with increases in the tax rate. However, when tax rates become too high (beyond point B), they discourage workers and busi-

results of high marginal tax rates
less work

less investment risk

more unproductive "tax shelters"

a large "underground economy" hiding income

Laffer curve
lower tax rates may increase government revenue

high marginal tax rates actually reduce government revenue by discouraging production and investment

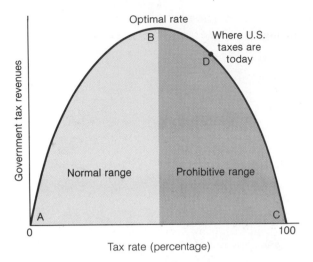

FIGURE 6-3 The Laffer curve

nesses from producing and investing. When discouragement occurs, the economy declines, and government revenues fall. Indeed, if the government imposed a 100-percent tax rate (if the government confiscated everything anyone produced), then everyone would quit working and government revenues would fall to zero (point C).

When the Reagan administration arrived in Washington in 1981, its first priority was to reduce high marginal rates of income taxation in the hope of stimulating **Economic Recovery** economic growth. The *Economic Recovery Tax Cut Act of 1981* pushed through **Tax Cut Act of 1981** Congress by President Reagan reduced marginal tax rates from a range of 14 to 70 **Tax Reform Act of** percent to a range of 11 to 50 percent; this was only a minor reduction at the bottom **1986** end of the income bracket, but it was a significant reduction in the highest income bracket. The *Tax Reform Act of 1986* set marginal tax rates at 15 and 28 percent. A zero bracket plus personal exemptions ensured that poor working families would pay no income taxes. (However, they still had to pay Social Security taxes.) Again, the incentive effect of this reduction in rates was greatest in the top bracket. Indeed, considering both the 1981 and 1986 tax law changes, the top marginal rate came down from 70 to 28 percent during the Reagan years.

tax cut results These tax rate reductions succeeded in stimulating the economy. The United economic growth States experienced the longest period of continuous GNP growth in its history. Run-more jobs away inflation was halted, unemployment was reduced from double-digit levels, huge government defi- and the number and proportion of Americans with jobs reached all-time highs. cits However, the incentive effects of the tax cuts did not produce enough new tax revenues to make up for lower rates. Tax revenues lagged far behind federal expenditures. Neither President Reagan, President Bush, nor Congress was willing to cut expenditures enough to reduce the gap between lower taxes and continued high spending levels. This resulted in the largest deficits in the nation's history.

By 1990 the pressure of these government deficits forced President Bush to abandon his campaign pledge, "Read my lips: no new taxes!" and agree to increase the top tax rate from 28 to 31 percent. But the ensuing recession caused government revenues to stagnate despite the higher tax rate, and government deficits soared to new heights.

Measuring America's Wealth: National Income Accounting

Underlying the power of nations is the strength of their economy—their total productive capacity. The United States can produce nearly $6 trillion worth of goods and services in a single year for its 250 million people. This is approximately $22,000 worth of output per person. To understand America's vast wealth, we must learn how to measure it. We need to know where the wealth comes from and where it goes. The system of *national income accounts* provides these measures.

Let us begin with the gross national product. *The GNP is the nation's total production of goods and services for a single year valued in terms of market prices.* It is the sum of all the goods and services that people have been willing to pay for, from wheat production to bake sales, from machine tools to maid service, from aircraft manufacturing to bus service, from automobiles to chewing gum, from wages and salaries to interest on bank deposits.

The GNP is also the total income received by all sellers of goods and services. It really does not matter whether we view the GNP as the *value* of all goods and services *produced*, or the sum of all *expenditures* on these goods and services, for they are the same thing. (See Box 6-2 for a discussion of the relationship between a nation's GNP and its standard of living.)

To compute the GNP, economists sum up all the expenditures on goods and services, plus government purchases. Care is taken to count *only the final product* sold to consumers so that raw materials will not be counted twice, that is, in the original sale to a manufacturer and in the final price of the product. Business investment includes *only new investment goods* (buildings, machinery, and so on) and does not include financial transfers such as the purchase of stocks and bonds. Government purchases for goods and services include the money spent on *goods* (weapons, roads, buildings, parks, and so on), as well as the *wages* paid for the *services* of government employees. "Transfer payments" such as welfare payments, unemployment insurance, and Social Security payments are *not* part of the GNP because they are not payments for currently produced goods or services. Thus, the GNP becomes a measure of the nation's production of goods and services. It can be thought of as the total national pie for a given year, and it is the most widely used measure of total national production.

National income accounting helps us understand the circular flow that makes up the *income* and *expenditure* sides of the GNP. Figure 6-4 shows the circular flow of goods and services. Note that the GNP is composed of consumer outlays, plus business investment, plus government purchases of goods and services. Table 6-2 shows national income accounting figures for 1990. The *net national product* is the sum of all goods and services produced (GNP) less "depreciation," that is, the wearing out of producer goods that must be replaced to maintain the nation's productive capacities. The *national income* is the total of all income earned by the

GNP (gross national product)
total value of nation's production of goods and services for a year

computing the GNP

GNP – depreciation = net national product

net national product – indirect business taxes = national income

TABLE 6-2 National Income Accounting and the GNP, 1990

	Billions of dollars
Gross national product	5,519
Less capital consumption (depreciation of capital goods that must be replaced)	− 585
Net national product	4,934
Less indirect business taxes (sales, excise, property taxes)	− 482
National income	4,452
Less corporate profit taxes	− 301
Net interest	− 468
Social Security taxes	− 511
Plus government transfer payments (Social Security, welfare)	661
Personal interest income	685
Dividends	125
Business transfer payments	35
Personal income	4,678
Less personal taxes	− 710
Disposable personal income	3,968
Personal savings	− 166
Consumer outlays	3,802

Source: Economic Report of the President 1991.

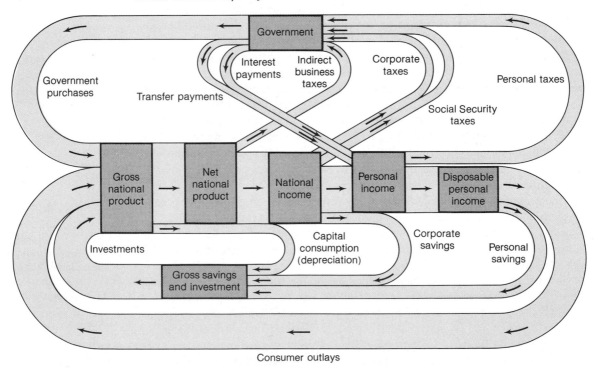

FIGURE 6-4 Circular flow of goods and services

basic factors of production—land, labor, capital, and management—less indirect business taxes. The national income is always less than the net national product because the factors of production do not actually receive the full value of their output; businesses must pay many indirect taxes to the government, which cuts down on the income left to pay for the factors of production. *Personal income* is the total received by all individuals in the country—the amount people actually have to spend or to save to pay their taxes. Personal income includes government transfer payments to individuals, mainly Social Security and welfare payments. Personal income is what remains of national income after corporations have paid their income taxes, made their Social Security contributions, and decided on their corporate savings (that is, how much they want to plow back into the business rather than pay out to stockholders). *Disposable personal income* is what people have left after they pay their taxes. Disposable personal income goes either to *personal savings* or to *consumer outlays.*

personal income – personal taxes = disposable personal income

disposable personal income – personal savings = consumer outlays

Because prices have increased over time through inflation, to get a meaningful measure of actual growth and output we must view the gross national product in

---

BOX 6-2

Cross-National Perspective: GNP and Standards of Living

A nation's GNP is the most common measure of its total production of goods and services. National income accounting is highly refined in the Western industrialized nations. But figures for Third World nations are often estimates by agencies of the United Nations or the United States. In the past, the Soviet Union and other communist nations were very secretive about economic data, and they frequently misrepresented economic statistics in order to conceal weaknesses in their system. (For example, the GNP figure in Table 6-3 for the Soviet Union, $2,460 billion for 1987, may overestimate output for that year by $600 to $800 billion.) Nonetheless, we can compare the relative size of national economies, as well as the distribution of some key consumer items, by observing Table 6-3, which presents selected data from the UN *Statistical Yearbook.*

The United States is the world's largest national economy. However, the European Economic Community, which promises to eliminate national trade barriers between the Western European nations and to create a single united economy, may eventually create a larger market than the United States. Third World nations, despite accounting for three-fourths of the world's population, have very modest GNPs.

Productivity, or economic output per person, is frequently measured by GNP per person. Note that although the United States has the largest economy, productivity in several nations equals or exceeds productivity in the United States. Japan, for example, has an economy slightly over half the size of the United States; but Japan has a population of only 125 million, compared to 250 million in the United States. This means that productivity in Japan, measured by GNP per capita, is slightly greater than in the United States.

The United States is the most consumer-oriented society in the world. Americans enjoy more consumer items—automobiles, telephones, television sets, and many other goods—than any other people. Note that the Japanese, despite their high per capita aggregate output, do not generally enjoy the same high standard of living as the average American. Many consumer items that Americans consider necessities are rarities in Third World countries. For example, although there is one automobile for every 1.8 Americans, there is only one automobile for every 1,075 Chinese.

(continued)

BOX 6-2

(continued)

TABLE 6-3 Cross-National Perspective: GNP and Standards of Living in Selected Nations, 1987

	GNP (billions of dollars)	GNP (per capita)	Automobiles (persons per car)	Telephones (per 100 people)	Television sets (per 1,000 people)
United States	4,527	18,570	1.8	76.0	811
Brazil	291	1,980	16.0	9.3	191
Canada	402	15,550	2.2	78.0	577
China	470	438	1,075.0	0.7	17
France	868	15,620	2.5	60.8	333
India	246	307	566.0	0.6	7
Italy	703	13,010	2.5	48.8	257
Japan	2,369	19,410	4.2	55.5	587
Mexico	139	1,701	16.0	9.6	120
Pakistan	34	327	404.0	0.7	14
Philippines	35	563	173.7	1.5	36
Poland	260	6,879	9.6	12.2	263
South Korea	118	2,796	54.0	25.5	194
Soviet Union	2,460	6,662	22.0	11.3	194
Spain	284	7,282	3.9	39.6	314
Turkey	66	1,235	46.0	9.1	172
United Kingdom	667	11,730	2.8	52.4	434
Germany	1,075	18,450	2.1	65.0	395

Source: Statistical Abstract of the United States 1990, pp. 840, 843, 844.

actual and "dollar" increases

constant dollars. Doubling the GNP merely by doubling prices signifies no real gain in production, so in order to separate *actual increases* in the GNP from mere *"dollar" increases,* we must adjust for changes in the value of the dollar over the years. Economists account for changes in the value of a dollar by establishing the value of a dollar in a particular time base (for example, 1982) and then using constant dollars to measure the value of goods over time. Figure 6-5 shows that the GNP has grown both in current dollars *and* in constant dollars. Thus, America's economic growth is not just a product of inflation. Between 1970 and 1990 the gross national product in current dollars rose from $1 trillion to $5.5 trillion. Even with inflation taken into account, the growth is still real: in constant dollars, from about $2.4 trillion to $4.2 trillion. GNP growth reflects economic cycles, growing over 4 percent a year on the upswing and actually declining during recessions.

Public Sector Economics

Governments in the United States—the federal government, together with fifty state governments and eighty thousand local governments—account for about 35

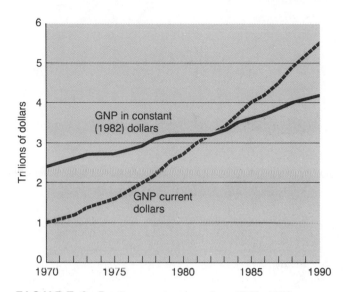

FIGURE 6-5   Gross national product, 1970–1990.
Source: Statistical Abstract of the United States 1988. Washington, D.C.: U.S. Government Printing Office, 1988, p. 406.

percent of the gross national product. The goods and services produced by these governments include Social Security and welfare, health and hospitals, education, highways, police and fire protection, and national defense (see Figure 6-6).

Government employment—federal, state, and local—constitutes more than 15 percent of the total civilian labor force. About one of every six workers is employed by the government.

Obviously, government plays a very important role in our economy. Nonetheless, the United States remains primarily a private, free enterprise economy. In Great Britain and France, the governmental proportion of the GNP is 40 to 45 percent; in Sweden and Israel, it is 55 to 60 percent; and in socialist bloc nations, Cuba and the Soviet Union, the governmental percentage of the GNP is 85 to 90 percent.

The federal government itself accounts for nearly two-thirds of all government spending in the United States. Washington's *trillion*-dollar budgets of recent years have funded national defense (20%); Social Security, Medicare, and welfare benefits paid to individuals (41%); grants to state and local governments (12%); and interest on the national debt (14%).

Federal spending far outstrips federal taxing each year. The federal government must borrow new money each year to make up the difference. This borrowing expands the national debt and forces the federal government to pay more money in interest to lenders (see Figure 6-7). The lenders include banks, insurance companies, trust funds, and private individuals—anyone who buys government bonds.

Federal, state, and local government revenues now amount to over one-third of the gross national product. Americans may consider their tax burden a heavy one, but taxes range between 35 and 51 percent of the GNP in Western European nations.

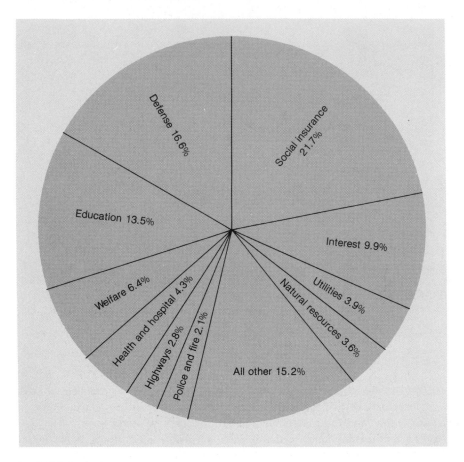

FIGURE 6-6   Total government spending (federal, state, and local) by function

The federal government relies primarily on the individual income tax and the Social Security payroll tax for its income. State governments rely primarily on sales taxes, although forty-three states also tax personal income. Local governments rely primarily on property taxes.

governing the corporation

"inside" and "outside" directors

The modern corporation is governed by its board of directors. The directors include the chairman of the board, the president, selected senior vice-presidents, and some "outside" members who are not managers of the corporation. The "inside" directors, who are also full-time presidents or vice-presidents of the corporation, tend to dominate board proceedings because they know more about the day-to-day operations of the corporation than the outside directors do. Outside directors may sit on the corporate board as representatives of families who still own large blocks of stock or of banks that have lent money to the corporation. Occasionally, outside directors are prominent citizens, women, members of minorities, or representatives of civic associations. Outside directors are usually chosen by inside directors. All directors are officially elected by the corporation's stockholders. However, the inside directors draw up the "management slate," which almost

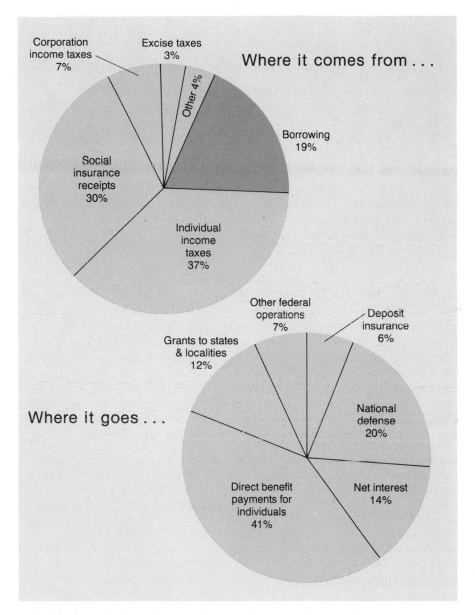

FIGURE 6-7   The federal government dollar
Source: Budget of the United States Government, 1992.

always wins, because top management (the presidents and vice-presidents) cast many "proxy" votes, which they solicit in advance from stockholders.

A. A. Berle, Jr., a corporate lawyer and director himself, referred to the corporate directors as "a self-perpetuating oligarchy."[4] Corporate power does *not* rest in the hands of masses of corporate employees or even in the hands of millions of middle- and upper-middle-class Americans who own corporate stock.

Power in the corporate boardroom.
Source: Spencer Grant/Photo Researchers

**interlocking director-
ates**
a director of one corpo-
ration is also a director
of other corporations

Corporate power is further concentrated by a system of *interlocking directorates,* in which a director of one corporation also sits on the boards of other corporations, and by a *corporate ownership* system in which control blocks of stock are owned by financial institutions rather than by private individuals. Interlocking directorates enable the key corporate elite to wield influence over a large number of corporations. It is not uncommon for members of the top elite to hold six, eight, or ten directorships.

Berle argues that *managers,* rather than major stockholders, have come to exercise dominant influence in American corporations:

management control
stock ownership is
scattered among many
small investors and
management controls
the corporation itself

> Management control is a phrase meaning merely that no large concentrated stock-holding exists which maintains a close working relationship with the management or is capable of challenging it, so that the board of directors may regularly expect a majority, composed of small and scattered holdings, to follow their lead. Thus, they need not consult with anyone when making up their slate of directors, and may simply request their stockholders to sign and send in a ceremonial proxy. They select their own successors. . . . Nominal power still resides in the stockholders; actual power in the board of directors.[5]

The Corporate Managers

Today the requirements of technology and planning have greatly increased industry's need for specialized talent and skill in organization. Capital is something a corporation can now supply to itself. Thus, there is a shift in power in the American economy from capital to management.

**decline of the individ-
ual investor**

Individual capitalists are no longer essential to the accumulation of capital for investment. Approximately three-fifths of industrial capital now comes from retained earnings of corporations rather than from the investments of individual capitalists. Another one-fifth of industrial capital is borrowed, chiefly from banks. Even though the remaining one-fifth of the capital funds of industry comes from

BOX 6-3

The Concentration of Corporate Power

Control over the nation's economic resources is becoming increasingly concentrated in the hands of very few people, largely because of the *consolidation of economic enterprise* into a small number of giant corporations. The following statistics can only suggest the scale and concentration of modern corporate enterprise in the United States: there are over 200,000 industrial corporations in the United States, but the 100 largest corporations hold over half of the nation's industrial assets. Indeed, just ten industrial corporations hold 24 percent of the nation's industrial assets (see Table 6-4). Concentration in banking is even greater. There are nearly fifteen thousand banks in the United States, but the ten largest banks hold 36 percent of all banking assets (see Table 6-5). The rate of corporate mergers in recent years suggests that this concentration of economic resources is increasing.

TABLE 6-4 The Concentration of Economic Power (Industrial Corporations)

Rank	Corporation	Assets (millions of dollars)	Cumulative % of all U.S. industrial assets
1	General Motors	180,237	7.5
2	Ford Motor	173,663	14.7
3	General Electric	153,884	21.1
4	Exxon	87,707	24.8
5	International Business Machines	87,568	28.5
6	Philip Morris	46,569	30.4
7	Chrysler	46,374	32.3
8	Mobil	41,665	34.0
9	Du Pont	38,128	35.6
10	Chevron	35,089	37.1
11	RJR Nabisco	32,915	38.5
12	Amoco	32,209	39.8
13	Xerox	31,495	41.1
14	Shell Oil	28,496	42.3
15	Texaco	25,975	43.4
16	Eastman Kodak	24,125	44.4
17	Dow Chemical	23,953	45.4
18	Atlantic Richfield	23,864	46.4
19	Westinghouse	22,033	47.3
20	Occidental Petroleum	19,743	48.1
21	Tenneco	19,034	48.9
22	Procter & Gamble	18,487	49.7
23	USX	17,268	50.4
24	Pepsico	17,143	51.1
25	Weyerhaeuser	16,356	51.8

Total of all U.S. industrial assets = $2,397,942

Source: Data derived from "Rank 1990," *Fortune* Vol. 120, April 23, 1990.

(continued)

BOX 6-3

(continued)

TABLE 6-5   The Concentration of Economic Power (Banks)

Rank	Corporation	Assets (millions of dollars)	Cumulative % of all U.S. industrial assets
1	Citicorp	216,986	6.9
2	BankAmerica	110,728	10.4
3	Chase Manhattan	98,064	13.5
4	J P Morgan	93,103	16.5
5	Security Pacific	84,731	19.2
6	Chemical Bank	73,019	21.5
7	NCNB Corp.	65,284	23.6
8	Bankers Trust	63,596	25.6
9	Manufacturers Hanover	61,530	27.6
10	Wells Fargo	56,198	29.4
11	First Interstate	51,356	31.0
12	C & S	51,237	32.6
13	First Chicago	50,779	34.2
14	PNC Financial	45,533	35.7
15	Bank of New York	45,389	37.1
16	First Union	40,781	38.4
17	Suntrust	33,411	39.5
18	Bank of Boston	32,529	40.5
19	Fleet/Norstar	32,507	41.5
20	Barnett	32,214	42.5
21	Norwest	30,626	43.5
22	Banc one	30,336	44.5
23	Republic New York	29,597	45.5
24	First Fidelity	29,110	46.4
25	Mellon Bank	28,762	47.4

Total assets (millions of dollars) = 3,130.8
Domestic assets (millions of dollars) = 2,726.1

Source: Data derived from "Rank by Assets 1990," *Fortune* Vol. 120, May 10, 1990.

"outside" investments, the bulk of these funds is from large insurance companies, mutual funds, and pension trusts rather than from individual investors. Thus *the individual capitalist investor is no longer in a position of dominance in American capital formation.* (See Box 6-3.)

Corporate power is exercised by managers of large corporations and financial institutions (see Box 6-4). Stockholders are supposed to have ultimate power over management, but individual stockholders seldom have any control over the activities of the corporations they own. Usually "management slates" for the board of

BOX 6-4

The CEOs: Who's at the Top

Who are the people who run corporate America? What are they like? Where did they go to school? *Business Week* magazine surveyed the chief executive officers (CEOs) of the nation's one thousand largest corporations. (See Tables 6-6 and 6-7). Here are some of the results:

Age   The average CEO is fifty-six years old; only nineteen were under forty; seventy were over sixty-five.

Place of birth   Nearly 40 percent were born in one of five states—New York, New Jersey, Pennsylvania, Illinois, and Ohio. Other large states, California and Texas, contributed less than 3 percent each.

Salary   The CEOs' average paycheck was $651,000 in 1986, with a high of $13 million.

Family   Ninety-nine percent were married; ninety percent had children, and sixty-three percent had three or more children. In a country where nearly 40 percent

of marriages end in divorce, 84 percent of CEOs have intact first marriages.

Education   Only 5 percent never attended college. Nearly half have graduate degrees, and half of these graduate degrees are MBAs. Leading undergraduate universities include Yale, Princeton, Harvard, Northwestern, University of Pennsylvania, Cornell, University of Wisconsin, Stanford, University of Michigan, and MIT. Leading graduate schools include Harvard, Columbia, University of Pennsylvania, MIT, and Stanford.

None of the CEOs of the one thousand largest corporations were African American, and only two, Katherine Graham of the Washington Post Company and Liz Claiborne of Liz Claiborne clothing, were women.

TABLE 6-6   The Most Powerful People in Corporate America

Industrial corporation	Chief executive/age (1990)	Education (undergraduate/graduate)	Total compensation (1990)
General Motors	Roger Smith/65	Michigan '47 M.B.A., Michigan '49	$1,629,000
Exxon	Lawrence G. Rawl/63	Oklahoma '52	1,385,000
International Business Machines	John F. Akers/57	Yale '56	713,000
Ford Motor	Harold Poling/66	Monmouth '49 M.B.A., Indiana '51	2,149,000
Mobil	Allen E. Murray/62	New York University '56	1,675,000
General Electric	John F. Welch/55	Massachusetts '57 Ph.D., Illinois '60	2,649,000
American Telephone and Telegraph	Robert E. Allen/56	Wabash '57	1,744,000
Chevron	Kenneth T. Derr/55	Cornell '59 M.B.A., Cornell '60	948,000
Texaco	James W. Kinnear/63	U.S. Naval Academy '50	1,793,000
E. I. du Pont de Nemours	Edgar S. Woolard, Jr./57	North Carolina State '56	1,474,000

(continued)

BOX 6-4

(continued)

TABLE 6-6   *(continued)*

Industrial corporation	Chief executive/age (1990)	Education (undergraduate/graduate)	Total compensation (1990)
Amoco	Richard M. Morrow/65	Ohio State '48	1,559,000
Atlantic Richfield	Lodwrick M. Cook/63	Louisiana State '50 M.B.A., SMU '65	1,916,000
Chrysler	Lee A. Iacocca/67	Lehigh '45 M.E., Princeton '46	1,414,000
USX	Charles A. Corry/59	University of Cincinnati '55 J.D., Cincinnati Law '59	1,347,000
Philip Morris	Hamish Maxwell/65	Cambridge '49	1,877,000
Tenneco	James L. Ketelsen/61	Northwestern '52	1,636,000
Occidental Petroleum	Armand Hammer/93	Columbia '19 M.D., Columbia '21	2,334,000
Eastman Kodak	Kay R. Whitmore/59	University of Utah '57 M.B.A., Indiana State '59	963,000
Procter & Gamble	Edwin L. Artzt/61	University of Oregon '51	1,436,000
ITT	Rand V. Araskog/60	U.S. Military Academy '53	2,388,000
Sun	Robert McClements/63	Drexel '52	938,000
Boeing	Frank A. Shrontz/60	Idaho '54 M.B.A., Harvard '58	910,000
Phillips Petroleum	C. J. Silas/59	Georgia Tech '53	1,240,000

TABLE 6-7   The Most Powerful People in Commercial Banking

Commercial bank	Chief executive/age	Education (undergraduate/graduate)	Total compensation
Citicorp	John S. Reed/52	MIT '61 M.S., MIT '65	$1,484,000
BankAmerica Corp.	Richard M. Rosenberg/ 61	Suffolk '52 M.B.A., Golden Gate '63 L.L.B., Golden Gate '66	1,250,000

(continued)

BOX 6-4

(continued)

TABLE 6-7 *(continued)*

Commercial bank	Chief executive/age	Education (undergraduate/graduate)	Total compensation
Chase Manhattan Corp.	Thomas G. Labrecque/ 53	Villanova '60	942,000
Manufacturers Hanover Corp.	J. F. McGillicuddy/61	Princeton '52 L.L.B., Harvard '55	1,680,000
Security Pacific Corp.	Robert H. Smith/56	USC '57 J.D., Van Norman Law '66	1,028,000
Chemical New York Corp.	Walter V. Shipley/56	New York University '61	1,120,000
Bankers Trust New York Corp.	Charles S. Sanford/55	Georgia '58 M.B.A., Pennsylvania '60	1,500,000
First Interstate Bancorp.	Edward M. Carson/62	Arizona State '51	731,000
Wells Fargo & Co.	Carl E. Reichhardt/60	USC '56	1,523,000
First Chicago Corp.	Barry F. Sullivan/61	Columbia '55 M.B.A., Chicago '57	1,461,000
Mellon Bank Corp.	Frank V. Cahouet/59	Harvard '54 M.B.A., Pennsylvania '59	1,062,000
Bank of Boston Corp.	Ira Stepanian/55	Tufts '58 M.B.A., Boston College '71	1,248,000
Continental Illinois Corp.	Thomas C. Theobald/ 54	Holy Cross '58 M.B.A., Harvard '60	1,150,000
First Bank System	John F. Grundhoffer/52	Loyola '60 M.B.A., USC '64	NA
NCNB Corp.	Hugh L. McColl/62	North Carolina '57	1,500,000
First Union Corp.	Edward E. Crutchfield/ 50	Davidson '63 M.B.A., Pennsylvania '65	1,020,000
Suntrust Banks	James B. Williams/58	Emory '55	471,000
PNC Financial Corp.	Thomas H. O'Brien/54	Notre Dame '58 M.B.A., Harvard '62	1,489,000
Norwest Corp.	Lloyd P. Johnson/61	Carleton '52 M.B.A., Stanford '54	1,291,000
NBD Bancorp.	Charles T. Fisher/62	Georgetown '51 M.B.A., Harvard '53	1,210,000

directors are selected by management and automatically approved by stockholders. Banks and financial institutions and pension-trust or mutual-fund managers occasionally get together to replace a management-selected board of directors. But, more often than not, banks and trust funds sell their stock in corporations whose management they distrust, rather than using the voting power of their stock to replace management. Generally, banks and trust funds vote their stock for the management slate. This policy of *nonaction by investors* means that the directors and management of corporations become increasingly self-appointed and unchallengeable; and this policy freezes absolute power in the corporate management.

nonaction by investors

Of course, the *profit motive* is still important to the corporate managers because profits are the basis of capital formation within the corporation. Increased capital at the disposal of corporate managers means increased power; losses mean a decrease in the capital available to the managers, a decrease in their power, and perhaps eventual extinction for the organization.

profit motive

But there is increasing evidence that the corporate managers put *personal motives,* especially their own pay, benefits, and perquisites, above the interests of their corporation and its stockholders. The pay of CEOs of America's largest corporations has mushroomed in recent years, as has the pay of corporate directors. A $5 million annual salary is no longer uncommon, even in corporations that are losing money. The average CEO in the 365 largest corporations in 1990 took home nearly $2 million in pay and benefits.[6]

personal motive

The average CEO of a large American corporation makes eighty-five times the pay of the average factory worker. (In Japan, by contrast, the average CEO receives only seventeen times the pay of an ordinary worker.) This executive pay gap has widened each year over the last decade. Of course, it can be argued that entertainment and sports stars earn even more than CEOs. Madonna reportedly earned $25 million in 1990; Arnold Schwartzenegger, $32 million; and baseball pitchers Roger Clemens and Dwight Gooden, over $5 million. But these incomes were directly related to the ability of these persons to attract fans, audiences, viewers, and customers, and thus to make profits for the companies that paid their salaries. In contrast, CEO salaries have gone up even when corporate profits have gone down. Boards of directors are supposed to oversee top executive pay and protect stockholders, but CEOs generally win approval for their own salaries from compliant directors.

Notes

1. Adam Smith, *The Wealth of Nations* (New York: Modern Library), p. 423.
2. J. Roland Pennock, *Liberal Democracy: Its Merits and Prospects* (New York: Holt, 1950), p. 333.
3. Richard Hofstadter, *American Political Tradition* (New York: Knopf, 1948), p. 332.
4. A. A. Berle, Jr., *Economic Power and the Free Society* (New York: Fund for the Republic, 1958), p. 14.
5. A. A. Berle, Jr., *Power without Property* (New York: Harcourt Brace Jovanovich, 1959), p. 73. See also Ferdinand Lundberg, *The Rich and the Super Rich* (New York: Stuart, 1968).
6. *Business Week,* May 8, 1991, pp. 90–112.

About This Chapter

In this chapter we have examined the content of economic decisions and observed how individuals, government, and corporations make them. Now that you have read it, you should be able to

- describe the operation of the market in a private enterprise economy;
- define the various cycles an economy experiences;
- discuss the reasons that government intervenes in the economy, thus creating a "mixed" economic system, and some of the means by which government does this;

- define supply-side economics and discuss its policy implications;
- discuss the growth of multinational corporations;
- describe how the wealth of the United States is measured and discuss some of the shortcomings of this system of measurement;
- discuss personal wealth in the United States and the increasing concentration of corporate power; and
- discuss the causes of inflation and various proposals to deal with it.

Discussion Questions

1. Identify the components of an economic system. Discuss how the market in a private enterprise economy determines what is to be produced, how much it will cost, and who will be able to buy it. Comment on the roles that the following factors play in a market operation: consumer demands, profits, prices, willingness to pay and ability to pay, labor market, competition, product supply.

2. Describe the ideal conditions for a market operation in a free enterprise system. What are the reasons for government interference in such a system?

3. Discuss the similarities between laissez faire (classical) economics and a traditional democratic political system. Describe the conflict between laissez faire economics and Keynesian economics over the self-adaptability of the free enterprise system.

4. Describe the kinds of fiscal and monetary policies that a Keynesian economist would recommend during a recessionary period and an inflationary period. How do the automatic stabilizers work during each of these periods?

5. Discuss some of the problems the government has in using fiscal and monetary policies.

6. Define supply-side economics. What government policies are proposed by supply-side economists?

7. Explain how economists compute the gross national product (GNP). Differentiate between actual increases in the GNP and "dollar" increases in GNP. Describe some of the weaknesses of the GNP measure and some of the alternative measures that social scientists have suggested. What are the difficulties with *these* measures?

8. What proportion of the GNP is produced by all governments—federal, state, and local—in the United States? What are the major sources of revenue of the *federal* government, and what are its major spending categories?

9. Discuss the reasons for the increasing concentration of corporate power in the United States. Describe the factors contributing to the power of corporate management.

Power and

Government

Politics, Political Science, and Governmental Power

politics
the study of power

A distinguished American political scientist, Harold Lasswell, defined *politics* as "who gets what, when, and how." "The study of politics," he said, "is the study of influence and the influential. The influential are those who get the most of what there is to get. . . . Those who get the most are the *elite;* the rest are *mass.*" He went on to define *political science* as the study of "the shaping and sharing of power."

Admittedly, Lasswell's definition of political science is very broad. Indeed, if we accept Lasswell's definition of political science as *the study of power,* then political science includes cultural, economic, social, and personal power relationships—topics we have already discussed in chapters on anthropology, economics, sociology, and psychology.

Although some political scientists have accepted Lasswell's challenge to study power in all its forms in society, most limit the definition of political science to *the study of government.*

distinguishing governmental power
the legitimate use of force; coverage of the whole society

What distinguishes *governmental power* from the power of other institutions, groups, and individuals? The power of government, unlike that of other institutions in society, is distinguished by (1) *the legitimate use of physical force* and (2) *coverage of the whole society* rather than only segments of it. Because governmental decisions extend to the whole of society and because only government can legitimately use physical force, government has the primary responsibility for maintaining order and for resolving differences that arise *between* segments of society. Thus, government must regulate conflict by establishing and enforcing general rules by which conflict is to be carried on in society, by arranging compromises and balancing interests, and by imposing settlements that the parties in the dispute must accept. In other words, government lays down the "rules of the game" in conflict and competition between individuals, organizations, and institutions within society.

The Concerns of Political Science

Political scientists ever since Plato have constructed ideal political systems—notions of what a *good* "polity" should be. Today we refer to efforts to devise *good* political systems as *political philosophy.* Political philosophy concerns itself with political norms and values: criteria for judging the "rightness" or "wrongness" of governmental structures and actions. In Chapter 9 we discuss political ideologies—liberalism, conservatism, communism, socialism, and fascism—and examine these political philosophies more closely.

political philosophy
the study of political norms and values

Aristotle's classification of governments

Political science also concerns itself with describing *political systems.* Schemes for classifying political systems are as old as the study of politics itself. Aristotle, for example, produced a classification based on two criteria: (1) the number of citizens who could participate in making rules: one, few, or many; and (2) whether the rulers governed in "the common interest" or in their own selfish interest. Aristotle's classification system (Table 7-1) included six types of government. Note that Aristotle believed "democracy" was a corrupt form of government in which the

TABLE 7-1 Aristotle's Classification of
                      Governments

Number of persons who rule	Interests served	
	Common	*Selfish*
One	Monarchy	Tyranny
Few	Aristocracy	Oligarchy
Many	Polity	Democracy

masses pursued their selfish interests at the expense of the common good. Not until the nineteenth century did the word *democracy* come to have a positive connotation.

Political scientists are also concerned with the *political processes and behaviors* among individuals and groups. The study of political processes and behaviors goes beyond the study of political philosophy and the study of political systems. It asks how voters, interest groups, parties, legislators, executives, bureaucrats, judges, and other political actors behave and why. Social scientists who explore these questions are known as *behavioral* political scientists. Behavioral political scientists study the way individuals acquire political values and attitudes and how those values and attitudes shape their political activity; why people vote as they do or choose not to vote at all; how and why interest groups are formed and what influence they have on governments; how and why city council members and state and national legislators vote as they do on pieces of legislation; what motivates the actions of mayors, governors, and presidents; what influences the decisions of judges; what the attitudes and functions of political parties are before and after elections; and so on.

political processes and behaviors

But political philosophy and ideology, the structure of governments, and the behavior of political figures can seldom be studied separately. Discovering how these important areas of study interact is essential for a better understanding of power in society.

The Meaning of Democracy

Ideally, *democracy* means *individual participation* in the decisions that affect one's life. In traditional democratic theory, popular participation has been valued as an opportunity for individual self-development. Responsibility for governing one's own conduct develops character, self-reliance, intelligence, and moral judgment— in short, dignity. Even if a benevolent king could govern in the public interest, the true democrat would reject him.

1. popular participation in government

Procedurally, popular participation was to be achieved through *majority rule* and *respect for the rights of minorities*. Self-development means *self-government*, and self-government can be accomplished only by encouraging each individual to contribute to the creation of public policy and by resolving conflicts over public policy through majority rule. Minorities who had had the opportunity to influence policy but whose views had not succeeded in winning majority support would accept the decisions of majorities. In return, majorities would permit minorities to attempt

2. majority rule, with minority rights

Democracy means individual participation in government.
Source: Robert Fox/Impact Visuals

openly to win majority support for their views. Freedom of speech and press, freedom to dissent, and freedom to form opposition parties and organizations are essential to ensure meaningful individual participation.

3. the value of individual dignity

The underlying value of democracy is *individual dignity.* Human beings, by virtue of their existence, are entitled to life, liberty, and the pursuit of happiness. Governmental control over the individual should be kept to a minimum; this means the removal of as many external restrictions, controls, and regulations on the individual as possible without infringing on the freedom of other citizens.

4. equality of opportunity

Another vital aspect of classic democracy is a belief in the *equality* of all people. The Declaration of Independence expresses the conviction that "all men are created equal." The Founders believed in equality *before the law,* notwithstanding the circumstances of the accused. A person was not to be judged by social position, economic class, creed, or race. Many early democrats also believed in *political equality,* that is, equal opportunity to influence public policy. Political equality is expressed in the concept of "one person, one vote."

Over time, the notion of equality has also come to include *equality of opportunity* in all aspects of American life—social, educational, and economic, as well as political—and to encompass employment, housing, recreation, and public accommodations. All people are to have equal opportunity to develop their individual capacities to their natural limits.

In summary, democratic thinking involves the following ideas:

1. Popular participation in the decisions that shape the lives of individuals in a society;
2. Government by majority rule, with recognition of the rights of minorities to try to become majorities; these rights include the freedoms of speech, press, assembly, and petition, and the freedom to dissent, to form opposition parties, and to run for public office;
3. A commitment to individual dignity and the preservation of the liberal values of liberty and property;
4. A commitment to equal opportunity for all to develop their individual capacities.

Power in the American Constitution

The design of American federalism is found in the Constitution's division of governmental authority between the national and state governments. The Constitution sets out several types of powers: (1) the delegated powers of the national government, both enumerated and implied; (2) the reserved powers of the states; (3) concurrent powers, exercised by both national and state governments; and (4) powers denied to the national and state governments.

The Constitution also contains many specific restrictions on governmental power. The original text of the Constitution that emerged from the Philadelphia convention in 1787 did *not* contain a "Bill of Rights"—a listing of individual freedoms and restrictions on governmental power. The nation's founders argued that a specific listing of individual freedoms was unnecessary because the national government possessed only enumerated powers; the power to restrict free speech or press or religion was not an enumerated power, so the national government could not do these things. But Anti-Federalists in the state ratifying conventions were suspicious of the power of the new national government. They were not satisfied with the mere inference that the national government could not interfere with personal liberty; they wanted specific written guarantees of fundamental freedoms. The Federalist supporters of the new Constitution agreed to add a "Bill of Rights" as the first ten amendments to the Constitution in order to win ratification in the state conventions. This is why our fundamental freedoms—speech, press, religion, assembly, petition, and due process of law—appear in the Constitution as *amendments.*

States may not enter into relations with foreign states. They cannot make treaties or agreements (unless Congress consents) with other countries. In short, they have no foreign policy. Similarly, although the states have never completely given up their armies (they retain the state militia and the National Guard, with congressional consent), the national government can control these armies; and they have certainly become less significant than they once were. In the economic sphere, the states cannot coin money or create any new legal tender for payment of debts. In addition, the states cannot impair the obligation of contracts and hence cannot pass laws that invalidate private agreements. In effect, a limit is placed on changing the rules of the economic game. Finally, states may not levy import and export duties.

John Locke:
Constitutionalism

The potential power of governments has worried people for a long time. Indeed, since earliest recorded history, people have attempted to limit the powers of government, to set standards of legitimate authority, and to prevent the arbitrary use of governmental power. Of course, not all people or societies share the belief that governmental power should be limited. *Totalitarianism* is a belief that the state should be orderly, harmonious, and unified in purpose and values and that the power of government should be unlimited and all-embracing. In a totalitarian state, government exercises unlimited authority in all segments of life—the economy, education, the church, the family, and so on.

Constitutionalism is the belief that governmental power should be *limited.* A fundamental ideal of constitutionalism—"a government of laws and not of men"—suggests that those who exercise governmental authority are restricted in their use of it by a higher law. A *constitution* governs government. A constitution describes the offices and agencies of government, defines their prerogatives, prescribes how they should function, sets limits on the authority of government, and protects the freedoms of individual citizens. In other words, a constitution defines what governmental authority can and cannot do. A constitution should not be subject to change by the ordinary acts of government officials; change should come only through a process of general public consent. Most important, a constitution must truly *limit the exercise of authority by government;* the so-called constitutions of totalitarian states, which merely describe government offices and agencies but do not actually limit their powers, are not genuine constitutions.

A famous exponent of the idea of constitutional government was the English political philosopher John Locke (1632–1704). Perhaps more than anyone else, Locke inspired the political thought of our nation's founders in that critical period of American history in which the new nation won its independence and established its constitution. Locke's ideas are written into both the Declaration of Independence and the Constitution of the United States. His writings, particularly his *Essay Concerning Human Understanding* and his *Two Treatises on Civil Government,* were widely read in early America and even plagiarized in part by Thomas Jefferson in the Declaration of Independence.

According to Locke, all people possess natural rights. These rights are not granted by government but derive from human nature itself. Governments cannot deprive people of their "inalienable rights to life, liberty, and property." People are rational beings, capable of self-government and able to participate in political decision making. Locke believed that human beings formed a contract among themselves to establish a government in order to better protect their natural rights, maintain peace, and protect themselves from foreign invasion. The *social contract* that established government made for safe and peaceful living and for the secure enjoyment of one's life, liberty, and property. Thus, the ultimate *legitimacy* of government derived from a contract among the people themselves and not from gods or

(continued)

(continued)

kings. It was based on the *consent* of the governed. To safeguard their individual rights, the people agreed to be governed.

Because government was instituted as a contract to secure the rights of citizens, government itself could not violate individual rights. If government did so, it would dissolve the contract establishing it. Revolution, then, was justified if government was not serving the purpose for which it had been set up. However, according to Locke, revolution was justified only after a long period of abuses by government, not over any minor mismanagement.

Thomas Jefferson eloquently expressed Lockean ideals in the Declaration of Independence:

> We hold these truths to be self-evident, that all men are created equal, that they are endowed by their Creator with certain inalienable rights, that among these are life, liberty, and the pursuit of happiness. That to secure these rights, governments are instituted among men, deriving their just powers from the consent of the governed.

Notice that Jefferson varied slightly from Locke in his description of inalienable rights. While Locke had affirmed the right of the individual to "life, liberty, and *property,*" Jefferson substituted the more general idea in his famous formulation of the right to "life, liberty, and the *pursuit of happiness.*"

Powers Granted by the Constitution

To the National Government

Enumerated
- to coin money
- to conduct foreign relations
- to regulate interstate commerce
- to levy and collect taxes
- to declare war
- to raise and support military forces
- to establish post offices
- to establish courts inferior to the Supreme Court
- to admit new states

Implied
"To make all laws which shall be necessary and proper for carrying into execution the foregoing powers, and all other powers vested by this Constitution in the Government of the United States, or in any other department or officer thereof." (Article 1, Section 8:18)

To the National and State Governments
- to levy and collect taxes
- to borrow money

President Bush delivers the state of the union message to Congress.
Source: Doug Mills/AP/Wide World Photos

- to make and enforce laws
- to establish courts
- to provide for the general welfare
- to charter banks and corporations

TO STATE GOVERNMENTS
- to regulate intrastate commerce
- to conduct elections
- to provide for public health, safety, and morals
- to establish local governments
- to ratify amendments to the federal Constitution

Powers Denied by the Constitution

TO THE NATIONAL GOVERNMENT
- to tax articles exported from one state to another
- to change state boundaries

TO STATE GOVERNMENTS
- to tax imports or exports
- to coin money
- to enter into treaties
- to impair obligations of contracts
- to abridge the privileges or immunities of citizens

To the National and State Governments
- to grant titles of nobility
- to permit slavery
- to deny citizens the right to vote
- to deprive a person of life, liberty, or property without due process of law
- to deny any person equal protection of the law

Federalism and the Growth of Power in Washington

The Constitution *divides* power between two separate authorities, the nation and the states, each of which can directly enforce its own laws through its own courts. This arrangement is known as *federalism.*

American federalism differs from a "unitary" political system in which the central government can determine, alter, or abolish the power of the states. At the same time, American federalism differs from a "confederation of states," in which the national government depends on the states for power. In the American system, authority and power are *shared* by the national government and the states, constitutionally and practically.

The states are also units in the organizational scheme of the national government. The House of Representatives apportions members to the states by population, and state legislatures draw up their districts. Every state, regardless of population, has at least one House representative. Each state, regardless of population, elects two U.S. senators. The president is chosen by the electoral votes of the states; each state has as many electoral votes as it has senators and House representatives. Finally, three-fourths of the states must ratify amendments to the U.S. Constitution.

Over the nation's 200-year history, power has flowed toward the national government and away from the states. Major developments in the history of American federalism have contributed to national power:

1. *The Supreme Court's broad interpretation of the "necessary and proper" clause.* Chief Justice John Marshall added immeasurably to national power in *McCulloch* v. *Maryland* (1819) when he broadly interpreted the "necessary and proper" clause of Article I, Section 8, of the Constitution. In approving the establishment of a national bank (a power not specifically delegated to the national government in the Constitution), Marshall wrote:

> Let the end be legitimate, let it be within the scope of the Constitution, and all means which are appropriate, which are plainly adopted to that end, which are not prohibited but consistent with the letter and the spirit of the Constitution, are constitutional.

Since then, the "necessary and proper" clause has been called the "implied powers" clause or even the "elastic" clause, suggesting that the national government can do anything not specifically prohibited by the Constitution. Given this tradition, the courts are unlikely to hold an act of Congress unconstitutional simply because no formal constitutional grant of power gives Congress the power to act.

2. *The national government's victory in the Civil War.* The Civil War was the nation's greatest crisis in federalism. Did a state have the right to oppose federal action by force of arms? This issue was decided in the nation's bloodiest war. (Combined military and civilian casualties in the Civil War exceeded U.S. casualties

federalism
the division of power between national and state governments

sources of growing national power:

1. broad interpretation of national power in the Constitution

2. national military force

in World War II, even though the U.S. population in 1860 was only one-quarter of the population in 1940.) The same issue was at stake when the federal government sent troops to Little Rock, Arkansas, in 1957; to Oxford, Mississippi, in 1962; and to Tuscaloosa, Alabama, in 1963, to enforce desegregation; however, in these confrontations it was clear which side held the military advantage.

3. broad interpretation of interstate commerce

3. *The growth of a national economy and the broad interpretation of the interstate commerce clause.* The growth of national power under the interstate commerce clause is also an important development in American federalism. The Industrial Revolution created a national economy governable only by a national government. Yet, until the 1930s, the Supreme Court placed many obstacles in the way of government regulation of the economy. Finally, in *National Labor Relations Board* v. *Jones & Laughlin Steel Corporation* (1937), the Supreme Court recognized the principle that Congress could regulate production and distribution of goods and services for a national market under the interstate commerce clause. As a result, the national government gained control over wages, prices, production, marketing, labor relations, and all other important aspects of the national economy.

4. development of national system of civil rights enforceable in federal courts

4. *The development of a national system of civil rights and their enforcement by federal courts.* Over the years, the U.S. Supreme Court has built a national system of civil rights based on the Fourteenth Amendment. This amendment rose out of the Civil War: "No State shall . . . deprive any person of life, liberty, or property, without due process of law; nor deny to any person within its jurisdiction the equal protection of the laws." In early cases, the Supreme Court held that the general guarantee of *liberty* in the first phrase (the "due process" clause) prevents states from interfering with free speech, press, religion, and other personal liberties. Later, particularly after *Brown* v. *Board of Education of Topeka* in 1954, the Supreme Court also used the "equal protection" clause to ensure fairness and equality of opportunity throughout the nation.

5. growth of federal grants-in-aid money

5. *The growing financial power of the national government and its grants-in-aid programs for the states.* Money and power go together. The income tax (established in 1913) gave the federal government the authority to raise large sums of money, which it spent for the "general welfare," as well as for defense. Gradually the federal government expanded its power in states and communities by use of grants-in-aid. During the Great Depression of the 1930s, the national government used its taxing and spending powers in a number of areas formerly reserved to states and communities. Congress began grants-in-aid programs to states and communities for public assistance, unemployment compensation, employment services, child welfare, public housing, urban renewal, highway construction, and vocational education and rehabilitation.

Whenever the national government contributes financially to state or local programs, the state or local officials have less discretion in using the funds than they would have otherwise. Federal grants-in-aid invariably come with congressional standards or "guidelines" that states and communities must follow to receive their federal money. Often Congress delegates to federal agencies the power to establish the conditions attached to grants. Thus, through the power to tax and spend for the general welfare and through the conditions attached to federal grants-in-aid, the national government can exercise important powers in areas originally reserved to the states.

Under the banner of a "New Federalism," the Reagan and Bush administrations have sought to return some responsibilities to state and local governments. They succeeded in consolidating a number of separate and specific project grant programs into a few large *block grant* programs. Under the block grant idea, states and cities receive federal funds for broad purposes, for example, social services, community development, elementary and secondary education, maternal and child health, and community services. Instead of having to seek approval and funding from Washington for specific projects, states and cities can decide for themselves, within fairly broad limits, how to use block grant funds. Another important change under the New Federalism is a reversal of the historical trend toward greater dependence of state and local governments on federal grant money. Federal grants, which had risen to over 25 percent of all state and local government revenue in 1980, have now fallen to less than 20 percent today. This means that states and communities must increasingly finance their own services. Many mayors, governors, and state and local officials would like to be free from burdensome federal rules and regulations, but they welcome federal money.

"New Federalism" efforts to return some powers and responsibilities to state and local governments

block grants federal aid to state and local governments for broad purposes

The Separation of Powers

The *separation of powers* in the national government—separate legislative, executive, and judicial branches—was intended by the nation's founders as a bulwark against majoritarianism and an additional safeguard for liberty. The doctrine of separation of legislative, executive, and judicial powers derived from the French writer Montesquieu, whose *Spirit of the Laws* was a political textbook for these eighteenth-century statesmen. *The Federalist* paper No. 51 expresses the logic of the checks-and-balances system:

separation of powers the principle of dividing governmental powers among the executive, legislative, and judicial branches

> Ambition must be made to counteract ambition. . . . It may be a reflection on human nature, that such devices should be necessary to control the abuses of government. But what is government itself, but the greatest of all reflections on human nature? If men were angels, no government would be necessary. If angels were to govern men, neither external nor internal controls on government would be necessary. In framing a government which is to be administered by men over men, the great difficulty lies in this: you must first enable the government to control the governed; and in the next place oblige it to control itself.[1]

There are really *four* separate decision-making bodies in the national government: a *bicameral* Congress, which is divided into a House of Representatives and a Senate, together with the president and the Supreme Court. Each of these bodies is chosen in a separate fashion for different terms of office. In the *original* Constitution of 1787, only the House of Representatives was directly elected by the people; each House member serves a two-year term but can be reelected as often as his or her constituents wish. House members (435) are apportioned to the states on the basis of population. There are two U.S. senators for each state, regardless of the size of the state's population. Originally senators were selected by their state legislatures, but since the adoption of the Seventeenth Amendment to the Constitution (1913), U.S. senators have been elected by the people of their states. U.S.

bicameral legislature a legislature made up of two chambers or parts. The U.S. Congress, composed of the House of Representatives and the Senate, is a bicameral legislature

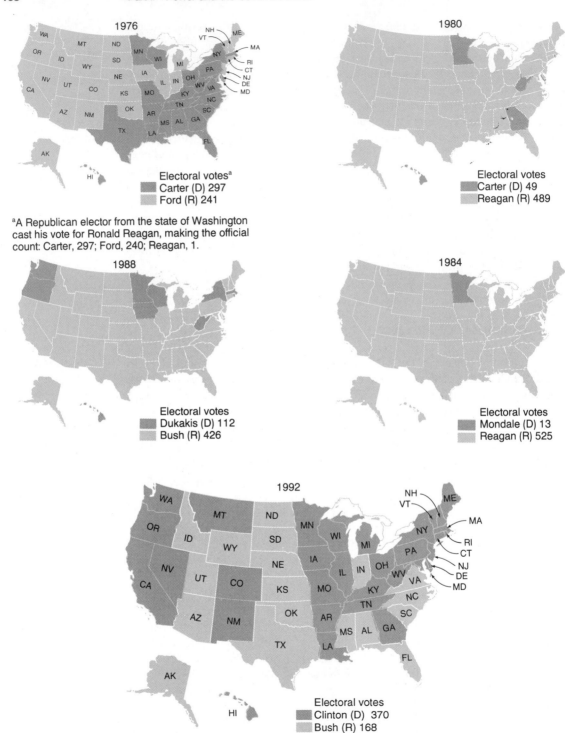

FIGURE 7-1   Electoral college votes

senators are elected for six-year terms, and there is no limit on the number of terms they may serve.

In the Constitution of 1787, the president was to be chosen by *electors*—prominent citizens in each state, selected as state legislatures provided. (Apparently the Founders did not believe the people should be directly involved in the choice of a president.) The *electoral college* system still remains in the Constitution, but it has been changed by custom and practice over the years. As early as 1800, presidential electors had begun running for their posts "pledged" to cast their votes for one party and candidate or another. This practice permitted popular participation in the selection of the president by enabling voters in each state to choose among electors pledged to particular candidates. The same practice holds today: voters in presidential elections actually cast their votes for slates of Democratic or Republican electors pledged to either the Democratic or Republican candidate. Each state has as many electors as it has U.S. senators and representatives combined. The District of Columbia was given three electors in the Twenty-third Amendment (1961). These electors compose the electoral college, which, according to the Constitution, actually elects the president. By custom, all of a state's electors cast their vote for the candidate who won their state (see Figure 7-1). But occasionally an elector violates this custom and casts a vote for someone else. (The most recent case of a "faithless elector" occurred in 1988, when a West Virginia elector pledged to that state's winning Democratic candidate, Michael Dukakis, voted instead for Lloyd Bentsen.) Moreover, in a close election it is possible for a candidate to lose the popular vote total nationwide but still win a majority in the electoral college. These problems have led to proposals to reform the electoral college system, but there has been no agreement on reform.

Each of the major decision-making bodies of American government possesses important *checks and balances* (see Figure 7-2) over the decisions of the others. No bill can become law without the approval of both the House and the Senate. The president shares in legislative power through the veto and the responsibility of the office to "give to the Congress information of the State of the Union, and recommend to their consideration such measures as he shall judge necessary and expedient." The president can also convene sessions of Congress. But the president's powers to make appointments and treaties are shared by the Senate. Congress can also override executive vetoes. The president must execute the laws, but to do so he or she must rely on the executive departments, and they must be created by Congress. Moreover, the executive branch cannot spend money that has not been appropriated by Congress.

Federal judges, including members of the Supreme Court, must be appointed by the president, with the consent of the Senate. Congress must create lower and intermediate courts, establish the number of judges, fix the jurisdiction of lower federal courts, and make "exceptions" to the appellate jurisdiction of the Supreme Court.

Perhaps the keystone of the system of checks and balances is the idea of *judicial review*, an original contribution by the nation's founders to the science of government. Judicial review is the power of the courts to strike down laws that they believe conflict with the Constitution. Article VI grants federal courts the power of judicial review of *state* decisions, specifying that the Constitution and the laws and treaties of the national government are the supreme law of the land, superseding anything in any state laws or constitutions. However, nowhere does the Constitution

electoral college
a group of persons called electors, selected by the voters in each state, that officially elects the president and vice-president

checks and balances
principle whereby each branch of the government exercises a check on the actions of the others, preventing too great a concentration of power in any one person or group of persons

judicial review
power of the Supreme Court or any court to declare federal or state laws unconstitutional

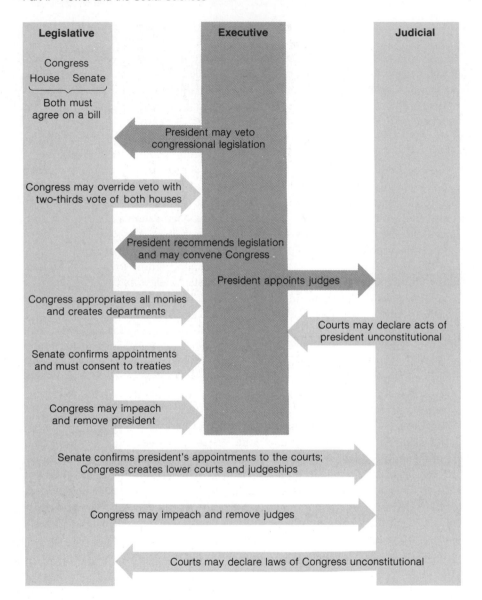

FIGURE 7-2 Checks and balances in the U.S. government

specify that the Supreme Court has power of judicial review of *executive* action or of laws enacted by *Congress*. This principle was instead established in the case of *Marbury* v. *Madison* in 1803, when Chief Justice John Marshall argued convincingly that the Founders had intended the Supreme Court to have the power of invalidating not only state laws and constitutions, but also any laws of Congress or executive actions that came into conflict with the Constitution of the United States. Thus, the Supreme Court stands as the final defender of the constitutional principles against the encroachments of popularly elected legislatures and executives.

The Power of the President

The responsibility for the initiation of public policy falls principally on the president, White House staff, and executive departments. Through the power of policy initiation alone, the president has considerable impact on American politics. The president sets the agenda for public decision making. The president dominates the nightly news and shapes policy debate. Presidential programs are presented to Congress in various messages and in the budget; thus, the executive office largely determines what the business of Congress will be in any session. Few major undertakings get off the ground without presidential initiation; the president frames the issues, determines their context, and decides their timing.

Presidential power has grown throughout the twentieth century. One reason is America's greater involvement in world affairs and the constant increase in the importance of military and foreign policy. The Constitution gives the president far-reaching powers in foreign and military affairs: the president is authorized to send and receive ambassadors and to make treaties (with the advice and consent of the Senate) and is made commander in chief of the armed forces. In effect, these powers put the president in almost exclusive control of foreign and military policy in the nation. The Congress has declared war only five times in U.S. history (the War of 1812, the Mexican War in 1845, the Spanish–American War in 1898, World War I in 1917, and World War II in 1941), but the president has ordered U.S. military forces into action on more than 150 occasions, including Korea, 1950–1953; Vietnam, 1965–1973; Grenada, 1983; and the Persian Gulf, 1991.

A second factor contributing to the power of the president in the twentieth century has been the growth of the executive branch, which the president heads. The federal bureaucracy has become a giant power structure, and constitutional powers as chief executive place the president at the top of that structure. The Constitution gives the president broad, albeit vague, powers to "take care that the laws be faithfully executed" and to "require the opinion, in writing, of the principal officer in each of the executive departments, upon any subject relating to the duties of their respective offices." By this clause the president has general executive authority over the nearly 3 million civilian employees of the federal bureaucracy. Moreover, the president has the right to appoint and remove the principal officers of the executive branch of government (the Senate consenting). Although Congress must appropriate all monies spent by executive departments, the president nonetheless has responsibility for formulating the budget, through the Office of Management and Budget (OMB). Congress may cut a presidential budget request and even appropriate more than the president asks for a particular agency or program, but by far the greatest portion of the president's budget is usually accepted by Congress.

The third reason for the importance of the presidency in the twentieth century can be traced to technological improvements in the mass media and the strengthening of the role of the president as molder of public opinion. Television brings the president directly in contact with the people, and the people have an attachment to the president that is unlike their attachment to any other public official or symbol of government. Fred I. Greenstein has classified the "psychological functions of the presidency." First, the president "simplifies perception of government and politics" by serving as "the main cognitive 'handle' for providing busy citizens with

growth of presidential power
international involvements and military action

expansion of executive branch and government spending

development of mass media and direct presidential communication with the people some sense of what their government is doing." Second, the president provides "an outlet for emotional expression" through public interest in the president's private and public life. Third, the president is a "symbol of unity" and of nationhood (as the national shock and grief over the death of a president clearly reveals). Fourth, the president provides the people with a "vicarious means of taking political action," in the sense that the president can act decisively and effectively while they cannot. Finally, the president is a "symbol of social stability," providing the people with a feeling of security and guidance. Thus, the president is the most visible symbol of government.[2] (For a discussion of presidential personalities, see Chapter 5, Box 5-3, "Power, Personality, and the Presidency.")

The president has many sources of power (see Table 7-2), as chief of state, chief administrator, chief diplomat, commander in chief, party leader, and voice of the people. But despite the great powers of the office, no president can monopolize policy making. (See Box 7-1, "The 'Best' and 'Worst' Presidents.") The president

TABLE 7-2   Presidential Powers

Chief of state and crisis manager
Direct national action ("The executive power shall be vested in a President")
Represent nation as chief of state
Provide leadership in national crises
Be a symbol of national unity

Chief administrator
Implement policy ("take care that the laws be faithfully executed")
Supervise executive branch of government
Appoint and remove policy officials
Prepare executive budget

Chief legislator
Initiate policy ("give to the Congress information of the State of the Union, and recommend to their consideration such measures as he shall judge necessary and expedient")
Veto legislation passed by Congress
Convene special sessions of Congress "on extraordinary occasions"

Chief diplomat
Make treaties ("by and with the advice and consent of the Senate")
Make executive agreements
Exercise power of diplomatic recognition—to send and receive ambassadors

Commander in chief
Command U.S. armed forces ("the President shall be Commander in Chief of the Army and Navy")
Appoint military officers
Direct military forces

Party leader
Control national party organization
Control federal patronage

Opinion leader
Provide reassurance and build national morale
Communicate regularly with nation through mass media
Set policy agenda and rally popular support

functions within an established political system and can exercise power only within its framework. The president cannot act outside existing political consensus, outside the "rules of the game." (See the case study, "Watergate and the Limits of Presidential Power.")

The Power of Congress

What are the powers of Congress in the American political system? Policy proposals are usually initiated *outside* Congress; it is the role of Congress to respond to proposals from the president, executive agencies, and interest groups. Congress does not merely ratify or "rubber-stamp" decisions; it plays an independent role in the policy-making process. But this role is essentially a deliberative one in which Congress accepts, modifies, or rejects the policies initiated by others. Congress functions as an *arbiter* rather than an *initiator* of public policy.

Congress is more influential in *domestic* than in foreign and military affairs. It is much freer to reject presidential proposals regarding business, labor, agriculture, education, welfare, urban affairs, civil rights, taxation, and appropriations. The president and executive departments must go to Congress for needed legislation and appropriations. Congressional committees can exercise power in domestic affairs

---

BOX 7-1

The "Best" and "Worst" Presidents

Evaluating presidential performance is no easy task. Too often the political views of the evaluator bias his or her judgment. Journalists often turn to public opinion polls, asking national samples of respondents, "Do you approve or disapprove of the way [the president] is handling his job as president?" (see the case study in Chapter 2, "Explaining Presidential Approval Ratings"). The resulting "presidential approval ratings" may measure a president's current popularity, but they do not really evaluate performance.

Occasionally leading political scientists and historians, who have studied and written about the presidency, are asked to render their judgments about presidential performance.

A 1982 survey of forty-nine leading presidential scholars (historians and political scientists) produced the following results:

THE 10 "BEST" PRESIDENTS
1. Abraham Lincoln
2. George Washington
3. Franklin D. Roosevelt
4. Theodore Roosevelt
5. Thomas Jefferson
6. Woodrow Wilson
7. Andrew Jackson
8. Harry S Truman
9. Dwight D. Eisenhower
10. James K. Polk

THE 10 "WORST" PRESIDENTS
1. Warren G. Harding
2. Richard M. Nixon
3. James Buchanan
4. Franklin Pierce
5. Ulysses S. Grant
6. Millard Fillmore
7. Andrew Johnson
8. Calvin Coolidge
9. John Tyler
10. Jimmy Carter

Note: The survey, by the *Chicago Tribune,* resembled polls taken in 1948 and 1962 by historian Arthur Schlesinger, Sr., for other publications. In all three surveys, Abraham Lincoln, George Washington, and Franklin D. Roosevelt led the list of "best" presidents, and Warren G. Harding was rated the very worst. The biggest shift was the rating for Dwight Eisenhower, who rose from the tenth-worst position in 1962 to ninth-best in the 1982 survey. Eisenhower's stature among scholars is believed to have grown in part because of the troubles of his more activist successors. Nixon's role in the Watergate scandal and his resignation from office, it was clear, led to his second-to-lowest rating. Jimmy Carter received one vote in the "ten best" category, but he received many votes for the bottom ten.

CASE STUDY

Election to the nation's highest office, even by an overwhelming majority, does not entitle the president to govern alone. It only gives the president the opportunity to engage in consultation, accommodation, and compromise with other elites. Richard Nixon was the only president ever to resign from office. His forced resignation in 1974 was not merely a product of specific misdeeds associated with Watergate. It also grew out of his general isolation from established elites, his failure to cooperate with Congress and the courts, and his disregard for the general "rules of the game."

On the night of June 17, 1972, five men with burglary and wiretapping tools were arrested in the offices of the Democratic National Committee in the Watergate apartments in Washington, together with E. Howard Hunt and G. Gordon Liddy, who directed the break-in. All pleaded guilty and were convicted, but U.S. District Court Judge John J. Sirica believed that the defendants were shielding whoever had ordered and paid for the bugging and break-in. The *Washington Post* reported that the defendants were under pressure to plead guilty, that they were still being paid by an unnamed source, and that they had been promised cash settlements and executive clemency if they remained silent and went to jail. Judge Sirica threatened the defendants with heavy sentences, and soon James W. McCord confessed to secret payments and a cover-up.

The Senate formed a Special Select Committee on Campaign Activities—the so-called Watergate Committee—headed by Sen. Sam J. Ervin, to delve into Watergate and related activities. The national press, led by the prestigious *Washington Post,* which had always been hostile to Richard Nixon, began its own "investigative reporting" and launched a series of damaging stories, reported nightly on the national television networks, involving former Attorney General John Mitchell, White House chief of staff H. R. Haldeman, and White House adviser John Ehrlichman.

President Nixon might have been able to stay in office if he had publicly repented his own actions and cooperated in the Watergate investigation by Congress and the courts. But Nixon increasingly viewed the Watergate affair as a test of his own strength and character; he perceived it as a conspiracy among liberal opponents in Congress and the news media to reverse the 1972 election outcome; he became rigid in his stance on withholding information. He came to believe he was defending the presidency itself by refusing to cooperate.

When the Senate Watergate Committee learned that the president regularly taped conversations in the Oval Office, it issued subpoenas for tapes that would prove or disprove charges of a cover-up. In response President Nixon chose to argue that the constitutional separation of powers permitted the president to withhold information from both Congress and the courts. But the Supreme Court, in *The United States* v. *Richard M. Nixon,* denied the president the power to withhold information that was essential to a criminal investigation. President Nixon publicly released the transcripts of the subpoenaed White House tapes in a national television broadcast

(continued)

(continued)

in which he claimed innocence of any wrongdoing. The conversations on the tapes are rambling, inconclusive, and subject to varied interpretations. But the most common interpretation is that President Nixon approved a payoff to a convicted burglar.

The Judiciary Committee of the House of Representatives, chaired by Rep. Peter Rodino of New Jersey, was convened in the spring of 1974 to consider a series of articles of impeachment against President Nixon. The release of the tapes failed to persuade this committee of Nixon's innocence. Indeed, it had the opposite effect. The committee passed two articles of impeachment: one accused the president of obstructing justice in the Watergate investigation; the other accused the president of misusing his executive power and disregarding his constitutional duties to take care that the laws be faithfully executed. Shortly thereafter, Nixon was informed by congressional leaders of his own party that impeachment by a majority of the House and removal from office by two-thirds of the Senate was assured. On August 9, 1974, President Nixon resigned his office—the first U.S. president ever to do so.

On September 8, 1974, new President Gerald R. Ford pardoned former President Richard Nixon "for all offenses against the United States which he, Richard Nixon, has committed or may have committed or taken part in" during his presidency. In accepting the pardon, Nixon expressed remorse over Watergate and acknowledged grave errors of judgment, but he did not admit personal guilt. Despite intensive questioning by the press and Congress, President Ford maintained that his purpose in granting the pardon was to end "bitter controversy and divisive national debate" and "to firmly shut and seal the book" on Watergate.

by giving or withholding the appropriations and the legislation these executive agencies want.

In the Constitution, the president and Congress share power over foreign and military affairs. The president is "Commander in Chief of the Armed Forces," but Congress "declares war." The president "sends and receives ambassadors" and "makes treaties," but the Senate must confirm appointments and "advise and consent" to treaties. Nevertheless, strong presidents have generally led the nation in both war and peace. (See the case study in Chapter 8, "Vietnam: A Political History," and the case study in Chapter 14, "American Military Power: Desert Storm.")

Until Vietnam, no congressional opposition to undeclared war was evident. But military failure and public opposition to the war in Vietnam led Congress to try to curtail the war power of the president. Congress passed the controversial War Powers Act in 1973 over a weakened President Nixon's veto. The act specifies that if the president sends U.S. troops into combat, this must be reported to Congress within forty-eight hours. American forces can remain in a combat situation for only sixty days unless Congress by specific legislation authorizes their continued

Senate confirmation hearings for Supreme Court Justice Clarence Thomas attracted heavy media coverage and national interest.
Source: Rick Reinhard/Impact Visuals

engagement. The act also states that Congress can withdraw troops at any time by passing a resolution in both houses, and the president cannot veto a resolution. Obviously the War Powers Act raises very serious constitutional questions, but they may never be tested in court. The U.S. Constitution makes the president, not Congress, commander in chief of the armed forces, and commanders may order their troops to go anywhere at any time. The act did not prevent President Ford from sending troops to Cambodia during the Mayaguez incident, President Carter from attempting a military rescue of the Iranian-held U.S. hostages, President Reagan from sending U.S. troops to Lebanon and Grenada, or President Bush from sending military forces to Panama and ordering U.S. forces into "Operation Desert Storm" to liberate Kuwait and destroy Iraq's war-making power.

The Power of the Courts

power of the courts   The founders of the United States viewed the federal courts as the final bulwark against threats to individual liberty. Since *Marbury* v. *Madison* first asserted the Supreme Court's power of judicial review over congressional acts, the federal courts have struck down more than eighty congressional laws and uncounted state laws that they believed conflicted with the Constitution. *Judicial review and the right to interpret the meaning and decide the application of law* are great sources of power for judges. Some of the nation's most important policy decisions have been made by courts rather than by executive or legislative bodies. The federal courts took the lead in eliminating racial segregation in public life, ensuring the separation of church and state, defining relationships between citizens and law

Custom, rather than the Constitution, dictates a nine-member Supreme Court of the United States.
Source: Courtesy, National Geographic Society/Supreme Court Historical Society

enforcers, and guaranteeing voters equal voice in government. Today the federal courts grapple with the most controversial issues facing the nation: abortion, affirmative action, the death penalty, religion in schools, flag burning, the rights of criminal defendants, and so on. Courts are an integral component of America's governmental system, for sooner or later most important policy questions are brought before them.

The undemocratic nature of judicial review has long been recognized in American politics. Nine Supreme Court justices—who are not elected to office, whose terms are for life, and who can be removed only for "high crimes and misdemeanors"—possess the power to void the acts of popularly elected presidents, Congresses, governors, and state legislators. The decision of the Founders to grant federal courts the constitutional power of judicial review of *state* decisions is easy to understand. Federal court power over state decisions is probably essential in maintaining national unity, for fifty different state interpretations of the meaning of the U.S. Constitution or of the laws and treaties of Congress would create unimaginable confusion. Thus, the power of federal judicial review over state constitutions, laws, and court decisions is seldom questioned.

However, at the national level, why should the views of an appointed court about the meaning of the Constitution prevail over the views of an elected Congress and president? Presidents and members of Congress are sworn to uphold the Constitution, and it can reasonably be assumed they do not pass laws they believe to be

democracy and the Supreme Court

judicial review of state laws

judicial review of federal laws

*un*constitutional. Why should the Supreme Court have judicial review of the decisions of these bodies?

The answer appears to be that the Founders distrusted both popular majorities and elected officials who might be influenced by popular majorities. They believed government should be limited so it could not attack principle and property, whether to do so was the will of the majority or not. So the courts were deliberately *insulated* against popular majorities; to ensure their independence, judges were not to be elected, but appointed for life terms. Only in this way, the writers of the Constitution believed, would they be sufficiently protected from the masses to permit them to judge courageously and responsibly. Insulation is, in itself, another source of judicial power.

insulation of the courts
appointed, not elected
judges serve life terms

The power of the courts, especially the U.S. Supreme Court, is limited only by the justices' own judicial philosophy. The doctrine of *judicial restraint* argues that because justices are not popularly elected, the Supreme Court should defer to the decisions of Congress and the president unless their actions are in clear conflict with the plain meaning of the Constitution. Justice Felix Frankfurter once wrote: "The only check upon our own exercise of power is our own sense of self-restraint. For the removal of unwise laws from the statute books, appeal lies not with the Courts but to the ballot and to the processes of democratic government."[3]

judicial restraint
judges should defer to the decision of elected representatives unless it is in clear conflict with the plain meaning of the Constitution

One should not confuse the wisdom of a law with its constitutionality; the courts should decide only the constitutionality of laws, not the wisdom or fairness. A related limitation on judicial power is the principle of *stare decisis,* which means the issue has already been decided in earlier cases. Reliance on precedent is a fundamental notion in law; it gives stability to the law. If every decision ignored past precedents and created new law, no one would know what the law is from day to day.

stare decisis
reliance on precedent to give stability to the law

However, the history of the Supreme Court, especially in the last few decades, has been one of *judicial activism,* not restraint. The dominant philosophy of the Supreme Court under Chief Justice Earl Warren (1953–1969) was that judges should interpret the meaning of the Constitution to fit the needs of contemporary society. By viewing the Constitution as a broad and flexible document, the nation can avoid new constitutional amendments and still accomplish changes in society. Precedents can be overturned as society grows and changes.

judicial activism
judges may interpret the meaning of the Constitution to fit the needs of contemporary society

Judicial activism was reflected in the Supreme Court's famous *Brown* v. *Board of Education of Topeka* decision in 1954 that declared that racially segregated schools violated the equal protection clause of the Fourteenth Amendment. The Supreme Court also overturned precedent in requiring that the states apportion their legislatures so as to guarantee equal voter representation in *Baker* v. *Carr* in 1962. It struck down long-established practices of prayer and Bible reading in public schools in *Engle* v. *Vitale,* also in 1962. The Court under Earl Warren also greatly expanded the rights of criminal defendants.

The Supreme Court under President Richard Nixon's appointee, Chief Justice Warren Burger (1969–1986), was only slightly less activist. The Court's 1973 decision in *Roe* v. *Wade,* declaring that abortion was a constitutional right of women, was perhaps the most sweeping reinterpretation of individual liberty in the Court's history.

Presidents Ronald Reagan and George Bush sought to strengthen the doctrine of judicial restraint in their appointments to the Supreme Court. The Court under

Chief Justice William Rehnquist (first appointed to the Court by President Nixon in 1971 and elevated to Chief Justice by President Reagan in 1986) may prove less activist than its predecessor. (See Table 7-3 for information about the current Supreme Court justices.) It has been willing to allow states to place some restrictions on abortion (see Chapter 10), and it has declined to extend any further the rights of criminal defendants (see Chapter 12). But it is unlikely that any of the major decisions of the Warren or Burger Courts will be reversed.

Political Behavior in the United States

Popular participation in the political system is the very definition of democracy. Individuals in a democracy may run for public office; participate in marches and demonstrations; make financial contributions to political candidates and causes; attend political meetings, speeches, and rallies; write letters to public officials and newspapers; belong to organizations that support or oppose particular candidates and take stands on public issues; wear political buttons and place bumper stickers on their cars; attempt to influence friends while discussing candidates and issues; vote in elections; or merely follow an issue or campaign in the mass media.

This list of activities constitutes a ranking of the *forms of political participation*, in inverse order of their frequency. The activities at the beginning of the list require greater expenditure of time and energy and greater personal commitment; consequently, far fewer people engage in those activities (see Figure 7-3). Less than 1 percent of the American adult population ever run for public office. Only about 5 percent are ever active in political parties and campaigns, and only about 10 percent make financial contributions. Only about 15 percent of the nation's autos will carry political bumper stickers, even in a presidential election. A few more people claim to have written or called a public official, but this figure includes local governments and school boards. About one-third of the adult population belong to organizations, including unions, that are politically active. But fully one-third of the population

forms of political participation

TABLE 7-3   Members of the U.S. Supreme Court

Name	Place of birth	Law school from which graduated	President who appointed
White, Byron Raymond	Fort Collins, CO	Yale	Kennedy (1962)
Blackmun, Harry A.	Nashville, IL	Harvard	Nixon (1970)
Rehnquist, William Hubbs*	Milwaukee, WI	Stanford	Nixon (1971) Reagan (1986)
Stevens, John Paul	Chicago, IL	Chicago	Ford (1975)
O'Connor, Sandra Day	El Paso, TX	Stanford	Reagan (1981)
Scalia, Antonin	Trenton, NJ	Harvard	Reagan (1986)
Kennedy, Anthony McLeod	Sacramento, CA	Harvard	Reagan (1988)
Souter, David H.	Melrose, MA	Harvard	Bush (1990)
Thomas, Clarence	Pinpoint, GA	Yale	Bush (1991)

*Rehnquist was nominated to the U.S. Supreme Court in 1971 by Richard Nixon; he was nominated as chief justice by Ronald Reagan in 1986.

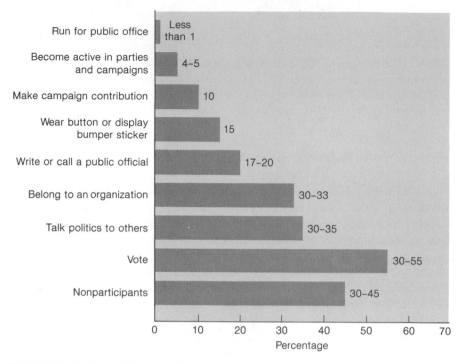

FIGURE 7-3 Political participation

are politically apathetic: they do not vote, and they are largely unaware of and indifferent to the political life of the nation.

Voter turnout is greatest in presidential elections, but even in those contests turnout is only about 50 percent of eligible people. Voter turnout has been declining slightly over the years (see Figure 7-4). "Off-year" congressional elections—congressional elections held in years in which there is no presidential election—attract only 35 or 40 percent of eligible people to the polls. Yet in these "off-year" contests the nation chooses all of its U.S. representatives, one-third of its U.S. senators, and about one-half of its governors. Local government elections—for mayor, council members, school board, and so forth—frequently attract only one-quarter to one-third of eligible voters.

Voting is the primary form of popular participation in a democracy, and voter participation is highly valued in American political theory. Popular control of government—the control of leaders by followers—is supposed to be accomplished through the electoral process. Voting requires an individual to make not one, but two decisions: the individual must choose whether to vote at all; and, if the individual decides to vote, he or she must choose between rival parties or candidates. Both decisions are equally important; decisions about whether or not to vote can clearly influence the outcome of elections.

The states administer national, state, and local elections. Most states have established a system of voting registration. Presumably, registration helps prevent fraud and multiple voting in elections, but many observers believe it also reduces voter turnout.

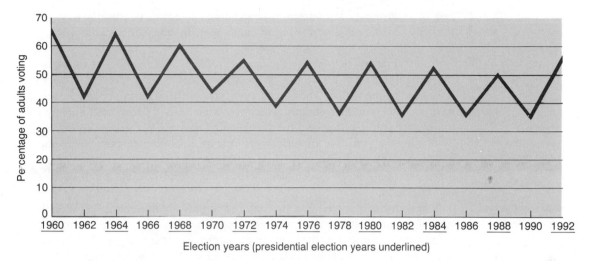

FIGURE 7-4   Voter turnout in presidential and congressional elections

State voting laws are now heavily circumscribed by national authority. Consider the following:

- Amendment XV: no denial of voting because of race
- Amendment XIX: no denial of voting because of gender
- Amendment XXIV: no poll taxes in federal elections
- Amendment XXVI: no denial of voting to persons eighteen years of age or older
- Civil Rights Act of 1964: no discrimination in the application of voter registration laws
- Voting Rights Act of 1965: attorney general may replace local voting officials with federal examiners on evidence of voter discrimination.

Democrats and Republicans—What's the Difference?

Democracy is ultimately based on majority rule, and one function of political parties is to *put majorities together.* Political parties organize voters for effective political expression at the polls. Voters, in turn, use party labels to help them identify the general political viewpoints of the candidates.

Because American parties are necessarily rather loose coalitions of interests, they do not command the total loyalty of every officeholder elected under a party's banner. The fact that candidates run under a Republican or Democratic label does not clearly indicate where they will stand on every public issue. Even so, these coalitions do have considerable cohesion and historical continuity. The party label *discloses the coalition of interests and the policy views* with which candidates have generally associated themselves. At the least, the party label tells more about a candidate's politics than would a strange name, with no party affiliation, on the ballot.

Especially in two-party systems, such as we have in the United States, parties also *limit the choice of candidates* for public office and thus relieve voters of the

functions of political parties

organize majorities

identify candidate's coalition of interests

limit choices

define issues

criticize officeholders

task of choosing among dozens of contending candidates on election day. The preliminary selecting and narrowing of candidates, by conventions and primary elections, is indispensable in a large society.

Political parties help *define the major problems and issues* confronting society. In attempting to win a majority of the voters, parties inform the public about the issues facing the nation. The comparisons parties make during political campaigns have an important educational value: voters come to "know" the opposing candidates for public office, and the problems of national interest are spotlighted.

Finally, the party *out* of office performs an important function for democratic government by *criticizing officeholders.* Moreover, the very existence of a recognized party outside the government helps make criticism of government legitimate and effective.

It is sometimes argued that there are few significant differences between the two main American parties. It is not uncommon in European nations to find authoritarian parties competing with democratic parties, capitalist parties with socialist parties, Catholic parties with secular parties, and so on. However, within the context of American political experience, the Democratic and Republican parties can be clearly differentiated. There are at least three ways in which to discern the differences: (1) by examining differences in the *coalitions of voters* supporting each party, (2) by examining differences in the *policy views of the leaders* in each party, and (3) by examining differences in the *voting records of the representatives and senators* of each party.

In ascertaining party differences according to support from different groups of voters, we must note first that major groups are seldom *wholly* within one party or the other. For example, in presidential elections all major social groups divide their votes between the parties (see Table 7-4). Yet differences between the parties are revealed *in the proportions of votes given by each major group to each party.* Thus, the Democratic party receives a disproportionate amount of support from Catholics, Jews, blacks, lower-income groups, blue-collar workers, union members, and big-city residents. The Republican party receives disproportionate support from Protestants, whites, higher-income groups, professionals and managers, white-collar workers, nonunion members, and rural and small-town residents.

The second way of discerning Democratic and Republican party differences involves an examination of the political opinions of the leaders of each party. Political scientists have studied party differences by presenting a series of policy questions to the delegates to the Democratic and Republican national conventions. They have found substantial differences of opinion between Democratic and Republican leaders on important public issues, including governmental regulation of the economy, civil rights issues, social welfare programs, tax policy, and foreign policy (see Table 7-5 on page 189). Political scientist Herbert McClosky concludes:

> Democratic leaders typically display the stronger urge to elevate the low-born, the uneducated, the deprived minorities, and the poor in general; they are also more disposed to employ the nation's collective power to advance humanitarian and social welfare goals (e.g., Social Security, immigration, racial integration, a higher minimum wage, and public education). They are more critical of wealth and big business and more eager to bring them under regulation. Theirs is the greater faith in the wisdom of using legislation for redistributing the national product and for furnishing social services on a wide scale. Of the two groups of leaders, the Democrats are more "pro-

---

criticism of the American two-party system
not enough differences

ascertaining the real party differences
differing coalitions of voters

differing views of party leaders

differing voting records in Congress

TABLE 7-4   Percentage of Vote by Groups in Presidential Elections since 1976

	1980			1984		1988		1992		
	Carter	*Reagan*	*Anderson*	*Mondale*	*Reagan*	*Dukakis*	*Bush*	*Clinton*	*Bush*	*Perot*
National	41	51	7	41	59	46	54	43	38	19
Gender										
Male	38	53	7	37	61	42	58	41	38	21
Female	44	49	6	42	57	49	51	46	37	17
Race										
White	36	56	7	34	66	40	60	39	41	20
Nonwhite	86	10	2	90	9	90	10	82	11	7
Occupation										
Prof. & business	33	55	10	37	62	35	65	36	48	16
White-collar	40	51	9	40	59	43	57	42	38	20
Blue-collar	48	46	5	46	53	51	49	59	23	18
Age										
Under 30 years	47	41	11	41	58	47	53	44	34	22
30–49	38	52	8	42	58	46	54	42	38	20
50 years & older	41	54	4	36	63	48	52	45	40	15
Religion										
Protestants	39	54	6	26	73	38	62	33	46	12
Catholics	46	47	6	44	55	54	46	44	36	20
Politics										
Republicans	8	86	5	7	92	8	92	10	73	17
Democrats	69	26	4	73	26	83	17	77	10	13
Independents	29	55	14	35	63	43	57	38	32	30
Region										
East	43	47	9	47	52	49	51	47	35	18
Midwest	41	51	7	38	61	47	53	42	37	21
South	44	52	3	36	63	41	59	42	43	16
West	35	54	9	40	59	47	53	44	34	22
Members of labor union families	50	43	5	53	45	56	44	55	24	21

Source: Based on data from the Gallup Poll Survey and *Public Opinion* (January/February 1989), and *New York Times* (November 5, 1992).

gressively" oriented toward social reform and experimentation. The Republican leaders, while not uniformly differentiated from their opponents, subscribe in greater measure to the symbols and practices of individualism, *laissez-faire,* and national independence. They prefer to overcome humanity's misfortunes by relying upon personal effort, private incentives, frugality, hard work, responsibility, self-denial (for both men and government), and the strengthening rather than the diminution of the economic and status distinctions that are the "natural" rewards of the differences in human character and fortunes.[4]

The third indication of party differences in the United States is the roll-call voting behavior of the representatives and senators of each party on controversial issues.

Political Power
and the Mass
Media

Television has helped reshape American politics. Over two-thirds of the American public report that they receive all or most of their news from television. Perhaps more important, television is the most trusted medium of communication. Television has thus become the focus of political campaigning. Candidates are no longer selected by party bosses in smoke-filled rooms. Instead of seeking meetings with party leaders, candidates now seek professional media experts to construct a popular image for the TV screen. Campaigns are organized as media events. The media have replaced the political party as the chief link between the citizen and government.

1980—Communicating Discontent

Americans take great pride in their country. They want to see their nation as strong, self-reliant, and prosperous, with a future even greater than its past. But during his presidency, Jimmy Carter talked about the limits of American resources and the limits of U.S. power in world affairs. The United States was unable to gain the release of its hostages in Iran through either diplomatic or military means. Rather than controlling its own affairs, the United States saw its economy, lifestyle, and foreign policy increasingly affected by Arab oil producers. Taxes, interest rates, and inflation were eroding the real incomes of American families.

Ronald Reagan lived his life in front of a camera. The camera was the principal tool of both his trades, actor and politician. Reagan's appeal to mass audiences had always been underestimated by the New York and Washington journalists and commentators. Reporters wrote down his commonplace observations and timeworn slogans. The printed messages were uninspiring. But reporters missed Reagan's true audience appeal—his folksy, warm, comfortable, and reassuring manner and the likable personality he projected to his audiences, whatever his words.

The task fell to Ronald Reagan to channel popular discontent into a rejection of the incumbent president. Jimmy Carter, of course, did not bear the sole responsibility for Americans' accumulated discontents. But Reagan knew that the past of the United States looked better than its present, that the "good old days" never seemed better than they did in 1980. Reagan benefited from the public identification of him as the good guy in old western movies and the genial host of the early television shows *G.E. Theatre* and *Death Valley Days*. His conservative political messages reinforced his image as guardian of traditional American values.

Although attacked by Carter as a threat to peace, Reagan, in their televised debate, seemed by contrast a pleasant, smiling, reassuring figure. Carter was clearly the master of substance: he talked about programs, figures, budgets. He talked rapidly and seriously. But during the ninety minutes of debate, Reagan was the master of the stage: he was relaxed, smiling, even joking. He never raised his voice or increased the tempo, and he managed in the process to treat the president of the

(continued)

(continued)

United States as an overly aggressive younger man, regrettably given to exaggeration. "There you go again."

Reagan never said anything of great importance. He merely asked: "Are you better off now than you were four years ago?" Simple, yet highly effective. When it was over, it was plain that Carter had been bested by a true professional in the media skills in which Carter himself had once claimed supremacy.

In the final few days before the election, the media decided to publicize the first anniversary of the Iranian hostage taking. That decision sealed Carter's fate. By reminding Americans of international humiliations, military weaknesses, and administration blunders during the Carter years, the media set the stage for the Reagan landslide.

1984—Communicating Confidence

Throughout Reagan's first term, whatever people thought about his tax cuts, his defense buildup, or the deficit, Reagan himself was perceived as a strong, decisive man who embodied the best of America's past. He was, above all else, a leader who commanded respect, who did not vacillate, who "stayed the course." Americans were feeling better about themselves and their country. They chanted "U-S-A" at the 1984 Los Angeles Summer Olympics and cheered the invasion of Grenada. Ronald Reagan became the benefactor of this new patriotism.

By 1984 the television debates had become the central focus of the presidential campaign. The debates reward appearance over content and quickness of thought over thoughtfulness. A televised debate is more like a pop quiz given by selected reporters than a serious discussion of the issues. Reagan's advisers would have preferred that he not debate at all. The debates always seem to favor the challenger by simply showing him in the same ring with the president. But the popularity of televised debates with 100 million viewers had gained nearly the force of a constitutional command by 1984.

In the first of the two televised debates with Democrat Walter Mondale, Reagan stumbled badly. The acquired skills of a lifetime deserted the president as he groped for words and thoughts, searching his mind and coming up empty. Mondale was respectful of the presidency, somewhat stiff and ill at ease but nonetheless clear-headed and effective in his responses to the questions. But it was not Mondale's performance that hurt Reagan, it was Reagan's own errors in preparation and performance. Reagan's poor performance raised the only issue that could defeat him: his age. The president had looked and sounded old. Postdebate polls showed Mondale the clear winner, and the challenger took a quick jump, although not a lead, in the voter polls.

The president decided on his own, without telling his aides, to lay the perfect trap for his questioners in the second debate. He knew the age question would be

(continued)

(continued)

raised against him early in the debate. He memorized his lines and played the bit perfectly. When asked about his age and capacity to lead the nation he responded to a hushed audience and a waiting America in a serious deadpan expression: "I want you to know that I will not make age an issue in this campaign. I am not going to exploit for political purposes [*pause*] my opponent's youth and inexperience." The studio audience broke into uncontrolled laughter. Even Mondale had to laugh. With a classic one-liner, the president buried the age issue and won not only the debate but the election.

The president's performance reassured the nation that he was not too old or out of touch to handle the job. He avoided his earlier mistake of trying to reel off statistics. He was relaxed again, flashing his folksy humor, and sounding hurt rather than angry at Mondale's charges. He was once again the Great Communicator.

1988—Battle of the Sound Bites

When the Bush team assembled for the 1988 presidential campaign, the outlook was gloomy. It was true that the nation was experiencing peace and prosperity, and historically, "good times" had favored the candidate of the party in power. But in the media age, candidate "image" dominates the voters' decision. Bush was behind in the polls by seventeen percentage points in early summer of the election year. He suffered from a "wimp" image, created by eight years of service as Reagan's vice-president.

The remaking of Bush's image began at the Republican national convention. His World War II Navy fighter pilot photos, and film of his dramatic rescue from the water by a submarine, helped overcome the wimp image. His support for President Reagan, even during the Iran-Contra scandal, was recast as a test of his loyalty to a popular president under fire. In his acceptance speech, an astonishingly new and telegenic George Bush emerged—warm, relaxed, authoritative, even presidential. He distinguished his own vision of America from that of Ronald Reagan, and he called for a "kinder, gentler nation."

At the Democratic National Convention, the Dukakis team chose "competence" as its theme. Dukakis intoned the theme in a very effective acceptance speech: "This election is about competence, not ideology." By casting the theme in this fashion, Dukakis hoped to deflect attention from his liberal positions on taxing, spending, the death penalty, and other unpopular social and domestic policies he had espoused. He wanted to sell himself as a pragmatist, not a liberal; as a manager, not an ideologue.

But the Bush team launched a series of "attack videos," paid television ads designed to link Dukakis with unpopular liberal policy positions. Bush's skilled handlers had previously identified "hot-button" issues by electronically recording the reactions to various themes of small "focus groups" of citizens. The most effective videos focused on the flag salute issue (Dukakis had vetoed a bill mandating

(continued)

(continued)

the flag salute in public schools); the furlough of murderers and rapists (a Massachusetts prison furlough program gave a convicted murderer, Willie Horton, the opportunity to rape and murder a woman while on furlough); and Dukakis's opposition to defense spending. Dukakis's lead in the polls evaporated.

In the first debate both Bush and Dukakis performed extraordinarily well. But in the second televised debate Michael Dukakis ensured his own defeat with a cold, impersonal performance. CNN anchorman Bernard Shaw opened with a question that touched on every viewer's raw emotions: "Governor, if Kitty Dukakis were raped and murdered, would you favor an irrevocable death penalty for the killer?" The question demanded an emotional reply, but the detached candidate responded with an impersonal recitation of his stock positions. Bush seized the opportunity to establish an intimate, warm, and personal relationship with the viewers. On the death penalty Bush quickly identified himself with the majority position of the electorate: "I do believe some crimes are so heinous, so brutal, so outrageous . . . I do believe in the death penalty." On abortion, Bush presented a sympathetic image.

On television, *image* triumphs over *issues*. And Bush emerged from the second debate as likable, occasionally goofy, warm, personal, and spontaneous. Dukakis emerged as competent yet cool, intense yet personally detached, almost arrogant. Bush leaped ahead in the polls.

1992—The TV Talk Show Campaign

It is easy to understand why candidates prefer the talk show format, with its "softball" questioning, to the abrasive interrogations of news shows such as "Meet the Press," "Face the Nation," and "60 Minutes." Talk shows hosts generally let guests tell their own story. Audience and call-in questions are generally less specific and less adversarial than reporters' questions. More important, candidates can communicate directly to talk show audiences without the "filters" of anchors, news reporters, and commentators.

Texas billionaire Ross Perot had been a frequent guest on CNN's "Larry King Live" over the years, so when King pressed him during an appearance in early February as to whether he would be a presidential candidate, Perot responded by saying "If the American people put me on the ballot in all fifty states, I'll be their candidate." The announcement set off "Perot mania," and poll ratings for the pint-sized tycoon soared. Perot detached many middle-class voters from President Bush with his message of America's economic decline and crippling government deficits. When Perot quit the race in July, his disappointed supporters turned to Democrat Bill Clinton and his promises of change.

Perot jumped back in the race in September, and in the first debate his Texas twang and down-home folksy style stole the show. Chided by his opponents for having no governmental experience, he shot back, "Well they have a point. I don't have any experience in running up a 4 trillion dollar debt!" Perot's popularity in

(continued)

CASE STUDY

(continued)

the polls, hardly visible at all following his abrupt withdrawal from the race, suddenly sprang to life again. With both spot ads and half-hour "informercials," Perot would outspend both Bush and Clinton before the campaign ended.

Bill Clinton took charge in the second debate with its talk show format. Comfortable and confident with a fifteen percentage-point lead in the polls, Clinton walked about the stage easily fielding audience "softballs." He knew how to make

his audience feel comfortable by sharing his personal problems; he "humanized" himself by talking about his stepfather's alcoholism and brother's drug addiction. When Bush stumbled trying to understand the question of a confused young woman who asked how the "national debt . . . has affected you personally," Clinton approached her with microphone in hand and asked sympathetically, "Tell me how it's affected you. . . . You know people who lost their jobs and lost their homes?"

The final debate attracted more viewers than any presidential debate in history, matching audiences for the World Series and the Superbowl! Bush seized the initiative from a cautious Clinton to warn Americans that "taxing and spending more" would not improve the economy. He hit home in describing Clinton as "waffling" on the issues, and ended with a plea to the viewers to keep their "trust" in him. Bush's performance, together with Perot's continuing rise in the polls, narrowed the huge gap between himself and Clinton.

Yet in the end Clinton prevailed because he effectively communicated compassion for economic hardship and the need for change. Clinton won 43 percent of the popular vote to Bush's 38 and Perot's 19. The television talk show campaign produced the highest voter turnout in several decades.

TABLE 7-5   How Democratic and Republican Leaders Differ over Issues

	All voters (%)	Democratic leaders (%)	Republican leaders (%)
Political philosophy			
Conservative	30	5	60
Liberal	20	39	1
Government role			
Prefer smaller government, fewer services	43	16	87
Prefer larger government, more services	44	58	3
Domestic policy			
Favor increased federal spending for day care	52	87	36
Abortion should remain legal	40	72	29
Government pays too little attention to blacks	34	68	14
Defense policy			
Keep defense spending at current levels	66	32	84

Source: Responses of Democratic and Republican delegates to 1988 presidential nominating conventions as reported in the *New York Times,* August 14, 1988.

Voters usually think of themselves as Democrats or Republicans, and their *party identification* is the single most important factor in voter decisions. Candidates and issues, two other bases of voter decisions, are influential in elections, but they do not provide the solid core of millions of party supporters who almost always vote for their party's nominees.

About half of all roll-call votes in Congress are party votes—votes in which a majority of Democrats oppose a majority of Republicans. Party votes occur most frequently on well-publicized, high-conflict issues, including social welfare and anti-poverty programs, medical care, business regulation, and the federal budget. Party voting also occurs on presidential recommendations, with the president's party in Congress supporting the president's position and the opposition party opposing it. Bipartisan votes, those roll calls in which party majorities are found on the same side, usually occur on less-publicized, low-conflict issues. On many issues, voting follows party lines during roll calls on preliminary amendments but swings to a bipartisan vote on the final legislation. This occurs when the parties disagree on certain aspects of a bill but compromise on its final passage.

For many years Democratic party identifiers in the electorate heavily outnumbered Republican identifiers. But during the administrations of Republican presidents Reagan and Bush, party identification shifted toward the Republicans, so the parties are now closer to parity (see Table 7-7). Republicans have made their greatest gains among younger voters and Southern white voters.

party identification
thinking of oneself as a Democrat or Republican and generally supporting one's party's candidates

party votes
roll call votes in Congress in which a majority of Democrats oppose a majority of Republicans

BOX 7-2

Cross-National Perspective: The Role of Government

The idea of *limited* government, found in the writings of John Locke and echoed by the founders of the American nation, continues to influence American politics. Indeed, public opinion in the United States about the role of government in society differs significantly from public opinion in other nations, even in other advanced Western industrial nations.

Americans generally believe they are individually responsible for their own well-being, while Europeans tend to look toward government as their protector and benefactor. For example, Americans are much less likely than Europeans to believe that government "should provide everyone with a guaranteed basic income" or

"reduce differences in income among people" (see Table 7-6). Americans are more likely than Europeans to believe their taxes are "too high," even though taxes in the United States are generally lower than those in European nations. Americans are also generally less supportive of governmental regulation, even for purposes of public safety and health. Americans seem to prefer that individuals, rather than governments, make the decisions that shape their lives. Table 7-6 contains information obtained during surveys when interviewees were asked to indicate how much they agreed or disagreed with specific statements related to the role of government.

TABLE 7-6 Results of Surveys Related to the Role of Government (Percentage Who "Strongly Agree" or "Agree" with Each Statement)

	Government should provide everyone with a guaranteed basic income	It is the responsibility of government to reduce differences in income between people	Government should provide a job for everyone who wants one	Taxes are much too high/too high
Switzerland	43	43	50	51
Great Britain	61	64	59	41
Netherlands	50	65	75	60
West Germany	56	61	77	52
Austria	57	81	80	47
Italy	67	82	82	62
Hungary	77	80	92	39
United States	21	29	45	70

Source: Derived from international surveys reported in *American Enterprise,* March/April 1990, pp. 113–115.

TABLE 7-7 Change in Party Identification in the Electorate

	1978	1984	1988	1991
Democrat	48%	43%	36%	34%
Republican	23%	26%	30%	33%
Independent, other	29%	31%	34%	33%

Source: From various Gallup surveys. Respondents were asked "As of today, do you consider yourself a Republican, a Democrat, or an Independent?" See *Public Opinion* (September/October 1988), p. 34; *The American Enterprise* (May/June 1991), p. 92.

Notes

1. The Federalist papers were a series of essays by James Madison, Alexander Hamilton, and John Jay, written in 1787 and 1788 to explain and defend the new Constitution during the struggle over its ratification (*The Federalist,* New York: Modern Library, 1937).
2. Fred I. Greenstein, "The Psychological Functions of the Presidency for Citizens," in *The American Presidency: Vital Center,* ed. Elmer E. Cornwell (Chicago: Scott, Foresman, 1966), pp. 30–36.
3. *West Virginia State Board of Education* v. *Barrett* 319 U.S. 624 (1943).
4. Herbert J. McClosky et al., "Issue Conflict and Consensus Among Party Leaders and Followers," *American Political Science Review* 54 (June 1960): 595.

About This Chapter

The power of government is truly awesome. Government power influences every facet of our lives "from the cradle to the grave." We eat government-inspected foods, which have been transported on government-regulated railroads and highways and grown on government-subsidized farms. We live in government-inspected homes, paid for by government-subsidized mortgages from government-regulated banks. We attend government-subsidized schools, or work in government-inspected shops, or manage government-regulated businesses. The awesome powers of government have worried people for centuries. How can governmental power be limited? How can we enjoy the benefits and protections of government yet not become slaves to it? How can government leaders be restrained? How can we guarantee that our personal liberties will not be threatened by governments?

These questions are the province of political science, and in this chapter we have examined the answers that political science provides. Now that you have read Chapter 7, you should be able to

- discuss the meaning of democracy;
- discuss the separation of powers around which our government is structured and the reasons the Founders designed it this way;
- understand the limits of presidential power, especially in relation to the forced resignation of Richard Nixon;
- describe changes in the structure of governmental power;
- discuss actual political behaviors and processes in America and describe their effect on the exercise of power;
- discuss the increasing power of the mass media in American politics.

Discussion Questions

1. Define *political science* and describe its areas of concern.

2. Describe John Locke's views on constitutionalism and constitutional government, natural law, and the social contract. Discuss the influence of Locke's ideas on the authors of the U.S. Constitution. Define what the nation's founders meant by *republican government, limited government,* and *a strong national government.*

3. Discuss the ideal and procedural meanings of democracy and the democratic values.

4. What are the foundations of national power, and how does the Constitution define and limit them? Contrast expressed (delegated) powers with implied powers and identify the clause on which implied powers are based.

5. Define *federalism* and discuss the change that has taken place in the American federal structure. Include in your discussion definitions of *grants-in-aid* and *guidelines,* as well as an identification of the delegated congressional power that has been responsible for the change in the federalist structure.

6. Discuss the rationale the Founders used for structuring the government around a separation of powers. Identify the separate power structures the Constitution created. Using the original constitutional provisions regarding elections as an illustration, describe how the Founders' philosophy conflicted with the concepts of democracy. Define *sharing of power.*

7. Discuss the sources of presidential power and the factors contributing to the growth of that power in the twentieth century. Briefly describe how Richard Nixon overstepped the boundaries or limitations of presidential power. Comment on how the system of checks and balances and Nixon's own failure to "play by the rules of the game" contributed to his downfall.

8. Identify the sources of judicial power. Define *judicial review* and explain why the nation's founders were in favor of this principle. Describe how and why the courts are "insulated."

9. Discuss participation and nonparticipation in democracy. Who participates, and how is it possible to participate? Identify the titles and contents of some of the congressional acts and constitutional amendments that have removed obstacles to voting.

10. Describe the functions of political parties. Compare the American two-party system with European political party systems. How is it possible to identify real party differences in America? Identify and describe the most important factor in voting behavior.

11. What has been the impact of television on politics, especially presidential elections?

Power and History

History and Social Science

Can history inform the social sciences? The purpose of this chapter is not to teach American history, but rather to examine the work of historians to see what contribution they can make to our understanding of power and the social sciences.

History refers to all *past human actions and events*. The study of history is the *recording, narrating, and interpreting of these events*. History includes the discovery of facts about past events, as well as the interpretation of the events. Many historians contend that their primary responsibility is the disclosure of facts about the past: the accurate presentation of what actually happened, unbiased by interpretive theories or philosophies.

history
the recording, narrating, and interpreting of all past human actions and events

But however carefully historians try to avoid bias, they cannot report *all* the facts of human history. Facts do not select and arrange themselves. The historians must select and organize facts that are worthy of interest, and this process involves personal judgment of what is important about the past. The historian's judgment about the past is affected by present conditions and by personal feelings about the future. So the past is continually reinterpreted by each generation of historians. History is "an unending dialogue" between the present and the past; it is "what one age finds worthy of note in another."

In selecting and organizing their facts, historians must consider the causes of wars and revolutions, the reasons for the rise and fall of civilizations, the consequences of great events and ideas. They cannot marshal their facts without some notion of *interrelations* among human events. Because they must consider what forces have operated to shape the past, they become involved in economics, sociology, psychology, anthropology, and political science. Historian Henry Steele Commager has observed that "no self-respecting modern historian is content merely with recording what happened; he wants to explain why it happened."[1] Thus, history and social science are intimately related.

History and the American Experience

approaches to American history
the "great man" approach

the democratic institutions approach

the western frontier approach

critical approaches

There is a great temptation to romanticize national history. Many national histories are self-congratulating, patriotic exercises. Many historical biographies paint their subjects as larger-than-life figures, free of the faults of common people, who shape the course of events themselves rather than merely respond to the world in which they live. National leaders of the past—Washington, Jefferson, Jackson, Lincoln, Franklin D. Roosevelt—are portrayed as noble people superior in character and wisdom to today's politicians. Even with the myth of the cherry tree discarded, generations of historians have looked with awe on the gallery of national heroes as almost superhuman individuals who gallantly saved the nation.

Some national histories do not rely on "great man" explanations, but instead emphasize the origin and growth of democratic institutions. Democracy is traced from its ancient Greek beginnings, through English constitutional development, to the colonies and the American constitutional system. Frequently these national histories reinforce reverence for existing political and governmental institutions. Some are written more to support than to explain the United States.

A bull train makes a treacherous climb over Ute Pass.
Source: State Historical Society of Wisconsin

In the 1890s historian Frederick Jackson Turner argued that the main influence on American history was not the development of political institutions from English or Greek origins, or even the actions of "great men," but the impact of the western frontier on American society. As historians explained (and occasionally exaggerated) Turner's thesis, they wrote new and even more nationalistic sagas of the American expansion. They hailed western settlement, the Indian wars, the development of transportation and communication, and the rugged individualism of the heroic democratic frontiersman.

But historians have also been critical of American institutions. At the beginning of the twentieth century, reform politicians and muckraking journalists brought a new skepticism to American life. The Progressive era was critical of the malfunctioning of many governmental institutions that had become sacred over time, and even of the Olympian position of the nation's founders. In 1913 Charles A. Beard created an uproar by suggesting that economic motives played a part in leading the Founders to write the Constitution.

Nevertheless, for the most part the quest for the American past has been carried on in a spirit of sentiment and nostalgia, rather than of critical analysis. Historical novels, fictionalized biographies, pictorial collections, and books on American regions all appeal to our fondness for looking back to what we believe was a better era. Americans have a peculiar longing to recapture the past, to try to recover what seems to have been lost.

Power and Change over Time

studying changes in sources of power over time

Our own bias about the importance of power in society leads us to focus attention on *changing sources of power over time* in American history and on the characteristics of the people and groups who have acquired power. We contend that the Constitution, and the national government it established, reflected the beliefs, values, and interests of the people of power—the elite—of the new republic. If we are to have a true understanding of the Constitution, we must investigate the political interests of the Founders and the historical circumstances surrounding the Philadelphia convention in 1787.

Power structures change over time. To understand power in society we have to explore the historical development of power relationships. Any society, to maintain stability and avoid revolution, must provide opportunities for talented and ambitious individuals to acquire power. As an expanding economy created new sources of wealth, power in the United States shifted to those groups and individuals who acquired the new economic resources. Western expansion and settlement, industrialization, immigration, urbanization, technological innovation, and new sources of wealth created new bases of power and new powerholders.

incremental change
slow and continuous rather than rapid or revolutionary

But power in the United States has changed slowly, without any serious break in the ideas and values underlying the American political and economic system. The nation has never experienced a true revolution, in which national leadership is formally replaced by groups or individuals who do not share the values of the system itself. Instead, *changes have been slow and incremental.* New national leaders have generally accepted the national consensus about private enterprise, limited government, and individualism.

Historian Richard Hofstadter argues effectively that many accounts of the American past overemphasize the political differences in every era:

historical consensus
beliefs shared over time

> The fierceness of the political struggles has often been misleading; for the range of vision embraced by the primary contestants in the major parties has always been bounded by the horizons of property and enterprise. However much at odds on specific issues, the major political traditions have shared a belief in the rights of property, the philosophy of economic individualism, the value of competition; they have accepted the economic virtues of capitalist culture as necessary qualities of man. Even when some property right has been challenged—as it was by followers of Jefferson and Jackson—in the name of the rights of man or the rights of the community, the challenge, when translated into practical policy, has actually been urged on behalf of some other kind of property.
>
> The sanctity of private property, the right of the individual to dispose of and invest it, the value of opportunity, and the natural evolution of self-interest and self-assertion, within broad legal limits, into a beneficent social order have been staple tenets of the central faith in American political ideologies; these conceptions have been shared in large part by men as diverse as Jefferson, Jackson, Lincoln, Cleveland, Bryan, Wilson, and Hoover.[2]

Charles Beard, historian and political scientist, provided the most controversial historical interpretation of the origin of American national government in his landmark book, *An Economic Interpretation of the Constitution.*[3] Not all historians agree with Beard's interpretation, particularly his emphasis on economic forces, but all concede that it is a milestone in understanding the American Constitution.

Beard argued that to understand the Constitution we must understand the economic interests of the national elite, which included the writers of the document:

> Did the men who formulated the fundamental law of the land possess the kinds of property which were immediately and directly increased in value or made more secure by the results of their labors in Philadelphia? Did they have money at interest [loans outstanding]? Did they own public securities [government bonds]? Did they hold Western lands for appreciation? Were they interested in shipping and manufactures?[4]

Beard was *not* charging that the Founders wrote the Constitution exclusively for their own benefit. But he argued that they personally benefited immediately from its adoption and that they did not act only "under the guidance of abstract principles of political science." Beard closely studied old unpublished financial records of the U.S. Treasury Department and the personal letters and financial accounts of the fifty-five delegates to the Philadelphia convention. Table 8-1 summarizes his findings of the financial interests of the nation's founders. Beard then turned to an examination of the *Constitution* itself, in the original form in which it emerged from the Convention, to observe the *relationship between economic interests and political power.*

The first, and perhaps the most important, enumerated power is the power to "lay and collect taxes, duties, imposts, and excises." The *taxing power* is, of course, the basis of all other powers, and it enabled the national government to end its dependence on the states. The taxing power was of great benefit to the holders of government bonds, particularly when it was combined with the provision in Article VI that "all debts contracted and engagements entered into, before the adoption of this Constitution, shall be as valid against the United States under this Constitution, as under the Confederation." This meant that the national government would be obliged to pay off all those investors who held bonds of the United States, and the taxing power would give the national government the ability to do so on its own.

Congress was also given the power to "regulate commerce with foreign nations, and among the several states." The *interstate commerce clause,* which eliminated state control over commerce, and the provision that prohibited the states from taxing exports, created a free-trade area, or "common market," among the thirteen states.

Following the power to tax and spend, to borrow money, and to regulate commerce in Article I, there is a series of *specific powers designed to enable Congress to protect money and property.* Congress is given the power to make bankruptcy

(continued)

(continued)

laws, to coin money and regulate its value, to fix standards of weights and measures, to punish counterfeiting, to establish post offices and post roads, to pass copyright and patent laws to protect authors and inventors, and to punish piracies and felonies committed on the high seas. Each of these powers is a specific asset to bankers, investors, merchants, authors, inventors, and shippers.

The Constitution provided an explicit advantage to slaveholders in Article IV, Section 2 (later altered by the Thirteenth Amendment, which abolished slavery):

> No person held to service or labour in one state, under the laws thereof, escaping into another, shall, in consequence of any law or regulation therein, be discharged from

TABLE 8-1   The Founders of the American Nation Classified by Known Economic Interests

Public security interests (owners of U.S. government bonds)		Real estate and land speculation	Lending and banking investments	Mercantile, manufacturing, and shipping interests	Plantations and slaveholdings
Major	*Minor*				
Baldwin	Bassett	Blount	Bassett	Broom	Butler
Blair	Blount	Dayton	Broom	Clymer	Davie
Clymer	Brearley	Few	Butler	Ellsworth	Jenifer
Dayton	Broom	FitzSimons	Carroll	FitzSimons	A. Martin
Ellsworth	Butler	Franklin	Clymer	Gerry	L. Martin
FitzSimons	Carroll	Gerry	Davie	King	Mason
Gerry	Few	Gilman	Dickinson	Langdon	Mercer
Gilman	Hamilton	Gorham	Ellsworth	McHenry	C. C. Pinckney
Gorham	L. Martin	Hamilton	Few	Mifflin	C. Pinckney
Jenifer	Mason	Mason	FitzSimons	G. Morris	Randolph
Johnson	Mercer	R. Morris	Franklin	R. Morris	Read
King	Mifflin	Washington	Gilman		Rutledge
Langdon	Read	Williamson	Ingersoll		Spaight
Lansing	Spaight	Wilson	Johnson		Washington
Livingston	Wilson		King		Wythe
McClurg	Wythe		Langdon		
R. Morris			McHenry		
C. C. Pinckney			Mason		
C. Pinckney			C. C. Pinckney		
Randolph			C. Pinckney		
Sherman			Randolph		
Strong			Read		
Washington			Washington		
Williamson			Williamson		

(continued)

(continued)

such service or labour, but shall be delivered up on claim of the party to whom such service or labour may be due.

Slaves were one of the most important forms of property in America at the time, and this constitutional provision was an extremely valuable protection for slave-holders. The slave trade was to end twenty years after the Constitution was written, but slavery as a domestic institution was better safeguarded under the new Constitution than under the Articles of Confederation.

The Constitution also forbids states to pass any law "impairing the obligation of contracts." The structure of business relations in a free enterprise economy depends on governmental enforcement of private contracts, and it is essential to the economic elite that the government be prevented from relieving persons of their obligations to contracts. If state legislatures could relieve debtors of their contractual obligations, or relieve indentured servants of their obligations to their masters, or prevent creditors from foreclosing on mortgages, or declare moratoriums on debt, or otherwise interfere with business obligations, the interests of investors, merchants, and creditors would be seriously damaged.

Some historians disagree with Beard's emphasis on the economic motives of the Founders. For example:

> The Constitution was adopted in a society which was fundamentally democratic, not undemocratic; and it was adopted by people who were primarily middle-class property owners, especially farmers who owned realty, not just by the owners of personalty. . . . The Constitution was not just an economic document, although economic factors were undoubtedly important. Since most of the people were middle-class and had private property, practically everybody was interested in the protection of property.[5]

Moreover, in the struggle over ratification of the Constitution, it is clear that some people of prestige, reputation, and property opposed accepting the new Constitution. Influential Anti-Federalists deplored the undemocratic features of the Constitution, and their criticism about the omission of a bill of rights led directly to the inclusion of the first ten amendments. Supporters of the Constitution were forced to retreat from their demand for unconditional ratification, and they agreed to add the Bill of Rights as amendments as soon as the first Congress was convened under the Constitution.

Over the years, America's political leadership has been essentially consensual. Whatever the popular label of the American political and economic system—Federalist, Democrat, Whig, Republican, Progressive, Conservative, or Liberal—American leaders have remained committed to the same values and ideas that motivated the Founders. Although major changes in public policy and in the structure of American government have indeed taken place over two centuries, these changes have been *incremental* rather than revolutionary.

Costs of preserving the Union—the scene after Antietam in "Bloody Lane," a sunken road where two Union regiments had trapped Confederates in a barrage of rifle fire. This photograph and others from Antietam, taken by Matthew Brady, the most famous Civil War photographer, were the first photos Americans had ever seen of wartime coverage. *Source:* Collections of the Library of Congress

The Civil War and Elite Division

division among the elite

Social scientists can gain insight into societal conflict and *the breakdown of elite consensus* through the study of history, particularly the history of the American Civil War. America's elite were in substantial agreement about the character and direction of the new nation during its first sixty years. In the 1850s, however, the role of African Americans in American society—the most divisive issue in the history of American politics—became an urgent question that drove a wedge between the elite groups and ultimately led to the nation's bloodiest war. The political system was unequal to the task of negotiating a peaceful settlement to the problem of slavery because America's elite was deeply divided over the question.

southern elite
plantation owners dependent on slave labor

It was the white southern elite and not the white masses who had an interest in the slave and cotton culture. On the eve of the Civil War probably not more than 400,000 southern families (approximately one in four) held slaves, and many of those families held only one or two slaves each. The number of great planters (men who owned fifty or more slaves and large holdings of land) was probably not more than 7,000. Yet the views of these planters dominated southern politics.

northern elite
manufacturers dependent on wage labor

The northern elite consisted of merchants and manufacturers who depended on free labor. However, the northern elite had no direct interest in the abolition of slavery in the South. Some northern manufacturers were making good profits from southern trade, and with higher tariffs they stood a chance to make even better profits. Abolitionist activities imperiled trade relations between North and South and were often looked on with irritation in northern social circles.

conflict over western land
plantations or small farms

Both the northern and the southern elite realized that control of the West was the key to future dominance of the nation. The northern elite wanted a West composed of small farmers who produced food and raw materials for the industrial and commercial East and provided a market for eastern goods. But southern planters feared the voting power of a West composed of small farmers and wanted western lands for the expansion of the cotton and slave culture. Cotton ate up the land, and because it required continuous cultivation and monotonous rounds of simple tasks, cotton growing was suited to slave labor. Thus, to protect the cotton economy, it was essential to expand westward and to protect slavery in the West. The conflict over western land eventually precipitated the Civil War.

Yet despite such differences, the underlying consensus of the American elite was so great that compromise after compromise was devised to maintain unity. Both the northern and the southern elite displayed a continued devotion to the principles of constitutional government and the protection of private property. In the *Missouri Compromise of 1820,* the land in the Louisiana Purchase exclusive of Missouri was divided between free territory and slave territory at 36°30′; and Maine and Missouri were admitted to the Union as free and slave states, respectively. After the war with Mexico, the elaborate *Compromise of 1850* caused one of the greatest debates in American legislative history, with Senators Henry Clay, Daniel Webster, John C. Calhoun, Salmon P. Chase, Stephen A. Douglas, Jefferson Davis, Alexander H. Stephens, Robert Toombs, William H. Seward, and Thaddeus Stevens all participating. Cleavage within the elite was apparent, but it was not yet so divisive as to split the nation. A compromise was achieved, providing for the admission of California as a free state; for the creation of two new territories, New Mexico and Utah, out of the Mexican cession; for a drastic fugitive slave law to satisfy southern planters; and for the prohibition of the slave trade in the District of Columbia. Even the *Kansas–Nebraska Act of 1854* was intended to be a compromise; each new territory was supposed to decide for itself whether it should be slave or free, the expectation being that Nebraska would vote free and Kansas slave. Gradually, however, the spirit of compromise gave way to divergence and conflict.

> **underlying elite consensus: attempts at compromise**
> Missouri Compromise of 1820
> Compromise of 1850
> Kansas–Nebraska Act

Beginning in 1856, proslavery and antislavery forces fought it out in "bleeding Kansas." Senator Charles Sumner of Massachusetts delivered a condemnation of slavery in the Senate and was beaten almost to death on the Senate floor by Congressman Preston Brooks of South Carolina. Intemperate language in the Senate became commonplace, with frequent threats of secession, violence, and civil war. In 1857 a southern-dominated Supreme Court decided, in *Dred Scott* v. *Sanford,* that the Missouri Compromise was unconstitutional because Congress had no authority to forbid slavery in any territory. Slave property, said Chief Justice Roger B. Taney, was as much protected by the Constitution as was any other kind of property. In 1859 John Brown and his followers raided the U.S. arsenal at Harper's Ferry, as a first step to freeing the slaves of Virginia by force. Brown was captured by Virginia militia under the command of Colonel Robert E. Lee, tried for treason, found guilty, and executed. Southerners believed that northerners had tried to incite the horror of slave insurrection, whereas northerners believed that Brown died a martyr.

> **compromises break down**

Abraham Lincoln never attacked slavery in the South; his exclusive concern was to halt the spread of slavery in the western territories. He wrote in 1845: "I hold it a paramount duty of us in the free states, due to the union of the states, and perhaps to liberty itself (paradox though it may seem), to let the slavery of the other states alone."[6] Throughout his political career Lincoln consistently held this posi-

> **Lincoln's views and slavery**

CASE STUDY

Frederick
Jackson Turner:
The Rise of the
West

As we have noted, power relationships change over time. Industrialization, urbanization, technological change, and new sources of wealth create new bases of power and new powerholders. The governmental structure of society must provide for changes in the distribution of power or suffer the threat of instability and even revolution. The political system must provide for the "circulation of the elite" as new bases of power and new powerholders emerge in society.

According to historian Frederick Jackson Turner, "The rise of the New West was the most significant fact in American history."[7] Certainly the American West had a profound impact on the political system of the new nation. People went west because of the vast wealth of fertile lands that awaited them there; nowhere else in the world could one acquire wealth so quickly. Because aristocratic families of the eastern seaboard seldom had reason to migrate westward, the western settlers were mainly middle- or lower-class immigrants. With hard work and good fortune, a penniless migrant could become a rich plantation owner or cattle rancher in a single generation. Thus, the West meant rapid upward social mobility.

A new elite arose in the West and had to be assimilated into America's governing circles. This assimilation had a profound effect on the character of America's elite. No one exemplifies the new entrants better than Andrew Jackson. Jackson's victory in the presidential election of 1828 was not a victory of the common man over the propertied classes, but a victory of the new western elite over established leadership in the East. It forced the established elite to recognize the growing importance of the West and to open their ranks to the new rich who were settling west of the Alleghenies.

Because Jackson was a favorite of the people, it was easy for him to believe in the wisdom of the masses. But "Jacksonian Democracy" was by no means a philosophy of leveling egalitarianism. The ideal of the frontier society was the self-made individual, and wealth and power won by *competitive skill* were much admired. Wealth and power obtained through special privilege offended the frontierspeople. They believed in a *natural aristocracy,* rather than an aristocracy by birth, education, or special privilege. It was *not* absolute equality that Jacksonians demanded but a *more open elite system*—a greater opportunity for the rising middle class to acquire wealth and influence through competition.

In their struggle to open America's elite system, the Jacksonians appealed to mass sentiment. Jackson's humble beginnings, his image as a self-made man, his military adventures, his frontier experience, and his rough, brawling style endeared him to the masses. As beneficiaries of popular support, the new western elite developed a strong faith in the wisdom and justice of popular decisions. The new western states that entered the Union granted universal white male suffrage, and gradually the older states fell into step. The rising elite, themselves often less than a generation away from the masses, saw in a widened electorate a chance for personal advancement they could never have achieved under the old regime. Therefore, the

(continued)

(continued)

Jacksonians became noisy and effective advocates of the principle that all men should have the right to *vote* and that no restrictions should be placed on *office-holding*. They also launched a successful attack on the congressional caucus system of nominating presidential candidates. Having been defeated in Congress in 1824, Jackson wanted to sever Congress from the nominating process. In 1832, when the Democrats held their first national convention, Andrew Jackson was renominated by acclamation.

Jacksonian Democracy also brought changes in the method of selecting presidential electors. The Constitution left to the various state legislatures the right to decide how presidential electors should be chosen, and in most cases the legislatures themselves chose the electors. But after 1832 all states elected their presidential electors by popular vote. In most states the people voted for electors who were listed under the name of their party and their candidate.

tion. On the other hand, with regard to the western territories, he said: "The whole nation is interested that the best use shall be made of these territories. We want them for homes and free white people. This they cannot be, to any considerable extent, if slavery shall be planted within them."[8] In short, Lincoln wanted the western territories to be tied economically and culturally to the northern system. As for Lincoln's racial views, as late as 1858 he said:

> I will say, then, that I am not, nor ever have been, in favor of bringing about in any way the social and political equality of the white and black races: that I am not, nor ever have been, in favor of making voters or jurors of negroes, nor of qualifying them to hold office, nor to intermarry with white people. . . .
>
> And inasmuch as they cannot so live, while they do remain together there must be the position of superior and inferior, and I as much as any other man am in favor of having the superior position assigned to the white race.[9]

Historian Richard Hofstadter believed that Lincoln's political posture was essentially *conservative:* he wished to preserve the long-established *order and consensus that had protected American principles and property rights* so successfully in the past. He was *not* an abolitionist, and he did *not* seek the destruction of the southern elite or the rearrangement of the South's social fabric. His goal was to bring the South back into the Union, to restore orderly government, and to establish the principle that states cannot resist national authority with force. At the beginning of the Civil War, Lincoln knew that a great part of conservative northern opinion was willing to fight for the Union but might refuse to support a war to free slaves. Lincoln's great political skill was his ability to gather all the issues of the Civil War into one single overriding theme: *the preservation of the Union.* However, he was bitterly attacked throughout the war by radical Republicans who thought he had "no antislavery instincts."

Lincoln's goal: to preserve the Union

As the war continued and casualties mounted, opinion in the North became increasingly bitter toward southern slaveowners. Many Republicans joined the abolitionists in calling for emancipation of the slaves simply to punish the "rebels." They knew that the power of the South was based on the labor of slaves. Lincoln also knew that if he proclaimed to the world that the war was being fought to free the slaves, there would be less danger of foreign intervention.

real origin of the Emancipation Proclamation

On September 22, 1862, Lincoln issued his preliminary Emancipation Proclamation. Claiming his right as commander in chief of the army and navy, he promised that "on the first day of January, . . . 1863, all persons held as slaves within any State or designated part of a State the people whereof shall then be in rebellion against the United States shall be then, thenceforward, and forever free." Thus, one of the great steps forward in human freedom in this nation, the Emancipation Proclamation, did not come about as a result of demands by the people, and certainly not as a result of demands by the slaves themselves. Hofstadter contended that *the Emancipation Proclamation was a political action taken by the president for the sake of helping to preserve the Union.* It was not a revolutionary action but a conservative one.

Power and the Industrial Revolution

the rise of the industrial elite

The importance of the Civil War for the power structure of the United States lay in the commanding position that the new industrial capitalists won during the course of that struggle. Even before 1860, northern industry had been altering the course of American life; the economic transformation of the United States from an agricultural to an industrial nation reached the crescendo of a revolution in the second half of the nineteenth century. Canals and steam railroads had been opening up new markets for the growing industrial cities of the East. The rise of corporations and of stock markets for the accumulation of capital upset old-fashioned ideas about property. The introduction of machinery in factories revolutionized the conditions of labor and made the masses dependent on industrial capitalists for their livelihood. Civil War profits compounded the capital of the industrialists and placed them in a position to dominate the economic life of the nation. Moreover, when the southern planters were removed from the national scene, the government in Washington became the exclusive domain of the new industrial leaders.

social Darwinism
competition selects the best; a philosophy justifying great accumulations of wealth

The new industrial elite found a new philosophy to justify its political and economic dominance. Drawing an analogy from Darwinian biology, Herbert Spencer undertook to demonstrate that, just as an elite was selected in nature through evolution, so also society would near perfection as it allowed a natural *social* elite to be selected by *free competition.* Spencer hailed the accumulation of new industrial wealth as a sign of "the survival of the fittest." The *social Darwinists* found in the law of survival of the fittest an admirable defense for the emergence of a ruthless ruling elite, an elite that defined its own self-interest more narrowly, perhaps, than any other in American history. It was a philosophy that permitted the conditions of the masses to decline to the lowest depths in American history.

the industrialists acquire political power

After the Civil War, industrialists became more prominent in Congress than they had ever been. They had little trouble in voting high tariffs and hard money, both

The ideal history, completely objective and dispassionate, is really an illusion. Consciously or unconsciously, all historians are biased. There is bias in their choice of subject, in their selection of material, in their organization and presentation of the material, and, inevitably, in their interpretation of it.

Let us consider the historical interpretation of the African American experience in America, particularly of the black experience in the Reconstruction era following the Civil War. Only a few years ago historians viewed the Reconstruction Congress as vindictive and sinful. The period as a whole was considered destructive, oppressive, and corrupt. Military rule was imposed on the South. "Carpetbaggers" and "scalawags" confiscated the property of helpless southerners and retarded the economic progress of the South for decades. Maladministration and corruption in the federal government were portrayed as being greater than ever before in American history. The role of African Americans in the Reconstruction years was regarded with ridicule: it was implied that blacks were pushed into positions of authority by spiteful military rulers in order to humiliate proud southern whites. The accomplishments of blacks during this period were overlooked. Finally, it was suggested that the separation of the races—segregation—was the "normal" pattern of southern life. The belief was fostered that blacks and whites in the South had never known any other pattern of life than slavery and segregation.

A new awareness of African American history in recent years has resulted in a thoroughgoing reinterpretation of the Reconstruction era. Historian C. Vann Woodward's work led the way in bringing new light to this important period. Woodward recorded the progress of blacks during Reconstruction, described the good-faith efforts of the Reconstruction Congress to secure equality for African Americans, and explained the reimposition of segregation in terms of class conflict among whites. (Alex Haley's popular book *Roots,* together with the dramatic television series based on it, is another example of historical interpretation. Whereas many older histories of the pre–Civil War South romanticized plantation life, *Roots* described the cruelties and brutality of slavery.)

A Revised View of Reconstruction: African American Progress

When the Republicans gained control of Congress in 1867, blacks momentarily seemed destined to attain their full rights as U.S. citizens. Under military rule southern states adopted new constitutions that awarded the vote and other civil liberties to blacks. Black men were elected to state legislatures and to the U.S. Congress. In 1865 nearly 10 percent of all federal troops were black. The literacy rate among blacks rose rapidly as hundreds of schools set up by the federal government's Freedmen's Bureau began providing education for ex-slaves.[10]

The first African American actually to serve in Congress was Hiram R. Revels

(continued)

(continued)

of Mississippi, who in 1870 took over the Senate seat previously held by Confederate President Jefferson Davis. In all, twenty-two southern blacks served in Congress between 1870 and 1901. All were elected as Republicans; thirteen were former slaves. Many of those men made substantial contributions to Reconstruction policy.

The accomplishments of the Reconstruction Congress were considerable. Even before the Republicans gained control, the Thirteenth Amendment, which abolished slavery, had become part of the Constitution. But it was the Fourteenth and Fifteenth Amendments and the important Civil Rights Act of 1875 that attempted to secure a place for the blacks in the United States equal to that of whites.

The Civil Rights Act of 1875 declared that all persons were entitled to the full and equal enjoyment of all public accommodations, inns, public conveniences, theaters, and other places of public amusement. In this act the Reconstruction Congress committed the nation to a policy of nondiscrimination in all aspects of public life.

But by 1877 support for Reconstruction policies began to crumble. In what has been described as the "Compromise of 1877," the national government agreed to end military occupation of the South, thereby giving up its efforts to rearrange southern society and lending tacit approval to white supremacy in that region. In return, the southern states pledged their support for the Union, accepted national supremacy, and enabled the Republican candidate, Rutherford B. Hayes, to assume the presidency following the much-disputed election of 1876, in which his opponent, Samuel Tilden, had received a majority of the popular vote.

The Development of the White Supremacy Movement

The withdrawal of federal troops from the South in 1877 did not bring about an instant change in the status of the blacks. Southern blacks voted in large numbers well into the 1880s and 1890s. Certainly we do not mean to suggest that discrimination was nonexistent during that period. Perhaps the most debilitating of all segregation—that in the public schools—appeared immediately after the Civil War under the beneficent sanction of Reconstruction authorities. Yet segregation took shape only gradually.

The first objective of the *white supremacy movement* was to disenfranchise blacks. The standard devices developed for achieving this feat were the literacy test, the poll tax, the white primary, and various forms of intimidation. Following the disenfranchisement of African Americans, the white supremacy movement established segregation and discrimination as public policy by the adoption of a large number of "Jim Crow" laws, designed to prevent the mingling of whites and blacks (Jim Crow was a stereotypical African American in a nineteenth-century song-and-dance show). Between 1900 and 1910, laws were adopted by southern state legislatures requiring segregation of the races in streetcars, hospitals, prisons, orphan-

(continued)

(continued)

Ku Klux Klan cross-burning intended to intimidate.
Source: AP/Wide World Photos

ages, and homes for the aged and indigent. A New Orleans ordinance decreed that white and black prostitutes confine their activities to separate districts. In 1913 the federal government itself adopted policies that segregated the races in federal office buildings, cafeterias, and restroom facilities. Social policy followed (indeed, exceeded) public policy. Little signs reading "White Only" or "Colored" appeared everywhere, with or without the support of law.

Response of Blacks to Segregation

Many early histories of Reconstruction paid little attention to the response of blacks to the imposition of segregation. But there were at least three distinct types of response: (1) accommodation to a subordinate position in society, (2) the formation of a black protest movement, and (3) migration out of the South to avoid some of the consequences of white supremacy.

(continued)

CASE STUDY

(continued)

The foremost African American advocate of accommodation to segregation was the well-known educator Booker T. Washington. Washington enjoyed wide popularity among both white and black Americans. He was an adviser to two presidents (Theodore Roosevelt and William Howard Taft) and was highly respected by white philanthropists and government officials. In his famous Cotton States' Exposition speech in Atlanta in 1895, Washington assured whites that blacks were prepared to accept a separate position in society:

> In all things that are purely social we can be as separate as the fingers, yet one as the hand in all things essential to mutual progress.[11]

Booker T. Washington's hopes for African Americans lay in a program of self-help through education. He himself had attended Hampton Institute in Virginia, where the curriculum centered around practical trades for blacks. Washington obtained some white philanthropic support in establishing his own Tuskegee Institute in Tuskegee, Alabama, in 1881. His first students helped build the school. Training at Tuskegee emphasized immediately useful vocations, such as farming, preaching, and blacksmithing. Washington urged his students to stay in the South, to acquire land, and to build homes, thereby helping to eliminate ignorance and poverty among their fellow African Americans. One of Tuskegee's outstanding faculty members was George Washington Carver, who researched and developed uses for southern crops. Other privately and publicly endowed black colleges were founded that later developed into major universities, including Fisk and Howard (both started by the Freedmen's Bureau) and Atlanta, Hampton, and Southern.

While Washington was urging blacks to make the best of segregation, a small band of blacks were organizing themselves behind a declaration of black resistance and protest that would later rewrite American public policy. The leader of this group was W. E. B. Du Bois, a brilliant historian and sociologist at Atlanta University. In 1905 Du Bois and a few other African American intellectuals met in Niagara Falls, Canada, to draw up a black platform intended to "assail the ears" and sear the consciences of white Americans. In rejecting moderation and compromise, the Niagara statement proclaimed: "We refuse to allow the impression to remain that the Negro American assents to inferiority, is submissive under oppression and apologetic before insults." The platform listed the major injustices perpetrated against blacks since Reconstruction: the loss of voting rights, the imposition of Jim Crow laws and segregated public schools, the denial of equal job opportunities, the existence of inhumane conditions in southern prisons, the exclusion of blacks from West Point and Annapolis, and the failure on the part of the federal government to enforce the Fourteenth and Fifteenth Amendments. Out of the Niagara meeting came the idea for a nationwide organization dedicated to fighting for blacks, and on February 12, 1909, the one-hundredth anniversary of Abraham Lincoln's birth, the National Association for the Advancement of Colored People (NAACP) was founded.

(continued)

(continued)

Du Bois himself was on the original board of directors of the NAACP, but a majority of the board consisted of white liberals. In the years to follow, most of the financial support and policy guidance for the association was provided by whites rather than blacks. However, Du Bois was the NAACP's first director of research and the editor of its magazine, *Crisis.* The NAACP began a long and eventually successful campaign to establish black rights through legal action. Over the years, hundreds of court cases were brought at the local, state, and federal court levels on behalf of blacks denied their constitutional rights.

World War I provided an opportunity for restive blacks in the South to escape the worst abuses of white supremacy by migrating en masse to northern cities. In the years 1916 to 1918, an estimated half-million blacks moved to the North to fill the labor shortage caused by the war effort. Most migrating blacks arrived in big northern cities only to find more poverty and segregation. But at least they could vote and attend better schools, and they did not encounter laws requiring segregation in public places.

The progressive "ghettoization" of African Americans—their migration from the rural South to the urban North and their increasing concentration in central-city ghettos—had profound political, as well as social, implications. The ghetto provided an environment conducive to political action. Even as early as 1928, the black residents of Chicago were able to elect one of their own to the House of Representatives. The election of Oscar de Priest, the first African American congressman from the North, signaled a new turn in American urban politics by announcing to white politicians that they would have to reckon with the black vote in northern cities. The black ghettos would soon provide an important element in a new political coalition that was about to take form: namely, the Democratic party of Franklin Delano Roosevelt.

of which heightened profits. Very little effective regulatory legislation was permitted to reach the floor of Congress. After 1881 the Senate came under the spell of Nelson Aldrich, son-in-law of John D. Rockefeller who controlled Standard Oil. Aldrich served thirty years in the Senate. He believed that geographical representation in that body was old-fashioned and openly advocated a Senate manned officially by representatives from the great business "constituencies"—steel, coal, copper, railroads, banks, textiles, and so on.

The *corporate form of business* facilitated the amassing of capital by limiting the liability of capitalists to their actual investments and thereby keeping their personal fortunes safe in the event of misfortunes to their companies. The corporate form also encouraged capitalists to take risks in expanding industrial capital through the stock market. "Wall Street," the address of the nation's busiest securities market, the New York Stock Exchange, became a synonym for industrial capitalism. The markets for corporation stocks provided a vast and ready money source for new enterprises or for the enlargement and consolidation of old firms.

the rise of the modern corporation

The growth of industry brought many people to urban areas.
Source: Brown Brothers

The New Deal and the Emergence of the "Liberal Establishment"

impact of the Great Depression

The *economic collapse of the Great Depression* undermined the faith of both rich and poor in the idea of social Darwinism. Following the stock market crash of October 1929, and in spite of assurances by President Herbert Hoover that prosperity lay "just around the corner," the American economy virtually stopped. Prices dropped sharply, factories closed, real estate values declined, new construction

President Franklin D. Roosevelt signs the Social Security Bill, 1935.
Source: UPI/Bettmann

practically ceased, banks went under, wages were cut drastically, unemployment figures mounted, and welfare rolls swelled.

The election of Franklin D. Roosevelt to the presidency in 1932 ushered in a new era in American political philosophy. The Great Depression did *not* bring about a revolution; it did *not* result in the emergence of a new elite; but it did have an important impact on the *thinking* of America's governing circles. The economic disaster that had befallen the nation caused the elite to consider the need for economic reform. The Great Depression also reinforced the notion that the elite must acquire a greater public responsibility. The victories of fascism in Germany and communism in the Soviet Union and the growing restlessness of the masses in the United States made it plain that *reform and regard for the public welfare* were essential to the continued maintenance of the American political system and the dominant place of the elite in it.

Roosevelt sought to elaborate a *New Deal philosophy* that would permit government to devote much more attention to the public welfare than did the philosophy of Hoover's somewhat discredited "rugged individualism." The New Deal was not a revolutionary system but rather a necessary *reform* of the existing capitalist system. In the New Deal, the American elite accepted the principle that the entire community, through the agency of the national government, has a *respon-*

new era in elite thinking
reform and welfare to preserve American democracy

Roosevelt and the New Deal
to reform capitalism, not replace it

CASE STUDY

Vietnam: A
Political
History[12]

In the immediate aftermath of the Vietnam war, many Americans preferred simply to forget their nation's unhappy experience. The memories were too painful. Liberals and conservatives, Democrats and Republicans were equally implicated in the defeat. No one debated "who lost the war." Only later would Americans begin to reflect on the experience, build a memorial to the men and women who died, and undertake to write histories of that conflict.

Histories of the Vietnam war, like all histories, reflect the historian's judgment about what facts are most important and how they should be interpreted. Perhaps the Vietnam experience is still too recent to expect dispassionate explanations— why it happened and why it turned out so badly for so many people. Histories of the war continue many of the same controversies that occurred during the war itself.

The account of the Vietnam war presented here reflects the writer's view that the war was a political, not a military, defeat, and that responsibility for the tragic results lies with the nation's political leadership.

> "You know you never defeated us on the battlefield," said the American colonel. The North Vietnamese colonel pondered this remark for a moment. "That may be so," he replied, "but it is also irrelevant."
>
> *Conversation in Hanoi, April 1975*[13]

America's failure in Vietnam—the nation's longest war and only decisive loss— was not a result of military defeat. Rather, it resulted from the failure of the nation's political leadership to set forth clear objectives in Vietnam, to develop a strategy to achieve those objectives, and to rally mass support behind the effort.

Initially the United States sought to resist communist aggression from North Vietnam and ensure a strong and independent democratic South Vietnamese government. President John F. Kennedy sent a force of more than 12,000 advisors and counterinsurgency forces to assist in every aspect of training and support for the Army of the Republic of Vietnam (ARVN). President Kennedy personally inspired the development and deployment of U.S. counterinsurgency Special Forces ("Green Berets") to deal directly with a guerrilla enemy and help "win the hearts and minds" of the Vietnamese people. Kennedy personally approved a military coup that ended in the assassination of the unpopular Catholic President Ngo Dinh Diem in the largely Buddhist nation. But one military coup followed another, and the South Vietnamese government never achieved stability or won popularity in the countryside.

By 1964 units of the North Vietnamese Army (NVA) had begun to supplement the communist guerrilla forces (Vietcong) in the South. President Lyndon B. Johnson, informed that the South Vietnamese government was on the "verge of collapse," authorized major increases in U.S. supporting forces and began planning for a U.S. combat role. Yet in the presidential election of that year, Johnson assumed the pose of a dove and portrayed his Republican opponent Barry Goldwater as a hawk.

(continued)

(continued)

U.S. objectives in Vietnam became even more confused over time. It was not clear whether the ARVN with U.S. support was fighting a guerrilla war or an invasion by the NVA. Communist propaganda added to the confusion by representing the war as an internal struggle by a "National Liberation Front" rather than an invasion by North Vietnam. In August 1964, unconfirmed reports of an attack on U.S. Navy vessels by North Vietnamese torpedo boats led to the "Gulf of Tonkin" resolution by the Congress, authorizing the president to take "all necessary measures" to "repel any armed attack" against any U.S. forces in Southeast Asia.

In February 1965 President Lyndon B. Johnson ordered U.S. combat troops into South Vietnam and authorized a gradual increase in air strikes against North Vietnam. Marines landing on the beaches near Da Nang on March 8 in full battle gear were greeted by young girls selling flowers, souvenirs, and themselves; the heavy fighting would come later.

The fateful decision to commit U.S. ground combat forces to Vietnam was made without any significant effort to mobilize American public opinion, the government, or the economy, for war. On the contrary, President Johnson minimized the U.S. military effort, placed numerical limits on U.S. troop strength in Vietnam, limited bombing targets, and underestimated North Vietnam's military capabilities, as well as expected U.S. casualties. No U.S. ground troops were permitted to cross into North Vietnam, and only once (in Cambodia in 1970) were they permitted to attack NVA forces elsewhere in Indochina.

The nation's political leadership also failed to recognize the new role of the mass media in war. Vietnam was the first war ever fought in American living rooms. Visual images of burned children, wounded American GIs, and body bags being loaded on aircraft dramatized the costs of the war in human terms. Television made the *costs* of the war very clear to the American people, but the *benefits* of war were always very vague.

U.S. ground combat troops were initially placed in the northernmost Quang Tri province of South Vietnam in order to block the march of North Vietnamese troops directly into the South. The United States built a large military port at Da Nang to supply its forces. In the important battle of Khe Sanh in January 1968, U.S. soldiers and Marines defeated NVA efforts to dislodge those blocking forces. But the NVA had already established its larger "Ho Chi Minh trail," which swung around the U.S. blocking position, through "neutral" Laos and Cambodia, into the Central Highlands, and eventually into the Mekong Delta near the South Vietnamese capital of Saigon. The U.S. commander, General William C. Westmoreland, dispersed his troops throughout South Vietnam in widespread "search and destroy" missions against infiltrating NVA forces. By late 1967 more than 500,000 U.S. troops were committed to Vietnam.

Washington committed these military forces to a war of attrition, a war in which U.S. firepower was expected to inflict sufficient casualties on the enemy to force them to negotiate a settlement. U.S. casualties were supposed to be minimal. "The

(continued)

CASE STUDY

(continued)

Marines in Vietnam—U.S. forces stressed mobility.
Source: AP/Wide World Photos

solution in Vietnam," said General Westmoreland, "is more bombs, more shells, more napalm . . . till the other side cracks and gives up."[14] U.S. forces stressed mobility, and the helicopter became a principal instrument of U.S. ground forces in carrying troops into battle, waging war at treetop levels, and evacuating the wounded. But the enemy retained the initiative throughout the war. The enemy could attack, then quickly melt into the civilian population, hide in tunnels, or retreat back to "sanctuaries" in Cambodia and Laos. With attrition defined as the military objective, the enemy "body count" became notoriously unreliable. Americanization of the war had a debilitating effect on the South Vietnamese army. Given only demeaning chores, the ARVN morale and leadership collapsed, while American GIs did the fighting. Moreover, a genuinely popular South Vietnamese government never emerged.

The failure of the nation's leadership to set forth a clear military objective in Vietnam made "victory" impossible. The failure to achieve any decisive military victories eroded support for the war among both elites and masses. The *Pentagon Papers,*[15] composed of official memos and documents of the war, reveal increasing disenchantment with military results throughout 1967 by Secretary of Defense Robert McNamara and others who had originally initiated U.S. military actions. But

(continued)

(continued)

Vietnam memorial in Washington, D.C., engraves the names of those who made the supreme sacrifice.
Source: Ellen Shub/Impact Visual

President Johnson sought to rally support for the war by claiming that the United States was "winning." General Westmoreland was brought home to tell Congress that there was light at the end of the tunnel. "We have reached an important point where the end begins to come into view."[16] But these pronouncements only helped set the stage for the enemy's great political victory—the Tet offensive.

On January 30, 1968, Vietcong forces blasted their way into the U.S. embassy compound in Saigon and held the courtyard for six hours. The attack was part of a massive, coordinated Tet offensive against all major cities of South Vietnam. The offensive caught the United States and ARVN forces off guard. The ancient city of Hue was captured and held by Vietcong for nearly three weeks. But U.S. forces responded and inflicted very heavy casualties on the Vietcong. The Vietcong failed to hold any of the positions they captured, the people did not rise up to welcome them as "liberators," and their losses were high. Indeed, after Tet the Vietcong were no longer an effective fighting force; almost all fighting would be conducted thereafter by regular NVA troops. (Hanoi may have planned the elimination of Vietcong forces this way in order to ensure its eventual domination of the South.) By any *military* measure, the Tet offensive was a "defeat" for the enemy and a "victory" for U.S. forces.

(continued)

(continued)

Yet the Tet offensive was Hanoi's greatest political victory. "What the hell is going on?" asked a shocked television anchorman, Walter Cronkite. "I thought we were winning the war."[17] Television pictures of bloody fighting in Saigon and Hue seemed to mock the administration's reports of an early end to the war. The media, believing they had been duped by Johnson and Westmoreland, launched a long and bitter campaign against the war effort. Elite support for the war plummeted.

The antiwar protesters had no significant effect on the course of the war. Indeed, if anything, the protesters strengthened the war effort. After a careful analysis of change in elite and mass opinion of the war, John F. Mueller concluded, "The protest against the war in Vietnam may have been counterproductive in its impact on public opinion: that is, the war might have been somewhat more unpopular if protest had not existed."[18] Most Americans disapproved of Jane Fonda's broadcasting enemy propaganda from Hanoi while U.S. prisoners were being tortured in prisons a few blocks away.

Deserted by the very elite who had initiated American involvement in the war, hounded by hostile media, and confronting a bitter and divisive presidential election, Lyndon Johnson made a dramatic announcement on national television on March 31, 1968: he halted the bombing of North Vietnam and asked Hanoi for peace talks, and concluded: "I shall not seek, and I will not accept, the nomination of my party for another term as your president." He also declined Westmoreland's request for more troops and for permission to attack North Vietnamese territory. U.S. ground operations were scaled down to reduce casualties. Formal peace talks opened in Paris on May 13.

American objectives in Vietnam shifted again with the arrival in Washington of the new president, Richard M. Nixon, and his National Security Advisor, Henry A. Kissinger. . . . Nixon and Kissinger knew the war must be ended. But they sought to end it "honorably." The South Vietnamese could not be abruptly abandoned without threatening the credibility of American commitments everywhere in the world. They sought a peace settlement that would give South Vietnam a reasonable chance to survive. They hoped that "détente" with the Soviet Union, and a new relationship with communist China, might help to bring about "peace with honor" in Vietnam. But even in the absence of a settlement, they began the withdrawal of U.S. troops under the guise of "Vietnamization" of the war effort. ARVN forces were required to take up the burden of fighting as U.S. forces withdrew.

Unable to persuade Hanoi to make even the slightest concession at Paris, President Nixon sought to demonstrate American strength and resolve. He wished to make clear to Hanoi that he would not necessarily be bound by his predecessors' restraints. In the spring of 1970 Nixon authorized an attack on an NVA sanctuary inside the territory of Cambodia—an area known as the Parrot's Beak—not far from Saigon. The Cambodian operation was brief and probably achieved very little militarily. (However, Henry Kissinger argues that "The attack on the sanctuaries

(continued)

(continued)

made our withdrawal from Vietnam easier; it saved lives."[19]) But it mobilized the antiwar movement in the United States. Demonstrations centered on American campuses, and four students were killed in an angry confrontation with National Guardsmen at Kent State University.

North Vietnam launched a new, massive, conventional invasion of the South in March 1972. Only 6,000 American combat troops remained, and Hanoi believed that the antiwar movement in the United States would prevent Nixon from reinforcing the ARVN. Spearheaded by Soviet tanks and artillery, NVA forces struck directly across the old 17th parallel and its "DMZ," or "demilitarized zone." At that time Nixon was just concluding the SALT I Agreement with the Russians, and a Moscow summit was planned. Dismissing advice that a strong U.S. response to the new NVA invasion might disrupt talks with the Russians, Nixon authorized the heaviest bombing campaign of the war, as well as a naval blockade of North Vietnam and the mining of its Haiphong Harbor. The ARVN fought better than either Hanoi or Washington had expected. The Soviets publicly denounced the renewed U.S. bombing, but they did not disrupt the SALT talks or Nixon's summit visit to Moscow.[20] The NVA suffered heavy casualties, and the attack was thrown back.

Meanwhile, National Security Advisor Henry Kissinger and Hanoi's Le Duc Tho had begun meeting secretly in Paris, away from the formal negotiations, to work out "the shape of a deal." U.S. prisoners of war were a major bargaining chip for Hanoi. After the heavy fighting of 1972 and the success of the ARVN and American airpower, Kissinger and Le Duc Tho began inching toward an agreement. In the presidential election of 1972, the war became a partisan issue. Democratic candidate George McGovern had earlier stated that he would "crawl on his hands and knees to Hanoi" for peace, while Nixon continued his "peace with honor" theme. Nixon's landslide reelection strengthened his position in negotiations. In October Kissinger believed he had worked out a peace agreement, and he announced prematurely that "peace is at hand." But the agreement collapsed, in part because of the reluctance of the South Vietnamese to go along with the provisions worked out between Hanoi and Washington and in part because of last-minute new demands by Hanoi.[21]

The United States unleashed a devastating air attack directly on Hanoi for the first time in December 1972. U.S. B-52s from Guam joined with bombers based in Thailand to destroy factories, power plants, and transportation facilities in Hanoi itself. Critics at home labeled Nixon's action "the Christmas bombing," and Congressional doves planned to end the war by law. But when negotiations resumed in Paris in January, the North Vietnamese quickly agreed to peace on the terms that Kissinger and Le Duc Tho had worked out earlier. Both Nixon and Kissinger contend that the Christmas bombing secured the final peace.[22]

The Paris Peace Agreement of 1973 called for a cease-fire in place, with NVA troops remaining in its areas of control in the South. The South Vietnamese gov-

(continued)

(continued)

ernment and the ARVN also remained in place. All U.S. forces were withdrawn from South Vietnam and U.S. prisoners returned. But the major question of the war—the political status of South Vietnam—was unresolved. The United States promised "full economic and military aid" to the South Vietnamese government and promised to "respond with full force" should North Vietnam violate the cease-fire. The U.S. also agreed to provide Hanoi with billions in aid for reconstruction.

The South Vietnamese government lasted two years after the Paris Agreement. The U.S. fulfilled none of its pledges, either to South or North Vietnam. Congress refused to provide significant military aid to the South Vietnamese. Congress passed the War Powers Act in 1973 over Nixon's veto, obligating the president to withdraw U.S. troops from combat within sixty days in the absence of an explicit Congressional endorsement. The Watergate affair forced Nixon's resignation in August 1974. In early 1975 Hanoi decided that the Americans would not "jump back in," and therefore "the opportune moment" was at hand. The NVA attacked first in the Central Highlands, and President Thieu unwisely ordered a withdrawal to the coast. But the retreat quickly became a rout. When NVA forces attacked Hue and Da Nang, the ARVN and thousands of civilians fled southward toward Saigon.

President Gerald Ford never gave serious consideration to the use of U.S. military forces to repel the new invasion, and his requests to Congress for emergency military aid to the South Vietnamese fell on deaf ears. U.S. Ambassador Graham Martin, embarrassed by his government's abandonment of Vietnam, delayed implementation of escape plans until the last moment. The United States abandoned hundreds of thousands of loyal Vietnamese who had fought alongside the Americans for years.[23] The spectacle of U.S. Marines using rifle butts to keep desperate Vietnamese from boarding helicopters on the roof of the U.S. embassy "provided a tragic epitaph for twenty-five years of American involvement in Vietnam."[24]

America's humiliation in Vietnam had lasting national and international consequences. The United States suffered 47,378 battle deaths and missing-in-action among the 2.8 million who fought in Vietnam. . . . Perhaps one million Vietnamese, military and civilian, in both the North and South, were killed during the war years. But the "peace" was more bloody than the war. In Cambodia more than two million people were murdered by victorious communist forces in genocidal "killing fields." More than 1.5 million South Vietnamese were forcibly relocated to harsh rural areas and "reeducation camps." Nearly one-half million "boat people" tried to flee their country; eventually the United States took in nearly 250,000 Vietnamese refugees. Unlike past wars, there were no victory parades, and no one could answer the question of the mother whose son was killed in Vietnam: "What did he die for?" . . .

A "Vietnam syndrome"—national guilt and self-doubt, disillusionment with political leadership, hostility toward the military, and reluctance to use force for

(continued)

CASE STUDY

(continued)

any purpose—dominated American foreign policy for over a decade following the war. The slogan "No more Vietnams" was used to oppose U.S. political and military intervention everywhere in the world, whether or not vital U.S. interests were at stake. Yet, over time, the scars of Vietnam faded. Americans came to have a new appreciation of the courage and sacrifice of the soldiers who fought the war.

sibility for mass welfare. Roosevelt's second inaugural address called attention to "one-third of a nation, ill housed, ill clad, ill nourished." Roosevelt succeeded in preserving the existing system of private capitalism and avoiding the threats posed to the established order by fascism, socialism, communism, and other radical movements.

Historian Richard Hofstadter commented on Roosevelt's liberal, public-regarding philosophy:

> At the beginning of his career he took to the patrician reform thought of the progressive era and accepted a social outlook that can best be summed up in the phrase "noblesse oblige." He had a penchant for public service, personal philanthropy, and harmless manifestos against dishonesty in government; he displayed a broad easygoing tolerance, a genuine liking for all sorts of people; he loved to exercise his charm in political and social situations.[25]

Roosevelt's personal philosophy was soon to become the prevailing ethos of the new liberal establishment.

Thus, *liberalism* in the United States today is a product of elite response to economic depression at home and the rising threats of fascism and communism abroad. Its historical origin can be traced to elite efforts to *preserve* the existing political and economic system through reform. This historical perspective on the liberal tradition gives us a better understanding of the origins of change and reform within society.

the origins of liberalism

Notes

1. Henry Steele Commager, *The Study of History* (Columbus, Ohio: Merrill, 1965), p. 79.
2. Richard Hofstadter, *The American Political Tradition and the Men Who Made It* (New York: Vintage Books, 1956), p. viii.
3. Charles Beard, *An Economic Interpretation of the Constitution* (New York: Macmillan, 1913).
4. Ibid., p. 73.
5. Robert E. Brown, *Charles Beard and the Constitution* (Princeton, N.J.: Princeton University Press, 1956), p. 200.
6. Richard Hofstadter, *The American Political Tradition* (New York: Knopf, 1948), p. 109.
7. Frederick Jackson Turner, "The West and American Ideals," in *The Frontier in American History* (New York: Holt, 1921).
8. Ibid., p. 113.
9. Ibid., p. 116.
10. For a general history of Reconstruction politics, see C. Vann Woodward, *Reunion and Reaction* (Boston: Little, Brown, 1951), and *The Strange Career of Jim Crow* (New York: Oxford University Press, 1957).
11. Quoted in Henry Steele Commager, ed., *The Struggle for Racial Equality: A Documentary Record* (New York: Harper & Row, 1967), p. 19.

12. Excerpted from Thomas R. Dye and Harmon Zeigler, *The Irony of Democracy,* 7th ed. (Pacific Grove, Calif.: Brooks/Cole, 1987), pp. 78–88.

13. See Harry G. Summers, Jr., *On Strategy: A Critical Analysis of the Vietnam War* (Novato, Calif.: Presidio Press, 1982), p. 21.

14. George C. Herring, *America's Longest War* (New York: Random House, 1979), p. 152.

15. *New York Times, The Pentagon Papers* (New York: Bantam Books, 1971).

16. Herring, *America's Longest War,* p. 182.

17. Ibid., p. 188.

18. John F. Mueller, *War, Presidents, and Public Opinion* (New York: Wiley, 1973), p. 164.

19. Henry Kissinger, *The White House Years* (Boston: Little, Brown, 1979), p. 507.

20. Nixon correctly judged that the Soviets would not jeopardize the SALT I treaty for North Vietnam. See *RN: The Memoirs of Richard Nixon,* vol. 2 (New York: Warner Books, 1978), pp. 59–87.

21. Kissinger, *The White House Years,* pp. 1301–1446.

22. Ibid., p. 1461; Nixon, *RN,* p. 251.

23. Frank Snepp, *Decent Interval* (New York: Random House, 1977).

24. Herring, *America's Longest War,* p. 262.

25. Hofstadter, *The American Political Tradition,* pp. 323–324.

About This Chapter

Over the ages, history seems to have had a variety of meanings for people:

> So very difficult a matter is it to trace and find out the truth of anything by history.
> *Plutarch (46–120)*

> History is little else than a picture of human crimes and misfortunes.
> *Voltaire (1694–1778)*

> Peoples and governments never have learned anything from history, or acted on principles derived from it.
> *Hegel (1770–1831)*

> The history of the world is but the biography of great men.
> *Thomas Carlyle (1795–1881)*

> The subject of history is the life of peoples and of humanity. To catch and pin down in words . . . to describe directly the life, not only of humanity, but even of a single people, appears to be impossible.
> *Tolstoy (1828–1910)*

Despite these somewhat gloomy views, we believe it is possible to learn something from history, and we hope you will agree. After you have read this chapter, you should be able to

- describe briefly the various approaches to American history;
- describe historian Charles Beard's "economic interpretation" of the Constitution;
- describe changes in the power elite of various periods of American history, from the Revolution through the New Deal;
- discuss the historical reinterpretation of the African American experience during the Reconstruction era;
- discuss the reasons for U.S. involvement in the Vietnam War and why the U.S. effort failed.

Discussion Questions

1. Describe the various approaches to studying history. Comment on the strengths or weaknesses of each.

2. What were Charles Beard's two main approaches to understanding the Constitution? Describe briefly how the following constitutional provisions were of immediate benefit to the nation's elite: taxing power; interstate commerce clause; congressional powers to protect money and property; Article IV, Section 2, which required the return of runaway slaves and indentured servants; prevention of laws impairing obligation of contracts. Discuss the criticisms of Beard's interpretation of the Constitution.

3. Describe the power elite that was created by expansion into the American West. What factors contributed to the emergence of this elite, and what was its power base? Describe the philosophy of this new elite and the impact it had on both the elite system and the electoral system.

4. Describe the economic interests of the northern and southern elite on the eve of the Civil War. What were their points of conflict and of agreement? Discuss at least one of the compromises they attempted. Describe Lincoln's attitude toward slavery and his attempts at preserving consensus. Why was the Emancipation Proclamation a conservative, rather than a revolutionary, document?

5. Describe the power elite that emerged in the aftermath of the Civil War. What factors contributed to the rise of this elite? Discuss the philosophy this elite adopted, as well as the influence this elite had on Congress.

6. Discuss the impact the Great Depression had on both elite and nonelite philosophy and the kind of elite

thinking that developed in this era. What foreign influences had an impact on this new thinking? Briefly describe Franklin Delano Roosevelt's New Deal philosophy.

7. Show how historical interpretations of the same historical events can radically differ by contrasting earlier interpretations of the Reconstruction era with the more recent interpretations of historian C. Vann Woodward.

8. What were the U.S. objectives in Vietnam? How did these objectives change over time? Do you agree with the author that America's political leadership was responsible for our nation's defeat?

THE USES
OF POWER

PART

In Part III we shall explore the major social problems confronting society. These problems are interdisciplinary in nature, not confined to any of the social science disciplines. The problem of crime and violence, for example, is of as much interest and concern to the psychologist as it is to the sociologist. Because it is a question of human behavior and its consequences, it is also of concern to the political scientist, the historian, the economist, and the anthropologist. Each of these social scientists would, of course, approach the study of crime and violence from a somewhat different perspective. Our unifying perspective will continue to be power in society, but our main focus here will be on how power can be used to confront the crises that afflict human societies, for the betterment or detriment of humanity.

In Chapter 9 we shall explore the power of ideology and some of the major ideological conflicts in the twentieth century. In Chapter 10 we shall examine powerlessness and discrimination on the bases of race and gender and the power of the protest movements by which blacks and women have gained some measure of equality. In Chapter 11 we shall look at the problem of poverty in an affluent nation and at governmental efforts to alleviate, prevent, or cure this type of powerlessness. In Chapter 12 we shall explore the ways in which the United States has struggled to maintain a balance between the exercise of its police powers and the safeguarding of individual freedom, and we shall look at the continuous role that violence has played in American struggles for power. In Chapter 13 we shall examine some of the problems that affect the quality of life in the nation's large metropolitan areas and how power is exercised at the community level. In Chapter 14 we shall consider the global struggle for power and the attempts to maintain peace in international relations.

Power and Ideology

The Power of Ideas

Ideology
an integrated system of ideas that rationalizes and justifies the exercise of power

Ideas have power. People are coerced by ideas—beliefs, symbols, doctrines—more than they realize. Indeed, whole societies are shaped by systems of ideas that we frequently refer to as *ideologies*. An *ideology* is an integrated system of ideas that provides society and its members with rationalizations for a way of life, guides for evaluating "rightness" and "wrongness," and emotional impulses to action. Power and ideology are intimately related. Ideology rationalizes and justifies the exercise of power. By providing a justification of power, ideology itself becomes a source of control over people. Without the added *legitimacy* provided by ideology, powerholders would be confronted by an aroused populace who strongly resented what they regarded as the naked power exercised over them. Nothing could be more dangerous to the stability of a power system. Yet the very ideology that legitimizes power also governs the *conduct of powerholders*. Once an ideology is deeply rooted in a society, powerholders themselves are bound by it if they wish to retain power.

the functions of ideology
describes human character and society

rationalizes and justifies a way of life

provides standards of right and wrong

motivates people to social and political action

Ideologies control people's behavior in several ways: (1) Ideologies affect perception. Ideas influence what people "see" in the world around them. Ideologies frequently describe the character of human beings in society; they help us become aware of certain aspects of society but often impair our ability to see other aspects. Ideologies may distort and oversimplify in their effort to provide a unified and coherent account of society. (2) Ideologies rationalize and justify a way of life and hence provide legitimacy for the structure of society. An ideology may justify the status quo, or it may provide a rationale for change, or even for revolution. (3) Ideologies provide normative standards to determine "rightness" and "wrongness" in the affairs of society. Ideologies generally have a strong moral component. Occasionally, they even function as "religions,"complete with prophets (Marx), scriptures (the *Communist Manifesto*), saints (Lenin, Stalin, Mao), and visions of utopia (a communist society). (4) Ideologies provide motivation for social and political action. They give their followers a motive to act to improve world conditions. Ideologies can even "convert" individuals to a particular social or political movement and arouse them to action.

It is difficult to summarize a modern ideology in a few brief paragraphs. The risk of oversimplification is great. And because ideologies themselves are oversimplifications, the problem is compounded. Moreover, ideologies are constantly changing. When old utopian hopes are disappointed, they are frequently revised or replaced by new ones. New ideologies compete with older ones in various stages of revision. To unravel the ideological forces operating in society at any given time is a highly complex affair. With these warnings in mind, however, let us consider some of the major ideologies that influence our contemporary world.

classical liberalism
asserts the dignity of the individual

Classical Liberalism: The Least Government Is the Best Government

Historically, *liberalism* has asserted the worth and dignity of the *individual*. It has emphasized the rational ability of human beings to determine their own destinies, and it has rejected ideas, practices, and institutions that submerge individuals into

The seventieth anniversary of the Bolshevik Revolution, celebrated at Red Square, 1987.
Source: Bernard Bisson/Thierry Orban/Sygma

a larger whole and deprive them of their essential dignity. Liberalism grew out of eighteenth-century Enlightenment, the Age of Reason in which great philosophers such as John Locke and Adam Smith affirmed their faith in reason, virtue, and common sense. Liberalism originated as an attack on hereditary prerogatives and distinctions of a feudal society, the monarchy, the privileged aristocracy, the state-established church, and the restrictions on individual freedom associated with the feudal order.

Classical liberalism helped motivate America's founders to declare their independence from England, to write the American Constitution, and to establish the Republic. It rationalized their actions and provided ideological legitimacy for the new nation. John Locke, the English political philosopher whose writings most influenced the founders of the United States, argued that even in a "state of nature"—that is, a world in which there were no governments—an *individual* possesses *inalienable rights* to life, liberty, and property. Locke spoke of a *natural law,* or moral principle, that guaranteed every person these rights. They were not given to the individual by government, and no government could legitimately take them away. Locke believed that the very purpose of government was to protect individual

related ideas
rights to life, liberty, and property

natural law

social contract

liberty. Human beings form a *social contract* with one another to establish a government to protect their rights; they agree to accept governmental authority in order to better protect life, liberty, and property. Implicit in the social contract and the liberal notion of freedom is the belief that governmental activity and restrictions over the individual should be kept to a minimum.

limited government

Thus, classical liberalism included a belief in *limited government.* Because government is formed by the consent of the governed to protect individual liberty, it logically follows that government cannot violate the rights it was established to protect.

Classical liberalism also affirmed the equality of all human beings. The Declaration of Independence expressed the conviction that "all men are created equal." The Founders believed in equality for all *before the law,* notwithstanding the accused's circumstances. Over time, the notion of equality has also come to include *equality of opportunity* in all aspects of life—social, educational, and economic.

equality of opportunity but not absolute equality

Each person should have an equal chance to develop individual capacities to his or her natural limits; there should be no artificial barriers to personal advancement. It is important to remember, however, that classical liberalism has always stressed *equality of opportunity* and not *absolute equality.* Thomas Jefferson recognized a "natural aristocracy" of talent, ambition, and industry, and classical liberals have always accepted inequalities that are a product of individual merit and hard work. Absolute equality, or "leveling," is *not* a part of classical liberalism.

classical liberalism and capitalism
political freedom and economic freedom related

Finally, classical liberalism as a *political* ideology is closely related to *capitalism* as an *economic* ideology. Capitalism asserts the individual's right to own private property and to buy, sell, rent, and trade in a free market. The economic version of freedom is the freedom to make contracts, to bargain for one's services, to move from job to job, to join labor unions, to start one's own business. Capitalism and classical liberal democracy are closely related as economic and political systems. Capitalism stresses individual rationality in economic matters; freedom of choice in working, producing, buying, and selling; and limited governmental intervention in economic affairs. Liberal democracy emphasizes individual rationality in voter choice; freedoms of speech, press, and political activity; and limitations on governmental power over individual liberty. In liberal politics, individuals are free to speak out, to form political parties, and to vote as they please—to pursue their political interests as they think best. In liberal economics, individuals are free to find work, to start businesses, and to spend their money as they please—to pursue their economic interests as they think best. The role of government is restricted to protecting private property, enforcing contracts, and performing only those functions and services that cannot be performed by the private market.

Modern Liberalism: Governmental Power to "Do Good"

modern liberalism
governmental power, a positive force in protecting the individual

Modern liberalism rationalizes and justifies much of the growth of governmental power in the United States in the twentieth century. Modern liberalism emphasizes the importance of the social and economic security of a whole population as a prerequisite to individual self-realization and self-development. Classical liberalism looked with suspicion on government as a potential source of "interference" with personal freedom, but modern liberalism looks on the *power of government as a positive force* to be used to contribute to the elimination of social and economic conditions that adversely affect people's lives and impede their self-development. The modern liberal approves of the use of governmental power to ensure the general social welfare and to correct the perceived ills of society.

Modern liberals believe they can change people's lives through the exercise of governmental power: end discrimination, abolish poverty, eliminate slums, ensure employment, uplift the poor, eliminate sicknesses, educate the masses, and instill humanitarian values in everyone. The prevailing impulse is to *do good,* to perform public services, and to assist the least fortunate in society, particularly minorities and the poor. Modern liberalism is impatient with what it sees as slow progress through individual initiative and private enterprise toward the solution of socioeconomic problems, so it seeks to use the power of the national government to find *immediate, comprehensive* solutions to society's troubles.

Modern liberalism is frequently critical of certain aspects of capitalism, but it proposes to *reform* capitalism rather than replace it with socialism. Modern liberalism continues to recognize the individual's right to own private property, but it imposes on the property owner many social and economic obligations. It assumes that business will be privately owned but will be subject to considerable governmental regulation. Thus, the government intervenes to ensure fair labor standards, minimum wages, healthy working conditions, consumer protection, environmental protection, and so forth. Modern liberals are committed to a significant *enlargement of the public (governmental) sector of society* in matters having to do with education, welfare, housing, the environment, transportation, urban renewal, medicine, employment, child care, and so on. Modern liberalism envisions a larger role for government in the future: setting new goals, managing the economy, meeting popular wants, and redirecting national resources from private wants toward public needs.

reform of capitalism

enlargement of the public sector

Modern liberalism defines equality somewhat differently than classical liberalism. Classical liberalism stresses the value of *equality of opportunity*: individuals should be free to make the most of their talents and skills, but differences in wealth or power that are a product of differences in talent, initiative, risk taking, and skill are accepted as natural. In contrast, modern liberalism contends that individual dignity and equality of opportunity depend in some measure on *reduction of absolute inequality* in society. Modern liberals believe that true equality of opportunity cannot be achieved where significant numbers of people suffer from hunger, remediable illness, or extreme hardships in the conditions of life. Thus, modern liberalism supports government efforts to reduce inequalities in society.

reduction of extreme inequalities

Modern Conservatism: Individualism and Traditional Values

modern conservatism
classical liberalism
tradition
evolutionary change
morality

In the United States today, *conservatism* is associated with classical liberalism. Conservatives in this country retain the early liberal commitment to individual freedom from governmental controls; maximum personal liberty; reliance on individual initiative and effort for self-development, rather than on governmental programs and projects; a free-enterprise economy with a minimum of governmental intervention; and rewards for initiative, skill, risk, and hard work, in contrast to government-imposed "leveling" of income. These views are consistent with the early classical liberalism of Locke, Jefferson, and the nation's founders. The result, of course, is a confusion of ideological labels: conservatives today charge modern liberals with abandoning the principles of individualism, limited government, and free enterprise, and today's conservatives claim to be the true "liberals" in society.

Modern conservatism does indeed incorporate much of classical liberalism, but conservatism also has a distinct ideological tradition of its own. Conservatism is not as optimistic as liberalism about human nature. Traditionally, conservatives realized that human nature includes elements of irrationality, intolerance, extremism, ignorance, prejudice, hatred, and violence. Thus, they were more likely to place their faith in *law* and *tradition* than in the popular emotions of mass movements. Without the protection of law and tradition, people and societies are vulnerable to terror and violence. The absence of law does not mean freedom, but rather, exposure to the tyranny of terrorism and violence.

Conservatism sets forth an *evolutionary* view of social progress. Revolutionary change is far more likely to set society back than to improve it. But over time, people can experiment in small ways with incremental changes; continued from generation to generation, this process of evolutionary change leads to a progressive improvement in the condition of humanity. No government possesses the wisdom to resolve all problems, but the cumulative experience of society does produce certain workable arrangements for the amelioration of social ills. Gradual progress is possible, but only if people do not destroy the painfully acquired wisdom of the past in favor of new, untried utopian solutions that jeopardize the well-being of society.

Conservatives hold that people are rational beings, but that they are also victims of passion. Without the guidance of *law, tradition,* and *morality,* people would soon come to grief by the unruliness of their passions, destroying both themselves and others in pursuit of selfish gain. Rationalism is far from a sufficient guide to action; law, tradition, and morality are also needed for the realization of human purposes. Strong institutions—*family, church,* and *community*—are needed to repress individuals' selfish and irrational impulses and to foster civilized ways of life. (See Box 9-1.)

margin notes:
- law and tradition
- preference for evolutionary change
- tradition and morality as guides
- family, church, and community

Fascism: The Supremacy of Race and Nation

Fascism
the supremacy of the nation over the individual

Fascism is an ideology that asserts *the supremacy of the nation or race over the interests of individuals.* In the words of Benito Mussolini, "Everything for the state; nothing against the state; nothing outside of the state." The state is the embodiment of a unifying, ethical "ideal" that stands above the materialistic class interest of a Marxist or the selfish individualism of the liberals.

the organic state

Fascism perceives the state as not merely a governmental bureaucracy but *the organic life* of a whole people. According to Mussolini, "The Italian nation is an organism having ends, life, and means of action superior to those of the separate individuals or groups of individuals which compose it." In *Mein Kampf,* written before his assumption of power, Adolf Hitler added to the concept of an organic state, with his idea of the *Volk* (people), in which race and nation are united. The central ideal of the *Volk* was that of a racial folk or an "organic people" with a life, will, and purpose of its own.

Volk
race and nation united

The *goal of the fascist state* is not the welfare of the mass of people but the *development of a superior type of human being.* The goal is the cultivation of the best qualities of a people: bravery, courage, creativity, genius, intelligence, and strength. Fascism values the superior individual who rises out of the mire of mass

the goal of the fascist state
the superior human being

BOX 9-1

Americans: Liberal or Conservative?

The terms *liberal* and *conservative* have been used with different meanings over the years, so it is difficult to know whether Americans are really liberal or conservative on the issues. One way of determining their stance is to ask questions such as "How would you describe your own political philosophy—conservative, moderate, or liberal?" As can be seen from the following results of recent surveys, self-described conservatives outnumber liberals, although it is important to note that many Americans prefer "moderate" and many others decline to label themselves at all (see Figure 9-1).

What do Americans mean when they label themselves "liberal," "moderate," or "conservative"? There is no clear answer to this question. People who called themselves "conservatives" did not consistently oppose social welfare programs or government regulation of the economy. People who called themselves "liberals" did not consistently support social welfare programs or government regulation of the economy.

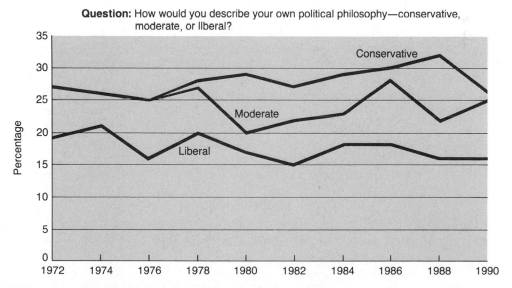

Question: How would you describe your own political philosophy—conservative, moderate, or liberal?

FIGURE 9-1   Americans' evaluation of their own political stance

Source: American National Election Studies, University of Michigan.

Hitler addressing battle-ready troops.
Source: The Bettmann Archive

mediocrity, and the superior nation that rises above the vast anthill of humankind. If life is a struggle for existence in which the fittest survive, then strength is the ultimate virtue and weakness is a fault. Good is that which survives and wins; bad is that which fails. Fascism admires heroism in individuals and nations. War frequently brings out the best in a nation: unity, bravery, strength, and courage.

triumph of will over reason

Fascism asserts the *superiority of will over reason*. The great deeds of history were performed not by reason, but by heroic will. Peoples are preserved *not* by rational thought, but by racial intuition. People rise to greatness when their will to power surmounts physical and worldly handicaps. Happiness is a poor motive in comparison with heroism, self-sacrifice, duty, and discipline.

Fascism offers itself as a *merger of nationalism and socialism*. Before World War II, fascism in Italy and Germany put itself forward as a socialist regime adopted to national purposes. The party of Adolf Hitler was the National Socialist, or "Nazi," party. Under fascism the nation is an organic whole; therefore, the econ-

a cooperative economy

omy ought to be *cooperative* rather than competitive. Every class and every interest ought to work together for the *good of the nation*. Against the rights of liberty or equality, national socialism established the duties of *service, devotion,* and *discipline*.

a totalitarian power structure

The power structure of a fascist regime is totalitarian. The unity of the fascist state requires "one people, one party, one leader." The fascist believes that a natural, superior, self-made leadership will emerge to provide intelligence and direction to the nation. At the head of the fascist elite is the leader—*Il Duce* in Italy or *Der Fuehrer* in Germany—in whose name everything is done, who is said to be "responsible" for all, but whose acts can nowhere be called into question. The leader is neither a scholar nor a theorist, but a charismatic man of action. Fascism strives for a *totality of power* in which all sectors of society—education, labor, art, science—are incorporated into the state and serve the purposes of the state.

Marxism: "Workers of the World, Unite"

Liberalism began as an eighteenth-century revolt against the aristocracy of a feudal system. Socialism represents a nineteenth-century revolt against the wealthy of a capitalist system. Communism is a violent strain of the larger ideological movement of socialism. Both socialism and communism arose out of the Industrial Revolution and the *social evils* it generated. Even though the Industrial Revolution led to a rapid rise in standards of living in western Europe, what impressed many early observers of this revolution was the economic inequalities it engendered. Throughout much of the nineteenth century, the real beneficiaries of the new industrialism seemed to be the successful manufacturers, bankers, merchants, and speculators; the lot of the slum-dwelling working classes showed little improvement. This was a bitter disappointment to the humanitarian hopes of many who had earlier embraced liberalism in the expectation that the rewards of economic progress would be shared by everyone. It appeared that liberalism and capitalism had simply substituted an aristocracy of wealth for an aristocracy of birth.

the roots of socialism and communism

Like many other socialists, Karl Marx (1818–1883) was an upper-middle-class intellectual. When his radicalism barred academic advancement, he turned to journalism and moved from Berlin to Paris. There he met Friedrich Engels, a wealthy young intellectual who supported Marx financially and collaborated with him on many of his writings. The *Communist Manifesto* (1848) was a political pamphlet— short, concise, and full of striking phrases, such as "Workers of the world, unite. You have nothing to lose but your chains." It provided an ideology to what had previously been no more than scattered protest against injustices. The *Manifesto* set forth the key ideas of Marxism, which would be developed twenty years later in great detail in a lengthy work, *Das Kapital.*

Karl Marx

Economic Determinism

Communism believes that the nature of the economy, or "mode of production," is basic to all the rest of society. The mode of production determines the class structure, the political system, religion, education, family life, law, and even art and literature. The economic structure of capitalism creates a class structure of a wealthy *bourgeoisie* (a property-owning class of capitalists) who control the government and exercise power over the *proletariat* (the propertyless workers).

economic determinism
the nature of the economy determines the social structure

Class Struggle

The first sentence of the *Communist Manifesto* exclaims, "The history of all hitherto existing society is the history of class struggles." The class that owns the mode

class struggle
the basic conflict in any society

of production is in the dominant position and *exploits* the other classes. Such exploitation creates antagonism, which gradually increases until it bursts into revolution. Just as the landed aristocracy was supplanted by the industrial bourgeoisie, so the bourgeoisie will in time be superseded by the proletariat. The capitalist exploits the worker to the point at which the worker is forced to revolt against the oppressors and overthrow the capitalist state.

Inevitability of Revolution

inevitability of revolution
by exploiting the workers, capitalism inspires revolution

Marx asserted that the proletariat revolution was inevitable. According to the *Communist Manifesto,* "What the bourgeoisie produces, above all, is its own gravediggers. Its fall and the victory of the proletariat are equally inevitable." As capitalists try to maximize their profits, the rich become richer and the poor become poorer. As capitalists drive wages down to maximize profits, capitalism becomes plagued by a series of crises or depressions, each one worse than the one before. The result of these "internal contradictions" in capitalism is a great deal of human misery, which eventually explodes in revolution. Thus, in their drive for profit, capitalists really dig their own graves by bringing the revolution ever closer.

Dictatorship of the Proletariat

dictatorship of the proletariat
a violent revolution will give all power to the workers and eliminate the bourgeoisie

Although Marx claimed that the coming of the revolution was inevitable, he nonetheless urged workers to organize for revolutionary action. The capitalists will never peacefully give up their ruling position. Only a violent revolution will place the proletarians in power. When the proletarians come to power, they, like ruling classes before them, will set up a state of their own—a dictatorship of the proletariat—to protect their class interests. This proletariat dictatorship will seize the property of the capitalists and place ownership of the mode of production in the hands of the proletariat. The bourgeoisie will be eliminated as a class.

Withering Away of the State

withering away of the state
after the revolution, a classless society will emerge; the need for government will disappear

After the revolution, as a result of *common ownership* of everything, a *classless* society will emerge. Because the purpose of government is to assist the ruling class in exploiting and oppressing other classes, once a classless society is established the government will have no purpose and will gradually "wither away." In the early stages of the revolution, the rule of distribution will be "from each according to his ability, to each according to his work." But after the victory of communism and the establishment of a full classless society, the rule of distribution will be "from each according to his ability, to each according to his need."

Socialism: Government Ownership, Central Planning

socialism
collective ownership of the means of production, distribution, and service

There are a bewildering variety of definitions of socialism. Communists employ the term as a label for societies that have experienced successful communist revolutions. Occasionally critics of governmental programs in the United States label as "socialist" any program or policy that restricts free enterprise in any way. But fundamentally, socialism means *public ownership of the means of production, dis-*

tribution, and service. Socialists agree on one point: private property in land, buildings, factories, and stores must be transformed into social or collective property. The idea of *collective ownership* is the core of socialism.

Socialism shares with communism a *condemnation of the capitalist system* as exploitive of the working classes. Communists and socialists agree on the evils of industrial capitalism: the exploitation of labor, the concentration of wealth, the insensitivity of the profit motive to human needs, the insecurities and sufferings brought on by the business cycle, the conflict of class interests, and the propensity of capitalist nations to involve themselves in war. In short, most socialists agree with the criticisms of the capitalist system set forth by Marx.

socialism and communism
condemnation of capitalism

However, socialists are committed to the *democratic process* as a means of replacing capitalism with collective ownership of economic enterprise. They generally reject the desirability of violent revolution as a way to replace capitalism and instead advocate peaceful constitutional roads to socialism. Moreover, socialists have rejected the idea of a socialist "dictatorship"; they contend that the goal of socialism is a *free society* embodying the democratic principles of freedom of speech, press, assembly, association, and political activity. They frequently claim that socialism in the economic sector of society is essential to achieving democracy and equality in the political sector of society. In other words, they believe that true democracy cannot be achieved until wealth is evenly distributed and the means of production are commonly owned.

democratic socialism
replacing capitalism through democratic processes

Wealth must be redistributed so that all persons can share in the benefits created by society. Redistribution means a transfer of ownership of all substantial economic holdings to the government. But the transfer must be accomplished in a democratic fashion, rather than by force or violence; and a socialist society must be governed as a true democracy.

government ownership of property

Socialism relies on central planning by government bureaucrats to produce and distribute goods and services. Free markets are either outlawed or restricted to a few consumer items. Government bureaucrats decide how many shirts, televisions, autos, and so on, should be produced. Factories are given quotas to meet, and their output is shipped to government stores. Workers' wages are also determined by government planners, as are decisions about new investments and developments. Government planners rely on their own judgment about what is needed, rather than relying on market demand. Planners set goals for each sector of the economy, usually in five-year plans.

central planning of economic activity

Socialists envision a gradual change from private to public ownership of property. Thus, socialists may begin by "nationalizing" the railroads, the steel industry, the automobile industry, privately owned public utilities, or other specific segments of the economy. (Nationalization involves governmental seizure of these industries from private owners.) Box 9-2 compares capitalist and socialist economies.

"nationalizing" industry

Why Communism Collapsed

Speculation about the causes of communism's collapse is risky. The fact that before 1989 very few Western social scientists had predicted these revolutionary events suggests that we do not fully understand their causes. Yet we can suggest some interesting hypotheses about the current crisis of communism.

Cuba's Fidel Castro—one of the last Communist dictators in the world.
Source: Reuters/Bettmann

BOX 9-2

Cross-National Perspective: Capitalism and Socialism in the World

In reality, all modern economies use some combination of capitalist and socialist economic organization. In primarily capitalist countries like the United States, the government protects private property, provides some public goods, and regulates and taxes business. In socialist countries, government ownership and central control of the economy exist side by side with a small but often significant free market.

Figure 9-2 presents a rough classification of current world governments according to their reliance on capitalist or socialist economic organization. Hong Kong has long been among the freest and most prosperous market systems in the world. The Japanese economy is dominated by large private corporations, although social custom and government persuasion result in a high degree of central coordination. Approximately thirty-five percent of the gross national product of the United States is produced by governments—federal, state, and local combined. European nations generally have larger public sectors than the United States. Government in Sweden and Israel produces over half of the output of these nations.

The collapse of communism in Eastern Europe has led to the introduction of market reforms in all of the nations of the former Soviet empire. Russia under President Boris Yeltsin is committed to market reforms, and that nation's economy is moving away from a centralized socialist system. In the past, 85 to 90 percent of the Russian economy was government-owned. China initiated market reforms in its agricultural sector as early as 1978, but movement toward a market economy in that nation has slowed since 1989. Communist Cuba and North Korea remain as socialist systems, wherein most private economic activity is suppressed by the government.

(continued)

BOX 9-2

(continued)

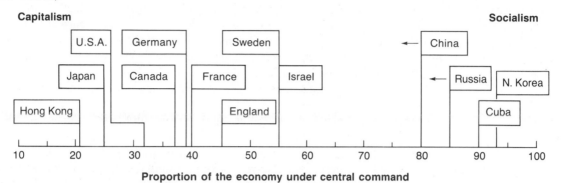

FIGURE 9-2 Economic organization of current world governments

CAPITALISM

- Productive resources owned by private individuals and firms
- Workers employed by private individuals and firms or self-employed
- Investment undertaken by private individuals and firms in search of profit
- Allocation of goods by market forces
- Income determined by market forces that reward productivity and ownership

Russia, Eastern Europe, and China, moving toward markets

SOCIALISM

- Productive resources owned by government
- Workers employed by government
- Investment ordered by government planners according to their own goals
- Allocation of goods by government planners according to their own goals
- Income determined by government planners who may seek to reward productivity or achieve equality or any other goals they desire

Socialist economies cannot provide an adequate standard of living for their people. The democratic revolutions in Eastern Europe and the Soviet Union were inspired principally by the realization that free market capitalism was providing much higher standards of living in the Western world. The economies of the socialist-bloc nations were falling further and further behind the economies of the capitalist nations of the West. Similar comparative observations of the successful economies of the free market "Four Dragons"—South Korea, Taiwan, Singapore, and Hong Kong—inspired Chinese leaders to experiment with market forces.

Socialist bureaucracies cannot determine production and allocate goods and services as effectively as free markets. In a socialist system, central bureaucracies, not consumers, determine production. Production for elite goals (principally, a strong military) comes first; production for individual needs comes last. People serve the system instead of the other way around. Consumer goods are shoddily made and always in short supply. This results in long lines at stores, rampant black marketeering, and frequent bribery of bureaucrats and managers to obtain necessary consumer items.

CASE STUDY

The Rise and
Fall of
Communism in
Russia

The task fell to Lenin to reinterpret Marxism as a revolutionary ideology, to carry out a successful communist revolution, and to construct a communist state in the Soviet Union after the 1917 Revolution. Lenin contributed a great deal to communist ideology, so much so that contemporary communist ideology is frequently referred to as *Marxism–Leninism.*

Marx believed the communist revolution would occur when capitalism itself had produced a class of factory workers that would be large enough to overcome its capitalist rulers. But this theory did not apply in 1917 in Russia, which was still a semifeudal society of peasants and landlords, with only a small number of factory workers and an even smaller number of capitalists. Lenin, however, believed that Russia could skip the capitalist stage of revolution and move directly from a feudal order to a communist society. His belief was based on the decay of the Russian state after decades of inefficient despotism under the czarist regime.

The Totalitarian Party

According to Lenin, the *key to a successful revolution* was the creation of a new and revolutionary type of totalitarian political party composed of militant professional revolutionaries. This party would be organized and trained like an army to obey the commands of superior officers. While western European socialist parties were gathering millions of supporters in relatively democratic organizations, Lenin constructed a small, exclusive, well-disciplined, elitist party. He described such a party in an early pamphlet, entitled *What Is to Be Done*; then he proceeded to organize it. Under his skilled leadership the Communist party of the Soviet Union became the first modern totalitarian party.

Lenin could justify the creation of a highly disciplined party elite on the basis of Marx's ambiguous attitudes toward democracy. Marx's idea of a *dictatorship of the proletariat,* and his phrase *vanguard of the proletariat,* revealed an *elitist* view of the revolutionary process. According to Lenin, the Communist party is the true "vanguard of the proletariat"—the most advanced and class-conscious sector of the proletariat—which has an exclusive right to act as spokesperson for the proletariat as a whole and to exercise the dictatorial powers of the proletariat over the rest of society.

The Theory of Imperialism

Lenin also tried to come to grips with two dilemmas: Why were capitalist societies still flourishing in the twentieth century, contrary to Marx's prediction? And why was the condition of the working classes improving, rather than deteriorating? Lenin's theory of *imperialism* was an attempt to answer these embarrassing questions. According to Lenin, when advanced capitalist countries were unable to find home

(continued)

Lenin statue, symbol of Communist rule, torn down by the people of Riga, Latvia.
Source: Reuters/Bettmann

markets for their products because of depressed worker income, they were obliged to turn outward and seize colonial markets. This maneuver enabled them, for the time being at least, to expand without forcing the wages of their own workers to go down to subsistence level.

Communism in One Country

After Lenin came to power in the Soviet Union in 1917, he found himself no longer in the position of revolutionary leader; he was the leader of a nation. Should the Soviet Union direct its energies toward immediate worldwide revolution, as envisioned by Marx? Or should it avoid confrontation with the Western world until it became a strong, self-sufficient nation? Gradually abandoning their original hopes for an immediate world revolution, Lenin and his successor, Stalin, turned to the task of creating "communism in one country." With the Communist party more centrally disciplined than ever, the Soviet leaders turned to the achievement of rapid industrialization through a series of five-year plans designed to convert a backward agrarian country into a modern industrial nation. The sweeping industrialization, brought about by the repression and terror of a totalitarian regime, came at great cost to the people.

(continued)

(continued)

The Police State

The Stalinist period saw brutality, oppression, imprisonment, purges, and murders—later officially admitted by the Soviet leaders. The Soviet regime held down the production of consumer goods in order to concentrate on the development of heavy industry. In part, the ideology of communism made it possible to call on the people for tremendous sacrifices for the good of the communist state.

Neither Marx nor Lenin proved successful as a political prophet. The state never withered away in communist Russia. Indeed, to maintain the communist government, a massive structure of coercion—informants, secret police, official terrorism, and a giant prison system—was erected. (The brutality of the system is described by Nobel Prize-winning author and former Soviet political prisoner Aleksandr Solzhenitsyn in *The Gulag Archipelago.*)

Militarism

Following the "Great Patriotic War"—the Russian name for World War II, in which more than 20 million Soviet citizens were killed and Nazi Germany was defeated—Stalin and his successors directed the Soviet economy primarily toward military purposes. The Soviets maintained the world's largest and most heavily armed military forces, and they built a nuclear missile force that surpassed that of the United States in size and numbers. (Their rapid progress in heavy missiles allowed them to place the first satellite in orbit in 1957 and the first man in space in 1962.) But the huge military establishment was a heavy economic burden; consumer goods in the Soviet Union were generally shoddy and always in short supply. Long waiting lines at state-run stores became the symbol of the Soviet economy.

Perestroika and Glasnost

Mikhail Gorbachev ascended to power in the Soviet Union in 1985, committed to *perestroika* ("restructuring")—the reform and strengthening of communism in the nation. Gorbachev deviated from many of the earlier interpretations of Marxism–Leninism. He increasingly turned to the principle of material interest—larger rewards for better labor and management performance. He also encouraged greater decentralization in industry and less reliance on centralized state direction. At the same time, he called for *glasnost* ("openness") in Soviet life and politics, removing many restrictions on speech, press, and religion and permitting free elections with noncommunist candidates running for and winning elective office.

Gorbachev also announced reductions in the size of the Soviet military and reached agreements with the United States and Western European nations on the reduction of both nuclear and conventional forces (see Chapter 14). Most importantly, he renounced the use of Soviet military force to keep communist govern-
(continued)

CASE STUDY

(continued)

ments in power in Eastern Europe. As result of this decision, communist governments were ousted in Poland, Czechoslovakia, Hungary, Bulgaria, Romania, and East Germany. The Berlin Wall was torn down and Germany was unified in 1990. New freedoms in the Soviet Union encouraged nationalities in the "republics" to demand independence from the central government in Moscow.

The Collapse of Communism

Gorbachev's economic and political reforms threatened powerful interests in the Soviet state — the Communist party "apparatchniks" (bureaucrats) who were losing control over economic enterprises; the military leaders, who opposed the withdrawal of Soviet troops from Germany and Eastern Europe; the KGB police, whose terror tactics were increasingly restricted; and cental government officials, who were afraid of losing power to the republics. These interests slowed *perestroika* and forced Gorbachev into many compromises; the results were a rapid deterioration of the Soviet economy and the emergence of disorders and disturbances in various republics seeking independence. Democratic and noncommunist forces, led by Boris Yeltsin, the first elected president of the Russian Republic, were strongly critical of Gorbachev's reluctance to speed reforms. But when hard-liners in the Communist party, the military, and the KGB attempted the forcible removal of Gorbachev in August 1991, the democratic forces rallied to his support. Led by Yeltsin, thousands of demonstrators took to the streets, Soviet military forces stood aside, and the coup crumbled. Gorbachev was temporarily restored as President, but Yeltsin emerged as the most influential leader in the nation. The failed coup hastened the demise of the Communist party. The party's offices and activities were suspended, and investigations of party complicity in the coup attempt were initiated. Clearly the party lost whatever legitimacy it had still retained with the peoples of Russia and the other republics.

The Disintegration of the Soviet Union

Strong independence movements in the republics of the former Union of Soviet Socialist Republics (USSR) emerged as the authority of the centralized Communist party in Moscow waned. Lithuania, Estonia, and Latvia—nations that had been forcibly incorporated into the Soviet Union in 1939—led the way to independence in 1991. Soon all of the fifteen republics of the USSR declared their independence, and the USSR officially ceased to exist after December 31, 1991. Its president, Mikhail Gorbachev, no longer had a government to preside over. The red flag with its hammer and sickle atop the Kremlin was replaced with the flag of the Russian Republic.

(continued)

CASE STUDY

(continued)   Today Russia, Ukraine, Byelorusse, and the other smaller republics of the former Soviet Union are struggling to overcome the disastrous effects of seventy-five years of communist rule. Their economies are shattered, and their experience in democratic politics is limited. They are trying to devise a new form of association, a Commonwealth of Independent States, which will achieve cooperation among republics yet avoid domination by a central authority.

BOX 9-3

Crisis of Communism: Chronology of Events

1978 Deng Xiaoping introduces market reforms in the communist system in the People's Republic of China. Output, especially in agriculture, rises rapidly.

1985 Mikhail Gorbachev assumes power in the USSR and introduces *perestroika.*

1987 The U.S. and the USSR sign the INF Treaty—the first arms-control agreement to achieve reductions, equality, and on-site verification.

1988 Gorbachev announces that the USSR will not use military force to keep communist governments in power in Eastern European nations.

1989 On January 1, 1989, communist parties were firmly entrenched in the USSR and the socialist-bloc nations of Eastern Europe—Poland, East Germany, Hungary, Czechoslovakia, Romania, and Bulgaria. The socialist military alliance, the Warsaw Pact, fielded military forces that vastly outnumbered those of the NATO nations. But by the end of the year the power balance of the world had changed radically:

Poland: The Solidarity movement, led by Lech Walesa, ousts communist rulers and establishes the first noncommunist government in the Warsaw Pact.

Czechoslovakia: Following mass anticommunist demonstrations in Prague, communist rulers resign, and Vaclav Havel, playwright and opposition leader, is elected president.

Hungary: Communist rulers are forced to share power with the democratic opposition.

East Germany: Following the flight of thousands of citizens through Hungary to Austria and anticommunist demonstrations in cities, hard-line communist leader Honnecker appeals to Gorbachev for military interven-

tion; Gorbachev declines, and the communists are ousted. In November the Berlin Wall, symbol of communist repression, is torn down.

Romania: Hundreds of protesters are killed by communist security forces, but the army joins the protesters. Communist dictator Nicolae Ceausescu is captured and executed.

USSR: The first multicandidate elections are held, and many Communist party officials are defeated. Opposition candidates are elected to the Congress of People's Deputies, although the Communist party retains a heavy majority.

China: Students lead massive "democracy movement" demonstrations in Tiananmen Square in Beijing. Demonstrations spread to other cities. Communist rulers call on the army to "restore order"; thousands of demonstrators are killed, injured, or arrested.

1990 Germany is officially reunified under the democratic government of Chancellor Helmut Kohl.

Lithuania declares its independence from the USSR, creating a crisis of national union.

Boris Yeltsin becomes the first elected president of the Russian Republic, posing a challenge to Gorbachev's leadership of the Soviet Union. Yeltsin renounces Communist party membership.

Albania: The last hard-line communist government of Eastern Europe is ousted.

1991 The Warsaw Pact, the military alliance of communist nations of Eastern Europe, is officially dissolved.

Hard-line communists in the Soviet Union, including
(continued)

BOX 9-3

(continued)

the defense minister, the chief of the KGB (secret police), and the vice-president of the Soviet Union, attempt a coup—a forceful overthrow of the legitimate government—in August. President Gorbachev is temporarily held at his house on the Black Sea, but Boris Yeltsin rallies "democratic" force in Moscow. The coup fails as thousands of demonstrators assemble in the streets of Moscow and Leningrad; Soviet troops and tanks patrol the streets but do not fire on the demonstrators. Gorbachev is quickly restored to his office

as President of the USSR, but Russian President Yeltsin emerges as the most influential leader.

The Communist party is deeply implicated in the coup attempt; Gorbachev resigns as General Secretary of the party, and its offices are officially closed.

Republics of the Soviet Union declare their independence.

The Union of Soviet Socialist Republics is officially dissolved December 31, 1991.

Socialism destroys the individual's incentive to work, produce, innovate, invent, save, and invest in the future. The absence of profit incentives leads to extravagant waste by enterprise managers. Employees have no incentives to work hard or to satisfy customers. Official prices are low, but shortages prevent workers from improving their standard of living. A common refrain among workers in socialist systems is: "The government pretends to pay me, and I pretend to work." Bureau-

Can the individual confront the power of the authoritarian state? A lone citizen in Peking, China, temporarily halted a column of tanks. Later, authoritarian rule was reimposed following a massacre of civilians in Tiananmen Square.
Source: Reuters/Bettmann

crats try to order innovation, but innovation requires individual creativity and reward, not conformity to a central plan.

Over time, socialist systems lose the trust of the people. Because the system promised a worker's paradise, the economic hardship imposed on the people inspires widespread cynicism. Because the system promised equality, the power and privilege enjoyed by the bureaucratic elite inspires resentment.

The concentration of both economic and political decision making in the hands of a central government bureaucracy is incompatible with democracy. Democracy requires limited government, individual freedom, and dispersal of power in society. In socialist nations, the government exercises virtually unlimited power over economic as well as political affairs, individual economic freedoms are curtailed, and great power is accumulated by the government bureaucracy. In contrast, in capitalist nations, governmental intervention in the marketplace is limited, individuals are free to make their own economic decisions, and power is dispersed among many groups and institutions: governments, corporations, unions, press and television, churches, interest groups, and so forth.

Thus, democracy is closely tied to capitalism. Capitalism does not *ensure* democracy; some capitalist nations are authoritarian. But capitalism is a necessary condition for democracy. *All existing democracies have free market economies, and no socialist system is a democracy.* In other words, capitalism is a necessary, although not a sufficient, condition for democracy.

Above all, the socialist system denies individual freedom, political pluralism, and democracy. Force, repression, and indoctrination can be ineffective over many years. But at some point, the universal human aspiration for personal freedom and dignity emerges to challenge the socialist order.

About This Chapter

When commanded by authority they perceive as legitimate, ordinary human beings may inflict extreme pain and suffering on their fellow humans. The experiments carried out by Stanley Milgram at Yale University served to confirm that observation; but indeed the pages of history are filled with similar evidence. It is difficult for us to comprehend the atrocities of World War II—six million Jews murdered; entire villages of Europe eradicated in acts of indiscriminate retaliation; millions of men, women, and children condemned to slave labor; untold numbers suffering the horrors of concentration camps; still others, suffering the hideous "medical experiments" that were surely the very definition of sadism. The list goes on. Incredibly enough, these were the acts of human beings. Not all of them could have been monsters. Many of them pleaded that they were just obeying "orders." Others revealed that despite their Nazi indoctrination, they felt a certain human aversion to their work. One German officer who had been in charge of an "extermination gang" testified at Nuremberg that to relieve the "psychological bur-

den" on his men, he had had them fire as a group, never as individuals, so they could avoid "personal responsibility."*

How is authority invested with such legitimacy that it has the power to command ordinary people to commit acts of such unthinkable brutality and inhumanity? At least part of the answer, but by no means all, may be found in the power of ideology. Ideology, it should be noted, may be used to further humanitarian as well as nonhumanitarian goals, but regardless of the purpose for which it is used, ideology can be an extremely powerful weapon. In this chapter we have examined the nature of that power and described some of the major ideological conflicts in the contemporary world. Now that you have read Chapter 9, you should be able to

• define *ideology* and describe its power to influence people's behavior;

*William L. Shirer, *The Rise and Fall of the Third Reich* (New York: Simon and Schuster, 1960), p. 959.

- compare and contrast classical liberalism, modern liberalism, and modern conservatism;
- discuss fascism, socialism, and communism;
- describe the development of Marxism–Leninism in the Soviet Union;
- describe the relationships between capitalism, socialism, and democracy;
- discuss the current crisis of communism and the possible reasons for the collapse of communist regimes in Eastern Europe.

Discussion Questions

1. Define ideology and describe its relationship to power. Discuss the ways in which ideology can control people's behavior. Identify the characteristics of modern ideologies.

2. Compare and contrast classical liberalism and modern liberalism. What is the attitude of each of these ideologies toward the individual? What is their approach to governmental power, the concept of equality, and the capitalist system?

3. Explain the confusion that arises from the ideological labels of *conservative* and *modern liberal*.

4. Describe the goal of the fascist state. What should the attitudes of a "good" fascist be toward "happiness" and rational thought, and toward the economy and the power structure?

5. Trace the development of socialism and communism. Discuss what Marx meant by economic determinism, class struggle, the inevitability of revolution, the dictatorship of the proletariat, and the withering away of the state.

6. Define *socialism* and discuss how this ideology differs from communism.

7. Describe how Lenin adapted the ideology of Marxism to conditions in the Soviet Union. Describe Lenin's totalitarian party and his theory of imperialism. Discuss the "communism in one country" created by Lenin and Stalin. How was the ideology of communism used during Stalin's regime, and what rather recent changes have the goals and methods of Soviet communism undergone?

8. What is meant by the statement, "Capitalism is a necessary, although not a sufficient, condition for democracy"?

9. What explanations might be given for the collapse of communist regimes in Eastern Europe, the rise of opposition to communism in the former Soviet Union, and the rise and repression of the "democracy movement" in China?

Power,
Race, and
Gender

10

Racism in American History

Racial conflict has been a central issue in American society throughout the nation's history. Black slavery was introduced to the earliest colonial settlements in 1619. In 1863 the Emancipation Proclamation, issued by President Abraham Lincoln in the midst of the Civil War, applied to slaves living in the Confederate states, and slavery was constitutionally abolished in the United States by the Thirteenth Amendment in 1865. But within a generation, racial segregation replaced slavery as a means of subjugation (see the case study "Reconstruction and Black History" in Chapter 8). Segregation won constitutional approval by the U.S. Supreme Court in 1896; not until the historic *Brown* v. *Topeka* case in 1954 did the Supreme Court formally reverse itself and declare segregation unconstitutional. Slavery and segregation left social scars that remain visible in American society today.

Following the Civil War, Congress passed, and the states ratified, the Fourteenth Amendment to the U.S. Constitution, declaring that

> no State shall make or enforce any law which shall abridge the privileges or immunities of citizens of the United States; nor shall any State deprive any person of life, liberty, or property, without due process of law; nor deny to any person within its jurisdiction the equal protection of the laws.

The language and historical context leave little doubt that the purpose of the Fourteenth Amendment was to secure for blacks a place in American society equal to that of whites. Yet for a full century these promises went unfulfilled. Segregation became the social instrument by which blacks were "kept in their place," that is, denied social, economic, educational, and political equality

Jim Crow
laws and social customs requiring separation of the races

Segregation was supported by a variety of social practices and institutions. In many states *Jim Crowism* followed blacks throughout life: birth in a segregated hospital ward, education in a segregated school, residence in segregated housing, employment in a segregated job, eating in segregated restaurants, and burial in a segregated graveyard. Segregation was enforced by a variety of private sanctions, from the occasional lynching mobs to country club admission committees. But government was a principal instrument of segregation both in the southern and in the border states of the nation. (School segregation laws in the United States in 1954 are shown in Figure 10-1.) In the northern states government was seldom used to enforce segregation, but it was also seldom used to prevent it. The results were often quite similar.

separate but equal
interpreting the equal protection clause of the Fourteenth Amendment to allow segregation of the races if facilities were equal (1896–1954)

The constitutional argument made on behalf of segregation—that the phrase "equal protection of the laws" did not prohibit the enforced separation of races so long as the races were treated equally—became known as the *separate-but-equal doctrine.* In 1896 the Supreme Court, in *Plessy* v. *Ferguson,* made this doctrine the official interpretation of the equal protection clause, thus giving segregation constitutional approval.

initial civil rights goal
elimination of segregation by law

The initial goal of the civil rights movement was the elimination of direct *legal segregation.* First, discrimination and segregation practiced by governments had to be prohibited, particularly in voting and public education. Then direct discrimination in all segments of American life, private as well as public, in transportation, theaters, parks, stores, restaurants, businesses, employment, and housing, came under attack.

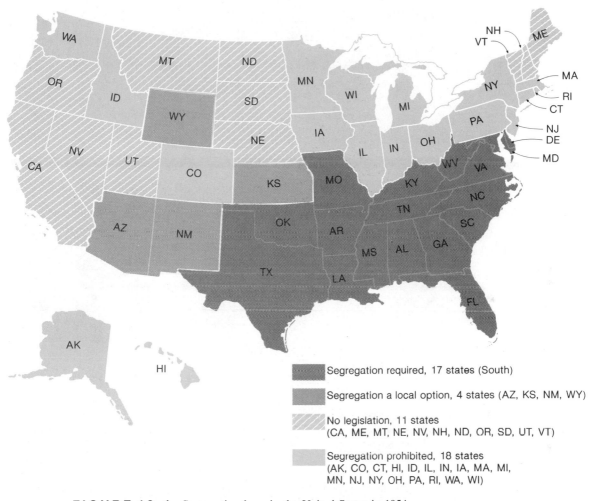

Segregation required, 17 states (South)

Segregation a local option, 4 states (AZ, KS, NM, WY)

No legislation, 11 states
(CA, ME, MT, NE, NV, NH, ND, OR, SD, UT, VT)

Segregation prohibited, 18 states
(AK, CO, CT, HI, ID, IL, IN, IA, MA, MI,
MN, NJ, NY, OH, PA, RI, WA, WI)

FIGURE 10-1   Segregation laws in the United States in 1954

Led by Roy Wilkins, executive director of the National Association for the Advancement of Colored People (NAACP), and Thurgood Marshall, chief counsel for the NAACP (who was later to become the first African American Supreme Court justice), the newly emerging civil rights movement of the 1950s pressed for a court decision that direct lawful segregation violated the guarantee of "equal protection of the laws" of the Fourteenth Amendment. The civil rights movement sought a complete reversal of the separate-but-equal interpretation of *Plessy* v. *Ferguson;* it wanted a decision that laws separating the races were *unconstitutional.*

On May 17, 1954, the Court rendered its historic *Brown* v. *Board of Education of Topeka, Kansas:*

Segregation of white and colored children in public schools has a detrimental effect upon the colored children. The impact is greater when it has the sanction of law, for the policy of separating the races is usually interpreted as denoting the inferiority of

Brown v. Board of Education of Topeka, Kansas
landmark Supreme Court decision declaring that segregation itself violates the equal protection clause of the Fourteenth Amendment (1954)

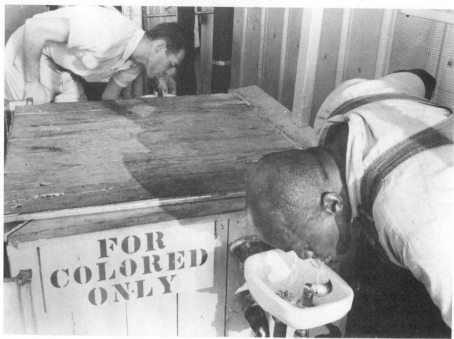

Jim Crow laws separated blacks and whites.
Source: The Bettmann Archive

the Negro group. A form of inferiority affects the motivation of a child to learn. Seg-regation with the sanction of law, therefore, has a tendency to retard the educational and mental development of Negro children and to deprive them of some of the ben-efits they would receive in a racially integrated school system. Whatever may have been the extent of psychological knowledge of the time of *Plessy* v. *Ferguson,* this finding is amply supported by modern authority. Any language in *Plessy* v. *Ferguson* contrary to this source is rejected.[1]

The Supreme Court's decision in *Brown* was symbolically very important. Although it would be many years before any significant number of black children would attend previously all-white schools, the decision by the nation's highest court stimulated black hopes and expectations. Indeed, *Brown* started the modern civil rights movement. The African American psychologist Kenneth Clark wrote: "This [civil rights] movement would probably not have existed at all were it not for the 1954 Supreme Court school desegregation decision which provided a tremendous boost to the morale of blacks by its *clear* affirmation that color is irrelevant to the rights of American citizens."[2]

The Civil Rights Movement

As long as the civil rights movement was combating *governmental* discrimination, it could employ the U.S. Constitution as a weapon in its arsenal. The Constitution governs the actions of governments and government officials. Because the Supreme

Court and the federal judiciary are charged with the responsibility of interpreting the Constitution, the civil rights movement could concentrate on *judicial* action to accomplish its objective of preventing governmental discrimination. But the Constitution does *not* directly govern the activities of private individuals. Thus, when the civil rights movement turned its attention to combating *private discrimination,* it had to carry its fight into the *legislative* branch of government. *Only* Congress could restrict discrimination practiced by private owners of restaurants, hotels, and motels; private employers; and other individuals who were not government officials.

Before 1964 Congress had been content to let other agencies, including the president and the courts, struggle with the problem of civil rights. Yet Congress could not long ignore the nation's most pressing domestic issue. The civil rights movement had stepped up its protests and demonstrations and was attracting worldwide attention with organized sit-ins, freedom rides, picketing campaigns, boycotts, and mass marches. After the massive "March on Washington" in August 1963, led by Martin Luther King, Jr., President Kennedy asked Congress for the most comprehensive civil rights legislation it had ever considered. After Kennedy's assassination, President Johnson brought heavy pressure on Congress to pass the bill as a tribute to the late president. The Civil Rights Act of 1964 finally passed both houses of Congress by better than a two-thirds vote and with the overwhelming support of members of both the Republican and Democratic parties. It can be ranked with the Emancipation Proclamation, the Fourteenth Amendment, and *Brown* v. *Board of Education* as one of the most important steps toward full equality for blacks in America.

The Act includes the following key provisions:

It is unlawful to discriminate against or segregate persons on the grounds of race, color, religion, or national origin in any place of public accommodation, including hotels, motels, restaurants, movies, theaters, sports arenas, entertainment houses, and other places offering to serve the public.

Each federal department and agency shall take appropriate action to end discrimination in all programs or activities receiving federal financial assistance in any form. These actions may include the termination of assistance.

It shall be unlawful for any firm or labor union to discriminate against any individual in any fashion because of his or her race, color, religion, sex, or national origins; an Equal Employment Opportunity Commission shall be established to enforce this provision by investigation, conference, conciliation, or civil action in federal court.

In 1965, following an organized march from Selma to Montgomery to protest voting inequities, Congress enacted the *Voting Rights Act of 1965,* which authorized the attorney general, upon evidence of voter discrimination in southern states, to replace local registrars with federal examiners, who were authorized to abolish literacy tests, waive poll taxes, and register voters under simplified federal procedures. The impact of the Voting Rights Act of 1965 can be observed in increased black voter registration figures in the South and election of African Americans to state legislatures in every southern state and to many city and county offices as well.

---

private discrimination
the need for legislative action

background

Civil Rights Act of 1964
prohibits discrimination in private employment and establishes the EEOC to enforce non-discrimination in employment

provisions:
prohibits discrimination in public accommodations

prohibits discrimination in programs receiving federal funds

Voting Rights Act of 1965

CASE STUDY

Martin Luther King, Jr.: The Power of Protest

The civil rights movement invented new techniques for minorities to gain power and influence in American society. *Mass protest* is a technique by which groups seek to obtain a bargaining position for themselves that can induce desired concessions from established powerholders. It is a means of acquiring a bargaining leverage for those who would otherwise be powerless. The protest may challenge established groups by threatening their reputations (unfavorable publicity), their economic position (a boycott), their peace and quiet (disruption of daily activities), or their security (violence or the threat of violence). The protest technique appeals to powerless minorities who have little to bargain with except their promise *not* to protest.

The nation's leading exponent of *nonviolent* protest was Dr. Martin Luther King, Jr. Indeed, King's contributions to the development of a philosophy of nonviolent, direct-action protest on behalf of African Americans won him international acclaim and the Nobel Peace Prize in 1964. King first came to national prominence in 1955, when he was only twenty-five years old; he led a year-long bus boycott in Montgomery, Alabama, to protest discrimination in seating on public buses. In 1957 he formed the Southern Christian Leadership Conference (SCLC) to provide encouragement and leadership to the growing nonviolent protest movement in the South.

In 1963 a group of Alabama clergymen petitioned Martin Luther King, Jr., to call off mass demonstrations in Birmingham, Alabama. King, who had been arrested in the demonstrations, replied in his famous "Letter from Birmingham Jail":

> You may well ask, "Why direct action? Why sit-ins, marches, etc.? Isn't negotiation a better path?" You are exactly right in your call for negotiation. Indeed, this is the purpose of direct action. Nonviolent direct action seeks to create such a crisis and establish such creative tension that a community that has constantly refused to negotiate is forced to confront the issue. It seeks to so dramatize the issue that it can no longer be ignored. . . .
>
> One may well ask, "How can you advocate breaking some laws and obeying others?" The answer is found in the fact that there are *unjust* laws. I would be the first to advocate obeying just laws. One has not only a legal but a moral responsibility to obey just laws. Conversely, one has a moral responsibility to disobey unjust laws. . . .
>
> One who breaks an unjust law must do it *openly, lovingly* . . . and with a willingness to accept the penalty. I submit that an individual who breaks a law that conscience tells him is unjust, and willingly accepts the penalty by staying in jail to arouse the conscience of the community over its injustice, is in reality expressing the very highest respect for law.[3]

Nonviolent direct action is a technique requiring direct mass action against laws regarded as unjust, rather than court litigation, political campaigning, voting, or other conventional forms of democratic political activity. Mass demonstrations, sit-ins, and other nonviolent direct-action tactics often result in violations of state and

(continued)

Martin Luther King, Jr.,
addresses a crowd of 70,000
people in Chicago.
Source: AP/Wide World Photos

local laws. For example, persons remaining in offices, halls, or buildings after being asked by authorities to leave ("sit-ins") may be violating trespass laws. Marching in the street may entail the obstruction of traffic, "disorderly conduct," or "parading without a permit." Mass demonstrations often involve "disturbing the peace" or refusing to obey the lawful orders of a police officer. Even though these tactics are nonviolent, they do entail *disobedience to civil law.*

Civil disobedience is not new to American politics. Its practitioners have played an important role in American history, from the patriots who participated in the Boston Tea Party, to the abolitionists who hid runaway slaves, to the suffragists who paraded and demonstrated for women's rights, to the labor organizers who picketed to form the nation's major industrial unions, to the civil rights marchers of recent years. Civil disobedience is a political tactic of minorities. (Because majorities can more easily change laws through conventional political activity, they seldom have to disobey them.) It is also a tactic attractive to groups wishing to change the social status quo significantly and quickly.

The political purpose of nonviolent direct action and civil disobedience is to call attention or "to bear witness" to the existence of injustices. Only laws regarded as unjust are broken, and they are broken openly, without hatred or violence. Punishment is actively sought rather than avoided because punishment will further emphasize the injustices of the law. The object of nonviolent civil disobedience is to stir the conscience of an apathetic majority and to win support for measures that will eliminate the injustices. By accepting punishment for the violation of an unjust law, persons practicing civil disobedience demonstrate their sincerity. They hope to shame the majority and to make it ask itself how far it will go to protect the status quo.

Clearly the participation of the mass news media, particularly television, contributes immeasurably to the success of nonviolent direct action. Breaking the law

(continued)

CASE STUDY

(continued)

makes news; dissemination of the news calls the attention of the public to the existence of unjust laws or practices; the public sympathy is won when injustices are spotlighted; the willingness of the demonstrators to accept punishment provides evidence of their sincerity; and the whole drama lays the groundwork for changing unjust laws and practices. Cruelty or violence directed against the demonstrators by the police or other defenders of the status quo plays into the hands of the demonstrators by stressing the injustices they are experiencing.

Perhaps the most dramatic application of nonviolent direct action occurred in Birmingham, Alabama, in the spring of 1963. Under the direction of Martin Luther King, Jr., the SCLC chose Birmingham as a major site for desegregation demonstrations during the centennial year of the Emancipation Proclamation. Birmingham was by its own description the "Heart of Dixie"; it was the most rigidly segregated large city in the United States. King believed that if segregation could be successfully challenged in Birmingham, it might begin to crumble throughout the South. Thousands of African Americans, including schoolchildren, staged protest marches in Birmingham from May 2 to May 7. In response, police and fire fighters, under the direction of Police Chief "Bull" Connor, attacked the demonstrators with fire hoses, cattle prods, and police dogs, all in clear view of national television cameras. Pictures of police brutality were flashed throughout the nation and the world, doubtless touching the consciences of many white Americans. The demonstrators conducted themselves in a nonviolent fashion. Thousands were dragged off to jail, including King. (It was at this time that King wrote his "Letter from Birmingham Jail," explaining and defending nonviolent direct action.)

The most massive application of nonviolent direct action was the great "March on Washington" in August 1963, during which more than 200,000 black and white marchers converged on the nation's capital. The march ended in a formal program at the Lincoln Memorial in which Martin Luther King, Jr., delivered his most eloquent appeal, entitled "I Have a Dream."

> I still have a dream. It is a dream deeply rooted in the American dream. I have a dream that one day this nation will rise up and live out the true meaning of its creed: "We hold these truths to be self-evident, that all men are created equal."

Despite its successes, nonviolent direct action does pose problems. If undertaken too frequently or directed against laws or practices that are not really serious injustices, it may have the effect of alienating the majority, whose sympathies are so essential to the success of the movement. A favorable outcome can be achieved by actions that arouse the conscience of a majority against the injustice or that discomfort a majority to the point that it is willing to grant the demands of the minority rather than experience further discomfort. But actions that provoke hostility or a demagogic reaction from the majority merely reduce the opportunities for progress.

(continued)

CASE STUDY

(continued)

Nonviolent direct action can be effective against direct discrimination or an obvious injustice. Few Americans approve of direct discrimination or cruelty against a nonviolent minority, and direct-action tactics that spotlight such injustice can arouse the conscience of the white majority. But the white majority is less likely to become conscience-stricken over subtle forms of discrimination, segregation, or inequalities that are not the immediate product of direct discrimination.

On April 4, 1968, Martin Luther King, Jr., was shot and killed in Memphis, Tennessee. The murder of the nation's leading advocate of nonviolence was a tragedy affecting all Americans. Before his death, King had campaigned in Chicago and other northern cities for an end to de facto segregation of blacks in ghettos and for the passage of legislation prohibiting discrimination in the sale or rental of houses and apartments. "Fair housing" legislation had consistently failed in Congress; there was no mention of discrimination in housing even in the comprehensive Civil Rights Act of 1964; and the prospects of a national fair housing law at the beginning of 1968 were not promising. With the assassination of Martin Luther King, Jr., however, the mood of the nation and of Congress changed dramatically. Congress passed a fair housing law as a tribute to the slain civil rights leader.

The *Civil Rights Act of 1968* prohibited the following forms of discrimination:

Civil Rights Act of 1968

- Refusal to sell or rent a dwelling to any person because of his race, color, religion, or national origin.
- Discrimination against a person in the terms, conditions, or privileges of the sale or rental of a dwelling
- Indication of a preference or discrimination on the basis of race, color, religion, or national origin in advertising the sale or rental of a dwelling

Continuing Inequalities

Despite progress toward equality in law, social and economic inequalities between blacks and whites persist. Median income of black families is only about 57 percent of that of white families, and this ratio has not improved over the past two decades (see Table 10-1). The black poverty percentage is over three times higher than the white poverty percentage. Blacks have made notable progress in education but the proportion of college graduates is still smaller than that of the white population. Female-headed households have increased among both whites and blacks, but today nearly 44 percent of all black households are headed by a woman with no spouse present. Life expectancy among blacks lags behind that of whites, although the gap is closing over time. The infant mortality rate for blacks remains twice as high as for whites.

TABLE 10-1 Continuing Racial Inequalities

	White	Black
Median family income (constant dollars)		
1970	$31,209	$19,144
1988	$33,715	$19,329
Poverty (percentage below poverty line)		
1970	9.9%	33.5%
1988	10.1%	31.6%
College education (percentage of population *25 years and over)*		
1970	11.3%	4.4%
1988	20.9%	11.3%
Female household, no spouse present *(percentage of all families)*		
1970	9.1%	28.3%
1988	12.9%	43.8%
Life expectancy		
1970	71.7%	64.1%
1988	75.5%	69.5%
Infant mortality (deaths per 1,000 live births)		
1970	17.8	32.6
1988	8.6	17.9

Source: U.S. Bureau of the Census, *Statistical Abstract of the United States 1990,* various pages.

Black Political Power

The Fifteenth Amendment (1870), ratified after the Civil War, stated that "the right of citizens of the United States to vote shall not be denied or abridged by the United States or by any State on account of race, color, or previous condition of servitude." Immediately after the adoption of this amendment, blacks in the South began to participate in political life. But their political power declined after 1877 when southern Democrats regained control of state governments. Social pressure, threats of violence, and the terrorist tactics of the Ku Klux Klan combined to dissuade blacks from voting. Southern states passed laws that effectively deprived blacks of the right to vote.

white primary
state primary elections for white voters only; outlawed in 1944

grandfather clause
intended to disenfranchise black voters, it allowed the vote only to those who could prove their grandfathers had voted before 1867

This was the era of the *white primary* and the *grandfather clause.* By using the ruse that party primaries were private, southern whites were allowed to exclude blacks. Indeed, it was not until 1944 in *Smith* v. *Allwright* that the U.S. Supreme Court finally declared the white primary a violation of the Fifteenth Amendment, reasoning that the political party was actually performing a state function in holding a primary election, not acting as a private group. Grandfather clauses, also later declared unconstitutional, prevented persons from voting unless they could prove that their grandfathers had voted before 1867.

Another device to prevent blacks from voting was the *poll tax,* requiring the payment of a fee in order to vote. This practice assured the exclusion of poor blacks from the political process. It wasn't until the passage of the Twenty-Fourth Amend-

Affirmative
Action or
Reverse
Discrimination?

The civil rights movement has opened new opportunities for minorities and women in America. But equality of *opportunity* is not the same as *absolute* equality. What public policies should be pursued to achieve greater equality in the United States? Is it sufficient that government eliminate discrimination, guarantee equality of opportunity for minorities and women, and apply "color-blind" standards to both blacks and whites? Or should government take "affirmative action" to overcome the results of past unequal treatment—preferential or compensatory treatment that would favor minority or women applicants for university admissions and scholarships, job hiring and promotion, and other opportunities for advancement in life?

The earlier emphasis of government policy was, of course, nondiscrimination. Over time, however, the goal of public policy shifted from the traditional aim of equality of opportunity through nondiscrimination, to absolute equality through "goals and timetables" established by affirmative action. Although carefully avoiding the term *quota,* the notion of affirmative action tests the success of equal employment opportunity by observing whether minorities and women achieve admissions, jobs, and promotions in proportion to their numbers in the population.

However, the *constitutional* question is whether affirmative-action programs discriminate against whites and therefore violate the equal protection clause of the Fourteenth Amendment. The U.S. Supreme Court has wrestled with this question in several interesting cases, including that of Allan Bakke. In 1972, after several years of premedical courses and volunteer work in a hospital, Bakke, a thirty-two-year-old white who was also a Vietnam veteran, applied to the University of California at Davis Medical School. He was rejected two years in a row. He later learned that his college grades and medical aptitude test scores ranked well above those of many who had been accepted. All who had been accepted with lower scores were black or Mexican American. Bakke filed a lawsuit arguing that the university had discriminated against him because of race—a violation of the Fourteenth Amendment's guarantee of "equal protection of the laws." The university, which accepted one hundred applicants to medical school per year, admitted that it set aside sixteen places for "disadvantaged students," a category that never included any whites. Candidates for those sixteen positions were placed in a separate admissions pool and competed only against each other. White applicants with grade point averages below 2.5 (out of a possible 4.0) were always rejected, but many minority students were accepted with averages as low as 2.1 and 2.2. Bakke's average was 3.5.

The university argued that using race as a favorable criterion was in the best interest of the state and the nation. By increasing the number of minority students, the university hoped eventually to improve medical care among the poor and the black. Minority doctors would also provide "role models" for young blacks and young Mexican Americans, giving them something to aspire to in their career development. The university contended that its separation of black and white can-

(continued)

CASE STUDY

(continued)

didates was "benign" discrimination (meant to help) rather than "invidious" (meant to hurt).

In *Regents of the University of California* v. *Bakke* (1978), the Supreme Court held that the affirmative-action program at the University of California at Davis Medical School violated Allan Bakke's rights to "equal protection of the laws" under the Fourteenth Amendment. The Court also held that the program violated Title VI of the Civil Rights Act of 1964 because Bakke was "subjected to discrimination under a program receiving federal financial assistance." The Supreme Court ordered the university to admit Bakke to medical school; Bakke was admitted in the fall of 1978 and began his studies six years after his original application.

The Supreme Court was careful to specify the discriminatory aspects of the university's affirmative action program:

> The Davis special admission program involves the use of an explicit racial classification. . . . It tells applicants who are not Negro . . . that they are totally excluded from a specific percentage of seats. . . . No matter how strong their qualifications . . . they [whites] are never afforded the chance to compete with applicants from the preferred groups for the special admission seats.

However, the Supreme Court went on to describe how an affirmative-action program *could* be constitutional:

> Race or ethnic background may be deemed a "plus" in a particular applicant's file, . . . [as long as] it does not insulate the individual from comparison with all other candidates for the available seats.

The Supreme Court generally approved of the goal of achieving racial and ethnic diversity in the student body.

In short, the U.S. Supreme Court indicated: (1) that affirmative-action programs that set aside specific numbers or percentages of positions for minorities violate the "equal protection" rights of majority candidates; but (2) that affirmative-action programs that consider race or ethnic origin as one of many factors in a competition and do not exclude anyone from competing for all available positions do not necessarily violate the constitutional rights of majority candidates. Thus, the *Bakke* case set some limits on affirmative-action programs, but it still permitted schools to consider race as a "plus" factor in competition for admission.

The Supreme Court has considered challenges to affirmative-action plans on a case-by-case basis. No clear or consistent policy has emerged. In some cases, racial quota systems have been upheld as constitutional, and in other cases they have been struck down as violations of the U.S. Constitution or the Civil Rights Act.[4] Many of these cases have been decided by close 5-to-4 votes of the Justices. Among the factors that seem to tip the voting in favor of racial quotas are the presence of a history of racial discrimination before the adoption of the quota system or voluntary agreement to the quota by employers and employees or their unions.

ment, ratified in 1964, that the poll tax was eliminated in federal elections as a precondition to voting. Literacy tests and other barriers were also used in the South to prevent blacks from voting. Frequently, literacy tests asked potential voters to interpret (not just read) complicated texts, such as sections of the state constitution, to the satisfaction of local registrars. Voters were sometimes asked to recite from memory parts of the Constitution. At times prospective voters even had to pass "good character" tests.

In 1965 Martin Luther King, Jr., took action to change all that. Selma, the county seat of Dallas County, Alabama, was chosen as the site to dramatize the voting rights problem. King organized a fifty-mile march from Selma to the state capital in Montgomery. He didn't get very far. Acting on orders of Governor George Wallace to disband the marchers, state troopers did so with a vengeance—with tear gas, nightsticks, and whips. Once again the national government was required to intervene to force compliance with the law. President Johnson federalized the National Guard, and the march continued. During the march the president went on television to address a special joint session of Congress, urging passage of new legislation to assure blacks the right to vote.

The Selma march resulted in the Voting Rights Act of 1965. The act had two major provisions. The first outlawed discriminatory voter registration tests like the literacy test. The second authorized federal registration of persons and federally administered voting procedures in any political subdivision or state that discriminated electorally against a particular group. As a result of that act and its extensions and of the large-scale voter registration drives in the South, the number of blacks registered to vote climbed dramatically.

Today there are more than 7,000 black elected officials, including 20 black members of Congress (see Table 10-2), more than 300 state legislators, more than 4,000 local officials, and 1,600 officials in various local school districts. Some of the largest cities in the United States have had black mayors: New York, Chicago, Los Angeles, Philadelphia, Atlanta, Detroit, New Orleans, and Washington, D.C.

Hispanic Power

The term *Hispanic* refers to Mexican Americans (sometimes called "Chicanos") and to Puerto Ricans, Cubans, and others of Spanish-speaking ancestry and culture. Hispanics are the nation's fastest-growing minority. In the 1990 census there were an estimated 22 million Hispanics, or 9.0 percent of the U.S. population. (There were 30 million blacks, or 12.1 percent of the population.) The largest subgroup is Mexican Americans. Some are descendants of citizens who lived in the Mexican territory annexed to the United States in 1848, but most have come to the United States in accelerating numbers in recent years. The largest Mexican American populations are found in Texas, Arizona, New Mexico, and California. Puerto Ricans constitute the second-largest subgroup (see Figure 10-2). Many still retain ties to the Commonwealth and move back and forth from the island to the mainland. Cubans make up the third-largest subgroup; most have fled from Castro's Cuba and live mainly in the Miami metropolitan area. Although these groups have different

poll tax
a special tax paid as a qualification for voting; outlawed in national elections and by the Twenty-Fourth Amendment; declared unconstitutional in 1966

TABLE 10-2 Growth in Numbers of Black Elected Officials

	1970	1980	1990
U.S. Congress	10	17	20
State government	169	326	441
City and county government	719	2,871	4,388
Judicial and law enforcement	213	534	759
Education	368	1,232	1,602
Total	1,479	4,963	7,190

Source: Joint Center for Political Studies, *Statistical Abstract of the United States 1990* (Washington, D.C.: U.S. Government Printing Office, 1990), p. 260.

experiences, they share a common language and culture, and they have encountered similar difficulties in making government responsive to their needs.

The progress of Hispanics in state and local politics in recent years is reflected in the election of several governors—Jerry Apodaca (D) and Toney Anayo (D) of New Mexico, Raul Castro (D) of Arizona, and Robert Martinez (R) of Florida.

Perhaps because of language barriers, Hispanic voter participation is lower than that of most other ethnic groups in America. However, Hispanic groups have made slow but steady progress toward national averages on education and income measures (see Figure 10-2).

Gender Inequality and the Economy

Gender roles involve power relationships. The traditional American family was patriarchal, and many cultural practices continue to reflect male dominance. (See the section headed "Power and Gender" in Chapter 3.) Men still hold most of the major positions in industry, finance, academia, the military, politics, and government. Authority in many families still rests with the man. Today more than half of all married women work; more than half of women with children under six years of age work (see Figure 10-3). Nonetheless, stereotyped gender roles continue to assign domestic service and child care to women, whether they work or not, and human achievement, interest, and ambition to men.

Despite these increases in the number and proportion of working women, the nation's occupational fields are still divided between traditionally male and female jobs. Women continue to dominate the traditional "pink-collar" jobs (see Table 10-3). Women have made important inroads in traditionally male white-collar occupations—doctors, lawyers, and engineers, for example—although men still remain in the majority in these professions. However, women have only begun to break into the "blue-collar" occupations traditionally dominated by men. Blue-collar jobs usually pay more than pink-collar jobs. This circumstance accounts for much of the earnings gap between men and women that we examined in Chapter 3 (see especially Figure 3-2). Box 10-1 describes the controversy over the handling of

Virginia was the capital of the Confederacy. For a century after the Civil War, it was a symbol of resistance to racial equality. Blacks were excluded from public office, discouraged from voting by the state poll tax, and denied educational equality through "massive resistance" to school integration. Yet in 1989 Virginia became the first state to elect a black governor. Douglas Wilder, grandson of slaves, governs a state with an 80-percent white population—from the domed capitol where Jefferson Davis once presided over the Confederacy.

Wilder grew up in segregated Richmond, one of eight children; his father worked as an insurance agent. Wilder waited tables while attending a local black college; as a U.S. Marine, he fought in the Korean War, winning a Bronze Star in combat; he returned to earn a law degree from Howard University. He became the first black elected to the Virginia state senate in 1969. His early political style was confrontational, but experience and success in the legislature brought greater maturity and moderation in his relations with white colleagues. By 1985 Virginia newspapers were ranking him among the state's most effective legislators. He had broadened his interests from racial affairs to a wide range of state issues. He embraced rather than ridiculed his state's historical symbols. Yet he was known as a tough negotiator within Democratic party circles.

In 1985 Wilder won the Democratic nomination for lieutenant governor. He was an effective campaigner, touring all of the state's ninety-five counties and running TV ads showing support from rural, conservative white policemen.

In contrast to practitioners of the often divisive politics of race, Douglas Wilder projected an image of statewide consensus and progress. "As a boy when I would read about an Abe Lincoln or a Thomas Jefferson . . . when I would read that all men are created equal . . . I knew it meant me."[5] With soft tones and a reassuring manner, Wilder moved to the center of Democratic politics in his state, becoming tough on crime and supporting the death penalty. Even while waging a successful battle to create a state holiday in honor of Martin Luther King, Jr., he solicited the support of moderate and conservative forces in Virginia. In 1989 Wilder easily captured the Democratic nomination for governor.

In winning the Virginia governorship, Douglas Wilder did more than any other elected public official to put race to rest as a political issue. Throughout the campaign Wilder insisted, "Race is not an issue."[6] He declined offers of help from Jesse Jackson. His Republican opponent attacked his earlier liberal record, charging that he had flip-flopped on the issues. It was a tough campaign: Wilder's millionaire legal and business interests, including his ownership of slum property, were the subject of negative TV ads. Wilder hit back hard and won support using conservative rhetoric. He won "pro-choice" votes on the abortion issue with the slogan "Keep politicians out of your personal life." A Labor Day riot of black students at Virginia Beach almost upset his mainstream campaign. But when the votes were

(continued)

Wilder of Virginia: Putting Race to Rest

(continued)

Governor Douglas Wilder of Virginia, the nation's first elected black governor.
Source: Jim West/Impact Visuals

counted, Wilder emerged with a razor-thin 50-percent margin of victory. He won over 40 percent of the white vote in the state and 90 percent of the black vote. His white running mate for lieutenant governor won 54 percent of the vote, suggesting perhaps that some white Democratic voters could not bring themselves to support Wilder.

Wilder's victory in a predominantly white southern state provides the model for successful statewide biracial politics. Political moderation, mainstream views, and a reassuring image can prevail where passionate rhetoric, left-leaning politics, and a flamboyant image will fail. Race can be put to rest by able and effective politicians.

this wage gap by government classification of traditionally male and female jobs according to their "comparable worth."

To supplement this discussion of women in the labor force, Box 10-2 offers a cross-national perspective of women in the work force in other nations.

The Roots of Sexual Inequality

How much of male dominance can be attributed to *biology* and how much to *culture*? Many scholars deny that biological differences necessitate any distinctions

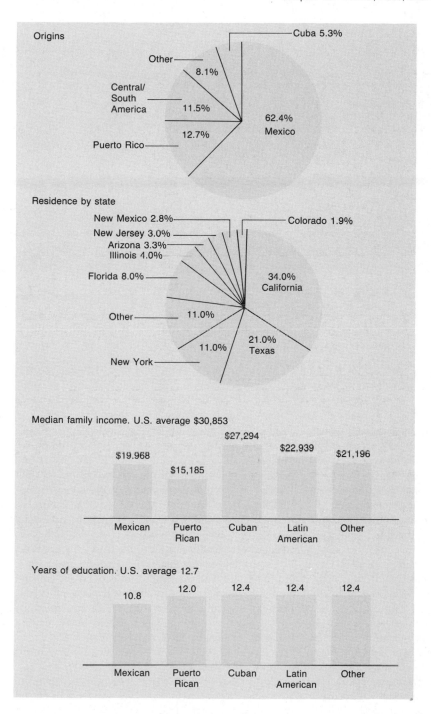

FIGURE 10-2   Hispanic Americans

Source: U.S. Bureau of the Census, *Statistical Abstract of the United States 1988* (Washington, D.C.: U.S. Government Printing Office, 1988).

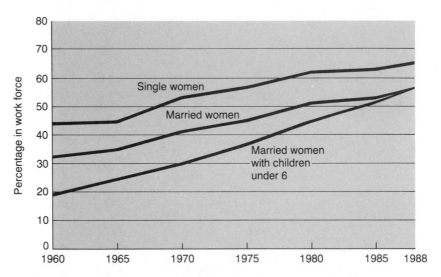

FIGURE 10-3   Increasing participation of women in the labor force
Source: Statistical Abstract of the United States 1991, p. 390.

BOX 10-1

The "Comparable Worth" Controversy

Federal laws guarantee equal pay for men and women doing the same work. Ever since passage of the Civil Rights Act of 1964, pay differences between men and women in the same job have been illegal. Yet, overall, women continue to earn less than men; the average woman in the work force today earns about 66 percent of the pay of the average man.[7] Most of this "wage gap" is a product of the concentration of women in traditionally lower-paid "pink-collar" occupations.

The initial efforts of the feminist movement were directed toward getting more women into traditionally male occupational fields; success would automatically narrow the "wage gap." But these efforts require time: Many years are required to recruit and train women as doctors, lawyers, or engineers. Moreover, efforts to recruit more women into blue-collar jobs have been only marginally successful.

Recently some feminist organizations adopted a new approach to the elimination of the wage gap—the demand that pay levels be determined by the "comparable worth" of various jobs rather than by the labor market. *Comparable worth* means more than paying men and women

equally for the same work; it means paying the same wages for jobs of comparable value to the employer. Comparable worth means that traditionally male and female jobs would be evaluated according to their "worth" to the employer, perhaps by considering responsibilities, effort, and knowledge and skill requirements. Jobs adjudged to be "comparable" would be paid equal wages. For example, the work of a secretary might be adjudged comparable in value to the work of a mechanic.

Comparable worth requires that a government agency, or perhaps the courts, determine for both private employers and government employers the value of various jobs. Decisions by the agencies would replace the determination of wage rates by the labor market. Many feminist groups charge that the labor market is really a "dual market" in which women's work is valued less than men's work.

Comparable worth raises problems of implementation: Who would decide what wages for various jobs should be? How would comparable worth be decided? What standards would be used to determine worth? If government

(continued)

BOX 10-1

(continued)

agencies set wage rates by law instead of the free market, would a black (illegal) market for labor arise? What penalties would be imposed on employers or employees who worked for wages different from those set by the government?

The U.S. Equal Employment Opportunity Commission

has rejected the notion of comparable worth and has declined to set wages for traditionally male and female occupations. However, a number of state governments have undertaken to review their own pay scales to determine if traditionally female occupations are underpaid.

TABLE 10-3 Women's Occupations, 1988

	Percentage female
"White collar"	
Women are increasingly entering white-collar occupational fields traditionally dominated by men:	
Architects	10
Computer analysts	34
College and university teachers	36
Engineers	6
Lawyers and judges	18
Physicians	18
"Pink collar"	
Women continue to be concentrated in occupational fields traditionally dominated by women:	
Nurses	94
Elementary school teachers	85
Librarians	86
Secretaries	99
Receptionists	97
Bookkeepers	92
Cashiers	83
Child-care workers	96
"Blue collar"	
Women continue to be largely shut out of blue-collar occupational fields traditionally dominated by men:	
Carpenters	1
Mechanics	4
Construction workers	2
Miners	2
Foresters	4
Truck drivers	4
Heavy-equipment operators	4

Source: U.S. Bureau of the Census, *Statistical Abstract of the United States 1988* (Washington, D.C.: U.S. Government Printing Office, 1988), pp. 376–377.

Focusing public attention on sexual harassment issues—law professor Anita Hill testifies at the Senate confirmation hearings of Justice Clarence Thomas.
Source: Rick Reinhard/Impact Visuals

inequality as a product of cultural conditioning

between male and female in domestic service or child-care responsibilities, authority in the family, economic roles in society, or political or legal rights. They contend that *existing gender differences are culturally imposed on women from earliest childhood.* The very first item in personality formation is the assignment of gender roles (you are a boy, you are a girl) and the encouragement of "masculine" and "feminine" traits. Aggression, curiosity, intelligence, initiative, and force are encouraged in the boy; passivity, refinement, shyness, and virtue are encouraged in the girl. Girls are supposed to think in terms of domestic and child-care roles, whereas boys are urged to think of careers in industry and the professions. Deeply ingrained symbols, attitudes, and practices are culturally designated as masculine or feminine ("What a big boy!" "Isn't she pretty!"). There are masculine and feminine subjects in school: science, technology, and business are male; teaching, nursing, and secretarial studies are female. Boys are portrayed in roles in which they master their environment; girls, in roles in which they admire the accomplishments of men. It is this *cultural* conditioning that leads a woman to accept a family- and child-centered life and an inferior economic and political role in society—not her *physiology.*

inequality as a product of social–psychological barriers

Many writers have deplored the *social–psychological barriers* to a woman's full human development. There is a double standard of sexual guilt in which women are subject to greater shame for any sexual liaison, whatever the circumstances. Yet, while denied sexual freedom herself, the woman is usually obliged to seek advancement through the approval of men. She may try to overcome her powerlessness by using her own sexuality, perhaps at the cost of her dignity and self-respect. The prevailing male attitude is to value women for their sexual traits rather than for their qualities as human beings. Women are frequently portrayed as "sex objects" in advertising, magazines, and literature. They are supposed to entertain, please, gratify, and flatter men with their sexuality; it is seldom the other way around. There is even evidence of self-rejection among women that is similar to that encountered among minority groups: female children are far more likely to wish they had been born boys than male children are to wish they had been born girls.[8] The power aspects of gender roles are also ingrained in male psychology. Young men are deemed feminine (inferior) if they are not sufficiently aggressive, physical, or violent.

In contrast to these arguments about *culturally* imposed gender roles, other observers have contended that *physiological differences* between men and women account for differential gender roles. The woman's role in the reproduction and care of the young is biologically determined. To the extent that she seeks to protect her young, she also seeks family arrangements that will provide maximum security and support for them. Men acquire dominant positions in industry, finance, government, and so forth, largely because women are preoccupied with family and child-care tasks. Men are physically stronger than women, and their role as economic providers is rooted in this biological difference. Whether there are any biologically determined mental or emotional differences between men and women is a disputed point, but the possibility of such differences exists. Thus, differential gender roles may be partly physical in origin.

inequality as a product of physiological differences

BOX 10-2

Cross-National Perspective: Women in the Labor Force

Women's progress in advanced democracies appears to be closely associated with their labor-force participation. Economic productivity leads to social and political power. In recent decades women have entered the labor force in increasing numbers and percentages in all the industrialized nations, not just in the United States (see Table 10-4). In some Western nations, notably Sweden, there is a longer tradition of women holding jobs outside of the home. For other nations, notably Japan, women in the work force is a more recent development. In Italy, female labor-force participation lags behind that of other industrialized nations. The United States is roughly comparable to other Western nations in its female labor-force participation rate.

TABLE 10-4 Percentage of Women in the Labor Force in Various Nations, 1980–1988

Percentage of women, ages 25–54, in labor force

	1980	1988
United States	63.8	72.5
Canada	60.1	73.1
France	63.0	71.2
Italy	39.9	47.8
Japan	56.7	62.2
Sweden	82.9	90.8
United Kingdom	63.4	70.2
West Germany	53.6	61.4

Source: Statistical Abstract of the United States 1991, p. 849.

Women in power: Palestinian spokesperson Hanan Ashrawi.
Source: Jacqueline Arzt/AP/Wide World Photos

The Power of Women's Protest Movements

Women in the United States have made great progress in acquiring equal rights over the years. The earliest active "feminist" organizations grew out of the pre–Civil War antislavery movement. The first generation of feminists, including Lucretia Mott, Elizabeth Cady Stanton, Lucy Stone, and Susan B. Anthony, learned to organize, to hold public meetings, and to conduct petition campaigns as abolitionists. After the Civil War, the feminist movement concentrated on winning civil rights and the franchise for women. The suffragettes employed mass demonstrations, parades, picketing, and occasional disruptions and civil disobedience—tactics similar to those of the civil rights movement of the 1960s. The more moderate wing of the American suffrage movement became the League of Women Voters; in addition to the women's vote, they sought protection of women in industry, child welfare laws, honest election practices, and the elimination of laws discriminating against the rights of women.

political equality
Nineteenth Amendment
(1920)

The culmination of the early feminist movement was the passage in 1920 of the Nineteenth Amendment to the Constitution:

> The right of citizens of the United States to vote shall not be denied or abridged by the United States or by any State on account of sex.

The movement was also successful in changing many state laws that abridged the property rights of the married woman and otherwise treated her as the "chattel" (property) of her husband. But active feminist politics declined after the goal of women's voting rights had been achieved.

Renewed interest and progress in women's rights came with the civil rights movement of the 1960s. The Civil Rights Act of 1964 prevents discrimination on the basis of gender, as well as of race, in employment, salary, promotion, and other conditions of work. The Equal Employment Opportunity Commission (EEOC), the federal agency charged with eliminating discrimination in employment, has established guidelines barring stereotyped classifications of "men's jobs" and "women's jobs." State laws and employer practices that differentiate between men and women in terms of hours, pay, retirement age, and so on, have been struck down. Under active lobbying from feminist organizations, federal agencies, including the U.S. Office of Education and the Office of Federal Contract Compliance, have established affirmative-action guidelines for government agencies, universities, and private businesses doing work for the government. These guidelines set goals and timetables for employers to alter their work force to achieve higher percentages of women at all levels.

equality in employment
Civil Rights Act of 1964

For many years feminist activity focused on the Equal Rights Amendment (ERA) to the Constitution, which would have struck down *all* existing legal inequalities in state and federal laws between men and women. The proposed amendment stated simply:

ERA
Equal Rights Amendment

> Equality of rights under the law shall not be denied or abridged by the United States or by any State on account of sex.

The ERA passed the Congress easily in 1972 and was sent to the states for the necessary ratification by three-fourths (thirty-eight) of them. The amendment won quick ratification by half of the states, but a developing "Stop-ERA" movement slowed progress after 1976. Both the ERA and Stop-ERA movements were led by women; they fought their battles over ratification in state legislatures across the nation. Despite an extension of time by Congress, ERA fell three states short of the necessary thirty-eight in 1982. Throughout the debates over ratification of ERA, opinion polls reported that a large majority of Americans favored it. Opponents argued that it might eliminate many legal protections for women: financial support by husbands, an interest in the husband's property, exemption from military service, and so forth. In addition to these specific objections, the opponents of the ERA and the feminist movement also charged that it would weaken the family institution and demoralize women who wish to devote their lives to their family and children. Supporters of the ERA argue that only a constitutional amendment can guarantee women full equality and that such a guarantee should be a part of the fundamental laws of the land.

Women are also acquiring greater power over their own lives through a series of *social and medical developments*. Advances in birth control techniques, including "the pill," have freed women's sexuality from the reproductive function. Abortions are now a recognized constitutional right. Women can determine for themselves whether and when they will undertake childbirth and child rearing.

changing mores and medical advances

Abortion controversy
continues in Washington and
state capitals throughout the
nation.
Source: Joel Gordon

Abortion and the Law

Abortion can dramatically affect a nation's birthrate, its population growth, and ultimately its whole structure and quality of life. For years, abortions in the United States for any purpose other than saving the life of the mother were criminal offenses under state laws. Then in the late 1960s about a dozen states acted to permit abortion in cases of rape or incest, or to protect the physical health of the mother and in some cases the mental health as well. However, relatively few abortions were performed under those laws because of the red tape involved—review of each case by several concurring physicians, approval of a hospital board, and so forth.

Abortion is a highly sensitive issue. It is not an issue that can be compromised. The arguments touch on fundamental moral and religious principles. Proponents of abortion argue that a woman should be permitted to control her own body and should not be forced by law to have unwanted children. They cite the heavy toll in lives lost because of criminal abortions and the psychological and emotional pain of an unwanted pregnancy. Opponents of abortion base their belief on the sanctity of life, including the life of the unborn child, which they insist deserves the protection of law—"the right to life." Many believe that the killing of an unborn child for any reason other than the preservation of the life or health of the mother is murder.

Roe **v.** *Wade*

One of the most controversial decisions in the Supreme Court's history was its ruling in *Roe* v. *Wade* (1973), which recognized abortion as a *constitutional* right of women. In this historic decision the Court determined that a fetus is not a "person" within the meaning of the Constitution, and therefore a fetus's right to life is not guaranteed by law. Moreover, the Court held that the "liberty" guaranteed by the Fifth and Fourteenth Amendments encompassed a woman's decision on whether or not to terminate her pregnancy. The Supreme Court decided that during the first three months of pregnancy the abortion decision must be left wholly to the woman and her physician; that during the second three months of pregnancy the state may not prohibit abortion, but only regulate procedures in ways reasonably related to maternal health; and that only in the final three months of pregnancy may the state prohibit abortion except when abortion is necessary for the preservation of life or health of the mother.

The Supreme's Court's decision did not end the controversy over abortion. Congress declined to pass a constitutional amendment restricting abortion or declaring that the guarantee of life begins at conception. However, Congress banned the use of federal funds under Medicaid (medical care for the poor) for abortions except to protect the life of a woman. The Supreme Court upheld the constitutionality of federal and state laws denying tax funds for abortions. Although women retained the right to an abortion, the Court held that there was no constitutional obligation for governments to pay for abortions:[9] the decision about whether to pay for abortion from tax revenues was left to Congress and the states.

About 1.5 million abortions are performed each year in the United States. This is about 43 percent of the number of live births. Most of these abortions are performed in the first three months; about 10 percent are performed after the third month.

Opponents of abortion won a victory in *Webster* v. *Reproductive Health Services* (1989), when the Supreme Court upheld a Missouri law sharply restricting abortions. The right to abortion under *Roe* v. *Wade* was not overturned but was narrowed in application. The Court held that Missouri could deny public funds for abortions that were not necessary for saving the life of the woman and could deny the use of public facilities or employees in performing or assisting in abortions. More importantly, the Court upheld the requirement for a test of "viability" after twenty weeks and a prohibition on abortion of a viable fetus except to save a woman's life. The Court recognized the state's "interest in the protection of human life when viability is possible."

Webster v. Reproductive Health Services

Again, in *Planned Parenthood* v. *Casey* (1992), the Supreme Court upheld *Roe* v. *Wade's* assertion that abortion was a personal liberty of women protected by the U.S. Constitution. However, four justices appeared to believe that no such right could be found in the text of the Constitution. Moreover, the Court upheld Pennsylvania's requirements for physician counseling prior to an abortion, a 24-hour waiting period, and parental notification when minors seek an abortion. It struck down a spousal notification requirement as too burdensome.

The effect of these decisions has been to inspire contentious debates over abortion in virtually all state capitols. Various legal restrictions on abortions have been passed in the states, including the following:

Restrictive laws in the states

1. *Public financing:* prohibitions on public financing of abortions
2. *Viability tests:* requirements for a test of viability and prohibitions on the abortion of a viable fetus

TABLE 10-5 Abortion Opinion

General

Should abortion be legal as it is now, or legal only in such cases as rape, incest, or to save the life of the mother, or should it not be permitted at all?

Legal as it is now	49%
Legal only in certain cases	39
Not permitted at all	9

Specific reasons

Do you think it should be possible for a pregnant woman to obtain a legal abortion:

	Yes	No
If the woman's health is threatened?	87%	7%
If there is a strong chance of serious defect in the baby?	69	21
If the family has a very low income and cannot afford any more children?	43	49
If the woman is unmarried and does not want to marry the man?	42	50
If the pregnancy interfered with work or education?	26	65

Restrictions

Would you support or oppose the following restrictions on abortion that may come before state legislatures?

	Support	Oppose
Medical tests must show fetus unable to survive outside womb	54%	33%
Teenagers must have parent's permission	75	22
Women seeking abortions must be counseled on the dangers and on alternatives to abortion	88	9
No public funds for abortion except to save a woman's life	61	34
No abortions in public facilities except to save a woman's life	54	41
Public employees may not perform, assist in, or advise abortion	40	50

Source: Data derived from reports in *New York Times,* April 26, 1989; and *Newsweek,* July 17, 1989.

3. *Conscience laws:* laws granting permission to doctors and hospitals to refuse to perform abortions

4. *Fetal disposal:* laws requiring humane and sanitary disposal of fetal remains

5. *Informed consent:* laws requiring physicians to inform patients about the development of the fetus and the availability of assistance in pregnancy

6. *Parental notification:* laws requiring that parents of minors seeking abortion be informed

7. *Spousal verifications:* laws requiring that spouses of women seeking abortion be informed

8. *Hospitalization requirement:* laws requiring that late abortions be performed in hospitals

9. *Clinic licensing:* laws setting standards of cleanliness and care in abortion clinics

10. *Gender selection:* laws prohibiting abortion based on the gender of the fetus

Public opinion is deeply divided over the issue of abortion. Although both "pro-choice" and "pro-life" forces claim to have public opinion on their side, in fact public opinion is almost equally split over when abortions should be permitted (see Table 10-5). Many of the specific restrictions under consideration in state legislatures have majority support, including the prohibition of public funding for abortion. Yet a majority of Americans want to "keep abortion legal."

Notes

1. *Brown* v. *Board of Education of Topeka, Kansas,* 347 U.S. 483 (1954).
2. Kenneth B. Clark, *Dark Ghetto: Dilemmas of Social Power* (New York: Harper & Row, 1965), p. 75.
3. A public letter by Martin Luther King, Jr., Birmingham, Alabama, April 16, 1963; the full text is reprinted in Thomas R. Dye and Brett Hawkins, eds., *Politics in the Metropolis* (Columbus, Ohio: Merrill, 1967), pp. 100–109.
4. See *Congressional Quarterly Weekly Report,* November 15, 1986.
5. *Time,* November 20, 1989, p. 54.
6. *New York Times,* September 16, 1989, p. A-10.
7. U.S. Bureau of the Census, *Statistical Abstract of the United States 1990* (Washington, D.C.: U.S. Government Printing Office, 1990), p. 411.
8. Goodwin Watson, "Psychological Aspects of Sex Roles," in *Social Psychology, Issues, and Insights* (Philadelphia: Lippincott, 1966), p. 477.
9. *Harris* v. *McRae,* 448 U.S. 297 (1980).

About This Chapter

The United States has a long history of protest. The nation was in fact born as a protest against the injustices of colonialism—against powerlessness and the lack of a "voice" in controlling its own affairs. Despite that heritage, America's women and racial minorities have had a long and continuing fight against the inequalities imposed on them by their nation's laws and customs.

In 1776 Abigail Adams wrote to her husband John, who was then a delegate to the Continental Congress, cautioning him and his fellow delegates that when framing the new nation's laws they should "Remember the Ladies. . . . Do not put such unlimited power into the hands of the Husbands." She added, probably in jest, "If particular care and attention is not paid to the Ladies we are determined to foment a Rebellion, and will not hold ourselves bound by any Laws in which we have no voice, or Representation."* The "Ladies" did not find that voice until

*L. H. Butterfield, Marc Friedlander, and Mary-Jo Kline, eds., *The Book of Abigail and John* (Cambridge, Mass.: Harvard University Press, 1975), p. 121.

1920, when the Nineteenth Amendment finally guaranteed women the right to vote. And the struggle for sexual equality continues today.

In this chapter we explored the struggles and triumphs of both blacks and women in the United States, as well as some of the inequalities these groups suffer. Now that you have read it, you should be able to

- discuss the civil rights movement of the 1950s and 1960s and the changes that it brought about in the laws;
- describe the inequalities against which American blacks and American women have protested;
- describe the philosophy of nonviolent direct action advocated by Martin Luther King, Jr.;
- discuss the controversy over "affirmative action" goals and timetables;
- describe the historical obstacles to black political participation, as well as recent black gains in political power;
- describe economic inequality between the sexes and various theories purporting to explain sexual inequality;
- describe the Supreme Court's reasoning in *Roe* v. *Wade* regarding the constitutionality of abortion.

Discussion Questions

1. Identify the initial goal of the civil rights movement. Discuss the Supreme Court case that marked the first step in attaining that goal and the constitutional amendment upon which the civil rights movement based its arguments. Why was the Supreme Court unable to implement its decision by itself?

2. Identify the key provisions of the Civil Rights Act of 1964.

3. Describe *nonviolent direct action* as advocated by Martin Luther King, Jr., its political purpose, and factors important to its success.

4. Describe how King and his followers were instrumental in the passage of the Voting Rights Act of 1965

and the Civil Rights Act of 1968. Briefly describe the content of each act.

5. Describe the purpose of affirmative-action programs. How does affirmative action differ from "color-blind" standards?

6. Describe some of the early obstacles to blacks' acquisition of political power.

7. Discuss the "cultural" and "biological" explanations of male dominance in society. Describe some of the important landmarks for women's protest movements.

8. Discuss the *Bakke* case. How may affirmative action conflict with the concept of equality of opportunity? How may it be in violation of the Fourteenth Amendment?

Poverty and Powerlessness

Poverty as Powerlessness

powerlessness
the inability to control the events that shape one's life

Powerlessness is the inability to control the events that shape one's life. The poor lack economic resources and are hence largely dependent on others for the things they need. Their lack of power derives from their *dependency*. But powerlessness is also an attitude, a feeling that no matter what one does it will have little effect on one's life. An *attitude* of powerlessness *reinforces* the *condition* of powerlessness among the poor. Their experiences generate a lack of motivation and feelings of meaninglessness, hopelessness, distrust, and cynicism. Constant defeat causes many of the poor to retreat into a self-protective attitude characterized by indifference and a pervasive sense of futility.

alienation
a feeling of separation from society

The poor often feel *alienated*—separated from society—because of their lack of success in obtaining important life goals. Persons who are blocked consistently in their efforts to achieve life goals are most likely to express powerlessness and alienation. These attitudes in turn become barriers to effective self-help, independence, and self-respect. Poverty can lead to apathy, aimlessness, and a lack of motivation.

To be *both* black and poor in a predominantly white, affluent society magnifies feelings of powerlessness and alienation. Social psychologists are not always certain about the processes by which social inequalities are perceived or how these perceptions influence attitudes and behaviors. But African American sociologist Kenneth B. Clark has provided some interesting insights into "the psychology of the ghetto."[1]

self-hatred and self-doubt
victims of poverty begin to blame themselves and see themselves as inferior

Professor Clark argues that human beings who live apart from the rest of society, who do not share in society's affluence, and who are not respected or granted the ordinary dignities and courtesy accorded to others will eventually begin to doubt their own worth. All human beings depend on their experiences with others for clues to how they should view and value themselves. Black children who consistently see whites in a superior position begin to question whether they, or their family, or blacks in general really deserve any more respect from the larger society than they receive. These doubts, Clark maintains, become the seeds of "a pernicious self- and group-hatred."[2]

the search for self-esteem
a poor environment leads to aggressive and self-destructive behavior

But all human beings search for self-esteem. According to Clark, teenage ghetto blacks often pretend to knowledge about illicit activities and to sexual experiences they have not really had. Many use as their models the petty criminals of the ghetto, with their colorful, swaggering style of cool bravado. The inability to succeed by the standards of the wider society leads to a peculiar fascination with individuals who successfully defy society's norms. Some young black men seek their salvation in aggressive and self-destructive behavior. Because the larger society has rejected them, they reject—or at least appear to reject—the values of that society.

Professor Clark believes that the explanation for violence and crime in the ghetto lies in the conscious or unconscious belief of many young blacks that they cannot hope to win meaningful self-esteem through the avenues available to middle-class whites, so they turn to "hustling"—pimping, prostitution, gambling, or drug dealing. They are frequently scornful of what they consider the hypocrisy and dishonesty of the larger society. They point to corruption among respected middle-class whites, including the police force.

Homeless families seek
temporary shelter; others sleep
on the streets.
Source: Mary Ellen Mark/Library

Poverty and discrimination have also taken their toll on black family life. Professor Clark observed that under the system of slavery, the only source of family continuity was through the female; children were dependent on their mothers rather than their fathers. Segregation relegated the black male to menial and subservient jobs. He could not present himself to his wife and children as a consistent wage earner. Many black women were obliged to hold the family together, to set its goals and encourage and protect its boys and girls. Many young black males had no responsible father figure upon which to model their behavior. The result was a high rate of family instability.

family instability

Poverty in the United States

How much poverty really exists in America? Conflict over the definition of poverty and over estimates of the number of poor is common. Liberal proponents of large-scale government programs for the poor frequently make broad definitions of poverty and high estimates of the number of poor people. They view the problem as a persistent one, even in an affluent society. They contend that millions suffer from hunger, exposure, and remediable illness. Their definition of the problem of poverty practically mandates immediate and massive governmental programs to assist the poor.

conflict over the nature and extent of poverty in the United States

On the other hand, conservative opponents of large-scale governmental welfare programs frequently minimize the number of poor in America. They view the poor in the United States as considerably better off than the middle class was fifty years ago—and even wealthy by the standards of most other societies in the world. They view government welfare programs as causes of poverty, destroying family life and robbing the poor of incentives to work, save, and assume responsibility for their own well-being. They deny that Americans need to suffer from hunger, homelessness, or remediable illness, if they make use of the services and facilities available to them. Their definition of the problem of poverty minimizes the need for massive public programs to fight poverty.

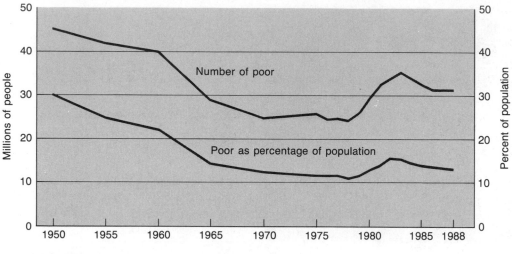

FIGURE 11-1   Poverty in the United States

Source: Statistical Abstract of the United States 1990 (Washington, D.C.:
U.S. Government Printing Office, 1990), p. 458.

**official definition of
poverty**
government estimates
each year of the mini-
mum costs required to
maintain families of various sizes

**liberal objections to
official definition of
poverty**

**conservative objec-
tions to official defi-
nition of poverty**

According to the U.S. Social Security Administration, in 1988 there were about
32 million poor people (those below the official poverty level) in the United States,
or approximately 13 percent of the population (see Figure 11-1). The poverty level
is set by the Social Security Administration. It is derived by calculating the minimum costs required to maintain families of different sizes. The dollar amounts
change each year to take into account the effect of inflation. In 1988 the poverty
line for a family of four was an income of approximately $12,092.

This official definition of poverty emphasizes *subsistence levels;* it seeks to
describe poverty objectively as the lack of enough income to acquire the minimum
necessities of life. Liberals frequently view the subsistence definition of poverty as
insensitive to a variety of needs, including entertainment, recreation, and the relief
of monotony. Items that were "luxuries" a generation ago are now considered
"necessities." Liberals also note that the official definition *includes* cash income
from welfare and Social Security. Without this government assistance, the number
of poor would be higher.

Conservatives also challenge the official definition of poverty: it does not
include the value of family assets. People (usually older people) who own their
own houses and automobiles may have incomes below the poverty line yet not
suffer any real hardship. (More than 50 percent of the official "poor" own their
own homes and more than 65 percent own automobiles.) Many persons who are
ranked as poor do not think of themselves as "poor people"—students, for example. More important, the official definition of poverty *excludes* "in-kind" (noncash)
benefits provided by government, benefits that include, for example, free medical
care under Medicaid and Medicare, food stamps, public housing, and school
lunches. If these benefits were "costed out" (that is, calculated as cash income),
there might be fewer persons classified as poor. The U.S. government itself esti-

mates that if all government benefits to the poor are costed out, the percentage of poor in the country is about 9 percent rather than the official 13 percent.[3] Box 11-1 discusses the categories of people that make up "the poor."

Is There a Culture of Poverty?

It is sometimes argued that the poor have a characteristic lifestyle or *culture of poverty* that assists them in adjusting to their world. Like other aspects of culture it is passed on to future generations, setting in motion a self-perpetuating cycle of poverty. The theory of the poverty cycle is as follows: deprivation in one generation leads, through cultural impoverishment, indifference, apathy, or misunderstanding of their children's educational needs, to deprivation in the next generation. Lacking the self-respect that comes from earning an adequate living, some young men cannot sustain responsibilities of marriage, and so they hand down to their children the same burden of family instability and female-headed households that they themselves carried. Children born into a culture of alienation, apathy, and lack of moti-

the culture-of-poverty thesis
the idea that a lifestyle of poverty, alienation, and apathy is passed on from one generation to another

---

BOX 11-1

Who Are the Poor?

Poverty occurs in many kinds of families and in all races and ethnic groups. However, some groups experience poverty in proportions that are greater than the national average. The following statistics indicate the percentage of Americans in various groups who were living below the poverty level in 1988. The figures are from *Statistical Abstract of the United States 1990*.

Total population	13.1
Husband–wife families	7.1
Families with female heads	33.6
White	10.1
African American	31.6
Hispanic	26.8
Over age 65	12.2
Under age 18	20.4

Poverty is most common among female-headed families. In 1988 the incidence of poverty among these families was 33.6 percent, compared with only 7.1 percent for married couples. These women and their children constitute over 66.7 percent of all of the persons living in poverty in the United States. These figures describe the "feminization of poverty" in America. Clearly, poverty is

closely related to family structure. Today the disintegration of the traditional husband–wife family is the single most influential factor contributing to poverty.

Blacks experience poverty in much greater proportions than whites. Over the years the poverty rate among blacks in the United States has been almost three times higher than the poverty rate among whites. Poverty among Hispanics is also significantly greater than among whites.

The aged in America experience *less* poverty than younger people. The aged are not poor, despite the popularity of the phrase "the poor and the aged." The poverty rate for persons over sixty-five years of age is *below* the national average. Moreover, the aged are much wealthier than younger age groups. They are more likely than younger people to own homes with paid-up mortgages. Medicare pays a large portion of their medical expenses. With fewer expenses, the aged, even with relatively smaller cash incomes, experience poverty in a different fashion than a younger mother with children. The declining poverty rate among the aged is a relatively recent occurrence. Continuing increases in Social Security benefits over the years are largely responsible for this singular "victory" in the war against poverty.

Finally, we should note that about one of every five children in the United States lives in poverty.

Poverty is also found in rural America.
Source: Mary Ellen Mark/Library

vation learn these attitudes themselves. Thus, the poor are prevented from exploiting any opportunities that are available to them.

It is probably more accurate to talk about a *subculture* of poverty. The prefix *sub* is used because most of the poor subscribe to the "middle-class American way of life," at least as a cultural ideal and even as a personal fantasy. Most poor people do not reject American culture but strive to adapt its values to the realities of economic deprivation and social disorganization in their own lives.

the culture of poverty as present-orientedness
the inability to plan or sacrifice for the future

Another view of the culture of poverty emphasizes the *present-orientedness* of many poor people. Professor Edward C. Banfield argues that the culture of poverty is primarily an effect produced by extreme present-orientedness rather than a lack of income or wealth. Individuals caught up in the culture of poverty are unable to plan for the future, to sacrifice immediate gratifications in favor of future ones, or to exercise the discipline that is required to get ahead. Banfield admits that some people experience poverty because of involuntary unemployment, prolonged illness, death of the breadwinner, or some other misfortune. But even when severe, this kind of poverty is not self-perpetuating. It ends once the external cause no longer exists. According to Banfield, other people will be poor no matter what their "external" circumstances are. They live in a culture of poverty that continues for generations because they are psychologically unable to provide for the future. Improvements in their circumstances may affect their poverty only superficially. Even increased income is unlikely to change their way of life. The additional money will be spent quickly on nonessential or frivolous items. This culture of poverty may involve no more than 10 or 20 percent of all families who live below the poverty line, but it generally continues regardless of what is done in the way of remedial action.[4]

Opponents of the idea of a culture of poverty argue that this notion diverts attention from the *conditions* of poverty that foster family instability, present-orientedness, and other ways of life. The question is really whether the conditions of poverty create a culture of poverty or vice versa. Reformers are likely to focus on the conditions of poverty as the fundamental cause of the social pathologies that afflict the poor. They note that the idea of a culture of poverty can be applied only to groups who have lived in poverty for several generations. It is not relevant to those who have become poor during their lifetime because of sickness, accident, or old age. The cultural explanation basically involves *parental transmission of values and beliefs,* which in turn determines behavior of future generations. In contrast, the situational explanation of poverty involves social conditions—differences in financial resources—that operate directly to determine behavior. In this view the conditions of poverty can be seen as affecting behavior directly, as well as *indirectly* through their impact on succeeding generations. Perhaps the greatest danger in the idea of a culture of poverty is that poverty in this light can be seen as an unbreakable, puncture-proof cycle, which may lead to a relaxation of efforts to ameliorate the conditions of poverty. In other words, a "culture" of poverty may become an excuse for inaction.[5]

> **poverty**
> a result of current social conditions or parental transmission?

Whether or not there is a culture of poverty is a perplexing question. The argument resembles the classic exchange between F. Scott Fitzgerald and Ernest Hemingway. When Fitzgerald observed, "The rich are different from you and me," Hemingway retorted, "Yes, they have more money." Observers who believe they see a distinctive lower-class culture will say, "The poor are different from you and me." But opponents may reply, "Yes, they have less money." In other words, are the poor poorly educated, underskilled, poorly motivated, "delinquent," and "shiftless" because they are poor, or are they poor because they are poorly educated, underskilled, unmotivated, "delinquent," and "shiftless"?

> **do the poor have a separate culture or simply less money than most other Americans?**

Government Policy as a Cause of Poverty

Does the government itself create poverty by fashioning social welfare programs and policies that destroy incentives to work, encourage families to break up, and condemn the poor to social dependency? Does the current social welfare system unintentionally sentence to a life of poverty many people who would otherwise form families, take low-paying jobs, and perhaps, with hard work and perseverance, gradually pull themselves and their children into the mainstream of American life?

Poverty in America steadily *declined* from 1950, when about 30 percent of the population was officially poor, to 1970, when about 13 percent of the population was poor. During this period of progress toward the elimination of poverty, government welfare programs were minimal. There were small AFDC (Aid to Families with Dependent Children) programs for women who lived alone with their children; eligibility was restricted, and welfare authorities checked to see if an employable male lived in the house. Further, there were federal payments for the aged, blind, and disabled poor. Welfare roles were modest; only about 1 to 2 percent of American families received AFDC payments.

The addition of many new Great Society welfare programs ended the downward trend in poverty. Indeed, the number and proportion of the population living in poverty began to move upward in the 1970s and early 1980s (see Figure 11-1). This was a period in which AFDC payments were significantly increased and eligibility rules were relaxed. The Food Stamp program was initiated in 1965 and became a major new welfare benefit. Medicaid was initiated in the same year and by the late 1970s became the costliest welfare program. Federal aid to the aged, blind, and disabled was merged into a new Supplemental Security Income (SSI) program. The number of recipients of this program quadrupled.

Did poverty increase in spite of, or because of, these new social welfare programs? Poverty increased in the 1970s despite a reasonably healthy economy. Discrimination did not become significantly *worse* during this period; on the contrary, the civil rights laws enacted in the 1960s were opening up many new opportunities for African Americans. Finally, poverty was reduced among the aged due to generous increases in Social Security benefits. The greatest increases in poverty

BOX 11-2

Cross-National Perspective: Tax Burdens

TABLE 11-1   Tax Burdens of Various Nations

Country	% of gross domestic product
Sweden	56.7
Denmark	52.0
Norway	48.3
Netherlands	48.0
Belgium	46.1
France	44.8
Austria	42.3
New Zealand	38.6
Germany	37.6
Britain	37.5
Greece	37.4
Italy	36.2
Finland	35.9
Canada	34.5
Switzerland	32.0
Portugal	31.4
Australia	31.3
Japan	30.2
United States	30.0
Turkey	24.1

Source: U.S. Bureau of the Census, *Statistical Abstract of the United States 1990* (Washington, D.C.: U.S. Government Printing Office, 1990), p. 845.

Americans sometimes complain bitterly about their taxes. Yet many nations impose heavier tax burdens on their citizens than the United States. Table 11-1 compares tax burdens as a percentage of gross domestic product—GNP minus the value of goods produced outside the country. The percentages include national, state, and local taxes and social security contributions. By this measure, the U.S. government extracts less in taxes from its citizens than the governments of most other democratic nations. At the top of the list stands Sweden, well known as a "social welfare" state, which consumes over 50 percent of its gross domestic product in taxes.

occurred in families headed by *working-age persons*. In short, it is difficult to find alternative explanations for the rise in poverty. We are obliged to consider the possibility that *policy* changes—new welfare programs, expanded benefits, and relaxed eligibility requirements—contributed to increased poverty.

According to Charles Murray, the persons hurt most by current welfare policies are the poor themselves. In his well-titled yet controversial book, *Losing Ground,* he argues that current social welfare policy provides many disincentives to family life.[6] Nearly everyone agrees that the breakup of the family is closely associated with poverty. Murray argues that generous welfare programs encourage poor young women to start families before they have sufficient job skills to support them, and poor young men are allowed to escape their family responsibilities. Surveys show that the poor prefer work over welfare, but welfare payments may subtly affect the behavior of the poor. Persons unwilling to take minimum-wage jobs may never acquire the work habits required to move into better-paying jobs later in life. Welfare may even help create a dependent and defeatist subculture, lowering personal self-esteem and contributing further to joblessness, illegitimacy, and broken families.

Murray's policy prescription is a drastic one. He recommended:

> . . . scrapping the entire federal welfare and income-support structure for working-age persons. It would leave the working-age person with no recourse whatever except the job market, family members, friends, and public or private locally funded services . . . cut the knot, for there is no way to untie it.[7]

The result, he argued, would be less poverty, less illegitimacy, more upward mobility, freedom, and hope for the poor. "The lives of large numbers of poor people would be radically changed for the better." The obstacle to this solution is not only the army of politicians and bureaucrats who want to keep their dependent clients but, more important, the vast majority of generous and well-meaning middle-class Americans who support welfare programs because they do not understand how badly these programs injure the poor.

Government Policy as a Remedy for Poverty

Public welfare has been a recognized responsibility of government in English-speaking countries for many centuries. As far back as the Poor Relief Act of 1601, the English Parliament provided workhouses for the "able-bodied poor" (the unemployed) and poorhouses for widows and orphans, the aged, and the handicapped. Today nearly one-third of the U.S. population receives some form of government benefit: Social Security, Medicare or Medicaid, disability insurance, unemployment compensation, government employee retirement, veterans' benefits, food stamps, school lunches, job training, public housing, and cash public assistance payments (see Table 11-2). The total cost of these social welfare programs is now approximately 18 percent of the gross national product.[8] Thus, the "welfare state" now encompasses a very large part of our society. Yet tax burdens in the United States remain well below other industrialized nations with more extensive welfare services (see Box 11-2).

TABLE 11-2   Major Government Social Insurance and
Public Assistance Programs

Social insurance programs	Beneficiaries (millions)
Retirement	
OASDHI[a]	26.8
Public employee	5.9
Railroad	3.4
Disability	
OASDHI[a]	4.0
Public employees	0.7
Veterans	2.9
Survivors	
OASDHI[a]	7.2
Public employees	1.0
Veterans	1.0
Unemployment	2.0
Public assistance programs	
Cash aid	
AFDC	11.0
SSI	4.5
Needy veterans	1.3
General assistance	0.9
Income tax credit	18.8
Medicare care	
Medicaid	23.3
Veterans	0.4
Native Americans	1.0
Community health centers	5.5
Food benefits	
Food stamps	20.6
School lunches	11.6
Women, infants, children	3.4
Elderly nutrition	3.5
Housing benefits	
Total	3.7
Education aid	
Pell Grants	2.7
Student loans	3.3
Head Start	0.4
Work–study	0.8
Education opportunity grants	0.7
Job training	
Total	1.8
Energy assistance	
Total	6.3

[a]Old-Age, Survivors, Disability, and Health Insurance

Source: U.S. Bureau of the Census, *Statistical Abstract of the United States 1990* (Washington, D.C.: U.S. Government Printing Office, 1990), pp. 353, 354, 365, and 367.

In the Social Security Act of 1935 the federal government undertook to establish a basic framework for social welfare policies at the federal, state, and local levels in America. The *social insurance* concept was designed to *prevent* poverty resulting from individual misfortune—unemployment, old age, death of the family bread-winner, or physical disability. Social insurance was based on the same notion as private insurance: the sharing of risks, the setting aside of money for a rainy day, and legal entitlement to benefits on reaching retirement or on occurrence of specific misfortunes. Social insurance was *not* to be charity or public assistance. Instead, it relied on people's (compulsory) financial contribution to their own protection.

social insurance
compulsory savings for all with legal entitlement to benefits

The key feature of the Social Security Act is the Old-Age, Survivors, Disability, and Health Insurance (OASDHI) program; this is a compulsory social insurance program financed by regular deductions from earnings, which gives individuals the legal right to benefit in the event that their income is reduced by old age, death of the head of the household, or permanent disability. It is not public charity but a way of compelling people to provide insurance against loss of income. Another feature of the Social Security Act was that it induced states to enact unemployment compensation programs. Unemployment compensation is also an *insurance* pro-gram, only in this case the costs are borne solely by the employer. In 1965 Congress amended Social Security to add comprehensive medical care for persons over sixty-five Medicare. Medicare provided for prepaid hospital insurance for the aged under Social Security and for low-cost voluntary medical insurance for the same group under federal administration. Medicare, too, is based upon the insurance prin-ciple: individuals pay for their medical insurance during their working years and enjoy its benefits after age sixty-five. Thus, the program resembles private medical hospital insurance, except that it is compulsory.

major social insur-ance programs
Social Security
unemployment com-pensation
Medicare

The distinction between the *social insurance* program and a *public assistance* (welfare) program is an important one that has on occasion become a major political issue. If the beneficiaries of a government program are required to have made con-tributions to it before claiming any of its benefits, and if they are entitled to the benefits regardless of their personal wealth, the program is said to be financed on the *social insurance* principle. If the program is financed out of general tax reve-nues, and if the recipients are required to show that they are poor before claiming its benefits, the program is said to be financed on the *public assistance* principle.

social insurance ver-sus public assistance
social insurance
contributions required
all are entitled to bene-fits

In addition to these insurance programs, the federal government also undertakes to provide public assistance payments to needy persons to alleviate the conditions of poverty. The strategy of public assistance is clearly *alleviative*. There is no effort to prevent poverty or to attack its causes; the idea is simply to provide a minimal level of subsistence to certain categories of needy persons. The federal government, under its Supplemental Security Income (SSI) program, directly aids three cate-gories of recipients: the aged, the blind, and the disabled. The federal government, under its Aid to Families with Dependent Children (AFDC) program, gives money to the states to assist them in providing welfare payments to families with children under eighteen. Welfare aid to persons who do not fall into any of these categories but who, for one reason or another, are poor is referred to as *general assistance* and is paid for entirely from state funds. SSI, AFDC, and general assistance all provide cash benefits.

public assistance
financed out of tax rev-enues
benefits paid only to persons who are poor

major public assis-tance cash programs
SSI
AFDC
general assistance

The federal government also provides many *in-kind (noncash) welfare benefits.*[9] The Food Stamp program was begun in 1965; originally the poor were allowed to

CASE STUDY

Senior Power

Senior citizens are the most politically powerful age group in the population. They constitute 28 percent of the voting-age population, but more important, because of their high voter turnout rates, they constitute over one-third of the voters on election day. Persons over sixty-five average a 68-percent turnout rate in presidential elections and a 61-percent rate in congressional elections. This compares, for example, with a turnout rate of 36 percent in presidential elections and 19 percent in congressional elections for persons eighteen to twenty-one years old. In short, the voting power of senior citizens is twice that of young people. No elected officials can afford to offend the seniors, and seniors strongly support generous Social Security benefits.

The Aged Today

There are about 31 million people aged sixty-five or over in the United States; this is 12.6 percent of the population. The aged are mostly women: 18 million women and only 13 million men. At age sixty-five, women have an added life expectancy of 18.4 years, and men have 14.0 remaining years.

The Aged in the Future

The "baby boom" from 1945 to 1960 produced a large generation of people who crowded schools and colleges in the 1960s and 1970s and encountered stiff competition for jobs in the 1970s and 1980s. During the baby boom, women averaged 3.5 births during their lifetime. Today the birth rate is only 1.8 births per woman; this is less than the 2.1 figure required to keep the population from declining. The baby-boom generation will be retiring beginning in 2010, and by 2030 they will constitute more than 20 percent of the population (see Figure 11-2). Changes in lifestyle—less smoking, more exercise, better weight control—may increase the aged population even more. So, too, may medical advances extend life expectancy.

Social Security and Medicare

Social Security was begun as a "trust fund" with the expectation that a reserve would be built up from "social insurance premiums" (taxes) from working persons. The reserve would earn interest, and the interest and principal would be used in later years to pay benefits. Benefits for individuals would be in proportion to their contributions. But it did not work that way at all. The social insurance system is now financed as a pay-as-you-go, rather than a reserve, system. Political pressure to raise benefit levels while keeping payments low reduced the reserve to a very minor role in Social Security finance. Today's generation of workers is paying for the benefits of the last generation, and it is hoped that this generation's benefits will be financed by the next generation of workers.

(continued)

(continued)

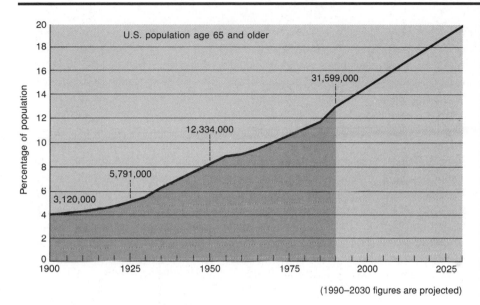

(1990–2030 figures are projected)

FIGURE 11-2   The graying of America
Source: U.S. Bureau of the Census, *Statistical Abstract of the United States 1988* (Washington, D.C.: U.S. Government Printing Office, 1988), p. 15.

Because current workers must pay for the benefits of current retirees and other beneficiaries, the "dependency ratio" becomes an important component of evaluating the future of Social Security.

The Social Security tax (the FICA deduction from paychecks) has risen from 1 percent of employee earnings and a maximum of $30 per year when the program began to 7.65 percent and a maximum of approximately $3,500 per year today. Employers must match these contributions, so the true tax on a worker's earnings is 15.30 percent or a maximum of $7,000 per worker per year. Low- and middle-income workers now pay more in Social Security taxes than in federal income taxes.

The Social Security system is now considered financially stable. However, the Medicare program is less financially secure, due to the unpredictability of rising medical costs. But in spite of assertions that the Social Security program is on stronger footing, many young people doubt that Social Security will provide them an adequate living in their old age. Some argue that Social Security was never intended to support people fully during their retirement years; it was intended to

(continued)

CASE STUDY

(continued)

help, not to fully subsidize elderly citizens. Up until now, however, almost everyone who has retired has received Social Security benefits that have greatly exceeded what he or she contributed in Social Security taxes over the years. This helps to explain the political popularity of the Social Security program among its millions of beneficiaries.

But what about today's workers? They are not likely to get back as much as they will pay into the system during their working years. For example, if you are now twenty-seven, your contributions and those of your employer, from now until your retirement at age sixty-five, will likely total over $225,000! But if these same monies were set aside in a private fund in your own name, such as an individual retirement account (IRA), and allowed to accumulate tax-free at even a low interest rate of 7.5 percent, you would wind up with a nest egg at age sixty-five of over $1 million. Needless to say, Social Security benefits will never amount to $1 million for an individual. So today's young workers are indeed paying a price far in excess of anything they might hope to regain. In addition to paying Social Security taxes, many young workers feel they must also invest in other retirement plans for fear that Social Security benefits will hardly be adequate in the twenty-first century.

Today there are fewer poor among the aged than among younger age groups, thanks largely to generous Social Security payments. And the aged have accumulated more wealth over the years than the average young family. Serious questions are now being raised about "intergenerational equity"—whether the burden currently placed on young workers to support senior citizens is fair. But as long as senior citizens remain politically powerful and unified in support of government benefits, Social Security will remain unchanged.

major public assistance in-kind programs
food stamps
school lunches
Medicaid
public housing

purchase food stamps at large discounts and use the stamps to buy food at stores; after 1977 the stamps were distributed free. Free school lunches (and in some cities breakfasts as well) are made available to children of the poor by federal payments to school districts. In 1965 Congress also authorized federal funds to enable states to guarantee medical services to all public assistance recipients. This program is known as Medicaid. Unlike Medicare, Medicaid is a welfare program designed for needy persons; no prior contributions are required, but recipients of Medicaid must be eligible for welfare assistance. In other words, they must be poor. Finally, the federal government assists in providing job training and low-cost public housing for the poor and educational programs for needy students. (See Box 11-3 for public opinion about poverty.)

Homelessness

For a pitiful few in America, sickness, hardship, and abandonment have risen dramatically in recent years. These few are the nation's homeless "street people," suf-

Social welfare is slowed by bureaucracy for this queue of unemployed.
Source: Nancy D'Antonio/Photo Researchers

fering exposure, alcoholism, drug abuse, and chronic mental illness while wandering the streets of the nation's larger cities.

The issue of homelessness has become so politicized that an accurate assessment of the problem and a rational strategy for dealing with it have become virtually impossible.[10] The term *homeless* is used to describe many different situations. There are the street people who sleep in subways, bus stations, parks, or the streets. Some of them are temporarily traveling in search of work; some have left home for a few days or are youthful runaways; others have roamed the streets for months or years. There are the sheltered homeless who obtain housing in shelters operated by local governments or private charities. As the number of shelters has grown in recent years, the number of sheltered homeless has also grown. But most of the sheltered homeless come from other housing, not the streets. These are people who have been recently evicted from rental units or have previously lived with family or friends. These sheltered homeless often include families with children; the street homeless are virtually all single persons.

The ranks of the street homeless expand and contract with the seasons.[11] These homeless are difficult subjects for systematic interviewing; many do not wish to admit to alcoholism, drug dependence, or mental illness. The television networks sensationalize the topic, exaggerate the number of homeless, and incorrectly portray the homeless as middle-class white families victimized by economic misfortune and the high cost of housing.

Serious studies indicate that close to half of the street homeless are chronic alcohol and drug abusers, and an additional one-fourth to one-third are mentally ill.[12] The alcohol and drug abusers, especially "crack" cocaine users, are the fastest-growing groups among the homeless. Moreover, the alcohol and drug abusers and

homeless
person living in streets and public places

persons accepting housing in public shelters

mentally ill among the homeless are likely to remain on the streets for long periods of time. Among the 15 to 25 percent of the homeless who are neither mentally ill nor dependent on alcohol or drugs, homelessness is more likely to be temporary.

deinstitutionalization
release of mental patients who pose no threat to others

Deinstitutionalization was a reform advanced by mental health care professionals and social welfare activists in the 1960s and 1970s to release chronic mental patients from state-run mental hospitals. It was widely recognized that aside from

---

BOX 11-3

Public Opinion about Poverty

Americans believe in individual responsibility. They believe that people should take care of themselves rather than rely on the government to take care of them. Yet Americans are a generous people and support government spending for the poor. Indeed, they support more federal spending for the poor rather than less, and they do *not* believe that welfare payments are overly generous.

Question: Which statement comes closer to your position: "The government is responsible for the well-being of all its citizens and it has an obligation to take care of them," or "People are responsible for their own well-being and they have an obligation to take care of themselves"?

Government responsible	26%
People responsible	74

Question: Generally speaking, do you think the federal government should spend a great deal more money on poverty programs, somewhat more, somewhat less, or do you think the federal government should spend a great deal less money on poverty programs?

Should spend more	59%
Should spend less	29
Not sure	12

Question: Do you think we're coddling the poor—that poor people live well on welfare—or do you think poor people can hardly get by on what the government gives them?

Live well	25%
Can hardly get by	75

On the other hand, Americans are concerned that welfare programs make poor people dependent and encourage them to stay poor. They also worry that welfare programs often contribute to the breakup of poor families.

Question: Do you think welfare benefits give poor people a chance to stand on their own two feet and get started again, or do you think they make poor people dependent and encourage them to stay poor?

Make poor people dependent	59%
Give poor people a chance to stand on their own	19
Neither	11
Not sure	11

Question: Some people think welfare encourages husbands to avoid their family responsibilities because it's easier for wives to get aid for their children if the father has left. How often do you think that happens in poor families: almost always, often, seldom, or do you think welfare almost never encourages husbands to avoid their family responsibilities?

Almost always	10%
Often	54
Seldom	29
Almost never	7

Most Americans believe that antipoverty programs seldom or never succeed. They doubt that giving direct money payments to the poor, providing social services, or creating government jobs is the best approach to ending poverty. Instead, they strongly favor education and training for jobs in the private sector.

Question: Would you say that antipoverty programs have almost always worked, have often worked, have seldom worked, or would you say that antipoverty programs have almost never worked?

Almost never worked	18%
Seldom worked	47

(continued)

BOX 11-3

(continued)

Often worked	28
Almost always worked	8

Question: There are only a certain number of things that can be done about the poverty problem. But which is best? We can make poor people less poor by giving them money. Or we can care for poor people by providing services like food, clothing, health care, and so forth. Or we can create government jobs and give them to poor people. Or we can educate people and train them so they can get jobs for themselves in the private sector. Or we can do nothing and wait for a strong economy to lift poor people out of poverty. In your opinion, which one of those is the best thing to do about the poverty problem?

Give money	1%
Provide services	5
Create government jobs	20
Give education and training for private-sector jobs	72
Wait for strong economy	2

Source: Public Opinion (June/July 1985), pp. 24–25. Reprinted by permission of the American Enterprise Institute for Public Policy Research.

drugs, no psychiatric therapies have much success among the long-term mentally ill. Drug therapies can be administered on an outpatient basis; they usually do not require hospitalization. So it was argued that no one could be rightfully kept in a mental institution against his or her will; people who had committed no crimes and who posed no danger to others should be released. The nation's mental hospitals were emptied of all but the most dangerous mental patients. The population of mental hospitals declined from over 500,000 in 1960 to about 100,000 in 1984.[13]

Vagrancy (homelessness) and public intoxication are no longer crimes. Involuntary confinement has been abolished for the mentally ill and for the substance abuser unless such a person is adjudged in court to be "a danger to himself or others." This means a person must commit a serious act of violence before the courts will intervene. For many homeless this means the freedom to "die with their rights on." The homeless are victimized by cold, exposure, hunger, the availability of alcohol and illegal drugs, and violent street crimes perpetrated against them, in addition to the ravages of illness itself.

decriminalization
abolishing confinement for vagrancy or public intoxication of persons who pose no danger to others

Social welfare programs are frequently irrelevant to the plight of the chronic mentally ill persons and alcohol and drug abusers in the streets. Most are "uncooperative"; they are isolated from society; they have no family members, doctors, or counselors to turn to for help. The nation's vast social welfare system provides them little help. They lose their social security, welfare, and disability checks because they have no permanent address. They cannot handle forms, appointments, or interviews; the welfare bureaucracy is intimidating. Welfare workers seldom provide the "aggressive care management" and mental health care these people need.

Notes

1. Kenneth B. Clark, *Dark Ghetto: Dilemmas of Social Power* (New York: Harper & Row, 1965).
2. Ibid. p. 67.
3. U.S. Bureau of the Census, *Statistical Abstract of the United States 1988* (Washington, D.C.: U.S. Government Printing Office, 1988), p. 437.

4. Edward C. Banfield, *The Unheavenly City* (Boston: Little, Brown, 1968), ch. 6.
5. Jack L. Roach and Orville R. Gursslin, "An Evaluation of the Concept Culture of Poverty," *Social Forces* 45 (March 1967): 384–392.
6. Charles Murray, *Losing Ground* (New York: Basic Books, 1984).
7. Ibid., pp. 227–228.
8. U.S. Bureau of the Census, *Statistical Abstract 1988,* p. 554.
9. For a description of all federal welfare programs, see A. Levitan, *Programs in Aid of the Poor in the 1980s* (Baltimore: Johns Hopkins University Press, 1980).
10. Robert C. Ellickson, "The Homelessness Muddle," *The Public Interest* (Spring 1990): 45–60.
11. No one knows the total number of homeless, but the systematic estimate is 250,000 to 350,000.
12. As reported in a survey of twenty-seven cities conducted by the U.S. Conference of Mayors. See *U.S. News and World Report,* January 15, 1990, pp. 27–29.
13. *Newsweek,* January 6, 1985, p. 16.

About This Chapter

Captain John Smith's ultimatum to his starving band of settlers in Jamestown in 1609 that "he who would not work must not eat" is probably the first recorded American welfare policy statement. It reflects an attitude that prevailed for many years. It was not until the western frontier had finally closed and the Great Depression of the 1930s had reduced many of the prosperous to the ranks of the paupers that there was any discernible change in the American attitude toward poverty. When poverty exists in the midst of plenty, it is more difficult for the poor to bear.

In this chapter we have explored various definitions of poverty, as well as some recent efforts to lift the poor from their position of powerlessness. Now that you have read it, you should be able to

- discuss various definitions of poverty and describe the characteristics of the poor,
- discuss the theory of a subculture of poverty,
- describe the relationship between poverty and powerlessness,
- describe the changing age composition of the American population and how this will affect Social Security in the future,
- discuss how government policies might contribute to poverty,
- identify major social insurance and public assistance programs and distinguish between the two types of programs.

Discussion Questions

1. Discuss the criteria used by the U.S. Social Security Administration to define the poverty line. Describe the emphasis of this official definition of poverty on subsistence levels. What are the criticisms of this definition of poverty?

2. Identify the groups of people who experience poverty in greater proportions than the national average.

3. Discuss the relationship between poverty and feelings of powerlessness. What are the feelings of the poor about themselves? What are their attitudes toward the larger society? Describe some of the forms of personal adjustment to poverty and the effect of poverty and discrimination on family life.

4. What is meant by the expression *culture of poverty*? Comment on Edward C. Banfield's view of the culture of poverty as "present-orientedness." What are the policy implications of a culture of poverty? Discuss the arguments of those who oppose the idea of a culture of poverty.

5. Identify the two basic strategies that are embodied in the Social Security Act of 1935. Differentiate between social insurance programs and public assistance programs in terms of who pays, who benefits, and when they benefit. Give examples of each type of program and specify the type of strategy each expresses.

6. Discuss the criticisms of current public assistance (welfare) programs.

7. What changes are occurring in the age composition of the nation's population? What do these changes mean for Social Security? How can the Social Security program be preserved?

Power,
Crime, and
Violence

12

Power and Individual Freedom

For thousands of years people have wrestled with the question of balancing social power against individual freedom. How far can individual freedom be extended without undermining the stability of a society, threatening the safety of others, and risking anarchy? The early English political philosopher Thomas Hobbes (1588–1679) believed that society must establish a powerful "Leviathan"—the state—in order to curb the savage instincts of human beings. A powerful authority in society was needed to prevent people from attacking each other for personal gain—"war of every man against every man" in which "notions of right and wrong, justice and injustice, have no place." According to Hobbes, without law and order there is no real freedom. The fear of death and destruction permeates every act of life: "Every man is enemy to every man"; "Force and fraud are the two cardinal virtues"; and "The life of man [is] solitary, poor, nasty, brutish, and short." Freedom, then, is *not* the absence of law and order. On the contrary, law and order are required if there is to be any freedom in society at all.[1]

Thomas Hobbes
freedom is not the absence of law; law is required to protect individual freedom. Governments are formed for collective self-protection

To avoid the brutal life of a lawless society, where the weak are at the mercy of the strong, people form governments and endow them with powers to secure peace and self-preservation. Hobbes believed that "the social contract"—the agreement of human beings to establish governments and grant them the powers to maintain peace and security—is a collective act of self-preservation. People voluntarily relinquish some of their individual freedom to establish a powerful government that is capable of protecting them from their neighbors as well as from foreign aggressors. This government must be strong enough to maintain its own existence or it cannot defend the rights of its citizens. But what happens when a government becomes too strong and infringes on the liberties of its citizens? People agree to abide by law and accept restrictions on their personal freedom for the sake of peace and self-preservation; but how much liberty must be surrendered to secure an orderly society? This is the *classic dilemma of free government:* people must create laws and governments to protect freedom, but the laws and governments themselves restrict freedom.

dilemma of free government
a government strong enough to protect its citizens may threaten their liberty

The Problem of Crime

Crime rates are the subject of a great deal of popular discussion. Very often they are employed to express the degree of social disorganization or even the effectiveness of law enforcement agencies. Crime rates are based on the Federal Bureau of Investigation's *Uniform Crime Reports,* but the FBI reports themselves are based on figures supplied by state and local police agencies. The FBI has established a *uniform classification* of the number of serious crimes per 100,000 people that are known to the police—murder and nonnegligent manslaughter, forcible rape, robbery, aggravated assault, burglary, larceny, and theft, including auto theft (see Table 12-1).

crime rates
reported serious crimes per 100,000 people

FBI classification
criminal homicide
forcible rape
robbery
assault
burglary
larceny
auto theft

We should be cautious in interpreting official crime rates. They are really a function of several factors: the diligence of police in detecting crime, the adequacy of the system for reporting and tabulating crime, and the amount of crime itself.

TABLE 12-1   Crime Rate—Number of Offenses Known to Police per 100,000 Persons

Year	Total	Criminal homicide	Forcible rape	Robbery	Assault	Burglary	Larceny	Auto theft
1960	1,126	5.0	10	60	85	502	283	182
1965	1,516	5.0	12	71	110	653	410	255
1970	3,985	7.9	19	172	165	1,025	2,079	457
1972	3,961	9.0	22	180	187	1,141	1,994	426
1976	5,266	8.8	26	196	229	1,439	2,921	446
1980	5,931	10.2	37	248	292	1,697	3,164	500
1983	5,159	8.3	34	214	273	1,334	2,866	429
1986	5,480	8.6	37	225	346	1,345	3,010	508
1989	5,741	8.7	38	233	383	1,276	3,171	630

Source: U.S. Bureau of the Census, *Statistical Abstract of the United States 1990* (Washington, D.C.: U.S. Government Printing Office, 1991), p. 176.

The official FBI crime rate rose dramatically in the United States in the twenty years prior to 1980. Increases occurred in both violent crime—murder, rape, robbery, and assault (see Figure 12-1)—and nonviolent crime—burglary, larceny, and theft. Certainly some of the increase was a result of improved reporting. As more people insure their property, they file more police reports in order to make insurance claims. The introduction of computers and sophisticated police data collection sys-

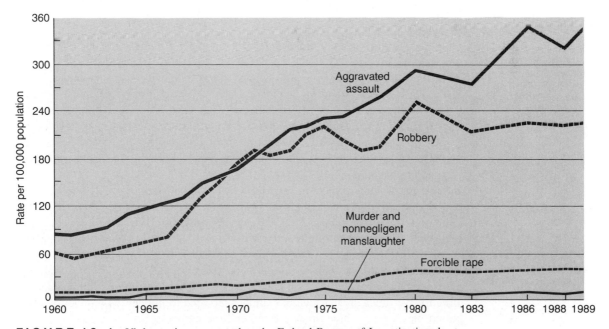

FIGURE 12-1   Violent crimes reported to the Federal Bureau of Investigation, by type.
Source: U.S. Bureau of the Census, *Social Indicators III* (Washington, D.C.: U.S. Government Printing Office, 1980); *Statistical Abstract of the United States 1991,* p. 176.

Police officers search a suspect.
Source: N. R. Rowan/Stock, Boston

tems may also have contributed to the increases. But unquestionably crime itself was also on the rise.

In the early 1980s crime rates declined slightly. Many commentators attributed this success to the changing age structure of the population: The most "crime-prone" age group, persons fifteen to twenty-four years old, was no longer increasing as a percentage of the population. Recently, however, crime rates have begun to surge again. This newest crime wave is frequently attributed to the expanding use of cocaine; drug users turn to crime to support their habit, and drug trafficking is a violent business.

How much crime is there in America today? We know that the FBI official crime rate understates the real amount of crime. Many crimes are not reported to the police and therefore cannot be counted in the official crime rate. In an effort to learn the real amount of crime in the nation, the U.S. Justice Department regularly surveys a national sample of people, asking whether they have been a victim of a crime during the past year.[2] These surveys reveal that the "victimization rate" is many times greater than the official crime rate. The number of forcible rapes is three to five times greater than the number reported to police, the number of unreported burglaries is three times greater, and the number of robberies is over twice that of the reported rate. Only auto theft and murder statistics are reasonably accurate, indicating that most people call the police when their car is stolen or someone is murdered. (For cross-national comparisons of murder rates see Box 12-1.)

victimization rates
national survey responses to the question of whether one has been the victim of a crime in the past year

Why do people fail to report crime to the police? The most common reason interviewees give is the feeling that police cannot be effective in dealing with the crime (see Box 12-2). Other reasons included the feeling that the crime was "a private matter" or that the victim did not want to harm the offender. Fear of reprisal was mentioned much less frequently, usually in cases of assaults and family crimes.

If law enforcement is to be a deterrent to crime, punishment must be (1) fairly certain, (2) swift enough to establish a link between the crime and its consequences, and (3) severe enough to outweigh the benefits of the crime. These criteria for an effective deterrent policy are ranked in the order of their probable importance. It is most important that punishment for crime is certain in the minds of potential criminals. The severity of the punishment is probably less important than its certainty or swiftness.

deterring crime in theory
punishment must be certain, swift, and severe enough to outweigh benefits

BOX 12-1

Cross-National Perspective: Murder and Homicide

The United States is one of the more violent societies in the world. Crimes of violence—murder, homicide, rape, robbery, and assault—appear to be more common in the United States than in other advanced nations. Indeed, in acts of violence per capita, the United States resembles many troubled, less-developed nations.

Reliable crime statistics that permit comparisons across nations are generally unavailable. Nations not only differ in reporting crime, but also in their definitions of crime itself. However, the United Nations World Health Organization reports homicides per million population—cases of death per million inhabitants that have been caused during a year by homicides or injuries deliberately inflicted by other persons. This statistic suggests the extent of violence in a society and may be used as an indicator of crime in general.

Whereas most advanced nations experience only 10 to 15 homicides per million persons in a year, the United States experiences over 100 homicides per million persons (see Table 12-2). The homicide rate in the United States more closely resembles rates in troubled nations of South America (Colombia and Venezuela for example) than rates in European nations. Only nations in the turmoil of civil war, El Salvador for example, suffer substantially more homicides than the United States.

TABLE 12-2   Cross-National Perspectives: Homicide Rates, 1970–1980

| Country | Homicides per 1 million population | | Country | Homicides per 1 million population | |
	1970	1980		1970	1980
United States	82.2	105.3	Germany, Federal Republic	13.9	11.5
Australia	15.3	19.1	Hungary	19.5	25.8
Austria	15.1	12.1	Israel	11.8	10.7
Belgium	11.0	16.1	Japan	13.3	9.5
Bulgaria	22.3	25.1	Netherlands	5.0	7.9
Canada	20.3	20.6	Norway	6.2	11.2
Colombia	144.5	183.0	Spain	6.3	10.6
Denmark	6.7	13.1	Sweden	8.3	11.7
El Salvador	312.5	329.8	United Kingdom	7.5	13.3
France	7.4	10.1	Venezuela	75.1	117.4

Source: United Nations, World Health Organization, as reported in George Mueller, *Comparative World Data: A Statistical Handbook for Social Science* (Baltimore: Johns Hopkins University Press, 1988).

failure of deterrence
the likelihood of punishment for crime is small

But the current system of criminal justice is certainly no *serious deterrent to crime*. The best available estimates of the ratio between crime and punishment suggest that the likelihood of an individual's being jailed for a serious crime is less than one in a hundred (see Figure 12-2). Many crimes are not even reported by the victim. Police are successful in clearing fewer than one in five reported crimes by arresting the offender. The judicial system convicts fewer than half of the persons arrested and charged; others are not prosecuted, are handled as juveniles, are found not guilty, or are permitted to plead guilty to a lesser charge and released. Only about one-fourth of convicted felons are given prison sentences.

The Constitutional Rights of Defendants

Guarantee of the Writ of Habeas Corpus

habeas corpus
police may not hold a defendant without showing cause before a judge

An ancient right in English common law is the right to obtain a *writ of habeas corpus*, a court order directing a public official who is holding a person in custody to bring the prisoner into court to explain the reasons for the confinement. If a judge finds that the prisoner is being unlawfully detained, or that there is not sufficient evidence that a crime has been committed or that the prisoner committed it, the judge orders the prisoner's immediate release.

BOX 12-2

What Police Do

At least three important functions in society are performed by police: enforcing the law, keeping the peace, and furnishing services. Actually, law enforcement may take up only a small portion of a police officer's daily activity.[a] The service function is far more common—attending accidents, directing traffic, escorting crowds, assisting stranded motorists, and so on. The function of peacekeeping is also very common—breaking up fights, quieting noisy parties, handling domestic or neighborhood quarrels, and the like. It is in this function that the police exercise the greatest discretion in the application of the law. In most of these incidents, it is difficult to determine blame. Participants are reluctant to file charges, and police must use personal discretion in handling each case.

Police are on the front line of society's efforts to resolve conflict. Indeed, instead of a legal or law enforcement role, the police are more likely to adopt a peacekeeping role. Police are generally lenient in their arrest practices; that is, they use their arrest practice less often than the law allows.[b] Rather than arresting people, the police prefer first to reestablish order. Of course, the decision to be more or less lenient in enforcing the law gives the police a great deal of discretion—the police exercise decision-making powers on the streets.

What factors influence police decision making? Probably the first factor to influence police behavior is the attitude of the other people involved in police encounters. If a person adopts an acquiescent role, displays deference and respect for the police, and conforms to police expectations, he or she is much less likely to be arrested than a person who shows disrespect or uses abusive language toward police.[c] This is not just an arbitrary response of police. They learn through training and experience the importance of establishing their authority on the streets.

[a]James Q. Wilson, *Varieties of Police Behavior* (Cambridge, Mass.: Harvard University Press, 1968), p. 18.

[b]See Donald J. Black, "Social Organization of Arrest," in *The Criminal Justice Process,* ed. William B. Sanders and Howard C. Davidstel (New York: Holt, Rinehart & Winston, 1976).

[c]Stuart A. Sheingold, "Cultural Cleavage and Criminal Justice," *Journal of Politics* 40 (November 1978): 865–897.

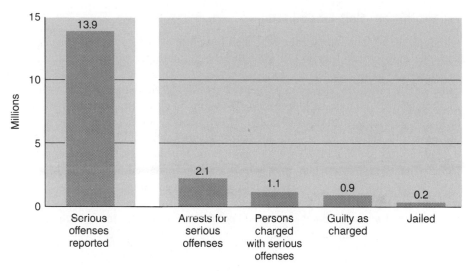

FIGURE 12-2 Law enforcement in relation to reported crime. (Actual crime is estimated to be two-and-a-half times the reported offenses.)
Source: U.S. Bureau of the Census, *Statistical Abstract of the United States 1990* (Washington, D.C.: U.S. Government Printing Office, 1990).

Prohibition of Bills of Attainder and of Ex Post Facto Laws

Protection against bills of attainder and against ex post facto laws was, like the guarantee of habeas corpus, considered so fundamental to individual liberty that it was included in the original text of the Constitution. A *bill of attainder* is a legislative act that inflicts punishment without judicial trial. An *ex post facto law* is a retroactive criminal law that works to the detriment of the accused—for example, a law that makes an act a criminal one *after* the act is committed, or a law that increases the punishment for a crime and applies it *retroactively*.

bill of attainder
a legislative act that inflicts punishment without a trial

ex post facto law
making an act criminal after it is committed or retroactively increasing punishment

Prohibition of "Unreasonable" Searches and Seizures

The Fourth Amendment provides: "The right of the people to be secure in their persons, houses, papers, and effects, against unreasonable searches and seizures, shall not be violated, and no warrants shall issue, but upon probable cause, supported by oath or affirmation, and particularly describing the place to be searched, and the persons or things to be seized." The requirement that the things to be seized must be described in the warrant is meant to prevent "fishing expeditions" into an individual's home and personal effects on the possibility that some evidence of unknown illegal activity might crop up. An exception to the requirement for a warrant is made if the search is "incident to a lawful arrest." A "lawful arrest" can be made by the police if they have "probable cause" to believe a person has committed a felony or if a misdemeanor is committed in their presence; a search of the person and the person's property is permitted without a warrant at the time of such an arrest.

unreasonable search
search without lawful warrant by judge, unless "incident to a lawful arrest"

Freedom from Self-Incrimination

freedom from self-incrimination
no physical or psychological force can be used to obtain confession or incriminating evidence from a defendant

Although the Fifth Amendment establishes a number of procedural guarantees, perhaps the most widely quoted clause of that amendment guarantees that no person "shall be compelled in any criminal case to be a witness against himself." The sentence "I refuse to answer that question on the ground that it might tend to incriminate me" is, today, a household expression. Freedom from self-incrimination has its origins in English resistance against torture and confession. It now embodies the ideas that individuals should not be forced to contribute to their own prosecution and that the burden of proof of guilt is on the state. The constitutional protection against self-incrimination applies not only to accused persons in their own trials but also to witnesses testifying in any public proceedings, including criminal trials of other persons, civil suits, congressional hearings, or other investigations. The silence of an accused person cannot be interpreted as guilt; the burden of proving guilt rests with the prosecution.

Guarantee of a Fair Jury Trial

fair jury trial
speedy
public
impartial

Trial by jury is guaranteed in both the original text of the Constitution and the Sixth Amendment: "In all criminal prosecutions, the accused shall enjoy the right to a speedy and public trial, by an impartial jury . . . and to be informed of the nature and cause of the accusation; to be confronted with the witnesses against him; to have compulsory process for obtaining witnesses in his favor. . . ." The requirement of a *speedy* trial protects the accused from long pretrial waits; but the accused may ask for postponements in order to prepare a defense. A *public* trial prevents secret proceedings, and *impartial* means that each juror must be able to judge the case objectively. Discrimination in the selection of the jury is forbidden. The guarantee of a fair trial can be violated if sensational pretrial publicity or an unruly courtroom hinders the jury from making an unbiased verdict. By old canon law a jury consisted of twelve persons, and the vote of the jurors had to be unanimous. This is still the requirement in most cases, but recently the Supreme Court indicated that unanimity might not be required in some cases.

unanimous jury not required in all cases

burden of proof on prosecution
"beyond reasonable doubt"

The burden of proof rests with the prosecution. It is up to the prosecution to convince a jury "beyond reasonable doubt" that the accused is guilty. Witnesses must appear in person against the accused. The accused or the counsel for the accused has the right to cross-examine those witnesses and may present witnesses on behalf of his or her own case. The accused may even obtain a "summons" to compel people to testify at the trial. If a guilty verdict is rendered, the defendant may appeal any errors in the trial to a higher court.

Protection against Double Jeopardy

no double jeopardy
if found not guilty, a person cannot be tried again for the same crime

The Fifth Amendment states: "Nor shall any person be subject for the same offense to be twice put in jeopardy of life or limb. . . ." Once a person has been tried for a particular crime and the trial has ended in a decision of not guilty, that person cannot be tried again for the same crime. However, this right does not prevent a new trial if the jury cannot agree on a verdict (a "hung jury"), or if the verdict is reversed by an appeal to a higher court because of a procedural error. Moreover, an individual may be tried by different jurisdictions on slightly different charges stemming from the same act.

Protection against Excessive Bail

Arrested persons are considered innocent until tried and found guilty. They are entitled to go free prior to trial unless their freedom would unreasonably endanger society or unless there is reason to believe they would not appear for trial. Bail is supposed to ensure that the accused will appear. Bail may be denied for major crimes, but most accused persons are entitled to be released on bail pending their trial. The Eighth Amendment states that bail must not be "excessive," although there are no fixed standards for determining what "excessive" is.

bail
money held by court to ensure that defendant will appear for trial

The Right to Counsel

The Sixth Amendment states: "In all criminal prosecutions, the accused shall enjoy . . . the assistance of counsel for his defense." In a series of cases in the 1960s, the Supreme Court, under the leadership of Chief Justice Earl Warren, greatly strengthened the Sixth Amendment's guarantee of the right to counsel:

- *Gideon* v. *Wainwright* (1963)—Ruling that equal protection under the Fourteenth Amendment requires that free legal counsel be appointed for all indigent defendants in all criminal cases.
- *Escobedo* v. *Illinois* (1964)—Ruling that a suspect is entitled to confer with counsel as soon as police investigation focuses on him or her, or once "the process shifts from investigatory to accusatory."
- *Miranda* v. *Arizona* (1966)—Ruling that police, before questioning a suspect, must inform the suspect of all his or her constitutional rights, including the right to counsel, appointed free if necessary, and the right to remain silent (see Figure 12-3). Although the suspect may knowingly waive these rights, the police cannot question anyone who at any point asks for a lawyer or indicates "in any manner" that he or she does not wish to be questioned. If the police commit an error in these procedures, the accused goes free, regardless of the evidence of guilt.

right to counsel
the right to an attorney in all criminal cases

right to free counsel for indigent defendants

counsel provided at beginning of investigation

defendants must be informed of rights upon arrest

The Exclusionary Rule

The exclusionary rule prevents illegally obtained evidence from being used in a criminal case. The rule, unique to the courts in the United States, was adopted by the U.S. Supreme Court in *Mapp* v. *Ohio* in 1961. Although illegally seized evidence may prove the guilt of the accused, it cannot be used in court, and the accused may go free because the police committed a procedural error. The Fourth Amendment's prohibition against "unreasonable searches and seizures" has been interpreted to mean that police cannot conduct a search on private property without a court warrant. To obtain a warrant from a judge, police must show "probable cause" for their search and describe "the place to be searched and the persons or things to be seized." Errors on warrants are not infrequent; the addresses may be

DEFENDANT | LOCATION

SPECIFIC WARNING REGARDING INTERROGATIONS

1. YOU HAVE THE RIGHT TO REMAIN SILENT.
2. ANYTHING YOU SAY CAN AND WILL BE USED AGAINST YOU IN A COURT OF LAW.
3. YOU HAVE THE RIGHT TO TALK TO A LAWYER AND HAVE HIM PRESENT WITH YOU WHILE YOU ARE BEING QUESTIONED.
4. IF YOU CANNOT AFFORD TO HIRE A LAWYER ONE WILL BE APPOINTED TO REPRESENT YOU BEFORE ANY QUESTIONING, IF YOU WISH ONE.

SIGNATURE OF DEFENDANT DATE

WITNESS TIME

☐ REFUSED SIGNATURE SAN FRANCISCO POLICE DEPARTMENT PR.9.1.4

FIGURE 12-3 The "Miranda card" used by San Francisco police to inform suspects of their rights at the time of arrest

wrong or the names of the persons incorrect, or the articles misspecified. Any error results in exclusion of the evidence. There can be no blanket authorizations in a warrant to find evidence of *any* crime. Police cannot arrest persons without a warrant unless police have "probable cause" to believe that a crime has been committed. Immediately after making a warrantless arrest, police must take the accused before a magistrate to decide whether a probable cause existed to justify the arrest.

Most trial proceedings today are not concerned with the guilt or innocence of the accused, but instead center on possible procedural errors by police or prosecutors. If the defendant's attorney can show that an error was committed, the defendant goes free, regardless of his or her guilt or innocence. Supreme Court Justice Felix Frankfurter wrote many years ago: "The history of liberty has largely been the history of procedural safeguards." These safeguards protect us all from the abuse of police powers. But Chief Justice Warren Burger attacked the exclusionary rule for "the high price it extracts from society—the release of countless guilty criminals." Why should criminals go free because of police misconduct? Why not punish the police directly, perhaps with disciplinary measures imposed by courts that discover procedural errors, instead of letting guilty persons go free? Releasing criminals because of police misconduct punishes society, not the police.

Plea Bargaining

Most convictions are obtained by guilty pleas. Indeed, about 90 percent of the criminal cases brought to trial are disposed of by guilty pleas before a judge, not trial by jury. The Constitution guarantees trial by jury (Sixth Amendment) and protects against self-incrimination (Fifth Amendment). All defendants have the right to a trial by jury to determine guilt or innocence. But guilty pleas outnumber jury trials by ten to one.[3]

"Plea bargaining," in which the prosecution reduces the seriousness of the charges, drops some but not all charges, or agrees to recommend lighter penalties, in exchange for a guilty plea by the defendant, is very common. Some critics of plea bargaining view it as another form of leniency in the criminal justice system that reduces its deterrent effects. Other critics view plea bargaining as a violation of the Constitution's protection against self-incrimination and guarantee of a fair jury trial. Prosecutors, they say, threaten defendants with serious charges and stiff penalties in order to force a guilty plea. Still other critics see plea bargaining as an "under-the-table" process that undermines respect for the criminal justice system.

Although the decision to plead guilty or go to jury trial rests with the defendant, the decision is strongly influenced by the policies of the prosecutor's office. A defendant may plead guilty and accept the certainty of conviction with whatever reduced charges the prosecutor offers, or accept the prosecutor's pledge to recommend a lighter penalty, or both. Or the defendant may go to trial, confronting serious charges with stiffer penalties with the hope of being found innocent. However, the possibility of an innocent verdict in a jury trial is only one in six. This apparently strong record of conviction comes about because prosecutors have already dismissed charges in cases where the evidence is weak or illegally obtained. Thus, most defendants confronting strong cases against them decide to "cop a plea."

It is very fortunate for the nation's court system that most defendants plead guilty. The court system would quickly break down from overload if any substantial proportion of defendants insisted on jury trials.

Crime and the Courts

Former Chief Justice Warren E. Burger has argued persuasively that rising crime in the United States is due partly to inadequacies in our system of criminal justice. "The present system of criminal justice does not deter criminal conduct," he said in a special State of the Federal Judiciary message. "Whatever deterrent effect may have existed in the past has now virtually vanished."[4] He urged widespread reforms in law enforcement, courts, prisons, probation, and parole.

A major stumbling block to effective law enforcement is the current plight of U.S. judicial machinery:

Congestion on court dockets that delays the hearing of cases for months or even years. Moreover, actual trials are now twice as long on the average as they were ten years ago.

Increased litigation in the courts. Not only are more Americans aware of their rights, but more of them are also using every avenue of appeal. Seldom do appeals concern the guilt or the innocence of the defendant; usually they focus on procedural matters.

Excessive delays in trials. "Defendants, whether guilty or innocent, are human; they love freedom and hate punishment. With a lawyer provided to secure release without the need for a conventional bail bond, most defendants, except in capital cases, are released pending trial. We should not be surprised that a defendant on

inadequacies of the criminal justice system

congestion in court system

increased litigation, including appeals on procedural grounds

excessive delays: trials and appeals

variations in sentences

plea bargaining

bail exerts a heavy pressure on his court-appointed lawyer to postpone the trial as long as possible in order to remain free. These postponements—and sometimes there are a dozen or more—consume the time of judges and court staffs as well as of lawyers. Cases are calendared and reset time after time while witnesses and jurors spend endless hours just waiting."[5]

Excessive delays in appeals. "We should not be surprised at delay when more and more defendants demand their undoubted constitutional right to trial by jury because we have provided them with lawyers and other needs at public expense; nor should we be surprised that most convicted persons seek a new trial when the appeal costs them nothing and when failure to take the appeal will cost them freedom. Being human, a defendant plays out the line which society has cast him. Lawyers are competitive creatures and the adversary system encourages contention and often rewards delay; no lawyer wants to be called upon to defend the client's charges of incompetence for having failed to exploit all the procedural techniques which we have deliberately made available."[6]

Excessive variation in sentencing. Some judges let defendants off on probation for crimes that would draw five- or ten-year sentences by other judges. Whereas flexibility in sentencing is essential in dealing justly with individuals, perceived inconsistencies damage the image of the courts in the public mind.

Excessive plea bargaining between the prosecution and the defendant's attorney, in which the defendant agrees to plead guilty to a lesser offense if the prosecutor will drop more serious charges.

Crime and Drugs

variation in laws regarding substances
alcohol, tobacco, marijuana, cocaine, heroin

Laws in the United States treat various drugs quite differently, even though all of these drugs have harmful effects. Alcohol and cigarettes are legal products, although the Office of the Surgeon General of the United States has undertaken educational campaigns to reduce their use, and Congress has banned the advertising of liquor and tobacco on radio and television. Marijuana has been "decriminalized" in several states, making its use or possession a misdemeanor comparable to a traffic offense; a majority of states, however, have retained criminal sanctions against marijuana, and its manufacture and distribution are prohibited everywhere. The potential for drug abuse is found in many prescription medicines such as amphetamines, barbiturates, and tranquilizers. These may not be sold anywhere in the United States without a medical prescription. The use and possession of cocaine is a criminal offense everywhere in the United States, yet this drug is very popular. Heroin is a physically addictive drug; its use in the United States declined somewhat with the widespread introduction of cocaine.

It is difficult to estimate the various forms of drug use. According to the U.S. National Institute on Drug Abuse, there are 12 to 14 million "problem drinkers," or about 6 percent of the population. There are an estimated 60 million cigarette smokers, or about 30 percent of the adult population (significantly less than the 45 percent of the population who smoked cigarettes in the 1940s and 1950s). An estimated 16 million, or about 7 percent of the population, are current users of marijuana, although many more have smoked it at least once. Cocaine use is reportedly on the decline. In 1985 current use was estimated to be as high as 12 million persons, or about 5 percent of the population; in 1990 it was estimated to be under 5 million, or about 2 percent of the population. There are an estimated half million users of heroin in the country.[7]

Marijuana

The medical evidence on the health effects of marijuana is mixed; conflicting reports have been issued about whether or not it is more dangerous than alcohol.[8] The manufacture and sale of marijuana is illegal in all U.S. jurisdictions. "Decriminalizing" marijuana does not make its production or sale legal, but it makes its possession (generally of an ounce or less) a civil offense, much like a traffic offense. In 1973 Oregon became the first state to decriminalize marijuana possession and use. Most Americans oppose legalization of marijuana, but a majority believe that "the possession of small amounts" should not be "treated as a criminal offense."[9]

Heroin

Since the Harrison Narcotic Act of 1916, heroin use has been considered a major law enforcement problem. Over the years, in the United States the extent of heroin addiction has varied with the success or failure of law enforcement efforts. During the 1930s and 1940s, with strong law enforcement (almost one-third of all federal prisoners in 1928 were violators of the Harrison Act), heroin use declined. It rose again in the 1960s and early 1970s, when over one million persons were estimated to be current users. But with the widespread introduction of cocaine into the drug world in the 1980s, heroin use reportedly declined, to about half a million people.

Cocaine

Cocaine is made from coca leaves and imported into the United States. Cocaine is not regarded as physically addictive, although the psychological urge to continue use of the drug is strong.

In the 1980s the widespread distribution of a relatively inexpensive yet potent form of "crack" cocaine expanded the market from middle- and upper-class users to the streets of most large cities. Crack cocaine can be either smoked or injected. The health problems associated with its continuous use are fairly serious, as reported by the National Institute on Drug Abuse. Death, although rare, can occur from a single ingestion. An estimated 25 percent of all AIDS victims acquired the disease through intravenous drug abuse. The power of the coca leaf has been known for hundreds of years: Coca-Cola originally contained cocaine, although the drug was removed from the popular drink in 1903.

Drug Use in Decline?

It is difficult to estimate drug use, to measure whether it is rising or falling over time, or to assess the effectiveness of antidrug efforts. The U.S. National Institute

Cocaine use spread from upper-middle-class recreational use to wider street use with the introduction of smokable "crack."
Source: Joel Gordon

on Drug Abuse (NIDA) annually surveys households in the United States, asking respondents whether they have used drugs in the past month, the past year, or ever in their lifetime. Past-month, or "current," use is the most widely cited NIDA statistic. Based on this survey evidence, overall drug use has declined significantly in recent years (see Figure 12-4). The NIDA also sponsors a national high school survey that indicates student drug use has declined dramatically in recent years. But survey responses may reflect popular attitudes toward drug use rather than actual abuse. As a result of educational campaigns on television and in the schools, public approval of drug use has declined, and social disapproval may cause some respondents to understate their drug use in interviews. However, NIDA bolsters its argument that drug use is declining by citing modest declines in patients admitted to hospitals for drug-related emergencies.

Trafficking

Crime associated with drug trafficking is a serious national problem, whatever the health effects of various drugs. The world of drug trafficking is fraught with violence. Sellers rob and murder buyers and vice versa; neither can seek the protection of police or courts in their dealings with the other. Although some citizens might want simply to allow dealers to wipe each other out, the frequency with which innocent bystanders are killed must be considered.

It is very difficult to estimate the total size of the drug market, but $20 to $25 billion per year is a common figure.[10] This would suggest that the drug business

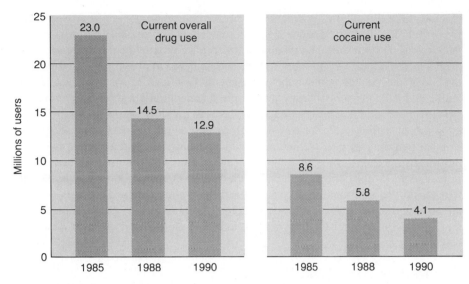

FIGURE 12-4   Declines in reported drug use

Source: National Institute on Drug Abuse, *National Drug Control Strategy* (Washington, D.C.: U.S. Government Printing Office, February 1991).

is comparable in size to one of the ten largest U.S. industrial corporations. More important, perhaps, drugs produce huge profit margins: a kilo of cocaine sold in Colombia may cost only $3,600; when sold in the United States, that kilo may retail for $80,000 to $120,000.[11] The price of smuggling a single, easily concealable kilo may run to $15,000. These huge profits allow drug traffickers to corrupt police and government officials as well as private citizens in the United States and other nations.

Public Policy

Federal antidrug efforts can be divided into three categories: interdiction, enforcement, and education. *Interdiction:* Efforts to seal U.S. borders against the importation of drugs have been frustrated by the sheer volume of smuggling. Each year increasingly larger drug shipments are intercepted by the U.S. Drug Enforcement Administration, the U.S. Customs Service, the Coast Guard, and state and local agencies. Yet each year the volume of drugs entering the country seems to increase. Drug "busts" are considered just another cost of business to the traffickers. It is not likely that the use of U.S. military forces to augment other federal agencies can succeed in sealing our borders. American pressure against Latin American governments to destroy coca crops and assist in interdiction has already resulted in strained relationships. Our neighboring countries wonder why the U.S. government directs its efforts at the suppliers, when the demand for drugs arises within the United States itself. *Enforcement:* The FBI and state and local law enforcement agencies already devote great effort to combating drugs; an estimated 40 percent of all arrests in the United States are drug-related. Federal and state prisons now hold a larger percentage of the nation's population than ever before. Sentences have lengthened for drug trafficking, and prisons are overcrowded as a direct result of drug-related convictions. Drug testing in government and private employment is increasing, but unless it is random it is not very useful, and some courts have prevented random testing of individuals without their consent. *Education:* Efforts at educating the public about the dangers of drugs have inspired many public and private campaigns, from former First Lady Nancy Reagan's "Just say no" to Jesse Jackson's "Up with hope, down with dope." But it is difficult to evaluate the effects of these efforts.

Although opinion polls show that Americans consistently rank drugs as one of the most important problems confronting the nation, no effective public policies appear likely to be adopted. As a nation the United States is both wealthy and free, two conditions that make it a perfect market for illicit drugs. The costs of truly effective enforcement, both in terms of dollar expenditures and, more important, in terms of lost individual liberty, may be more than our society wishes to pay.

Violence in American History

violence as a source of power and change

Violence is not uncommon in American society. The nation itself was founded in armed revolution, and violence has been a *source of power* and a *stimulus to social change* ever since. Violence has been associated with most of the important movements in American history: the birth of the nation (revolutionary violence), the freeing of the slaves and the preservation of the union (Civil War violence), the westward expansion of the nation (Indian wars), the establishment of law and order in frontier society (vigilante violence), the organization of the labor movement (labor–management violence), the civil rights movement (racial violence), and attempts to deal with the problems of cities (urban violence). History reveals that the patriot, the humanitarian, the pioneer, the lawman, the laborer, the African American, and the urban dweller have all used violence as a source of power. Despite pious pronouncements against it, Americans have frequently employed violence even in their most idealistic endeavors.

major instances of violence in American history
guerrilla warfare in the Revolution

Shays's Rebellion

violence of the Civil War era

the Indian wars

vigilante violence

labor–management violence

racial violence

political violence—assassinations

Perhaps the most famous act of organized mob violence occurred in 1773 when a group of "agitators" in Boston, Massachusetts, illegally destroyed 342 chests of tea. The early Revolutionary War fighting in 1774 and 1775, including the battles of Lexington and Concord, was really a series of small guerrilla skirmishes designed more to intimidate Tories than to achieve national independence. The old American custom of tarring and feathering was a product of the early patriotic campaign to root out Tories. Aside from the regular clash of Continental and British armies, a great deal of violence and guerrilla strife occurred during the Revolution. Savage guerrilla forays along the eastern coast resulted in the killing of thousands of Tory families and the destruction of their property. The success of this violence enshrined it in our traditions.

After the Revolutionary War many armed farmers and debtors resorted to violence to assert their economic interests. If taxes owed to the British government and debts owed to British merchants could be denied, why not the taxes owed to state governments and the debts owed to American merchants? In several states debtors had already engaged in open rebellion against tax collectors and sheriffs.

The most serious rebellion broke out in the summer of 1786 in Massachusetts, when a band of insurgents, composed of farmers and laborers, captured courthouses in several western districts of that state and momentarily held the city of Springfield. Led by Daniel Shays, a veteran of Bunker Hill, the insurgent army posed a direct threat to the governing elite of the new nation. Shays's Rebellion, as it was called, was put down by a small mercenary army paid for by well-to-do citizens who feared that a wholesale attack on property rights was imminent. The growing domestic violence in the states contributed to the momentum leading to the Constitutional Convention of 1787, where propertied men established a new central government with the power to "ensure domestic tranquility," guarantee "the republican form of government," and protect "against domestic violence." Thus, the Constitution itself reflects a concern of the nation's founders about domestic violence.

The Civil War was the bloodiest war the United States ever fought. Total casualties of the northern and southern armies equaled American casualties in World War II; but when the Civil War occurred, the nation was only one-third as large as it was during the latter conflict. There were few families that did not suffer the loss of a loved one during the Civil War. In addition to military casualties, the toll in lives and property among civilians was enormous. A great deal of domestic violence also occurred both before and after the war. Beginning in 1856, proslavery and antislavery forces fought in "bleeding Kansas." In 1859 John Brown led a raid at Harpers Ferry, meant to start the freeing of the slaves in Virginia. Brown's capture, trial for treason, and execution made him a hero to many abolitionists, though Southerners believed that he had tried to incite slave uprisings. The guerrilla war that took place in the West during the Civil War has seldom been equaled for savagery; the fearsome Kansas Jayhawkers traded brutalities with Confederate guerrillas headed by William Quantrell. Later, western bandits, including Frank and Jesse James and the Younger brothers, who had fought as Confederate guerrillas, continued their forays against banks and railroads and enjoyed considerable popular prestige and support. Moreover, after the war, racial strife and Ku Klux Klan activity became routine in the old Confederate states. The Ku Klux Klan was first used to intimidate the Republicans of the Reconstruction era by violence and threats, and later to force blacks to accept the renewed rule of whites.

Unquestionably the longest and most brutal violence in American history was that between whites and Native Americans. It began in 1607 and continued with only temporary truces for nearly three hundred years, until the final battle at Wounded Knee, South Dakota, in 1890. The norms of Indian warfare were generally more barbaric than those in other types of warfare, if such a thing is possible. Women and children on both sides were deliberately and purposefully killed. Torture was accepted as a customary part of making war. Scalping was a frequent practice on both sides.

Vigilante violence (taking the law into one's own hands) arose as a response to a typically American problem: the absence of effective law and order in the frontier region. Practically every state and territory west of the Appalachians had at one time or another a well-organized vigilante movement. The first vigilante movement appeared in 1767–1769 in South Carolina, where the vigilantes were known as *regulators*—a term later used by San Francisco vigilantes in the 1850s. Vigilantes were frequently backed by prominent men; many later became senators, representatives, governors, judges, businessmen, and even clergy. Like Indian-fighters, vigilantes became great popular heroes. Antitheft and antirustling associations flourished in the West until World War I. Vigilantes often undertook to establish law and order and to regulate the morals of the citizens, punishing drunks, vagrants, ne'er-do-wells, and occasional strangers.

Violence was also a constant companion of the early labor movement in the United States. Both management and strikers resorted to violence in the struggles accompanying the Industrial Revolution. In 1887, in the bitter railroad strike in Pittsburgh, Pennsylvania, an estimated sixteen soldiers and fifty strikers were killed, and locomotives, freight cars, and other property were destroyed. The famous Homestead strike of 1892 turned Homestead, Pennsylvania, into an open battlefield. The Pullman strike of 1893 in Chicago resulted in twelve deaths and the destruction of a great deal of railroad property. In 1914, Ludlow, Colorado, was the scene of the famous Ludlow Massacre, in which company guards burned a miner tent city and killed nearly a hundred persons, including women and children. The Molly Maguires were a secret organization of Irish miners who fought their employers with assassination and mayhem. The last great spasm of violence in the history of American labor came in the 1930s with the strikes and plant takeovers ("sit-down strikes") that accompanied the successful drive to unionize the automobile, steel, and other mass-production industries.

The long history of racial violence in the United States continues to plague the nation. Slavery itself was accompanied by untold violence. It is estimated that one-third to one-half of those captured in African slave raids never survived the ordeal of forced marches to the sea, with thirst, brutalities, and near starvation the rule; the terrible two-month voyage in filthy holds packed with squirming and suffocating humanity; and the brutal "seasoning" whereby African blacks were turned into slaves. Nat Turner's slave insurrection in 1831 resulted in the deaths of fifty-seven white persons and the execution of Turner and his followers. Following the end of slavery the white-supremacy movement employed violence to reestablish the position of whites in the southern social system. Racial violence directed against blacks—whippings, torture, and lynching—was fairly common from the 1870s to the 1930s. During World War II serious racial violence erupted in Detroit. Black and white mobs battled each other in June 1943, causing thirty-five deaths and hundreds of injuries, more than a thousand arrests, and finally the dispatching of federal troops to restore order.

Political assassinations have not been uncommon. Four presidents (Lincoln, Garfield, McKinley, and Kennedy) have fallen to assassins' bullets, and others were the intended objects of assassination. Only Lincoln was the target of a proven assassination conspiracy; the other presidential victims were the prey of presumably freelance assassins in varying states of mental instability. In the 1930s Senator Huey P. Long of Louisiana was murdered, and a bullet narrowly missed President Franklin Delano Roosevelt and killed Mayor Anton Cermak of Chicago, who was standing near the president. The wave of political assassinations and assassination attempts in more recent years, which cut down John F. Kennedy, Robert F. Kennedy, and Martin Luther King, Jr.; crippled George C. Wallace; and threatened the life of Ronald Reagan, may represent a "contagion phenomenon," unstable indi-

viduals being motivated to violence by highly publicized and dramatic acts of violence. But an even grimmer possibility is that political assassination may become
a persistent feature of American society.

Social, Psychological, and Political Perspectives on Violence

Social psychologists have various explanations of violence. One explanation relies
heavily on learning theory (stimulus–response theory); we shall refer to this as the
frustration–aggression explanation. Another relies on Freudian notions of instinctual behavior in the "unlocking" of inhibitions; we shall call this the *aggressive-
instinct* explanation. Yet another explanation focuses on the violence that is trig-
gered when rising hopes and expectations outstrip the ability of the system to fulfill
them. We shall refer to this as the *relative-deprivation* explanation.

   The frustration–aggression explanation is perhaps the most popular explanation
of social violence—of political turmoil, racial conflict, urban disorders, even crime
and juvenile delinquency. Psychologist John Dollard and several colleagues set
forth the proposition that "aggression is always the result of frustration."[12] They
argued, "The occurrence of aggressive behavior always presupposes the existence
of frustration and, contrariwise, the existence of frustration always leads to some
form of aggression." Frustration occurs when there is a blocking of ongoing, goal-
directed activity, and it evokes a characteristic reaction—aggression—whereby the
individual seeks to reduce the emotional anxiety produced by this blocking. Aggression helps to lessen frustration brought on by the blocking of the original need, but
it fails to satisfy the original need. The aggressive behavior merely copes with the
emotional reaction to the blocking. The degree of frustration is affected by the
intensity of the original need and by the degree of expectation that the goal-directed
activity would be successful. Aggressive behavior is a function of this degree of
frustration, which in turn is determined by the strength of the original need, the
degree of interference with its satisfaction, and the number of times its satisfaction
has been blocked. Minor frustrations added together can produce a stronger aggressive response than would normally be expected from a frustrating situation that
appears immediately before aggression. Thus, frustration can build up over time.

   Acts of physical violence are the most obvious forms of aggression. But other
forms include fantasies of "getting even," forays against the frustrating persons
(stealing from them or cheating them, spreading malicious rumors about them, or
making verbal assaults), and generalized destructive outbursts. Dollard contended
that frustration and aggression can characterize group action as well as individual
action: "Remonstrative outbursts like lynchings, strikes, and certain reformist campaigns are clearly forms of aggression as well." Aggression is generally directed
at the person or object that is perceived as causing the frustration, but it may also
be *displaced* to some altogether innocent source, or even toward the self, as in
masochism, martyrdom, and suicide. The act of aggression is presumed to reduce
the emotional reaction to frustration. Aggression turned against the self may occur
when other forms of expression are strongly inhibited.

contrasting explanations of violence
frustration and aggression

aggressive instincts

relative deprivation

the frustration–aggression explanation
goal-directed activity is blocked, resulting in anxiety

aggression may reduce anxiety but fails to satisfy original need

displaced aggression is directed against something other than the cause of the frustration

suicide may be aggression turned against the self

explanations of violence related to political ideology

the aggressive-instinct explanation
instinct for aggression is genetically based

civilization has inhibited the expression of aggressive instincts

"safe" outlets for aggression may release instinctual drive

The frustration–aggression explanation of violence is frequently espoused by political liberals because it implies that violence is best avoided by eliminating barriers to the satisfaction of human needs and wants. In other words, liberals believe that violence can be reduced if human needs and wants are satisfied and aggression-producing frustration is reduced. In contrast, if it should turn out that aggressive behavior is innate, then no amount of satisfaction of needs or wants would eliminate it. Only strong inhibiting forces would be able to cope effectively with innate aggressive instincts. This is frequently the view of political conservatives.

The research on the innate aggressive tendencies of organisms—human beings as well as animals, fish, and birds—suggests that aggressive behavior may be deeply rooted in human genetic history. In his interesting book *On Aggression*, eminent zoologist Konrad Lorenz argued that aggressive behavior is rooted in the long human struggle for survival.[13] The human being is by nature an aggressive animal. The external stimulus that seems to produce aggressive behavior only "unlocks" inhibitory processes, thereby "releasing" instinctual aggressive drives. Aggressive behavior is not just a reaction to some external condition but an inner force or instinct that is let loose by the stimulus. "It is the spontaneity of the (aggressive) instinct that makes it so dangerous." Aggressive behavior "can explode without demonstrable external stimulation" merely because inner drives for aggression have not been discharged through some previous behavior. Lorenz believed that "present day civilized man suffers from insufficient discharge of his aggressive drive." Civilization has inhibited people from expressing themselves aggressively; for the greatest part of human history, people released their aggressive drives in hunting, killing, and the struggle for survival. Now, however, these drives must be checked. The instincts that helped people survive millions of years in a primitive environment today threaten their very existence. Lorenz believed that frustrations are, at best, an unimportant source of aggression. According to this formulation, an excellent way to prevent people from engaging in aggression is to provide them with "safe" ways of venting their aggressive urges. For example, competitive, body-contact sports provide "safe" outlets; even observing these activities, as in the case of televised professional football, affords some release of aggressive drives.

a contrary view
learning can contribute to aggression

A number of experimental psychologists disagree with Lorenz's proposed remedy for aggression. Laboratory experiments have indicated that attacks on supposedly safe targets do not lessen, and can even increase, the likelihood of later aggression. Angry people may perhaps feel better when they can attack a safe target, but their aggressive tendencies are not necessarily reduced thereby. For example, laboratory studies have demonstrated that giving children an opportunity to play aggressive games does not decrease the attacks they will later make on another child, but in fact actually increases the strength of subsequent attacks.[14] These studies do not rule out the notion of innate determinants of aggression; indeed, there is today among social psychologists much greater recognition of the role of inherent determinants of human behavior. However, it is clear that other factors, such as fear of punishment or learning to respond in nonaggressive ways to frustrations, can prevent the human potential for violence from being realized.

Another explanation of violence centers in the relative deprivation of individuals and groups. Relative deprivation is the discrepancy between people's expectations about the goods and conditions of life to which they feel justifiably entitled and

The Death
Penalty

One of the more heated debates in correctional policy today concerns capital punishment. Opponents of the death penalty argue that it is "cruel and unusual punishment," and is thus in violation of the Eighth Amendment of the Constitution. They contend that nations and states that have abolished the death penalty have not experienced higher homicide rates, and hence there is no concrete evidence that the death penalty discourages crime. They also argue that the death penalty is applied unequally. A large proportion of those executed have been poor, uneducated, and nonwhite.

In contrast, there is a strong sense of justice among many Americans that demands retribution for heinous crimes—a life for a life. A mere jail sentence for a multiple murderer or a rapist-murderer seems unjust compared with the damage inflicted on society and the victims. In most cases, a life sentence means less than ten years in prison, under the current parole and probation policies of many states. Convicted murderers have been set free, and some have killed again. Moreover, prison guards and other inmates are exposed to convicted murderers who have "a license to kill" because they are already serving life sentences and have nothing to lose by killing again.

For nearly 200 years there was general agreement that death was not "cruel" or "unusual" unless it was carried out in a particularly bizarre or painful fashion. Most executions were by hanging; the electric chair was introduced in the 1920s as a "humane" alternative, and the gas chamber followed in some states. (Today, Texas employs a "lethal injection.") Before 1972 the death penalty was officially approved by thirty states; only fifteen states had abolished capital punishment. Federal laws also retained the death penalty. However, no one had actually suffered the death penalty since 1967 because of numerous legal tangles and direct challenges to the constitutionality of capital punishment.

In *Furman* v. *Georgia* (1972) the Supreme Court ruled that capital punishment *as then imposed* violated the Eighth and Fourteenth Amendments in that it constituted cruel and unusual punishment and denied due process of law. The decision was made by a 5-to-4 vote of the justices, and the reasoning in the case is very complex. Only two justices—Brennan and Marshall—declared that capital punishment itself is cruel and unusual. The other three justices in the majority—Douglas, White, and Stewart—felt that death sentences had been applied unfairly; a few individuals were receiving the death penalty for crimes for which many others were receiving lighter sentences. These justices left open the possibility that capital punishment would be constitutional if it were specified for certain kinds of crime and applied uniformly.

After this decision, a majority of states rewrote their death penalty laws to try to ensure fairness and uniformity of application. Generally, these laws mandate the death penalty for murders committed during rape, robbery, hijacking, or kidnapping; murders of prison guards; murder with torture; and multiple murders. Two

(continued)

(continued)

The electric chair—a
"humane" alternative.
Source: AP/Wide World Photos

trials must be held, one to determine guilt or innocence and another to determine the penalty. At the second trial evidence of "aggravating" and "mitigating" factors is presented; if there are aggravating factors but no mitigating factors, the death penalty is mandatory.

In a series of cases in 1976 (*Gregg* v. *Georgia, Profitt* v. *Florida, Jurek* v. *Texas*), the Supreme Court finally held that "the punishment of death does not invariably violate the Constitution." The Court upheld the death penalty with the following rationale: the men who drafted the Bill of Rights accepted death as a common sanction of crime. It is true that the Eighth Amendment prohibition against cruel and unusual punishment must be interpreted in a dynamic fashion, reflecting changing moral values. But the decisions of more than half of the nation's state legislatures to reenact the death penalty since 1972, as well as the decisions of juries to impose the death penalty on more than 450 persons under these new laws, were evidence

(continued)

(continued)

that "a large proportion of American society continues to regard it as an appropriate and necessary criminal sanction." Moreover, said the Court, the social purposes of retribution and deterrence justify the use of the death penalty. This ultimate sanction is "an expression of society's moral outrage at particularly offensive conduct."

The Court reaffirmed that *Furman* v. *Georgia* (1972) only struck down the death penalty where it was inflicted in "an arbitrary and capricious manner." The Court upheld the death penalty in states where the trial was a two-part proceeding, the second part of which provided the judge or jury with relevant information and standards for deciding whether to impose the death penalty. The Court approved the consideration of "aggravating and mitigating circumstances." The Court also approved automatic review of all death sentences by state supreme courts to ensure that the sentences were not imposed under the influence of passion or prejudice, that aggravating factors were supported by the evidence, and that the sentences were not disproportionate to the crimes.

Today there are about two thousand prisoners nationwide on "death row," that is, persons convicted and sentenced to death. But only about ten executions are actually carried out each year. The strategy of death-row prisoners and their lawyers, of course, is to delay indefinitely the imposition of the death penalty with stays and appeals. So far the strategy has been successful for all but a few luckless murderers. As trial judges and juries continue to impose the death penalty and appellate courts continue to grant stays of execution, the number of prisoners on death row grows. The few who have been executed have averaged ten years of delay between trial and execution.

The death penalty as it is employed today—inflicted on so few after so many years following the crime—has little deterrent effect. Nonetheless, proponents say the death penalty serves several purposes. It gives prosecutors some leverage in plea bargaining with murder defendants. The defendants may choose to plead guilty in exchange for a life sentence when confronted with the possibility that the prosecutor may win a conviction and the death penalty in a jury trial. Most importantly, however, the death penalty is symbolic of the value society places on the lives of innocent victims. The death penalty dramatically signifies that society does not excuse or condone the taking of innocent lives. It symbolizes the potential for society's retribution against heinous crime. Public opinion favors the death penalty by three to one. Only for a few years during the mid-1960s did public opinion appear to oppose the death penalty. With increases in the crime rate in the 1970s, heavy majorities swung back in favor of the death penalty. Public support for capital punishment remains high today.

what they perceive to be their chances of getting and keeping them. Relative deprivation is not merely a complicated way of saying that people are deprived and therefore angry because they have less than they want. Rather, it focuses on (1) what people think they deserve, not just what they want in an ideal sense; and (2)

**the relative–
deprivation
explanation**

individual and group
expectations and
entitlements

perceived chances of
actually obtaining
benefits

focus on difference
between current status
and expectation

poverty itself does not
inspire violence, but
rather, differences
between conditions and
expectations

revolution of rising
expectations: violence
occurs when expecta-
tions rise faster than
conditions

what they think they have a chance of getting, not just what they have. According to this theory, it is *relative* deprivation that creates aggression.

Relative deprivation is an expression of the distance between current status and levels of expectation. According to this explanation, neither the wholly downtrodden (who have no aspirations) nor the very well-off (who can satisfy their aspirations) represent a threat to civil order; that threat arises from those whose expectations of what they deserve outdistance society's capacity to satisfy them. Often rapid increases in expectations are the product of symbolic or token improvements in conditions. This situation leads to the apparent paradox of the eruption of violence and disorder precisely when conditions are getting better. Hope, not despair, generates civil violence and disorder. As Bowen and Masotti observed, "The reason why black Americans riot is because there has been just enough improvement in their condition to generate hopes, expectations, or aspirations beyond the capacity of the system to meet them."[15]

The political counterpart of this explanation of violence is frequently referred to as *the revolution of rising expectations.* Poverty-stricken people who have never dreamed of owning automobiles, television sets, or new homes are not frustrated merely because they have been deprived of these things; they are frustrated only after they have begun to hope that they can obtain them. Once they have come to believe that they can get them and have anticipated having them, the inability to fulfill their anticipations is a frustrating experience. The dashing of hopes is more likely to breed violence than privation itself. Political scientist James C. Davies has employed this type of reasoning in developing a theory of revolutions.[16] Revolutions do not arise because people are subjected to long, severe hardships. Revolutions occur when there is a sudden, abrupt thwarting of hopes and expectations that had begun to develop during the course of gradually improving conditions. Thus, modernization in traditionally backward societies is associated with a great increase in political instability. Hope outstrips reality, and, even though conditions are improving in society as a whole, many people become frustrated.

Notes

1. Thomas Hobbes, *Leviathan*, ed. Michael Oakeshott (New York: Crowell-Collier, 1962).
2. U.S. Department of Justice, *Criminal Victimization in the United States* (Washington, D.C.: Bureau of Justice Statistics, published annually).
3. U.S. Department of Justice, Bureau of Labor Statistics, *The Prevalence of Guilty Pleas* (December 1984).
4. Chief Justice Warren E. Burger, address on the State of the Federal Judiciary to the American Bar Association, August 10, 1970.
5. Ibid.
6. Ibid.
7. National Institute on Drug Abuse, *National Survey on Drug Abuse 1986 and 1990* (Washington, D.C.: U.S. Government Printing Office).
8. For a summary of this evidence and references to the relevant health literature, see Richard C. Schroeder, *The Politics of Drugs,* 2nd ed. (Washington, D.C.: Congressional Quarterly, 1980).

9. *The Gallup Report* (July 1980), p. 15.
10. *Congressional Quarterly Weekly Report*, June 25, 1988.
11. Ethan A. Nadelman, "U.S. Drug Policy," *Foreign Policy* 70 (Spring 1988): 83–108.
12. John Dollard et al., *Frustration and Aggression* (New Haven, Conn.: Yale University Press, 1939), p. 1.
13. Konrad Lorenz, *On Aggression* (New York: Harcourt Brace Jovanovich, 1966).
14. For an excellent review of the implications of laboratory studies on frustration and aggression, see Leonard Buckewitz, "The Study of Urban Violence," in *Riots and Rebellion,* ed. Louis H. Masotti and Don R. Bowen (Newbury Park, Calif.: Sage, 1968).
15. Don R. Bowen and Louis H. Masotti, "Civil Violence: A Theoretical Overview," in *Riots and Rebellion*, pp. 24–25.
16. James C. Davies, "Toward a Theory of Revolution," *American Sociological Review* 27 (February 1962): 1–15.

About This Chapter

More than 2,000 years ago Aristotle wrote of the problem of crime that "the generality of men are naturally apt to be swayed by fear rather than by reverence, and to refrain from evil rather because of the punishment that it brings, than because of its own foulness." Power must be exercised by society for the very basic purposes of maintaining order and protecting the citizenry. A free democratic society must struggle with maintaining a balance between its exercise of police power and its safeguarding of individual freedom. In this chapter we have examined America's struggles with this problem. We have also examined the violence that has been a part of most of the important social movements in American history.

Now that you have read Chapter 12, you should be able to

- describe the current status of crime and punishment in the United States as evidenced by crime rates, the constitutional rights of defendants, and judicial decisions regarding defendants' rights and capital punishment;
- describe the current legal status of various potentially harmful substances: alcohol, tobacco, marijuana, cocaine, and heroin;
- describe the basic protections afforded to persons accused of crime;
- discuss the history of violence in the United States and some of the social–psychological explanations of violence;
- discuss violence as a form of political protest;
- discuss the constitutional issues arising from capital punishment.

Discussion Questions

1. Discuss the "classic dilemma" of a free government and Thomas Hobbes's ideas regarding the need for a powerful state.

2. Discuss crime rates. How are they used, how are they determined, and what factors contribute to their inaccuracy? What is their current trend?

3. Suppose you have just been arrested by the police. Describe how the following constitutional rights of defendants would be of use to you: guarantee of the writ of habeas corpus; prohibition of bills of attainder and of ex post facto laws; prohibition of "unreasonable" searches and seizures; freedom from self-incrimination; the right to counsel; guarantee of a fair jury trial; protection against double jeopardy; protection against excessive bail.

4. Choose two of the following cases that were decided by the Warren Court and discuss how each of them strengthened the rights of accused persons in criminal cases: *Mapp* v. *Ohio* (1961); *Gideon* v. *Wainwright* (1963); *Escobedo* v. *Illinois* (1964); *Miranda* v. *Arizona* (1966).

5. Discuss the judicial stumbling blocks to law enforcement that Chief Justice Warren E. Burger outlined in his State of the Federal Judiciary message. What are some of the difficulties that the *police* may encounter in their law enforcement function?

6. Describe the major drug threats confronting the United States today. What is the legal status of various potentially harmful substances: alcohol, tobacco, marijuana, cocaine, and heroin?

7. Discuss the history of violence in the United States. Using at least three specific eras or social movements as examples, describe the type of violence that was used and the kind of social change that was its goal.

8. Discuss two of the following social–psychological explanations of violence: the frustration–aggression explanation, the aggressive-instinct explanation, the relative-deprivation explanation.

9. Discuss the arguments for and against capital punishment. Describe the 1972 Supreme Court decision regarding the constitutionality of capital punishment and the changes in state laws that followed it. Discuss the reasoning of the justices in the 1976 Court decision on capital punishment.

Power and Community

13
CHAPTER

Where Do Americans Live?

Three out of four Americans live in population clusters called *metropolitan areas.* Most of the nation's population increase is occurring in the suburbs of these areas. Approximately 44 percent of all Americans live in these suburbs, 32 percent live in central cities, and 24 percent live outside metropolitan areas.

MSA
metropolitan statistical area, a city of 50,000 or more, plus surrounding urban population

CMSA
metropolitan complex of connecting MSAs

central-city versus suburban growth

What is a metropolitan area? Briefly, it consists of a central city of 50,000 or more persons and the surrounding suburbs, which are socially and economically tied to the city (see Figure 13-1). The U.S. Census Bureau refers to metropolitan areas as *Metropolitan Statistical Areas (MSAs)* or, in the case of large metropolitan complexes with connecting metropolitan areas, *Consolidated Metropolitan Statistical Areas (CMSAs).* The nation's largest metropolitan areas are listed in Table 13-1.

Very few large *central cities* are growing. Metropolitan areas are growing because their *suburbs* are growing. In the nineteenth century, industrial workers had to live within walking distance of their places of employment. Hence, the nineteenth-century American city crowded large masses of people into relatively small central areas, often in tenement houses and other high-density neighborhoods. But new modes of transportation—the streetcar, the private automobile, and, finally, the expressway—eliminated the necessity for workers to live close to their jobs. Now an individual can work in a central business district office or industrial plant and spend his or her evening in a residential suburb miles away. The same technology that led to the suburbanization of residences has also influenced commercial and industrial location. Originally industry was tied to waterways or railroads for access to supplies and markets. Its dependence has been reduced by the development of motor truck transportation, the highway system, and the greater mobility of the labor force. Now many industries can locate in the suburbs, particularly light industries, which do not require extremely heavy bulk shipment that can be handled only by rail or water. When industry and people move to the suburbs, commerce

TABLE 13-1 Metro-America: Metropolitan Areas with One Million or More Residents (in Millions)

New York	18.0	St. Louis	2.4	Norfolk (Va.)	1.4
Los Angeles	14.5	Seattle	2.6	Sacramento	1.5
Chicago	8.1	Minneapolis	2.5	New Orleans	1.3
San Francisco	6.3	Baltimore	2.4	Columbus (Ohio)	1.4
Philadelphia	5.9	Pittsburgh	2.2	San Antonio	1.3
Detroit	4.6	San Diego	2.5	Indianapolis	1.2
Boston	4.2	Tampa	2.0	Buffalo (N.Y.)	1.2
Dallas	3.9	Phoenix	2.1	Providence (R.I.)	1.1
Washington, D.C.	3.9	Cincinnati	1.7	Charlotte (N.C.)	1.2
Houston	3.7	Denver	1.8	Hartford (Conn.)	1.1
Miami	3.2	Milwaukee	1.6	Salt Lake City	1.1
Cleveland	2.8	Kansas City	1.6	Orlando	1.1
Atlanta	2.8	Portland (Ore.)	1.5	Rochester	1.0

Source: U.S. Bureau of the Census, figures for July 1, 1990.

follows. Giant suburban shopping centers have sprung up to compete with downtown stores. Thus, metropolitan areas are becoming decentralized as people, business, and industry spread over the suburban landscape.

The Sociology of Urban Life

What is the impact of urbanism on the way people interact? To deal with this question, sociologists first had to formulate a *sociological definition of urbanism*, one that would identify those characteristics most affecting social life. Sociologist Louis Wirth provided the classic definition of urbanism over fifty years ago: "For sociological purposes a city may be defined as a relatively large, dense, and permanent settlement of socially heterogeneous individuals."[1] Thus, according to Wirth, the distinguishing characteristics of urban life were *numbers, density,* and *heterogeneity*—large numbers of people, living closely together, who are different from one another.

Large numbers of people involve a great range of individual variation. The modern economic system of the metropolis is based on a highly specialized and complex division of labor. We are told that in early farm communities a dozen occupations exhausted the job opportunities available to people. In a simple agricultural society nearly everyone was a farmer or was closely connected to or dependent on farming. But in the modern metropolis there are tens of thousands of different kinds of jobs. An industrial economy means highly specialized jobs; hence the *heterogeneity* of urban populations. Different jobs result in different levels of income, dress, and styles of living. People's jobs shape the way they look at the world and their evaluations of social and political events. To acquire a job, one attains a certain level and type of education that also distinguishes one from those in other jobs with other educational requirements. Differences in educational level in turn produce a wide variety of differences in opinions, attitudes, and styles of living. Urban life concentrates people with all these different economic and occupational characteristics in a very few square miles.

Ethnic and racial diversities are also present. At the beginning of this century, opportunities for human betterment in the cities attracted immigrants from Ireland, Germany, Italy, Poland, and Russia; later the city attracted African Americans, Hispanics, and rural families. Newcomers bring with them different needs, attitudes, and ways of life. The "melting pot" tends to reduce some of the diversity over time, but the pot does not melt people immediately, and there always seem to be new arrivals.

Increasing the numbers of people in a community limits the possibility that each member of the community will know everyone else personally. Multiplying the number of persons with whom an individual comes into contact makes it impossible for that individual to know everyone very well. The result is a *segmentalization of human relationships,* in which an individual comes to know *many* people but only in highly *segmental, partial* roles. According to Wirth:

> The contacts of the city may indeed be face-to-face, but they are nevertheless impersonal, superficial, transitory, and segmental. The reserve, the indifference, and the

sociological theory of urbanism
urbanism distinguished by numbers, density, and heterogeneity

heterogeneity
diversity in occupation, income, education
ethnic and racial diversity

segmental relationships
knowing many people, but only in their partial roles

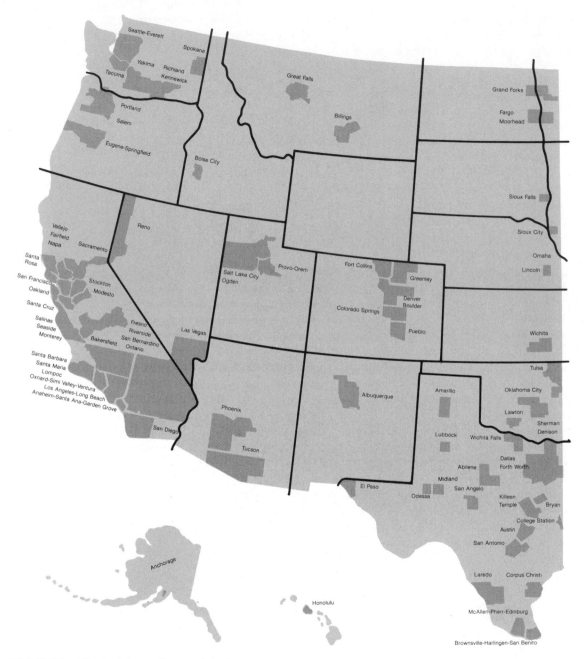

FIGURE 13-1 Metropolitan statistical areas
Sources: U.S. Bureau of the Census.

FIGURE 13-1   *(continued)*

Morning commuters on the San Francisco/Oakland Bay Bridge.
Source: Joe Munroe/Photo Researchers

blasé outlook that urbanites manifest in their relationships may thus be regarded as devices for immunizing themselves against the personal claims and expectations of others.[2]

Moreover, urban dwellers frequently interact with others by utilizing them as means to an end, thus giving a *utilitarian* quality to interpersonal relations.

Large numbers mean a certain degree of freedom for the individual from the control of family groups, neighbors, churches, and other community groups. But urbanism also contributes to a sense of *anomie*—a sense of social isolation and a loss of the personal recognition, self-worth, and feeling of participation that comes with living in a small integrated society. The social contacts of urban dwellers are

utilitarian relationships
interaction with others as a means to an end

anomie
a sense of social isolation and loss of personal recognition and self-worth

more anonymous than those of rural dwellers; they interact with persons who have little if any knowledge of their life histories.

Rural life emphasized *primary group ties*—interactions within the extended family. Many sociologists believe that urban life emphasizes *secondary group ties*—interactions among members of age and interest groups rather than among families and neighbors. Urban life is said to center around voluntary associations and secondary group memberships—crowds, recreational groups, civic clubs, business groups, and professional and work groups. Sociologists believe that urban dwellers have a greater number of interpersonal contacts than rural dwellers and that urban dwellers are more likely to interact with people as occupants of specific social roles. In contrast, rural dwellers are more likely to interact with individuals as full personalities.

primary groups
family and neighborhood groups known personally

secondary groups
interest or voluntary groups

Urban society also presents problems of social control. The anomie of urban life is believed to weaken social mores and social group controls. External controls through a series of formal institutions, such as laws, and organizations, such as the courts and the police, become more essential. Thus, *social control* in the cities depends in large degree on *formal mechanisms.* But laws generally express the minimum behavioral standard, and urban life involves a much wider range of behavior than rural life. Moreover, laws do not always succeed in establishing minimum standards of behavior; crime rates increase with increases in urbanism.

social control in urban society based more on formal institutions than on social groups

Another characteristic of urban life is *mobility,* or ease of movement. Urban mobility is both *physical* (from one geographic area to another) and *social* (from one position of social status to another). Rural communities are more stable than urban communities in both respects. Traditionally rural dwellers were more likely to stay near the place of their birth. In contrast, urbanites frequently move from city to city, or from one section of a city to another. Social mobility is also greater in the city, because of the wider range of economic opportunities there. Moreover, urban dwellers are judged far less by their family backgrounds (which are unknown) than by their own appearances, occupational accomplishments, incomes, and lifestyles. Although mobility creates opportunities for individuals, it weakens the sense of community. City dwellers do not think of their city as a community to which they belong but rather as a place they happen to live—a geographical entity commanding little personal allegiance (see Box 13-1).

social mobility
movement from one social status to another

physical mobility
movement from one location to another

both kinds of mobility greater in urban than in rural societies

Urban life presents a serious problem in *conflict* management. Because a metropolitan area consists of a large number of different kinds of people living closely together, the problem of regulating conflict and maintaining order assumes tremendous proportions. Persons with different occupations, incomes, and educational levels are known to have different views on public issues. The way that persons well equipped to compete for jobs and income in a free market view government housing and welfare programs may differ from the way that others not so well equipped view them. People at the bottom of the social ladder look at police—indeed, governmental authority in general—differently from the way those on higher rungs do. Persons who own their homes and those who do not own their homes regard taxation in a different light. Families with children and those without children have different ideas about school systems. And so it goes. Differences in the way people make their living, in their income and educational levels, in the

political conflict
heterogeneity of urban life presents greater potential for conflict among diverse peoples

color of their skin, in the way they worship, in their style of living—all are at the roots of political life in the metropolis.

summary   Thus, sociological theory provides us with a series of characteristics to look for in urban life:

BOX 13-1

The Social Psychology of Urban Life—Calling Aunt Sally

One of the more persistent views of life in big cities is that social relations are impersonal, indifferent, and unfriendly. It has been argued that because city dwellers come into close contact daily with thousands of strangers on the streets, in stores, at work, and at play, city dwellers unconsciously develop superficial, transitory, and impersonal modes of social interaction.[3] Since it is impossible to know personally all or even most of the people we come into contact with each day in the city, we learn to deal with fellow city dwellers with reserve, if not indifference. In contrast, in small towns and rural areas, we see other people less frequently, but we know most people we see on a personal basis. We can all think of personal stories of ill treatment in big cities, but is there really any systematic evidence to support the view that big-city dwellers are habitually indifferent to others? Unfortunately, there is.[4]

One interesting test of the urban indifference theme, conducted by social psychologists, is the "Aunt Sally call." Experimenters randomly call big-city and small-town dwellers and ask to speak to "Aunt Sally." When the respondent tells the experimenter that a wrong number has been reached, the experimenter says: "Oh, I'm sorry. But this is my last dime and I'm at the airport [in a city, or bus stop in a town]. Could you do me a favor and call my aunt for me and let her know my plane [or bus] has

come in early? She is supposed to pick me up here." If the respondent agrees, the experimenter gives a local phone number where another experimenter waits to see if the respondent actually calls. One test of this technique produced the results shown in Table 13-2.[5]

Scholars do not always agree on whether it is big-city life itself that creates impersonality or whether it is mobility, rapid change, and social disorganization. Some social psychologists link urban life to a wide variety of personal problems and social pathologies: mental illness, sexual deviance, crime and delinquency, suicide, high death rates, alcoholism and drug abuse, and violence in politics. Marshall Clinard traces social disorganization to urbanization: "Urbanism with mobility, impersonality, individualism, materialism, norm and role conflicts, and rapid social change appears to be associated with higher incidence of deviant behavior."[6] However, other scholars believe that there is no necessary relationship between urbanization and personal or social problems. It is true that rapid change and social disorganization are associated with social deviance, but these conditions can occur in rural as well as urban areas and in big cities as well as small towns. In other words, it is not city life itself that produces deviance, but rather mobility, social change, poverty, racism, unemployment, ignorance, and ill health.

TABLE 13-2   Calling Aunt Sally: "Could You Do Me a Favor and Call My Aunt for Me . . . ?"

Response	Big-city percentage	Small-town percentage
1. Subject hangs up	35	10
2. Subject hears request, refuses to help	15	20
3. Subject fulfills request	30	45
4. Subject offers assistance beyond what is requested	20	25
	100	100

- large numbers of people
- population density
- social and economic heterogeneity
- ethnic and racial diversity
- numerous but superficial, segmental, utilitarian relationships
- impersonality and anonymity
- greater interaction in secondary groups
- reliance on formal mechanisms of social control
- physical and social mobility
- greater potential for conflict

Not all these characteristics of urban life have been documented. Indeed, in a highly industrialized and urbanized society such as the United States, it is difficult to discern any differences between rural and urban dwellers. Furthermore, urban dwellers display a great range and variation in lifestyle; some reflect the "typical" style described by sociological theory, and others do not. Many retain their commitment to the extended family, and many city neighborhoods are stable and socially cohesive communities. Despite the plausibility of the hypothesis that urban life leads to anonymity, impersonality, and segmentalization in social relationships, it is hard to prove systematically that urban dwellers are becoming more impersonal or anonymous than are rural dwellers. Finally, sociologists can no longer focus on central-city lifestyles in describing urban living. We must now take account of suburban lifestyles because more people live in suburbs than in central cities. And the suburban way of life is in many ways quite different from the way of life described in early sociological theory.

weaknesses of early theory

The Suburban Trend: Escape from the City

One explanation of the suburbanization of America is that people strive to avoid many of the unpleasant characteristics of urban life. The move to the suburbs is in part generated by a desire to get away from the numbers, density, and heterogeneity of big-city life, the problems created by large numbers of people: the crowds, dirt, noise, smog, congestion, gas fumes, crime, and delinquency. People move to the suburbs seeking amenities: more land on which to build their own homes, enjoy backyard recreation, and give their children more room in which to play; they want sunshine, fresh air, quiet, privacy, and space.

Moreover, people often move to the suburbs to place physical distance between themselves and those whose cultures and lifestyles are different from theirs: the poor, the black, the lower class. They seek to replace the *heterogeneity* of big-city life with the *homogeneity* of the small suburban community: congenial neighbors, people like themselves who share their interest in good schools, respectable neighborhoods, and middle-class lifestyles. The suburban community, with a local government small in scale and close to home, represents a partial escape from the anonymity of mass urban life. A separate suburban government and a separate school district provide suburbanites with a sense of personal effectiveness in the management of public affairs.

why people move to the suburbs
amenities

neighbors like themselves

small-scale communities

"escape" social problems of cities

Suburbs offer escape from the worst problems of urban life: racial conflict, crime, violence, poverty, slums, drugs, congestion, pollution, and so forth. (See Box 13-2 for a comparison of the stress levels in some U.S. cities.) A move to the suburbs permits a family, for the time being at least, to avoid the problems of poor schools, deteriorating housing, expanding welfare rolls, muggings and robberies, and violence and rioting in the central cities. Yet at the same time suburbanites retain the positive benefits of urban life. The city offers economic opportunity: high-paying jobs, openings for highly skilled professionals and technicians, and upward social and economic mobility. This is the reason most people come to the city in the first place. The big city also offers theater and entertainment, professional sports, civic and cultural events, specialized shops and stores, and a host of other attractions. Suburban living allows people to enjoy the advantages of urban life while avoiding some of its hardships.

Is "escape" possible?

Of course, it is not really possible to argue that the major social problems of urban society—racial conflict, poverty, drugs, crime, undereducation, slum housing, and so on—are problems of central cities and not of suburbs. John C. Bollens and Henry J. Schmandt in *The Metropolis* addressed themselves to this point very effectively:

> Some myopic defenders of suburbia go so far as to say that the major socioeconomic problems of urban society are problems of the central city, not those of the total metropolitan community. Where but within the boundaries of the core city, they ask, does one find an abundance of racial strife, crime, blight of housing, and welfare recipients? Superficially, their logic may seem sound, since they are in general correct about the prevalent spatial location of these maladies. Although crime and other social problems exist in suburbia, their magnitude and extent are substantially less than in the central city. But why in an interdependent metropolitan community should the responsibility for suburbanites be any less than that of the central city dwellers? Certainly no one would think of contending that residents of higher income neighborhoods within the corporate limits of the city should be exempt from responsibility for its less fortunate districts. What logic then is there in believing that neighborhoods on the other side of a legal line can wash their hands of social disorders in these sections?
> . . . No large community can hope to reap the benefits of industrialization and urbanization and yet escape their less desirable byproducts. The suburbanite and the central city resident share the responsibility for the total community and its problems. Neither can run fast enough to escape involvement sooner or later.[7]

Perhaps the most frequently mentioned reason for a move to the suburbs is the "kids." Family after family lists consideration of its young as the primary cause for the move to suburbia. The city is hardly the place for most child-centered amenities. A *familistic* or *child-centered lifestyle* can be identified in certain social statistics. There are proportionately more children in the suburbs than in the central cities; a larger proportion of suburban parents stay at home to take care of the children; and a larger proportion of suburban families are housed in single-family homes. A nonfamilistic lifestyle is characteristic of the central city, where there are proportionately fewer children, greater numbers of employed mothers, and more apartment dwellers.

family lifestyles

racial composition

But the most important difference between cities and suburbs is their contrasting *racial composition*. Although blacks constitute only 12.4 percent of the total pop-

BOX 13-2

Urban Stress

Although no statistics directly measure the psychological health of a city, there are important measures of psychosocial pathology, such as rates of alcoholism, suicide, divorce, and crime. These measures reflect both the causes and effects of psychological stress. By comparing U.S. metropolitan areas on the basis of these measures, it is possible to derive overall rankings that reflect the areas' psychological well-being.[a]

The 10 highest- and 10 lowest-stress metropolitan areas out of the 286 areas ranked are shown in Table 13-3.

It is interesting that higher stress ratings are *not* associated with unemployment or poverty levels of cities. On the contrary, higher stress levels were found in cities with milder climates and healthier economic conditions. Psychological well-being is not necessarily related to economic well being.

However, cities with a large proportion of new residents (migrants from other areas) appear to have higher rates of divorce, suicide, alcoholism, and crime. Thus, southern and western cities with higher rates of new arrivals display higher rates of these pathologies.

Moving to a new area may attract people who are having trouble in life and who think a fresh start will help turn their lives around. For many the move fails, and their residence in new areas drives up the stress ratings. Or the move itself, even for relatively stable individuals and families, may produce stress. New arrivals face new social strains and the pressures of adjustment. They have distanced themselves from their old friends and relations and do not have the psychological support that helped them in the past.

TABLE 13-3 Highest- and Lowest-Stress Metropolitan Areas

		Ranking			
Lowest stress		*Alcoholism*	*Crime*	*Suicide*	*Divorce*
1	State College, PA	1	33	8	20
2	Grand Forks, ND	38	9	1	52
3	Saint Cloud, MN	44	3	16	15
4	Rochester, MN	6	17	19	65
5	McAllen, TX	48	102	6	11
6	Altoona, PA	73	7	77	3
7	Bloomington, IN	4	61	3	182
8	Provo, UT	8	24	40	30
9	Utica, NY	29	8	26	34
10	Akron, OH	11	114	53	7
	Highest stress				
277	Los Angeles, CA	275	284	235	112
278	San Francisco, CA	267	276	268	174
279	Jacksonville, FL	262	227	262	274
280	Odessa, TX	178	279	217	280
282	Little Rock, AR	167	242	264	284
283	Lakeland, FL	280	250	219	282
284	Miami, FL	248	285	274	205
285	Las Vegas, NV	285	283	285	285
286	Reno, NV	286	201	286	286
287	Panama City, FL	260	246	250	278

[a] See Robert Levine, "City Stress Index," *Psychology Today,* November 1988, pp. 53–58.

ulation of the United States, they are a much larger proportion of the population in many of the nation's largest cities. Blacks are a majority in Atlanta, Baltimore, Birmingham, Detroit, Gary, Jackson, Memphis, New Orleans, Newark, Oakland, Richmond, Savannah, and Washington, D.C.; and they make up more than a third of the population of Chicago, Cleveland, Cincinnati, Columbus (Ga.), Dayton, Durham (N.C.), Flint, Greensboro, Hartford, Little Rock, Mobile, Macon, Montgomery, New Haven, Norfolk, Philadelphia, St. Louis, and Youngstown (Ohio).

black ghettos

The concentration of blacks in large central cities is a product of the availability of low-priced rental units in older sections and of discriminatory housing practices in real estate sales and rentals. Of course, underlying the concentration of many blacks in central cities is a lack of sufficient income to purchase housing in suburbs or in better city neighborhoods. The poverty and unemployment that contribute to the concentration of blacks in *ghettos* are in turn a product of a whole series of interrelated problems: discrimination, undereducation, lack of job skills, and family disintegration (see Chapter 11). It is difficult to talk about any one of these problems without reference to them all.

The migration of blacks into cities, particularly in the North, has been accompanied by an out-migration of whites fleeing to the suburbs for a variety of reasons. The total populations of many large central cities have remained stagnant in recent years or even declined slightly; black population percentages have increased because black in-migration has compensated for white out-migration.

emerging patterns
black cities, white suburbs

Thus American life is becoming more, not less, segregated. A pattern has emerged of racial ghettos in large central cities surrounded by white middle-class suburbs.

Governing Urban Communities

local governments are creatures of state governments; all their powers legally flow from state governments

Local government is not mentioned in the U.S. Constitution. Although we regard the American federal system as a mixture of federal, state, and *local* governments, from a constitutional point of view local governments are really a part of state governments. Communities have no constitutional right to self-government; all their governmental powers legally flow from state governments. Local governments— cities, townships, counties, special districts, and school districts—are *creatures of the states,* subject to the obligations, privileges, powers, and restrictions that state governments impose on them. The state, either through its constitution or its laws, may create or destroy any or all units of local government. To the extent that local governments can collect taxes, regulate their citizens, and provide services, they are actually exercising *state* powers delegated to them by the state in either its constitution or its laws.

functions of
rural counties
urban counties
cities
school districts
townships
special districts

The fifty states have created over 83,000 local governments (see Table 13-4). What do they all do? Different units of government are assigned different responsibilities by each of the states, so it is difficult to generalize about what each of these types of local government is supposed to do. Indeed, even in the same state there may be overlapping functions and responsibilities assigned to cities, counties, school districts, and special districts.

TABLE 13-4   Local Governments in the United States, 1987

Counties	3,042
Municipalities	19,205
Townships	16,691
School districts	14,741
Special districts	29,487
Total (including states and national government)	83,217

Source: U.S. Bureau of the Census, *Census of Government,* 1987.

Nevertheless, let us try to make some generalizations about what each of these types of government does, realizing, of course, that in any specific location the pattern of governmental activity may be slightly different:

Counties: rural—keep records of deeds, mortgages, births, marriages; assess and levy property taxes; maintain local roads; administer elections and certify election results to state; provide law enforcement through sheriff; maintain criminal court; maintain a local jail; administer state welfare programs.

Counties: urban—most of the same functions as the rural counties (except police and court systems, which often become city functions), together with planning and control of new subdivisions; mental health; public health maintenance and public hospitals; care of the aged; recreation, including parks, stadiums, and convention centers; and perhaps some city functions.

Cities—provide the "common functions" of police, fire, streets, sewage, sanitation, and parks; over half of the nation's large cities also provide welfare services and public education. (In other cities welfare is handled by county governments or directly by state agencies, and education is handled by separate school districts.)

School districts—organized specifically to provide public elementary and secondary education; community colleges may be operated by county governments or by special districts with or without state support.

Townships—generally subdivisions of counties with the same responsibilities as their county.

Special districts—may be as large as the Port Authority of New York with more than $1 billion in diversified assets. However, special districts are usually established for mass transit, soil conservation, libraries, water and irrigation, mosquito control, sewage disposal, airports, and so on.

American city government comes in three structural packages. There are some adaptations and variations from city to city, but generally one can classify the form of city government as mayor–council, commission, or council–manager. Approximately 51 percent of American cities have the mayor–council form of government; 6 percent have the commission form; and 43 percent have the council–manager form. Figure 13-2 shows the general organization of these three forms of government.

forms of city government
mayor–council
commission
council–manager

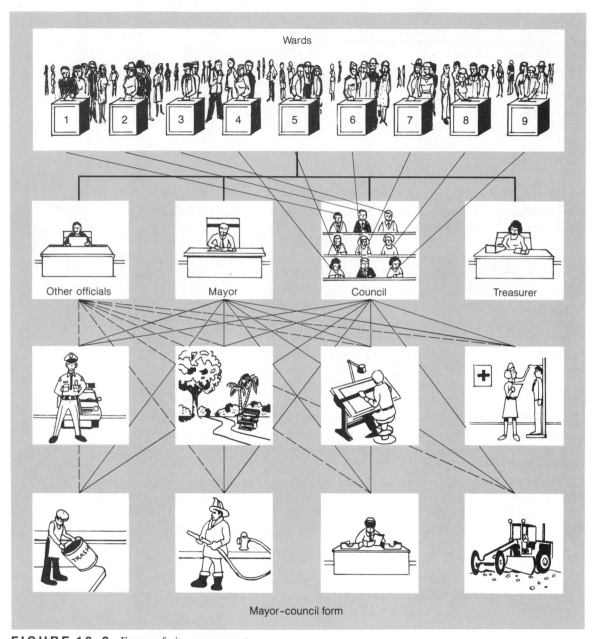

FIGURE 13-2 Forms of city government

Mayor-Council

The nation's largest cities tend to function under the *mayor–council* plan. This is the oldest form of American city government and is designed in the American tradition of separation of powers between legislature and executive. One may also

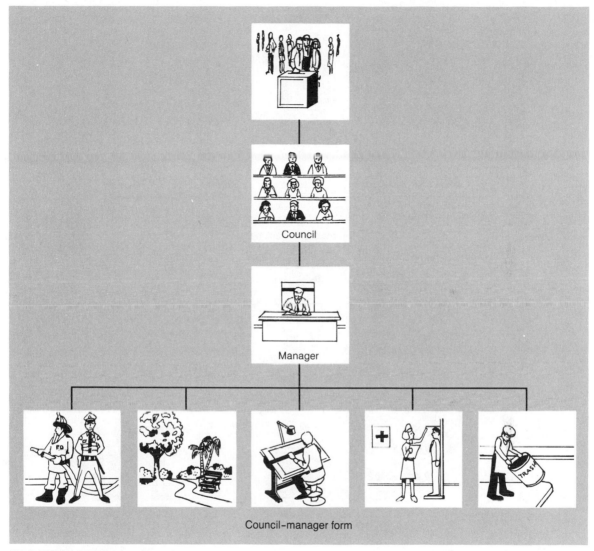

Council

Manager

Council-manager form

FIGURE 13-2 *(continued)*

establish subcategories of strong- or weak-mayor forms of mayor–council government. A strong mayor is the undisputed master of the executive agencies of city government and has substantial legislative powers in the form of budget making, vetoes, and opportunity to propose legislation. Only a few cities make the mayor the sole elected official among city executive officers; it is common for the mayor to share powers with other elected officials—city attorney, treasurer, tax assessor, auditor, clerk, and so on. Yet many mayors, by virtue of their prestige, persuasive abilities, or role as party leader, have been able to overcome most of the weaknesses of their formal office.

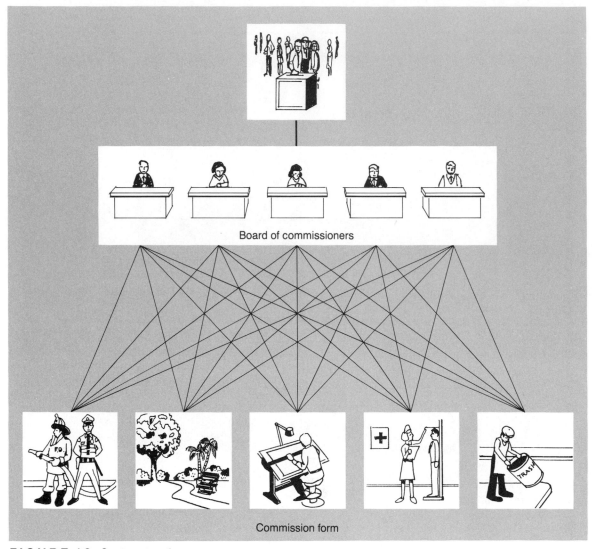

Board of commissioners

Commission form

FIGURE 13-2   (*continued*)

In recent years large cities have been adding to the formal powers of their chief executives. Cities have augmented the mayors' roles by providing them with direction over budgeting, purchasing, and personnel controls. Independent boards, commissions, and individual council members have relinquished administrative control over city departments in many cities. Moreover, many cities have strengthened their mayors' position by providing them with a chief administrative officer (CAO) to handle important staff and administrative duties of supervising city departments and providing central management services.

Who runs this town? Do the elected public officials actually make the important decisions? Or is there a "power structure" in this community that really runs things? If so, who is in the power structure? Are public officials "errand boys" who carry out the orders of powerful people who operate "behind the scenes"? Or are community affairs decided by democratically elected officials acting openly in response to the wishes of many different individuals and groups? Is city government of the people, by the people, and for the people? Or is it a government run by a small "elite," with the masses of people largely apathetic and uninfluential in public affairs? Do people who make the important decisions in business and banking also make the important decisions in urban renewal, public works, education, taxation, public charity, land development, and so on? Or are there different groups of people making decisions in each of these areas, with little or no overlap except for elected officials?

Social scientists have differed in their answers to these questions. Some social scientists (we shall call them *elitists*) believe that power in American communities is concentrated in the hands of relatively few people, usually top business and financial leaders. Elitists believe that this elite is subject to relatively little influence from the masses of people. Other social scientists (we shall call them *pluralists*) believe that power is widely shared in American communities among many leadership groups who represent segments of the community and who are held responsible by the people through elections and group participation. Interestingly, both elitists and pluralists seem to agree that decisions are made by small minorities in the community. Elitists describe a single structure of power, with a single leadership group making decisions on a variety of issues, whereas pluralists describe multiple structures of power, with different groups active in different issues and a great deal of competition, bargaining, and sharing of power among the elite.[8]

Power in "Middletown"

One of the earliest studies of American communities, the classic study of Middletown (actually Muncie, Indiana), conducted by Robert and Helen Lynd in the mid-1920s and again in the mid-1930s, tended to confirm a great deal of elitist thinking about community power.[9] The Lynds found in Muncie a monolithic power structure dominated by the owners of the town's largest industry. Community power was firmly entrenched in the hands of the business class, centering on but not limited to the "X family."[10] This group's power was based on its control over the economic life in the city, particularly its ability to control the extension of credit. The city was run by a "small top group [of] wealthy local manufacturers, bankers, the local head managers of . . . national corporations with units in Middletown, and . . . one or two outstanding lawyers." Democratic procedures and governmental institutions were so much window dressing for business control. The Lynds described the

(continued)

CASE STUDY

(continued)
typical city official as a "man of meager calibre" and as "a man whom the inner business control group ignore economically and socially and use politically." Perhaps the most famous quotation from the Lynds's study was a comment by a Middletown man made in 1935:

> If I'm out of work, I go to the X plant; if I need money I go to the X bank, and if they don't like me I don't get it; my children go to the X college; when I get sick I go to the X hospital; I buy a building lot or house in the X subdivision; my wife goes downtown to buy X milk; I drink X beer, vote for X political parties, and get help from X charities; my boy goes to the X YMCA and my girl to their YWCA; I listen to the word of God in X subsidized churches; if I'm a Mason, I go to the X Masonic temple; I read the news from the X morning paper; and, if I'm rich enough, I travel via the X airport.[11]

Noted sociologist W. Lloyd Warner studied Morris, Illinois, in the 1940s, and he describes a power structure somewhat similar to that encountered by the Lynds in Muncie.[12] Sociologist August B. Hollingshead studied the same town, and his findings substantially confirmed those of Warner.[13] (Sociologists seem to prefer to disguise the names of towns they are studying: Warner called the town "Jonesville," whereas Hollingshead called it "Elmtown.")

Power in "Regional City"

One of the most influential elitist studies of community politics was sociologist Floyd Hunter's *Community Power Structure,* a study of Atlanta, Georgia.[14] According to Hunter, no one person or family or business dominated "Regional City" (a pseudonym for Atlanta), as might be true in a smaller town. Instead, Hunter described several tiers of influentials, with the most important community decisions reserved for a top layer of the business community. Admission to the innermost circle was based primarily on one's position in the business world. These top decision makers were not formally organized but conferred informally and passed down decisions to government leaders, professional personnel, civic organizations, and other "front men." Hunter explained that the top power structure concerned itself only with major policy decisions; there were other substructures—economic, governmental, religious, educational, professional, civic, and cultural—that communicated and implemented the policies at the top levels. These substructures

> are subordinate, however, to the interests of the policy makers who operate in the economic sphere of community life in Regional City. The institutions of the family, church, state, education, and the like take their sustenance from economic institutional sources and are thereby subordinate to this particular institution more than any other. . . . Within the policy forming groups the economic interests are dominant.[15]

(continued)

(continued)

Top powerholders seldom operated openly. "Most of the top personnel in the power group are rarely seen in the meetings attended by the associational under-structure personnel in Regional City."[16]

In Hunter's description of community decision making, decisions tend to flow *down* from top policy makers, composed primarily of business and financial lead-ers, to civic, professional, and cultural association leaders; religious and education leaders; and government officials, who implemented the program; and the masses of people have little direct or indirect participation in the whole process. Policy does not go *up* from associational groupings or from the people themselves. According to Hunter, elected public officials are clearly part of the lower-level insti-tutional substructure, which "executes" policy rather than formulates it. Finally, Hunter found that this whole structure is held together by "common interests, mutual obligations, money, habit, delegated responsibilities, and in some cases, by coercion and force."

Power in New Haven

Perhaps the most influential of the pluralist community studies was Robert A. Dahl's *Who Governs?* a detailed analysis of decision making in New Haven, Con-necticut. Dahl chose to examine sixteen major decisions on redevelopment and pub-lic education in New Haven and on nominations for mayor in both political parties for seven elections. Dahl found a polycentric and dispersed system of community power in New Haven, in contrast to Hunter's highly monolithic and centralized power structure. Influence was wielded from time to time by many individuals, each exercising power over some issues but not over others. When the issue was one of urban renewal, one set of individuals was influential; in public education, a different group of leaders was involved. The business elite, said by Hunter to con-trol Atlanta, was only one of many different influential groups in New Haven. According to Dahl:

> The economic notables, far from being a ruling group, are simply one of many groups out of which individuals sporadically emerge to influence the politics and acts of city officials. Almost anything one might say about the influence of the economic notables could be said with equal justice about a half a dozen other groups in the New Haven community.[17]

The mayor of New Haven was the only decision maker who was influential in most of the issue areas studied, and his degree of influence varied from issue to issue.

> The mayor was not at the peak of a pyramid but at the center of intersecting circles. He rarely commanded. He negotiated, cajoled, exhorted, beguiled, charmed, pressed, appealed, reasoned, promised, insisted, demanded, even threatened; but he most

(continued)

(continued)

needed support and acquiescence from other leaders who simply could not be commanded. Because he could not command them, he had to bargain.[18]

Studying Community Power

Only by comparing structures of power and decision-making processes in a wide variety of communities can social scientists learn the actual extent of elitism or pluralism in American community life. Some communities may have concentrated, pyramidal structures of power, whereas others have diffused, multicentered power arrangements. For example, it is very likely that decision making in Atlanta is much more centralized than decision making in New Haven, Connecticut.

The key to understanding community power lies in identifying different types of community power structures and then relating them to social, economic, and political conditions in communities. For example, we may find that large communities with a great deal of social and economic diversity, a competitive party system, and a variety of well-organized competing interest groups tend to have *pluralistic* decision-making systems. On the other hand, small communities with a homogeneous population, a single dominant industry, nonpartisan elections, and few competing organizations may have power structures resembling the *elite* model.

Commission

The *commission* form of city government gives both legislative and executive powers to a small body, usually consisting of five members. The commission form originated at the beginning of the century as a reform movement designed to end a system of divided responsibility between mayor and council. One of the commission members is nominally the mayor, but he or she has no more formal powers than the other commissioners. The board of commissioners is directly responsible for the operation of city departments and agencies. In practice, one commission member will become responsible for the management of a specific department, such as finance, public works, or public safety. As long as the council members are in agreement over policy, there are few problems; but when commissioners differ among themselves and develop separate spheres of influence in city government, city government becomes a multiheaded monster, totally lacking in coordination. The results of the commission form of government were generally so disastrous that the reform movement abandoned its early support of this form of government in favor of the council–manager plan.

Council–Manager

The *council–manager* form of government revived the distinction between legislative "policy making" and executive "administration" in city government. Policy-making responsibility is vested in an elected council, and administration is assigned to an appointed professional administrator known as a manager, chosen by the council and responsible to it. All departments of the city government operate under the direction of the manager, who has the power to hire and fire personnel within the limits set by the merit system. The council's role in administration is limited to selecting and dismissing the city manager. The plan is based on the ideas that policy making and administration are separate functions and that the principal task of city government is to provide the highest level of services at the lowest possible costs—utilities, streets, fire and police protection, health, welfare, recreation, and so on. Hence, a professionally trained, career-oriented administrator is given direct control over city departments.

The City in History

The United States developed an anti-city bias in its rural beginnings and retained that bias long after it became a nation of city dwellers. When the first census was taken in 1790, a mere 5 percent of the nation's 4 million people lived in cities; there were only twenty-four towns with populations of 2,500 or more. A strong anti-city bias was already ingrained in the national character. In an age when technological progress was giving rise to the first industrial centers in Europe, the American social and economic outlook was decidedly agrarian. Most politicians and citizens distrusted cities, which Thomas Jefferson believed were not conducive to the exercise of virtue. Jefferson's warning notwithstanding, American cities steadily increased in population. The lure of urban life is reflected in the following Census Bureau figures showing the country's five most populous cities in 1820, 1870, 1950, and 1980.

from a rural to an urban America

1820	
New York	152,000
Philadelphia	65,000
Baltimore	63,000
Boston	43,000
New Orleans	27,000

1870	
New York	1,478,000
Philadelphia	674,000
St. Louis	311,000
Chicago	299,000
Baltimore	267,000

1950	
New York	7,896,957
Chicago	3,620,962
Philadelphia	2,071,605
Los Angeles	1,970,338
Detroit	1,849,568

1980	
New York	7,071,000
Chicago	3,005,000
Los Angeles	2,966,800
Philadelphia	1,688,200
Houston	1,594,100

First as seaports, then as trading and manufacturing centers, cities in the United States grew in response to economic needs. "Villages expanded into towns; towns became metropolises," historian Lewis Mumford wrote in *The City in History*.

economic needs fuel growth

Between 1820 and 1900, the destruction and disorder within cities was like that of a battlefield. . . . Industrialism, the main creative force of the nineteenth century, produced the most degraded urban environment the world had yet seen. . . . Men built in haste, and had hardly time to repent of their mistakes before they tore down their original structures and built again, just as heedlessly. The newcomers, babies, or immigrants, could not wait for new quarters: they crowded into whatever was offered. It was a period of vast urban improvisation: makeshift hastily piled upon makeshift.[19]

social stratification in cities

By the late nineteenth century most large American cities had become socially and economically stratified. The affluent lived in their posh neighborhoods, comfortably isolated from the poor in their ethnic ghettos, whereas the middle classes tended to move to the less-expensive outlying areas. As populations spread, many central cities simply annexed those areas to which the middle class had gravitated. New York, for example, added more than 250 square miles in 1891, and in 1941 Boston doubled its area. Some states established automatic annexation procedures. By 1920, however, political opposition to the absorption of fringe areas mounted, and large cities, especially in the congested northeast, found themselves unable to keep pace, through annexation or consolidation, with suburban migration.

automobiles encourage suburban growth

During the 1920s general prosperity and the increasing number of automobiles gave new impetus to the growth of the suburbs. In that decade, the suburban populations around the seventeen largest U.S. cities rose by nearly 40 percent, while the rate of growth for most cities fell sharply. But until the 1940s, the central city remained the focal point of business and industry; the surrounding suburbs were primarily commuter villages.

The Problems of the Inner City

The nation's largest cities have become the principal location of virtually all of the social problems confronting our society—poverty, homelessness, racial tension, family instability, drug abuse, delinquency, and crime. Some of these problems were discussed in previous chapters (especially in Chapter 11, "Poverty and Powerlessness," and in Chapter 12, "Power, Crime, and Violence"), but it is important to note here that these problems are all made worse by their concentration in large cities. The concentration of social ills in the nation's cities is a relatively recent occurrence; as late as 1970 there were higher rates of poverty in rural America than in the cities.

economic problems
fewer high-paying manufacturing jobs

migrating of jobs to suburbs

social problems
joblessness
poverty
family disintegration
welfare dependency

out-migration of working and middle class from inner city

Why has the "inner city" become the locus of social problems? It has been argued that changes in the labor market from industrial goods-producing jobs to professional, financial, and technical service-producing jobs is increasingly polarizing the labor market into low-wage and high-wage sectors.[20] The decline in manufacturing jobs, together with a shift in remaining manufacturing jobs and commercial (sales) jobs to the suburbs, has left inner-city residents with fewer job opportunities. The rise in joblessness in the inner cities has in turn increased the concentration of poor people, added to the number of poor single-parent families, and increased welfare dependency.

At the same time, inner-city neighborhoods have experienced an out-migration of working-class and middle-class families. The number of inner-city neighborhoods in which the poverty rate exceeds 40 percent has risen sharply.[21] The loss of working- and middle-class families creates further social instability. In earlier

Social problems are concentrated in the inner city.
Source: Harriet Gains/The Image Works

decades most inner-city adults were employed, and they invested their income and time in their neighborhoods, patronizing churches, stores, schools, and community organizations. Their presence in the community provided "role models" for youth. But their out-migration has decreased contact between the classes, leaving the poorest isolated and "truly disadvantaged." Inner-city residents now lack not only nearby jobs, but also access to job information, social learning through working role models, and (for some young women) suitable (that is, employed) marriage partners.

It is argued that joblessness and poverty are much more demoralizing when concentrated in the inner city. Neighborhoods that have few legitimate employment opportunities, inadequate job information networks, and poor schools not only weaken the work ethic, but also give rise to illegal income-producing activities in the streets—drugs, crime, prostitution. A jobless family living in a neighborhood where these ills are concentrated is influenced by the behaviors, beliefs, and perceptions of the people around them. These "concentration effects" make things worse. Moreover, the deterioration of inner-city neighborhoods saps the vitality of local businesses and public services, leading to fewer and shabbier movie theaters, restaurants, markets, parks, and playgrounds. Inner-city schools are particularly disadvantaged; as educational requirements for good jobs are rising, the quality of education available in the inner city is eroded by the concentration of children from poverty-impacted and disintegrating families. The fiscal burden on city governments increases: The cost of services to the inner city increases at the same time that the tax base is eroded by out-migrating businesses and working residents.

In short, the problems of the inner city are the problems of the nation in concentrated form. The United States is not the only country faced with the problems of its inner cities. Box 13-3 offers a cross-national perspective of urbanization.

"concentration effects"
absence of working role models

loss of job information

weakened work ethic

street-crime environment

deteriorating business and public services

BOX 13-3

Cross-National Perspective: Worldwide Urbanization

Urbanization is occurring worldwide. Cities throughout the world offer greater opportunities than rural areas. It is estimated that the world's urban areas are growing at twice the rate of the world's population generally. Millions of people migrate from the countryside in search of economic opportunity, health care, education, and higher standards of living in the world's largest cities. However poor and unpleasant life may be in many Third World cities, these cities hold the promise of a better life for rural migrants. Mexico City is rapidly growing into perhaps the world's largest city. Yet it is estimated that 10 percent of its residents have no running water and that 15 percent lack sewage facilities. Mountains of trash and garbage have become wretched shantytowns where the city's poor

pick through waste to survive and build shacks from discarded materials. The problems of Third World cities make those of the largest U.S. cities seem minor by comparison.

Yet it is likely that in the year 2000 most of the largest cities in the world will be found in less developed societies (see Table 13-5). Modernization brings urbanization, and as Third World nations move from agricultural to industrial economies, their cities grow exponentially. Only three of the world's largest cities are in the United States—New York, Los Angeles, and Chicago. By the year 2000, Third World cities will replace many Western cities in the list of the world's largest cities.

TABLE 13-5 The World's Twenty-Five Largest Cities (in Millions of People), 1985–2000

1985		2000	
Tokyo	19.0	Mexico City	24.4
Mexico City	16.7	São Paulo, Brazil	23.6
New York	15.6	Tokyo	21.3
São Paulo, Brazil	15.5	New York	16.1
Shanghai	12.1	Calcutta	15.9
Buenos Aires	10.8	Greater Bombay, India	15.4
London	10.5	Shanghai	14.7
Calcutta	10.3	Teheran	13.7
Rio de Janeiro	10.1	Jakarta, Indonesia	13.2
Seoul, S. Korea	10.1	Buenos Aires	13.1
Los Angeles	10.0	Rio de Janeiro	13.0
Osaka, Japan	9.6	Seoul, S. Korea	13.0
Greater Bombay, India	9.5	Delhi, India	12.8
Beijing	9.3	Lagos, Nigeria	12.5
Moscow	8.9	Cairo	11.8
Paris	8.8	Karachi, Pakistan	11.6
Tianjin, China	8.0	Beijing	11.5
Cairo	7.9	Manila	11.5
Jakarta, Indonesia	7.8	Dacca, Bangladesh	11.3
Milan	7.5	Osaka, Japan	11.2
Teheran	7.2	Los Angeles	10.9
Manila	7.1	London	10.8
Delhi, India	7.0	Bangkok	10.3
Chicago	6.8	Moscow	10.1
Karachi, Pakistan	6.2	Paris	8.8

Source: U.S. Bureau of the Census, *Statistical Abstract of the United States 1990* (Washington, D.C.: U.S. Government Printing Office, 1990), pp. 836–837.

Notes

1. Louis Wirth, "Urbanism as a Way of Life," *American Journal of Sociology* 44 (July 1938).
2. Ibid., p. 24.
3. Wirth, "Urbanism as a Way of Life"; Georg Simmel, *The Sociology of Georg Simmel,* ed. Kurt Wolff (New York: Free Press, 1950).
4. See, for example, S. Milgram, "The Experience of Living in Cities," *Science* 167 (1970); A. Lowin et al., "The Pace of Life and Sensitivity to Time in Urban and Rural Settings," *Journal of Social Psychology* 83 (1971); and C. Korte and N. Kerr, "Response to Activistic Opportunities under Urban and Rural Conditions," *Journal of Social Psychology* 32 (1975).
5. Derived from figures provided by Charles Korte, "The Impact of Urbanization on Social Behavior," *Urban Affairs Quarterly* 12 (September 1976).
6. Marshall Clinard, *Sociology and Deviant Behavior* (New York: Holt, Rinehart & Winston, 1968), p. 96.
7. John C. Bollens and Henry J. Schmandt, *The Metropolis* (New York: Harper & Row, 1965), pp. 249–250.
8. This literature is so voluminous that it seems appropriate to cite only some of the major summary pieces: Thomas J. Anton, "Power, Pluralism, and Local Politics," *Administrative Science Quarterly* 7 (March 1963); Lawrence Herson, "In the Footsteps of Community Power," *American Political Science Review* 55 (December 1961); Peter Bachrach and Morton S. Baratz, "Two Faces of Power," *American Political Science Review* 56 (December 1962); Peter Bachrach and Morton C. Baratz, "Decisions and Nondecisions," *American Political Science Review* 57 (September 1963); Herbert Kaufman and Victor Jones, "The Mystery of Power," *Public Administration Review* 14 (Summer 1954); Nelson Polsby, *Community Power and Political Theory* (New Haven: Yale University Press, 1963); Robert Presthus, *Men at the Top* (New York: Oxford University Press, 1964); Robert Dahl, *Who Governs?* (New Haven: Yale University Press, 1961); Floyd Hunter, *Community Power Structure* (Chapel Hill: University of North Carolina Press, 1953); and Robert Agger, Daniel Goldrich, and Bert Swanson, *The Rulers and the Ruled* (New York: Wiley, 1965); other citations are given in notes following.
9. Robert S. Lynd and Helen M. Lynd, *Middletown* (New York: Harcourt, Brace & World, 1929), and *Middletown in Transition* (New York: Harcourt, Brace & World, 1937).
10. The "X family," never identified in the Lynds's books, was actually the Ball family, glass manufacturers. Today it is headed by E. F. Ball, Chairman of the Board of the Ball Corporation, Ball Brothers' Foundation, Ball Memorial Hospital, Muncie Aviation Corp., and Muncie Airport, Inc., and a director of the American National Bank and Trust of Muncie, Borg-Warner Corp., Indiana Bell Telephone Co., Merchants National Bank of Muncie, and Wabash College. Ball State University in Muncie is named for the family.
11. Lynd and Lynd, *Middletown in Transition,* p. 74.
12. W. Lloyd Warner et al., *Democracy in Jonesville* (New York: Harper & Row, 1949).
13. August B. Hollingshead, *Elmtown's Youth* (New York: Wiley, 1949).
14. Hunter, *Community Power Structure.*
15. Ibid., p. 94.
16. Ibid., p. 90.
17. Dahl, *Who Governs?,* p. 72.
18. Ibid., p. 204.
19. Lewis Mumford, *The City in History* (London: Penguin Books, 1966), p. 11.
20. This thesis derives from sociologist William Julius Wilson, *The Truly Disadvantaged* (Chicago: University of Chicago Press, 1987).
21. See Christopher Jencks and Paul E. Peterson, eds., *The Urban Underclass* (Washington, D.C.: Brookings Institution, 1991).

About This Chapter

It has always been fashionable in the United States to deplore life in big cities. Thomas Jefferson believed cities were the source of human vice and that only a rural and small-town America could maintain democracy. When the first census of the United States was taken in 1790, only 5 percent of the American people lived in cities, whereas today three-quarters of our population live in large urban clusters known as metropolitan areas. We have changed from a rural society to an urban society. We are trying to cope with the social, psychological, economic, and political problems of urban life. We are particularly concerned with the deterioration of older central cities, the creation of African American ghettos in large cities, "white flight" to the suburbs, and financial and governmental problems posed by growth and decline in metropolitan areas.

In this chapter we have described where Americans live and the impact of urban life on social relations, psychological states of mind, government, and power relations. Now that you have read it, you should be able to

- describe changes over the past decade in central cities and suburbs of metropolitan areas and in nonmetropolitan areas,
- identify the social characteristics associated with urban life,
- discuss suburbanization and increasing separation of African American central cities from white suburbs in large metropolitan areas,
- discuss the social psychology of urban life,
- describe various structures of government found in American cities,
- describe "community power structures" and how they may vary from one city to another,
- describe the "concentration effects" of social problems in the inner city.

Discussion Questions

1. Describe overall growth and decline in central cities, suburbs, and nonmetropolitan areas of the United States. What is a CMSA?

2. According to sociologist Louis Wirth, what are the distinguishing characteristics of urban life?

3. Why do people choose to live in suburbs? What is meant by the statement "American life is becoming more, not less, segregated"?

4. How can we test the hypothesis that urban life is more impersonal than rural or small-town life?

5. What are the governmental functions of counties (rural and urban), cities, school districts, townships, and special districts?

6. What are the most common forms of city government?

7. Describe governmental programs designed to revive declining central cities.

8. What is meant by *elitist* and *pluralist* descriptions of community power structures?

9. What factors might account for the concentration of social problems in the inner city?

Power
and the
International
System

14

Relations among Nations

The distinguished political scientist Hans Morgenthau wrote:

international politics
the worldwide struggle
for power

International politics, like all politics, is a struggle for power. Whatever the ultimate aims of international politics, power is always the immediate aim. Statesmen and peoples may ultimately seek freedom, security, prosperity, or power itself. They may define their goals in terms of a religious, philosophic, economic, or social ideal. . . . But whenever they strive to realize their goal by means of international politics, they are striving for power.[1]

In brief, we are reminded that the struggle for power is global—it involves all the nations and peoples of the world, whatever their goals or ideals.

There are nearly 200 nations in the world today. Of these nations 159 are members of the United Nations. Others are too small or too poor to claim membership in that body. Yet all the nations of the world—inside and outside the UN, whatever their size, location, culture, politics, economic system, or level of technological development—claim *sovereignty*. Sovereignty means formal, legal power over internal affairs; freedom from external intervention; and political and legal recognition by other nations. Sovereignty is a legal fiction, of course: many nations have difficulty controlling their internal affairs; they are constantly meddling in each other's internal affairs and even trampling on each other's political and legal authority. Nonetheless, the *struggle* to achieve sovereignty is an important force in world politics.

sovereignty
legal power over internal affairs, freedom from external intervention, and legal recognition by other nations

Although sovereignty is highly valued by all nations, it creates an international system in which no authority—not even the United Nations—is given the power to make or enforce rules binding on all nations. There is *no world government.* Nations cooperate with each other only when it is in their own interests to do so. Nations can make treaties with each other, but there is no court to enforce the treaties, and they can be (and are) disregarded when it becomes advantageous for a nation to do so.

international law
a legal fiction that
guides relations among
nations

There is a series of customs and principles among nations—known as *international law*—that help to guide relations among nations. But international "law" is also a fiction: there is no international "police force" to enforce the law, and it is frequently broken or ignored. An International Court (at The Hague, the Netherlands) exists to decide conflicts according to international law, but nations do not have to submit to the authority of this court and can, if they wish, ignore its decisions. The United Nations, as we shall see, is largely a debating society. The UN has no real power to enforce its resolutions, unless one or more nations (acting in their own self-interest) decide to try to enforce a UN resolution with their own troops, or contribute troops to a joint "UN force." But UN forces are really the forces of sovereign nations that have voluntarily decided to contribute troops to enforce a particular resolution.

**international politics
as a serious game**

The international system can be viewed as a global game of power that is played continuously. All the players pursue different goals against all the other players. Some players are more powerful than others, and occasionally players team up against each other. (Some team up willingly, while others are coerced into doing it.) Periodically fights break out, but there is no referee with enough power to stop

President Bush and Russian President Boris Yeltsin meet at the White House.
Source: Patsy Lynch/Impact Visuals

the fighting (unless one or more stronger players step in to restrain the fighting nations). The players belong to a club called the United Nations, where they sit around and quarrel about the game. But the players never agree to a referee or to rules of the game for fear that a referee or rules might interfere with their own style of play. The game has been played for centuries. No one really knows all the goals that each player seeks (although we all know that power is the key instrument in achieving any goal). Yet all the players are deadly serious and play to win.

Bringing Order to International Relations

The instability and insecurity of "the global game of power" have led to many attempts over the centuries to bring order to the international system. Indeed, wars among nations have averaged one every two years,[2] and if "civil wars" and "indirect aggressions" are counted, the rate of armed conflict is even greater.[3]

The Balance-of-Power System—Nineteenth Century

One method of trying to bring order to international relations is the *balance-of-power system.* The nineteenth century saw a deliberate attempt to stabilize international relations by creating a system of alliances among nations that was designed to balance the power of one group of nations against the power of another and thus to discourage war. If the balance worked, war would be avoided and peace would

the balance-of-power system, 1815–1914

The United Nations General Assembly.
Source: Tannenbaum/Sygma

be assured. For almost an entire century, from the end of the Napoleonic Wars (1815) to World War I (1914), the balance-of-power system appeared to be at least partially effective in Europe. But an important defect in the balance-of-power system is that a small conflict between two nations that are members of separate alliances can draw all the member nations of each alliance into the conflict.

This defect can result in the rapid expansion of a small conflict into a major war between separate alliances of nations. Essentially this is what happened in World War I, when a minor conflict in the Balkan nations resulted in a very destructive **the Allies and the** war between the *Allies* (England, France, Russia, and eventually the United States) **Central Powers** and the *Central Powers* (Germany, Austria–Hungary, and Turkey).

Indeed, World War I proved so destructive (10 million men were killed on the battlefield between 1914 and 1918) that there was a worldwide demand to replace the balance-of-power system with a new arrangement—"collective security."

Collective Security—The United Nations

efforts at collective   *Collective security* originally meant that *all* nations would join together to guarantee **security** each other's "territorial integrity and existing political independence" against "external aggression" by any nation.[4] This concept resulted in the formation of the **the League of** League of Nations in 1919. However, opposition to international involvement was **Nations** so great in the United States after World War I that after a lengthy debate in the Senate, the United States refused to join the League of Nations. More important, the League of Nations failed completely to deal with rising militarism in Germany, Japan, and Italy in the 1930s. During that decade, Japan invaded Manchuria, Italy invaded Ethiopia, and Germany invaded Czechoslovakia; and the League of Nations failed to prevent any of these aggressions. Fascism in Germany and Italy and militarism in Japan went unchecked. The result was a war even more devastating than World War I: World War II cost more than 40 million lives, both civilian and military.

Yet even after World War II the notion of collective security remained an ideal of the victorious Allied powers, especially the United States, Great Britain, the

Soviet Union, France, and China. The Charter of the United Nations was signed in 1945. The new organization included fifty-one members. The UN provided for (1) a Security Council with eleven members, five of them being permanent members (the United States, the USSR, Britain, France, and China) and having the power to veto any action by the Security Council; (2) a General Assembly composed of all the member nations, each with a single vote; (3) a secretariat headed by a secretary-general with a staff at UN headquarters in New York; and (4) several special bodies to handle specialized affairs—for example, the Economic and Social Council, the Trusteeship Council, and the International Court at The Hague.

the United Nations
General Assembly
Security Council
secretary-general
specialized bodies
veto powers

The Security Council has the "primary responsibility" for maintaining "international peace and security." For this reason the world's most powerful nations—the United States, Russia, Great Britain, France, and China—have permanent seats on the council and veto powers over all but procedural matters. The General Assembly has authority over "any matter affecting the peace of the world," although it is supposed to defer to the Security Council if the council has already taken up a particular matter. No nation has a veto in the General Assembly; every nation has one vote, regardless of its size or power. Most resolutions can be passed by a majority vote.

Throughout most of its history, the United Nations has failed to bring order, stability, or security to the world. It has grown to a membership of 159 nations, but the majority of those nations are headed by authoritarian regimes of one kind or another. The Western democracies are outnumbered. Nonetheless, the United States, because of its wealth, pays the largest share of UN expenses. In the General Assembly the votes of tiny populations headed by absolute dictators count for just as much as the votes of large democracies, including the United States. "One person, one vote" does not operate in the General Assembly; there, the rule is "one country, one vote." Moreover, the General Assembly has been ineffective in dealing with many major international disputes. This is true largely because parties to these disputes have little confidence in the UN and decline to bring their problems to it. Except on rare occasions (in the Korean War, 1950–1953, when the Soviet Union boycotted the Security Council and China was not a member; and in the Gulf war, 1990–1991), member nations of the UN have failed to commit their troops to enforce UN decisions.

problems at the United Nations

The Security Council's strong resolutions against the Iraqi invasion of Kuwait, and its authorization for member nations to use "all available means" to expel Iraqi troops from Kuwait, was a significant improvement in the performance of that body. The success of the United Nations in uniting against Iraqi aggression may be attributed to improved relations between Russia and Western nations and to a desire on the part of China's leaders to improve relations with the West, as well as to the political skills of President George Bush, who had previously served as U.S. ambassador to the United Nations.

the UN in the Gulf war

Regional Security—NATO

The general disappointment with the United Nations as a form of collective security gave rise as early as 1950 to a different approach: *regional security*. In response to aggressive Soviet moves in Europe,[5] the United States, together with the nations

regional security

of Western Europe, created the North Atlantic Treaty Organization (NATO). In the NATO Treaty the United States made a specific commitment to defend Western Europe in the event of a Soviet attack. Indeed, fifteen Western nations agreed to collective regional security: They agreed that "an armed attack against one or more . . . shall be considered an attack against them all." Moreover, a joint NATO military command was established with a U.S. commanding officer (the first was General of the Army Dwight D. Eisenhower) to command and coordinate the defense of Western Europe. After the formation of NATO, the Soviets made no further advances into Western Europe. The Soviets themselves, in response to NATO, drew up a comparable treaty among their own Eastern European satellite nations: the

NATO and the Warsaw Pact

Warsaw Pact. Note that these regional security agreements—NATO and the Warsaw Pact—were more like the nineteenth-century *balance-of-power* alliances than like the true concept of *collective security*. The original notion of collective security envisioned agreement among *all* nations, whereas NATO and the Warsaw Pact were similar to the older systems of separate alliances.

The Warsaw Pact disintegrated following the dramatic collapse of the communist governments of Eastern Europe in 1989. Former Warsaw Pact nations—Poland, Hungary, Romania, Bulgaria, and East Germany—threw out their ruling communist regimes and began negotiations leading to the withdrawal of Soviet troops from their territory. The Berlin Wall was smashed in 1989, and Germany was formally reunified in 1990, bringing together 61 million prosperous people of West Germany with 17 million less affluent people of East Germany. United Germany continues as a member of NATO. The former Soviet Union pledged to remove its troops from Germany and from other former Warsaw Pact nations. These troops are gradually returning to Russia.

The reduced threat of a Soviet attack on Western Europe has raised a variety of questions regarding the future of NATO. Is NATO needed at all in view of the collapse of the Warsaw Pact? Or should it continue, perhaps with reduced military forces, as insurance against a future renewal of a Soviet-style threat? Should NATO guarantee the security of the emerging democracies of Eastern Europe against a possible renewed threat? Or should NATO be replaced with a new collective security arrangement, a Council on European Security that would include all European nations, including Russia, Ukraine, and other former states of the Soviet Union?

The Superpower Balance

the superpower balance

Since the end of World War II collective security and regional security concepts were overshadowed by the confrontation of the world's two *superpowers:* the United States and the Soviet Union. Indeed, international conflicts throughout the world—in the Middle East, Africa, Latin America, Southeast Asia, and else-

the old bipolar world

where—were affected by the superpower struggle. In this perceived *bipolar* world, the interests and aspirations of many peoples and nations were seen as secondary to the power struggle between the United States and USSR.

the new multipolar world

Today the international scene is more likely to be described as *multipolar,* with the interests of the United States and Russia competing on more equal terms with the interests of China; Japan; and a more united Europe led by Great Britain,

France, and Germany; and with the interests of Middle Eastern, African, Pacific Rim, and Latin American nations receiving greater attention.

Nonetheless, it is important to remember that the United States and Russia are distinguishable from the rest of the world by their capacity to destroy each other, and perhaps life on the planet, with nuclear weapons. Other nations—Great Britain, France, China, India, and perhaps Israel, South Africa, Pakistan, and North Korea—possess nuclear weapons, but none can deliver the kind of devastating nuclear attack that could destroy a large industrial society and endanger the world. In nuclear warmaking capability, the United States and Russia remain global superpowers.

nuclear superpowers: United States and Russia

Nuclear Peace and Deterrence

For nearly a half century, the United States has relied primarily on the notion of *deterrence* to avoid nuclear war. In a general sense, deterrence means that war can best be prevented by making its consequences unacceptably costly to rational leaders of other nations. Since the atomic attacks on Hiroshima and Nagasaki at the end of World War II in 1945, no nation has resorted to the use of nuclear weapons, despite huge nuclear arsenals and bitter wars. Nuclear war has been avoided not by treaties or agreements, nor by an absence of conflict, nor by compassion for humanity, but by *fear of nuclear retaliation.* This is the irony of nuclear deterrence: Massive destruction of civilization is avoided by maintaining nuclear weapons capable of inflicting the massive destruction they seek to prevent. The United States maintains a nuclear arsenal not to use *physically* against an enemy, but to use *psychologically* to inhibit a potential attacker from initiating a nuclear war.

deterrence
making the consequences of war unacceptably costly to rational leaders.

avoiding nuclear war by the threat of retaliation against potential attackers

Second-Strike Capability

The policy of deterrence is based on the notion that the United States can dissuade a potential enemy from nuclear war by maintaining the capacity to destroy the enemy's society even *after* we have suffered a well-executed surprise attack by the enemy. Deterrence assumes that the worst may happen—a surprise first strike against our own offensive forces. It emphasizes our *second-strike capability*—the ability of our forces to survive a surprise attack by the enemy and then to inflict an unacceptable level of destruction on the enemy's homeland. Deterrence, then, requires (1) that the United States maintain the *capability* to destroy an enemy even after absorbing a full-scale surprise attack (second-strike capability); (2) that the United States *communicate* its second-strike capability to the enemy (deterrence is achieved only if the enemy *knows* you have the capacity to deliver unacceptable damage even after absorbing a first strike); (3) that the United States make its threat *credible* (the enemy must believe that you would in fact retaliate if attacked); and (4) that the enemy is a *rational* decision maker (only an irrational nation would go to war knowing that its own society would be destroyed as a result). The *key component* of assured-destruction deterrence is the *survivability* of an effective strike force *after* a successful surprise attack by the enemy—that is, second-strike capability.

second-strike capability
the ability to retaliate even after absorbing an enemy's first strike

the key concept
survivability of forces

Strategic arms reductions will reduce the size of missile forces, but the United States will continue to rely on nuclear deterrence.
Source: UPI/Bettmann

The Triad

triad
separate land-based and submarine-launched missiles and manned aircraft to ensure survivability and discourage potential enemies from attempting a first strike

retaliatory systems
ICBMs

SLBMs

manned bombers

cruise missiles

MIRV
multiple nuclear warheads on a single missile

hard-target kill capability
ability to destroy missile silos and threaten retaliatory capability

American defense policy relies on a *triad* of land-based missiles, submarine-launched missiles, and manned bombers to provide deterrence. This combination of forces is believed to be a more effective deterrent than reliance on any single weapons system, because the diversity and multiplicity of forces makes it difficult for an enemy to develop a *first-strike capability*—the capability of destroying all three *retaliatory systems* simultaneously and thereby avoiding our second-strike retaliation.

ICBMs

The United States built 1,000 Minuteman intercontinental ballistic missiles (ICBMs) in the early 1960s. These missiles continue to be this nation's primary ICBM force. About half of the Minuteman force was modified so each Minuteman could carry three multiple independently-targeted reentry vehicles (MIRVs), which are smaller nuclear warheads that separate from the missile itself and can be accurately directed to separate targets.

However, over the years the Soviets were successful in developing large, accurate ICBMs carrying MIRVed warheads. These Soviet ICBM forces, especially their SS-18 ICBM, gave the Soviets "hard-target kill capability"—the ability to destroy U.S. missile silos and thus threaten to eliminate our retaliatory capability in a well-planned first strike. To partially restore the strategic imbalance created by the

SS-18, the United States developed the MX missile with hard-target kill capability. However, the central problem remained that of finding a *survivable* basing mode for land-based missiles. Congress refused to buy more than fifty MXs because they are vulnerable to attack. For over a decade various plans were discussed to make the MX survivable, but each plan was rejected.

MX
U.S. ICBM with hard-target kill capability

Midgetman proposed mobile ICBM

Manned Bombers

The second "leg" of the triad is the intercontinental bomber. Manned bombers can survive a first strike if they are in the air. A certain portion of a manned bomber force can be placed on alert or even kept in the air during crisis periods. The U.S. intercontinental manned bomber force is composed mainly of aged, slow, and large B-52s. This bomber was developed in 1952 and was predicted to "wear out" in the 1980s. Indeed, many of the original force of 600 B-52s have been cannibalized to keep 250 aircraft "operational." The B-52 has undergone eight major improvements (through the B-52G and B-52H models) in an attempt to offset improved enemy air defenses. The United States extended the life of the B-52 by arming many of them with cruise missiles. These are small guided missiles that can be launched from a B-52 well before it nears the target. The cruise missile will allow the old slow-flying, vulnerable B-52s to avoid flying over the heaviest enemy air defense.

B-52
aging strategic bomber

A more advanced manned bomber, the B-1 was developed and tested in the mid-1970s as a replacement for the aging B-52s. The B-1 is a supersonic bomber, designed for low-altitude penetration of modern air defenses. But successful penetration of enemy air defenses after the year 2000 will require highly sophisticated aircraft employing the most advanced "stealth" (radar-evading) technology. *Stealth technology* refers to airframe design and construction materials that minimize the aircraft's reflection on enemy radar screens. Beginning in the late 1970s, the United States made rapid strides in secret stealth research. A stealth fighter, the F117A was built in secret and later won fame attacking well-defended Iraqi targets during the Gulf war. In 1989 the Air Force rolled out its first stealth bomber, the B-2, with its revolutionary flying wing design. But the Air Force also revealed the high cost of the new bomber and its sophisticated technology. Only a small number of B-2s will be produced in an era of reduced defense spending.

stealth technology
minimizing aircraft
reflection on enemy
radar screens

SLBMs

The third leg of the triad is the submarine-launched ballistic missile (SLBM) force. This is the most "survivable" force and therefore the best second-strike component of the triad. Most defense analysts believe that antisubmarine warfare (ASW) capability is not now, nor will it be in the foreseeable future, capable of destroying a significant portion of our SLBM force on a surprise first strike.

The first SLBM-carrying submarines (SSBNs) went to sea in 1960. SSBNs are nuclear-powered; they can remain undersea for long periods and can launch missiles from underwater. Trident submarines will eventually replace earlier SSBNs (each with sixteen SLBM launch tubes) with the newer, quieter SSBNs (each with twenty-four launch tubes). Twelve Trident submarines are currently operational, out of a planned total of eighteen.

Trident
advanced U.S. nuclear missile-carrying submarine

Only limited numbers of advanced, stealthy B-2 bombers will be produced in an era of reduced defense spending.
Source: Sygma

Post–Cold War Changes

The strategic nuclear forces of the former Soviet Union consist of over 1,400 ICBMs (including modern rail-based and land mobile missiles built since 1985), over 900 SLBMs, and hundreds of manned bombers. These forces currently remain under centralized command of the elite Strategic Rocket Forces. They are located in four republics: Russia, Ukraine, Bylorusse, and Kazakstan.

The United States continues to rely on its strategic nuclear deterrent forces, although major modifications in all three legs of the triad are underway. The president canceled plans to place the MX on railroad cars and plans to build a small land mobile "Midgetman" missile; currently there are no plans to make the ICBM force more survivable. The president also ordered the early dismantling of 450 Minuteman II missiles. The manned bomber force was taken off alert status; no longer are American bombers parked at the end of runways, fueled and loaded with nuclear weapons, with crews ready for takeoff within minutes. The president also terminated the B-2 program at twenty aircraft and ended production of new nuclear warheads.

Democratic transformations in Russia are still underway. Powerful strategic nuclear forces still face the United States. There is the worrisome possibility that Russia may revert to a closed, authoritarian, and hostile regime, which once again may threaten its European neighbors and the United States. Additional reductions in U.S. strategic forces may await the institutionalization of democracy in Russia, its development of close ties to the Western democracies, and its compliance with all existing arms control agreements.

"Star Wars"

The Strategic Defense Initiative (SDI) is a research program designed to explore means of destroying enemy nuclear missiles in space before they can reach their targets. After President Ronald Reagan's initial announcement of SDI in March 1983, the press quickly labeled the effort "Star Wars." SDI, or "Star Wars," is only a research program; at present there is no way to intercept any significant portion of an enemy's missiles once they have been fired. Thus, for the present, U.S. defense continues to rest upon deterrence.

In theory, a ballistic missile defense (BMD) system could be based in space, orbiting over enemy missile-launching sites, and could be capable of destroying missiles shortly after they are fired. Destroying enemy missiles in their boost phase would mean that all the multiple warheads those missiles carry would be destroyed with a single hit. A ground-based BMD system would attempt to intercept enemy warheads in their terminal phase, when they reenter the atmosphere and approach their targets. Destroying a missile or warhead in flight is a challenging technical feat, comparable to "hitting a bullet with a bullet." SDI includes research on laser beams, satellite surveillance, computerized battle-management systems, and "smart" and "brilliant" weapons systems.

The success of the Patriot antiballistic missile in destroying Iraqi Scud missiles during the Gulf war demonstrated that a BMD system was indeed feasible. The Patriot is a ground-based weapon designed to protect specific military targets. It was developed by the Army rather than by SDI, but it silenced critics of SDI who claimed that a successful intercept of incoming missiles was impossible. But controversy over SDI continues. Should SDI focus on futuristic and sophisticated spaced-based BMDs designed to protect the entire nation from ICBM attack, or should SDI concentrate on ground-based BMDs, similar to the Patriot, that would be deployed in the near future?

Saddam Hussein's use of Scud missiles against Israel and Saudi Arabia warned the world that outlaw nations or terrorists can also threaten missile attacks. Fortunately, Saddam Hussein had not yet acquired nuclear warheads for his Scuds. But the Gulf war experience demonstrated that deterrence may not protect us against a nuclear attack by a terrorist regime. A ballistic missile defense will be required in the future if the nation is to be protected from irrational, terrorist, or accidental nuclear attacks.

Arms Control

The United States and the former Soviet Union engaged in negotiations over nuclear arms control for many years. The development of reconnaissance satellites in the 1960s made it possible for each nation to monitor the strategic weapons possessed by the other. Space photography made cheating on agreements more difficult and thus opened the way for the United States and the Soviet Union to seek stability through arms control.

Following the election of Richard Nixon as president in 1968, the United States, largely guided by former Harvard professor Henry Kissinger (National Security Advisor to the president and later Secretary of State), began negotiations with the Soviet Union over strategic nuclear arms. In 1972 the United States and the USSR concluded two-and-one-half years of Strategic Arms Limitation Talks (SALT) about limiting the nuclear arms race. The agreement, SALT I, consists of a treaty limiting antiballistic missiles (ABMs) and an agreement placing a numerical ceiling on offensive missiles. The ABM treaty limits each side to one ABM site for defense of its national capital and one ABM site for defense of an offensive ICBM field. Under the offensive-arms agreement, each side was frozen at the total number of offensive missiles completed or under construction. Both sides could construct new missiles if they dismantled an equal number of older missiles. Each nation agreed not to interfere in the satellite intelligence-gathering activities of the other nation. But there were no limitations on MIRV, and there were no limitations on advanced research on totally new weapons systems like the cruise missile. Both nations pledged to continue efforts at further arms control—the SALT II talks.

The United States and the Soviet Union signed the lengthy and complicated SALT II treaty in 1979. It set an overall limit on strategic nuclear launchers—ICBMs, SLBMs, bombers, and long-range cruise missiles—for each side. It also limited the number of missiles that could be MIRVed and banned new types of ICBMs, with the exception of one new type of ICBM for each side. But the Soviets were allowed to keep 314 very heavy SS-18 missiles for which the United States had no equivalent. When the Soviet Union invaded Afghanistan, President Carter withdrew the SALT II treaty from Senate consideration. However, President Carter, and later President Reagan, announced that the United States would abide by the provisions of the unratified SALT II treaty as long as the Soviet Union did so.

In negotiations with the Soviets, the Reagan administration pushed for *reductions* in missiles and warheads, not merely for limitations on future numbers and types of weapons as in previous SALT talks. To symbolize this new direction, President Reagan renamed the negotiations the *Strategic Arms Reductions Talks,* or *START.* The president emphasized that any new treaty must result in reductions of strategic arms to levels equal for both sides. The Soviets objected strongly to President Reagan's research efforts in the field of ballistic missile defense (SDI). In 1983 the Soviets walked out of the START talks and out of talks seeking to limit European nuclear weapons. But by 1985, after President Reagan's reelection, the Soviets returned to the bargaining table at Geneva, Switzerland.

The Intermediate-Range Nuclear Forces (INF) Treaty in 1987 was the first agreement between the superpowers that actually resulted in the destruction of nuclear weapons. It eliminated an entire class of nuclear weapons—missiles with an intermediate range, between 300 and 3,800 miles. It was also the first treaty that resulted in equal levels (zero) of arms for the United States and the USSR. To reach an equal level, the Soviets were required to destroy more missiles and warheads than the United States. Finally, INF was the first treaty to provide for on-site inspec-

SALT I

the ABM treaty

the offensive-arms agreement

SALT II

START talks
renamed arms control talks to emphasize reductions

INF Treaty
eliminated intermediate-range ballistic missiles

U.S. principles in arms control
reductions

equality

verification

tion for verification. The proportion of each side's nuclear weapons covered by the INF Treaty was small, but this treaty set the pattern for future arms control agreements in its provisions for *reductions, equality,* and *verification.*

The long-waited agreement on long-range strategic nuclear weapons was finally signed in Moscow in 1991 by Presidents George Bush and Mikhail Gorbachev. The START Treaty included the following: the total number of deployed strategic nuclear delivery systems (ICBMs, SLBMs, and manned bombers) would be reduced to no more than 1,600, a 30-percent reduction from the SALT II level; the Soviet Union would reduce by one-half its force of heavy SS-18 ICBMs; the total number of strategic nuclear warheads would be reduced to no more than 6,000, a reduction of nearly 50 percent.

The ink had not yet dried on the START treaty when Russia's first democratically elected president, Boris Yeltsin, agreed to even deeper cuts in nuclear weapons and, more importantly, to the eventual elimination of all land-based missiles with multiple (MIRVed) warheads. This historic agreement between Presidents Bush and Yeltsin in 1992, when fully implemented in 2003, will virtually eliminate the threat of a massive nuclear attack—a threat that had cast a menacing shadow over the world for decades.

Specifically, the Bush–Yeltsin agreement calls for the United States and Russia to:

- Reduce the total number of strategic warheads on each side to between 3,000 and 3,500 by the year 2003; this amounts to a 75 percent reduction from the levels existing in 1990;
- Eliminate all land-based missiles with multiple warheads, including the Russian 55-18 and the American Minuteman III and MX;
- Reduce the total number of MIRVed warheads on submarine-launched missiles to 1,750 for each side.

The elimination of land-based MIRVed missiles is a historic breakthrough in nuclear relations. Traditionally, the former Soviet Union had always relied more heavily on land-based missiles than the United States, which had most of its strategic warheads on submarine-based missiles. The United States always considered land-based MIRVed missiles, especially the Soviet SS-18, to be "destabilizing," that is, more likely to be employed in a first-strike nuclear attack. Because submarine-based missiles are more likely to survive an attack, the U.S. always considered them "stabilizing," that is, more likely to be used in a retaliatory second strike. But for decades the leaders of the Soviet Union believed that the U.S. proposal to limit land-based MIRVed missiles was a cynical ploy to weaken Soviet forces while maintaining strong U.S. submarine forces. And, indeed, the Bush–Yeltsin agreement requires the Russians to dismantle many more missiles and warheads than the United States.

The process will take over a decade; the Russians have requested the financial assistance of the United States in reducing their arsenal. Hard-liners in Russia have attacked Yeltsin for agreeing to scrap the SS-18, the heart of their country's nuclear arsenal. The future of nuclear relations between the United States and Russia depends heavily on that nation's continued progress toward democracy.

START Treaty
reduction to 6,000 warheads for each side

Soviets to reduce heavy SS-18's by one-half

reduction to 1,600 strategic nuclear delivery systems for each side

on-site verification

The New European Power Balance

The preservation of democracy in Western Europe has been the centerpiece of U.S. foreign and military policy for most of the twentieth century. The United States fought in two world wars and suffered one-quarter million battle deaths to preserve democracy in Europe.

reduced threat
end of communist rule in East Europe

collapse of Warsaw Pact

German unification

The dramatic collapse of the communist governments of Eastern Europe in 1989–Poland, Hungary, Romania, Bulgaria, and East Germany—vastly reduced the threat of a military attack on Western Europe. The dismantling of communist governments in Eastern Europe came about as a direct result of President Mikhail Gorbachev's decision to renounce the use of Soviet military force to keep those communist governments in power (a decision that earned him the Nobel Peace Prize). For over forty years the communist governments of Eastern Europe were kept in power by Soviet tanks; bloody Soviet military operations put down civilian uprisings in Hungary in 1956 and Czechoslovakia in 1968. The threat of Soviet military intervention crushed the Solidarity movement in Poland in 1981, yet that same movement became the government of Poland in 1989. Any effort today by a Russian leader to reimpose communist governments on Eastern European nations by military force would probably result in widespread bloodshed.

The destruction of the Berlin Wall in 1989 and the formal unification of Germany in 1990 rearranged the balance of military power in central Europe. West Germany, with 61 million people, is economically strong. Uniting with 17 million less prosperous people in East Germany is causing temporary economic dislocations; but over the long run a united Germany is likely to become the strongest power in Europe. Germany remains a member of NATO.

The United States and its NATO allies must always consider the possible "reversibility" of these changes. Democratically minded leaders in Russia could be replaced and traditional military doctrines reimposed. For the time being at least, the NATO alliance remains in place, although all of the member nations are reducing their military forces. The United States has withdrawn over half of its European-based forces, leaving about 100,000 troops as a "forward-based" presence on the continent.

Regional Balances of Power

The Gulf War

end of Cold War focuses new attention on regional conflicts

"New World Order"
ending of Cold War provides opportunity for stable world peace

The end of the Cold War does not ensure world peace. Iraq's invasion of Kuwait in 1990 and its threatened military takeover of Saudi Arabia and the Gulf states reminded the world that there are many other international conflicts and threats to peace. (See the case study, "American Military Power: 'Desert Storm.'") Regional struggles for power have their own roots. The easing of Cold War tensions focuses new attention on regional conflicts in Asia, Latin America, Africa, and especially the Middle East.

Regional powers can no longer drag the United States or the USSR into their disputes by playing one superpower against the other. The Western democracies, led by the United States, have been victorious in the Cold War, and now it is time

First we're going to cut it off, then we're going to kill it.

General Colin Powell, January, 1991 (televised speech)

America's victory in the Gulf war came about as a direct result of confident political leadership setting forth clear strategic objectives, allowing the military to design and execute a plan to achieve these objectives, and rallying political support for the war both at home and in world capitals. Clear strategic objectives in the Gulf war were set forth by President George Bush: to force the immediate and unconditional withdrawal of Iraqi troops from Kuwait; to destroy Saddam Hussein's nuclear, chemical, and biological weapons facilities; and to ensure that Iraqi military forces would no longer be capable of posing a threat to the region. The president relied on his military commanders to devise a plan to achieve these objectives, to assemble the necessary forces to carry out the plan without artificial ceilings or limitations, and to execute the plan effectively and with minimum casualties.

The U.S. military leadership had learned its lessons from Vietnam: Define clear military objectives, use overwhelming and decisive military force, move swiftly and avoid protracted stalemate, minimize casualties, and be sensitive to the image of the war projected back home.

Saddam Hussein's monumental miscalculations contributed heavily to the U.S. political and military victory. His invasion of Kuwait on August 2, 1990, was apparently designed to restore his military prestige following eight years of indecisive war against Iran, to secure additional oil revenues to finance the continued buildup of Iraqi military power, and to intimidate and perhaps invade Saudi Arabia and the Gulf states and thereby secure control over a major share of the world's oil reserves. The Iraqi invasion met with a surprisingly swift UN response in Security Council resolutions condemning the invasion, demanding an immediate withdrawal, and imposing a trade embargo and economic sanctions. President Bush immediately set to work to stitch together a coalition military force that would eventually include thirty nations.

On paper, Iraq possessed the fourth largest military force in the world, with one million troops, battle-hardened from eight years of war with Iran. Iraqi weapons included over 5,000 tanks, 10,000 other armored vehicles, 4,000 artillery pieces, 700 combat aircraft, and a heavy surface-to-air missile air defense system. Iraq also possessed over 1,000 Soviet-made Scud surface-to-surface missiles, and it had used deadly chemical weapons against Iran and its own Kurdish population.

Early on, the president described the U.S. military deployment as "defensive," but he soon became convinced that neither diplomacy nor an economic blockade would dislodge Saddam from Kuwait. Saddam moved forty-two divisions, nearly one-half million troops, including his elite Republican Guard, into Kuwait and southern Iraq. He dug ditches and planted mine fields, erected earth berms to stop

(continued)

(continued)

tanks, set up antiaircraft defense, and rigged Kuwait's oil wells with explosives. He took hundreds of foreign hostages as "insurance" against attack, but this brutality only hardened Western opinion. The president ordered the military to prepare an "offensive" option.

The top U.S. military commanders—including the Chairman of the Joint Chiefs of Staff, General Colin Powell; and the commander in the field, General Norman Schwarzkopf—had been field officers in Vietnam, and they were resolved not to repeat the mistakes of that war. They were reluctant to go into battle without the full support of the American people. If ordered to fight, they wanted to employ overwhelming and decisive military force; they wanted to avoid gradual escalation, protracted conflict, target limitations, and political inference in the conduct of the war. They presented the president with an "offensive" plan that called for a very large military buildup: elements of six Army divisions and two Marine divisions, with 1,900 tanks, 930 artillery pieces, and 500 attack helicopters; and over 1,000 combat aircraft. Coalition forces also included British and French heavy armored units, and Egyptian, Syrian, Saudi, and other Arab forces.

The president announced this massive buildup of forces on November 8 but immediately faced a barrage of criticism at home for abandoning his earlier defensive posture. U.S. Senator Sam Nunn, respected chairman of the Senate Armed Forces committee, opened hearings that urged the president to continue economic sanctions and avoid the heavy casualties that a land war was expected to produce. But the president was convinced that sanctions would not work, that Saddam would hold out for years, that eventually the political coalition backing the embargo would break up, and that Saddam would become increasingly powerful on the world stage. He argued that Saddam would soon acquire nuclear weapons, that if unchecked he would soon dominate the Arab world and Mideast oil reserves, and that aggression must not be allowed to succeed. Secretary of State James Baker convinced the UN Security Council members, including the Soviet Union (with China abstaining), to support a resolution authorizing states to "use all necessary means" against Iraq unless it withdrew from Kuwait by January 15.

From Baghdad, CNN reporters Bernard Shaw and Peter Arnett were startled the night of January 16 when *Operation Desert Storm* began with an air attack on key installations in the city. Iraqi forces were also surprised, despite the prompt timing of the attack; Saddam had assured them that the United States lacked the resolve to fight, and that even if war broke out, U.S. public opinion would force a settlement as casualties rose. The air war had three objectives: first, to win air supremacy by destroying radars, air defense control centers, and SAM launchers and airfields, as well as any Iraqi fighters that managed to get into the air; second, to destroy strategic targets, including nuclear facilities, chemical warfare plants, command centers, and military communications; third, to degrade Iraqi military forces by cutting off supplies, destroying tanks and artillery, and demoralizing troops with 'round-the-clock bombardment.

(continued)

(continued)

The performance of the coalition air force was spectacular. Over 110,000 combat missions were flown with only 39 aircraft losses, none in air combat. Most Iraqi aircraft were compelled to stay on the ground as runway and control facilities were destroyed; 38 Iraqi planes were shot down in combat, and 140 escaped to Iran. Smart weapons performed superbly, and American TV audiences saw videotapes of laser-guided smart bombs entering the doors and air shafts of enemy bunkers. Civilian damage was lower than in any previous air war. The Patriot antiballistic missile system proved very effective against Scuds; in over eighty firings at Israel and Saudi Arabia, only one effective strike occurred, killing twenty-seven in a Marine barracks. After five weeks of air war, intelligence estimated that nearly half the Iraqi tanks and artillery in the field had been destroyed, demoralized troops were hiding in deep shelters, and the battlefield had been isolated and "prepared" for ground operations.

General Schwarzkopf's plan for the ground war emphasized deception and maneuver. He wanted to make the Iraqi's believe that the main attack would come directly against Kuwait's southern border and would be supported by a Marine landing on the coast. While Iraqi forces prepared for attacks from the south and the east coast, General Schwarzkopf sent heavily-armed columns in a "Hail Mary" play—a wide sweep to the west, outflanking and cutting off Iraqi forces in the battle area. The Iraqi forces, blinded by air attacks and obliged to stay in their bunkers, would not be able to know about or respond to the flanking attack. On the night of February 24, the ground attack began with Marines easily breaching berms, ditches, and mine fields and racing directly to the Kuwait city airport; helicopter air assaults lunged deep into Iraq; armored columns raced northward across the desert to outflank Iraqi forces and then attack them from the west; and a surge in air attacks kept Iraqi forces holed up in their bunkers. Iraqi troops surrendered in droves, highways from Kuwait city were turned into massive junkyards of Iraqi vehicles, and Iraqi forces that tried to fight were quickly destroyed. After one hundred hours of ground fighting, President George Bush declared a cease-fire.

The United States had achieved a decisive military victory quickly and with precious few casualties. The president resisted calls to expand the original objectives of war; that is, to capture Baghdad, to destroy the Iraqi economy, to encourage Iraq's disintegration as a nation, or to kill Saddam, although it was expected that his defeat would lead to his ouster. Although the war left many political issues unresolved, it was the most decisive military outcome the United States had achieved since the end of World War II. President Bush chose to declare victory and celebrate the return of American troops.

The Gulf war taught the nation a number of lessons about the effective use of military power:

• The rapid employment of overwhelming force is both politically and militarily superior to gradual escalation and employment of minimum force. The use of over-

(continued)

CASE STUDY

(continued)

whelming force reduces total casualties and achieves an earlier and more decisive victory. It reduces the opportunity for diplomatic interventions that may produce compromised, indecisive resolutions.

• The nation's political leadership is vastly more effective when it concentrates on developing and maintaining foreign and domestic political support for the war while leaving the planning and execution of military operations to the military leadership.

• A rapid conclusion of hostilities ensures that public support will not erode over time and that protracted combat and a steady stream of casualties will not fuel antiwar sentiments.

• Television images of war influence mass opinion, and control of those images is vital to the successful outcome of war. The U.S. military believed that the media "lost" the war in Vietnam through hostile media reporting and televised pictures of battlefield carnage. In Grenada in 1983 and in the Gulf war, reporters were restricted to a representative "pool" that was supervised by military officers. Reports were generally limited to official military briefings. Saddam Hussein allowed CNN to remain in Baghdad, and reporter Peter Arnett broadcast the Iraqi version of the war. But the U.S. military largely controlled the flow of information; military briefing officers became media celebrities, and videotapes of precision bombing enthralled viewers. Thus, the military "won" the media war and the support of the American people.

• Air power can be decisive in determining the outcome of a war. "The efficient and precise application of contemporary air power was perhaps the most important factor contributing to this remarkable victory."[6]

• Technologically advanced weaponry grants a major military advantage. Among the U.S. successes: the Tomahawk cruise missiles; smart laser-guided bombs and missiles; electronic countermeasures that blind enemy radars and missiles; "stealth" aircraft that can attack heavily defended targets; the Patriot air defense system that proved the effectiveness of ballistic missile defenses; the AH64 Apache attack helicopter, the M1A1 tank, and other sophisticated Army weapons.

• A highly trained, well-led, motivated, volunteer, professional military can prevail over much larger armies of badly trained conscripts.

• U.S. sealift and airlift capabilities are inadequate for moving heavy forces rapidly to world trouble spots. If the United States had not had six months' preparation, the outcome of the Gulf war may have been different.

Perhaps the most important lesson is that the end of the Cold War does *not* mean that the United States no longer requires military power.

to build a stable world peace. Aggression must be met with united world opposition and superpower cooperation. Yet questions remain about when, where, and how the United States should use its power to oppose aggression and maintain peace. The United States does not wish to become the world's policeman; yet today only the United States has the capability to project military force worldwide.

The Middle East

Perhaps no regional power struggle is so volatile as that of the Arabs and Israelis. The end of the Cold War may have reduced the likelihood of direct confrontation between the United States and Russia through escalation of a Middle East conflict. Nonetheless, struggles in the Middle East continue to pose dangers to the United States.

The state of Israel was founded in 1948 after Britain withdrew from its old League of Nations "mandate" to govern Palestine. The United Nations recognized the new nation of Israel, but immediately thereafter, the Arab–Israeli conflict broke out into open warfare. Although vastly outnumbered, the Israelis were successful in their War of Independence. Palestinian Arabs who were displaced from Israel were never integrated into surrounding Arab nations, but were instead kept in squalid camps in Egypt, Jordan, and Syria. These camps nourished the growth of a Palestinian Liberation Organization (PLO) dedicated to the elimination of the state of Israel and willing to use political, military, and terrorist means to accomplish its goal.

In 1956, after Egyptian President Nasser seized the British-built Suez Canal, a combined force of British, French, and Israeli forces captured the canal, with Israelis doing most of the fighting in the Sinai Desert. The United States, seeking to maintain its influence in the oil-rich Arab world, forced a return of the canal and of all captured lands to Egypt. Nonetheless, Egypt and Syria turned increasingly to the Soviet Union for military aid. In 1967 Egypt and Syria, heavily armed by the Soviets, moved their armies to the Israeli frontier. But in the Six-Day War, in a lightning military strike, the Israelis, though heavily outnumbered, defeated the forces of Egypt, Syria, and Jordan. The Israeli border expanded to the Suez Canal in the west, the Jordan River in the east, and the Golan Heights in the northwest. The Israelis asked for a permanent peace agreement that would recognize the right of Israel to exist, but the defeated Arabs, having received a rapid influx of new Soviet arms, refused to negotiate.

By 1973 the Arabs were prepared for another major war with Israel, the fourth in twenty-five years. The Yom Kippur War resulted in yet another defeat for the Arab nations, but this time the Israelis suffered a greater loss of life and material than they had in previous wars. The Yom Kippur War also resulted in the direct involvement of the United States in negotiations. The Arab nations placed a temporary embargo on oil shipped to the United States as a way of forcing the United States to pressure Israel into concessions. When Egyptian armies were threatened with annihilation in the desert and the Syrian capital of Damascus was under Israeli attack, the Soviets prepared to send in their own troops. A direct confrontation with the Soviets was avoided only when Henry Kissinger succeeded in convincing the Israelis to pull back. Kissinger began to win the Egyptians away from the Soviets and to convince them that negotiations with Israel were more likely to win back the Sinai than military attacks.

President Anwar Sadat of Egypt surprised the world in 1977 by announcing that he was prepared to go to Jerusalem and talk with Israel's Prime Minister Menachem Begin in an effort to achieve a permanent peace. This announcement changed the long-standing Arab policy of refusing even to recognize the existence of Israel. The subsequent talks between Egypt and Israel did not bring "permanent peace to the Middle East.'' Hard-line Arab states, such as Iraq, Libya, and Syria, and the militant PLO denounced the Egyptian–Israeli talks. However, the signing of a peace treaty by Anwar Sadat and Menachem Begin (the "Camp David agreement" negotiated with the assistance of President Jimmy Carter) in 1979 brought a brief promise of hope to the embattled Middle East. The Israelis agreed to a withdrawal of all occupied Egyptian lands (the Sinai) and to open negotiations regarding the future of Arabs living in the Israeli-controlled areas of the West Bank of the Jordan River and the Gaza Strip. In exchange, Egypt agreed to recognize the right of Israel to exist and to exchange ambassadors. But even this limited agreement was denounced by other Arab states. Egypt and Israel have continued to abide by the Camp David agreement despite the assassination of Anwar Sadat in 1981.

For many years Lebanon had been the most advanced Arab nation and its capital Beirut the most cosmopolitan city in the Middle East. Its Christian Arabs shared power with its Moslem Arabs in a delicately balanced constitution. But Palestinian refugees destabilized the Christian–Moslem balance in Lebanon; the PLO became a separate government in Lebanon and launched many attacks on Israel from its bases in southern Lebanon. In 1984 Israel launched an attack on PLO forces in Lebanon that carried Israeli troops to the outskirts of Beirut. Syrian air forces were destroyed in the battle, but Syrian and Israeli ground troops avoided direct contact. The PLO was severely damaged, but other Moslem groups in Lebanon joined in a bloody guerrilla campaign against the Israeli occupiers. Israel eventually withdrew from Lebanon, and the country became a battleground in which many separate armed Christian and Moslem sects engaged in sporadic fighting against each other. American efforts to restore stability in Lebanon were defeated when terrorists killed 241 marines in a suicide car bombing of their barracks in Lebanon, and President Reagan withdrew all U.S. forces from that nation.

In the Gulf war in 1991, Israel was attacked by Iraqi Scud missiles, but President Bush convinced Israel to stay out of the war so as not to upset the Arab nations allied with the United States against Iraq. After the war the United States hoped to use its renewed political and military credibility to initiate a new Middle East peace process. But hostilities in the Middle East run deep. Conflicts over the boundaries of Israel, over the future of the city of Jerusalem, and over the future of the Palestinian people appear unresolvable. The United States continues to try to maintain a balanced approach toward Israel and the Arab states.

Notes

1. Hans Morgenthau, *Politics among Nations* (New York: Knopf, 1960), p. 27.
2. Quincy Wright, *A Study of War* (Chicago: University of Chicago Press, 1942), pp. 641–646.
3. Frederick H. Hartman, *The Relations of Nations,* 4th ed. (New York: Macmillan, 1973), p. 12.
4. Terms used in Article X of the Covenant of the League of Nations.
5. These moves included (1) the establishment of communist governments in Eastern European nations in violation of war-time agreements at Yalta and Potsdam to support "democratic" governments "broadly representative" of all factions; (2) military support of the communist takeover of Czecho-slovakia in 1948; (3) the breakup of a four-power control commission that was to govern the occupation of Germany and the sealing off of the Soviet sector of East Germany; (4) a military blockade of Berlin in 1948 designed to oust American, British, and French occupation authorities; (5) Soviet military support for armed communist troops in Greece and Turkey; and (6) the continued maintenance of a large Soviet army in Eastern Europe threatening the security of Western European nations.
6. International Institute for Strategic Studies, *Strategic Survey 1991* (London: IISS, 1991), p. 94.

About This Chapter

Since the earliest recorded times, and no doubt before, people have been fighting wars. They have fought them for every conceivable reason—and even for some reasons that may seem *in*conceivable. They have fought to defend themselves or to subjugate others; they have fought for territorial, economic, or political gain; they have fought for ideological reasons and for leaders whose sole reason was to secure a place for themselves in history; they have fought class wars and race wars; they have undoubtedly even fought just for excitement and glory. But in our age the threat of a nuclear holocaust makes it imperative that the world's superpowers avoid war. Nuclear war can have no meaning today, no reason worth the annihilation of civilization as we know it.

In this chapter we have explored some of the means, past and present, by which people have sought to avoid war. Now that you have read it, you should be able to

- discuss the meaning of sovereignty and describe the nature of international law;
- discuss the concepts of a balance of power, collective security, and regional security;
- discuss the concept of deterrence and the means by which this policy is implemented;
- discuss the *minibalances of power* and why superpowers must maintain conventional armed forces.

Discussion Questions

1. Define *sovereignty* and discuss the role it plays in international politics. Describe the nature of international law.

2. Describe various systems of international order, giving specific examples of each type of system. Compare and evaluate the relative effectiveness of a balance-of-power system, collective security, and regional security.

3. What is meant by the *triad* of strategic forces?

4. What is meant by "hard-target kill capability"? What plans have been developed to ensure the survivability of our land-based missiles? What is the most survivable "leg" of the triad?

5. Discuss the SALT I ABM treaty. Why was the SALT II Treaty never ratified by the U.S. Senate? What kinds of weapons are eliminated by the INF Treaty? What principles of arms control are incorporated into the INF Treaty?

6. Describe the major provisions of the START agreement.

7. What factors have combined to reduce the military threat to Western Europe?

8. In the context of the Middle East crises of 1956 (Suez Canal), 1967 (Six-Day War), and 1973 (Yom Kippur War), discuss the concept of *minibalances of power*. What is the danger of superpower intervention in local wars?

9. Discuss the political and military "lessons" of the Gulf war.

10. Compare presidential leadership in the Gulf war with presidential leadership in the Vietnam war (see Chapter 8). How did U.S. military strategy differ in these wars?

Index

TO THE OWNER OF THIS BOOK:

We hope you have found Thomas R. Dye's *Power and Society: An Introduction to the Social Sciences*, 6th edition, useful. So that this book can be improved in a future edition, would you please take the time to complete this sheet and return it? Thank you.

Instructor's name: _____

Department: _____

School and address: _____

_____

1. The name of the course in which I used this book is: _____

_____

2. My general reaction to this book is: _____

_____

_____

3. What I like most about this book is: _____

_____

_____

4. What I like least about this book is: _____

_____

_____

5. Were all of the chapters of the book assigned for you to read?   Yes   No

   If not, which ones weren't? _____

6. Do you plan to keep this book after you finish the course?   Yes   No

   Why or why not? _____

_____

7. On a separate sheet of paper, please write specific suggestions for improving this book and anything else you'd care to share about your experience in using the book.

Optional:

Your name: _____ Date: _____

May Wadsworth quote you, either in promotion for *Power and Society*, 6th edition, or in future publishing ventures?

Yes: _____ No: _____

Sincerely,

Thomas R. Dye

FOLD HERE

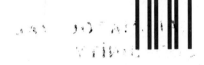

BUSINESS REPLY MAIL
FIRST CLASS   PERMIT NO. 34   BELMONT, CA

POSTAGE WILL BE PAID BY ADDRESSEE

Thomas R. Dye
Wadsworth Publishing Company
10 Davis Drive
Belmont, CA 94002

NO POSTAGE
NECESSARY
IF MAILED
IN THE
UNITED STATES